AS Business Studies

OCR

AS Business Studies

Andy Mottershead • Steve Challoner • Alex Grant

Philip Allan Updates
Market Place
Deddington
Oxfordshire
OX15 0SE

Orders

Bookpoint Ltd, 130 Milton Park, Abingdon, Oxfordshire, OX14 4SB
tel: (44) 01235 827720
fax: (44) 01235 400454
e-mail: uk.orders@bookpoint.co.uk
Lines are open 9.00 a.m. –5.00 p.m., Monday to Saturday, with a 24-hour
message answering service. You can also order through our website:
www.philipallan.co.uk

ISBN 13: 978-1-84489-404-8
ISBN 10: 1-84489-404-5

This textbook has been written specifically to support students studying
OCR AS Business Studies. The content has been neither approved nor
endorsed by OCR and remains the sole responsibility of the authors.

All efforts have been made to trace copyright on items used.

All website addresses included in this book are correct at the time of going
to press but may subsequently change.

Printed in Great Britain by CPI Bath.

Philip Allan Update's policy is to use papers that are natural, renewable
and recyclable products and made from wood grown in sustainable forests.
The logging and manufacturing processes are expected to conform to the
environmental regulations of the country of origin.

Contents

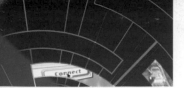

Contents

Accounting and Finance

People in Organisations

Operations Management

Introduction

This textbook has been written specifically to meet the needs of students following the OCR AS Business Studies course. It provides comprehensive coverage of the specification, and includes a wide range of up-to-date and real-life examples.

Special features

The book contains several special features designed to aid your understanding of the concepts and examination techniques required by OCR.

Examiner's voice

All three authors have many years' experience of examining for OCR and have used this to provide useful advice where appropriate. The advice concentrates on what you should do, although some advice highlights common pitfalls that should be avoided.

Your turn

All chapters have a questions section and/or one or more case studies. Some of the chapters also feature group tasks.

Questions

This section comprises short questions, which are intended for reinforcement and revision purposes, and longer questions requiring more detailed answers.

The mark scheme is provided as a guide to the amount of time you should spend on each question and the amount of detail required. The mark allocations are similar to those in the examination units.

Numerical questions are included where appropriate. These are in line with the type of questions set by OCR.

Case studies

Case studies are provided to help you to apply the newly acquired concepts in the context of a business. They also offer you an opportunity to practise your examination technique. The mark allocations and question styles are similar to those in the examination units.

The case studies are in accordance with OCR's introduction to the specifications: 'The fundamental philosophy of the specifications is that the study of Business Studies requires an integrated approach at all stages of the course.'

For this reason, some of the case studies include a wide range of material from various chapters. Furthermore, the case studies have been written to comply with OCR's statement that: 'The specifications require an approach which views business behaviour from a variety of perspectives.'

Group tasks

These are intended to stimulate debate and encourage you to learn the technique of justifying your view, which is necessary for evaluation.

Further sources

The majority of these are websites where you will find additional material and up-to-the-minute examples. Obvious websites such as Bized have not been included. Where appropriate, brief descriptions of the websites are given.

Key terms

These are included as summaries of the key concepts that you need to know.

The AS examinations

The examination format

You will have to sit three units.

Unit code	Unit name	Length of exam	Type of exam
2871	Businesses, Their Objectives and Environment	1 hour	Pre-issued case study
2872	Business Decisions	45 minutes	Data response
2873	Business Behaviour	1 hour 15 minutes	Pre-issued case study

Examination advice

The 'Examiner's voice' feature provides useful hints on issues and topics as they arise.

There are several other important factors for you to remember, which apply to all three AS units.

- When presented with a case study, it is important to answer in the context of the case.
- Read the case with care to ensure you are familiar with the type of business (its status, size and place in the market), its product or service, and its customers.
- Pay attention to the use of trigger terms, such as 'state', 'explain', 'outline', 'analyse', 'evaluate' and 'to what extent'. All these require different types and lengths of answers. Writing too much for a 'state' question could lose you time and therefore marks — a 'state' question requires you to write perhaps no more than a couple of words. An 'outline' question is asking you to show understanding of a concept and this can easily be done by offering a link. For example:

Outline why the government uses regional policy.

Answer: The government uses regional policy in order to encourage employment opportunities. In Scotland, there are areas of high unemployment and therefore grants will provide jobs.

■ Be careful when questions use phrases such as 'other than'. Many candidates miss the opportunity to gain marks by ignoring this instruction. For example, any references to taxation in answers to the following question will not gain marks:

Other than by taxation, suggest how a business may be affected by the government.

■ Notice the mark allocation. This will help you to write an appropriate amount for your answer.
■ The quality of language *is* important. Examiners are aware of the pressure under which students write their answers. Nevertheless, failing to use paragraphs and spelling words such as 'business' and 'interest' incorrectly is likely to mean that full marks will not be awarded.
■ Always try to write specific points related to the case, rather than general points that could apply to any business.
■ Answer the actual question rather than the one you prepared for or hoped would be there.
■ Take careful note of your time allocation. Many of the questions that offer a large number of marks are at the end of the exam papers. Unit 2872, which is only 45 minutes long, is not easy if you fail to watch the time. Remember to give yourself enough time to read the case properly.

Levels of response

Level	Key skill	Definition	Trigger words
1	Knowledge	• Business knowledge/facts	State, list
2	Explanation or application	• Knowledge of the issues and/or concepts • An explanation of the knowledge	Explain, outline, describe, how
3	Analysis	• The implication for the business • How the business is affected • How the business reacts • For Level 3, the points you make must be in the context of the business	Analyse
4	Evaluation	• Supported judgements and/or weighting of arguments and/or consideration of long- and short-term issues in context	Evaluate, to what extent, discuss, assess, recommend

Ensuring you reach the highest levels as quickly as possible will gain higher marks.

Analysis

There is no magic number of points that need to be analysed for you to reach Level 3. As long as you have shown how a particular point has affected the business or how the business is likely to react, you will gain Level 3 marks.

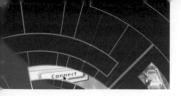

For example:

Analyse how the building company will be affected by a change in legislation.

Answer: If the government introduced further health and safety legislation, the building company would have to spend more money providing its employees with additional safety clothing. As a result, the business would have higher costs, which in turn would affect its profits. If it wanted to keep its profits at the previous level, it might have to increase its prices.

This answer shows how the business would be affected and how it would react (both are not essential — it depends on the question). Therefore, a Level 3 mark would be gained.

Evaluation

The key to making evaluative comments is to ensure that you offer a 'justified judgement'. Questions where evaluation is required are asking you to suggest:

- which factor is the most important to that particular business
- which factor is most likely to benefit the business
- which factor is most likely to occur
- which factor is going to damage the business the most
- whether the factor will occur in the short term or long term

To be evaluative, your answer needs to compare and weigh the evidence, considering the positives and the negatives for the business in the case. For example:

Evaluate how a change in interest rates might affect business X.

Answer: Of the two major ways in which business X will be affected, the increase in the cost of borrowing is the more significant. Although consumers may have less to spend because of an increase in mortgage rates, there are opportunities for them to increase their wages. However, business X will have to pay an increase in the cost of borrowing if it wants to expand its number of outlets. This consequence will take immediate effect on business X, whereas it is unlikely that a fall in consumer spending on business X's products will happen immediately, if at all.

In this answer, a clear judgement has been made and justified, and an attempt has been made to consider the short and long run. Consequently, this would gain a Level 4 mark.

Acknowledgements

The authors would like to express their thanks to numerous individuals who have contributed to the completion of this book.

A significant thank you to Judith Kelt for her suggestions to enhance the text and her ability to read at such a pace.

We are particularly grateful to Philip Cross for having faith in us from start to finish. His patience, continual support and his ability to cajole gently without creating ripples are much admired.

Andy would like to thank, yet again, Sheila for her understanding during the writing period, and Emma and Tim — particularly Tim, who frequently had to wait to use the computer! He is also grateful to the pupils of Tettenhall College, who have tested some of the case studies.

Steve would like to thank Benita, who offered continuous support and good humour, and Bethany and Daniel for their patience over being denied access to the computer for months on end.

Alex would like to thank his wife Kate and two sons James and Ben for putting up with his long absences in his study, and also MK Dons for being an inspiration in demonstrating that when life becomes difficult you don't give up.

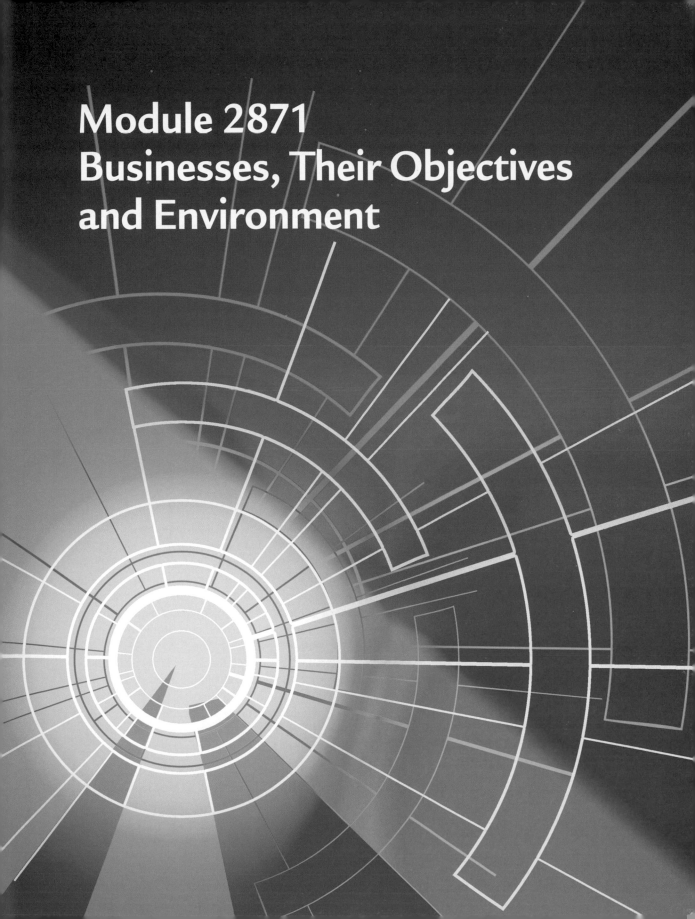

Module 2871
Businesses, Their Objectives and Environment

CHAPTER 1

The role of business

From the local corner-shop owner to BP, Shell and Cadbury-Schweppes, all are 'in business'. Being 'in business' is about taking risks in return for the possible reward of making a profit. It is often the case that the greater the risk, the greater is the potential reward of profit.

Inputs and outputs

The main role of business is to provide consumers with the goods and services they need. By using resources (**inputs**), it can produce the goods and services required (**output**) (see Figure 1.1).

The resources used are sometimes referred to as the factors of production: land, labour, capital and enterprise. Each of these can be used in various combinations in order to produce goods and services.

For example, bread is produced using the following factors:

■ **Land** is used for the factory and to grow the wheat.

■ **Labour** is used to drive the combine harvester, to collect the wheat, to operate the ovens, to pack the bread and to deliver it to the shops. The government, which is responsible for fixing the working age, determines the amount of labour within an economy. At present, the working age is between 16 and 65 for men, and between 16 and 60 for women. However, legislation is proposed to increase the retirement age for women to 65.

■ **Capital** — a combine harvester is used to collect the wheat, ovens and baking trays to cook the bread, packaging machines to pack the bread and vans to deliver it.

■ **Enterprise** — this factor is the owner and organiser of the bakery.

The key aspect for a business is to meet consumers' needs in a profitable way, by ensuring that the cost of producing and selling its goods and services is less than the money it gains from selling the goods (revenue).

Figure 1.1
Inputs and outputs

Inputs	Outputs
Raw materials Labour Money Owners/directors	Goods and services The needs and wants of consumers

INGRAM

- **Services** consist of all purchases that do not involve buying a tangible item. They are bought by both consumers and businesses, and include travel via trains and planes, advertising, banking, insurance, holidays and essential services such as the provision of gas and electricity. Some services are provided by the government (public sector), including defence, policing and local services such as libraries. Other services are provided by the private sector, which is made up of individual businesses.

Other functions of business

Business serves a number of other useful purposes:

- **Business as an employer.** Business provides a valuable source of employment, whether in the extraction of raw materials, the manufacturing of goods or the provision of services in the economy.
- **Business as a source of revenue.** Business is a large source of revenue for its owners, either as individuals or as shareholders. It is also a source of revenue for the government, which taxes company profits (corporation tax), puts taxes on goods and services (VAT) and imposes many additional taxes, such as the recent tax on company pension schemes. These taxes make a significant contribution to the government's expenditure programme (see Chapter 11).
- **Business helping the balance of payments.** Many businesses in the UK produce goods and services that are sold abroad. This means that money comes into the UK economy from the countries buying UK goods and services. This is good for the economy (see Chapters 10 and 12).

Further sources

www.dti.gov.uk

www.businesslink.org

YOUR TURN

Questions

Time allowed: 20 minutes

1 State which market best describes each of the following items, e.g. a Mars Bar is a consumer non-durable.

   a holiday abroad   **d** oven for a restaurant

   b shirt   **e** advertising agency

   c glass   **f** can of Redbull   *(6 marks)*

2 Explain how businesses help the economy.   *(5 marks)*

3 Name the four main departments or functions of a business organisation.   *(4 marks)*

4 Explain the role of one of the functions you named for question 3.   *(5 marks)*

                                                                     (20 marks)

Stakeholders

Business activity creates jobs, prosperity and wealth. Who benefits from this? One way of considering this question is to look at the concept of **stakeholders**. A stakeholder is a person, or party, with an interest (i.e. 'a stake') in the success of a business. Stakeholders want to see a business succeed because they will benefit from this success.

A consideration of how the needs of stakeholders affect a business can be used to create a framework to analyse both a business's objectives and the way it operates.

Stakeholders can be classified as internal or external. Internal stakeholders are found within the business and are the owners and employees, including managers. External stakeholders are suppliers, lenders, customers and the local community (see Figure 2.1).

Figure 2.1
The stakeholders in a business

Stakeholder objectives

In theory, all stakeholders will benefit from a business's success, but in reality they may not. Even if all stakeholders *do* benefit, they may not do so equally. In order to analyse why, it is necessary to consider the objectives of each stakeholder in the business.

Owners

A business might have a single owner if it is a sole trader, several if it is a partnership, or thousands of shareholders if it is a public limited company (see Chapter 5). The owner(s) will want the best possible return on the money they have invested in the business. They are also likely to want to see the business grow so that these returns increase.

The owners' pursuit of profit seems obvious, but this does not necessarily mean that they want 'immediate maximum profit'. Although a high rate of return is certainly a desirable long-run objective, in the short run a business may be pursuing the objective of growth via low prices. This will hopefully mean that it captures more of the market and that customers will stay loyal in the long term if it increases prices. In the immediate future, however, this tactic may reduce profits. This will obviously have implications for the other stakeholders.

Employees

As their livelihood depends on the business, it is not surprising that employees want the highest wage they can get, a bonus if possible, and job security. Employees also want the business to offer more than the legal entitlement to holidays, sick pay, and so on.

Most employees would like managers to organise their work so that it is interesting and challenging, and provides some job satisfaction. In addition, many will want to attend training courses to improve their skills and therefore their pay and promotion prospects. While it is clear that training courses will enable employees to work more effectively, their implementation will come at a cost to the business.

Hairdressing salons often have a single owner

Customers

Customers want the best-quality product(s) at the lowest possible price. They want products to be safe. They also want product innovation — each year's products should be better than the last. Other requirements are good customer service and credit facilities if the product is expensive, such as furniture or carpets. As well as these factors, customers are increasingly aware of ethical issues and are asking questions such as 'Were the products obtained from sustainable sources?' and 'Did any animals suffer in the making of the product?'

If consumers are fundamentally dissatisfied with quality, price, service or ethical behaviour, they will eventually stop buying from the business. If sufficient numbers of people do this, it can have a significant effect. Consumers may form pressure groups that try to influence the business by generating bad publicity.

Suppliers

If a business ceases trading, its suppliers lose a source of income. Therefore, a supplier would like to see its customers prosper so that it has a regular profit; it would like repeat orders rather than 'one-offs'. Furthermore, it hopes its customers will grow larger so that, in turn, it can increase its own sales to them. A supplier would also like to be paid as promptly as possible.

There is a difference between a supplier as 'a supplier' and a supplier as 'a stakeholder'. In the latter case, a business will try to build up a long-term relationship with its suppliers. This means using them regularly, paying them on time, and involving them in any plans for expansion. Suppliers who are treated as stakeholders are more likely to be loyal and committed because they have 'a stake' in the business in the true sense of the word.

A business that changes suppliers continually and tries to delay payment whenever possible may well be able to lower costs in the short term. However, it should not be surprised when, if it needs supplies of a particular kind at short notice, the firms that it has treated as suppliers rather than stakeholders are not prepared to drop everything in order to help out if they are already busy.

While it is sensible for any business to be trying to drive its costs down, this has to be balanced against the benefits of developing a long-term commitment with reliable suppliers — who may be crucial to success in the future.

Lenders

A supplier or a bank wants the agreed amount to be paid at the agreed time. These stakeholders do not want to receive less than expected or, alternatively, the correct amount but at a later date. The objective of a lender, such as a bank, is to get its money back at the agreed time.

The community

Businesses are chiefly interested in what their costs of production will be and what profit they will receive from their sales. These are known as **private costs and benefits**. However, the community is also affected by business activity. This 'community' might be defined as the people living in the area around the business.

While most people would welcome an increase in their quality of life, they may not all agree that business activity necessarily brings it about. On the one hand, businesses bring jobs; and a high level of employment brings prosperity and greater spending power. It also causes property prices to rise and crime levels to fall. Furthermore, many businesses are actively involved in community projects such as sponsoring sports teams. As more businesses move into an area, the local authority may improve the roads, making it easier for residents to drive around. These positive factors are brought to the community by businesses and are known as **social benefits**.

On the other hand, business activity can create external costs. These are costs which are not paid by the business itself in the same way that labour and raw material costs are. These external costs are costs on society and so are also known by the term **social costs**. For example, if a business producing chemical products locates in a particular area, there might be continual deliveries of raw materials. This will mean additional congestion and pollution on the roads as well as noise pollution for nearby residents. There may also be a smell from the factory. Property prices may fall. None of these is a cost to the firm, but will be 'paid' by the community.

KEY TERMS

private costs and benefits: costs that a business pays (e.g. labour costs) and the benefits it gets (e.g. profit)

social costs and benefits: costs of a business's actions that are 'paid' by society (e.g. pollution) and the benefits to society that business activity brings (e.g. lower crime levels due to increased employment)

When an area becomes prosperous, more people want to move there. This is quite natural; they want to work for growing businesses that offer good pay and conditions. This may mean that the area becomes overcrowded with congested roads and parking problems. The demand for improved roads and more housing may mean that parks and other green areas are sold off, denying the community recreational facilities. Increased numbers of people in the area, because of employment opportunities, can also put pressure on local schools and hospitals.

It is therefore important to identify *all* of the costs and benefits involved in a business's activities so that there can be a proper evaluation of whether or not they are beneficial to the community.

Pollution caused by a business is a social cost

The government

The government is not a direct stakeholder, but it does have an interest in any business's success. This is for several reasons:

- If more people are employed, the government pays out less on social security benefits.
- The government benefits from increased tax revenue, both from a business and from those whom the business is employing.
- As a business grows larger, it may start to export (sell goods abroad). When this happens, it helps to improve the UK's trading position with other countries.

Summary

Stakeholder objectives are summarised in Figure 2.2.

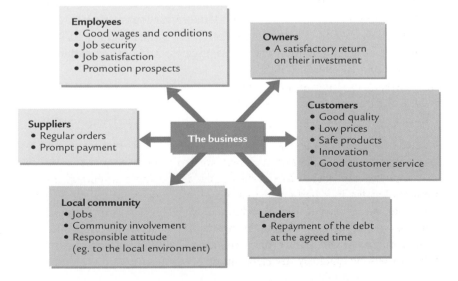

Figure 2.2 Summary of stakeholder objectives

CHAPTER 2

Conflict between stakeholders

In the light of these differing needs, there are likely to be conflicts between the various stakeholders. For example:

- higher expenditure on ethical initiatives (e.g. improving conditions in factories in less economically developed countries) could mean lower profits for owners and a slower growth in wages for any employees in the UK
- if telephonists are made redundant and replaced by an automated system, costs may fall and profits rise, but customer service could suffer
- the closure of a noisy and smelly factory might be a great benefit to local residents, but will mean that employees lose their jobs
- a financial business that deliberately sells savings schemes and pensions that are inappropriate will benefit owners and employees, but will negatively affect the customers who have bought them

Those who believe in the stakeholder approach to business argue that taking into account the needs of all stakeholders rather than only one group — usually the owners — will mean that, in the long run, all stakeholders will benefit. They say that concentrating on one group is counterproductive, as it will alienate the others. This may be true, but in the short term at least there will have to be trade-offs between the various groups. The fact that in the future there is the possibility that everyone will benefit is no consolation to someone who is likely to lose their job, or a consumer facing a large price rise.

The Co-operative movement

The term 'stakeholder' might be a fairly modern one, but the concept is not. One business that has been using it for over 150 years is the Co-operative movement. This began in Rochdale in 1844 when a group of workers who were fed up with poor-quality products and high prices set up their own grocery business. It was to be a 'co-operative business': that is, one that existed for the benefit of its users rather than some distant and uncaring owner. The co-operative idea was a great success and 'Co-op' supermarkets are now found all over the UK.

The group's website makes its approach clear:

> We aim to deliver a quality service to customers and to contribute to the well-being and enrichment of society through good operating practices and by re-investing our profits in the communities we serve...we aim to cater for the needs of the young, the old, those with disabilities. We recognise that commercial activity has an impact on the environment, but we are determined to measure and to minimise the adverse effects of our activities while positively contributing to environmental improvement.

The Co-operative Group now employs over 60,000 people and operates in many different business areas, including wholesaling, travel, funerals, insurance and banking.

EXAMINER'S VOICE

It is important that you understand the relationship and the interaction between a business and its stakeholders. This will enable you to evaluate whether or not pursuing a particular objective would be beneficial for a particular stakeholder.

Further sources

www.co-op.co.uk — homepage of the Co-operative Group. It contains information about the history and nature of the Co-operative movement and its stance on business practices and consumer issues

---

YOUR TURN

Questions

Time allowed: 20 minutes

1 State what is meant by the term 'stakeholder'. *(1 mark)*

2 List the likely stakeholders of a business. *(5 marks)*

3 State two likely objectives of each stakeholder. *(10 marks)*

4 Outline why a business might want to support projects in its local community, such as sponsoring a sports team or a theatre group. *(4 marks)*

(20 marks)

Case study

Time allowed: 35 minutes

Nissan 2000

As the car industry moved into the new millennium, Nissan threatened to switch production of its next Micra car away from the UK, raising the possibility of thousands of job losses in the car industry. The Japanese company, like other motor manufacturers, found its profits reduced by the high pound as well as other factors.

Nissan's Sunderland factory has received substantial financial assistance from the government and is Europe's most efficient. Even so, Nissan warned that unless there are further cost reductions of 30%, the next Micra will be built in the French and Spanish factories of Renault, with

which it has formed a joint venture. The Sunderland factory could lose up to 2,000 jobs unless the current production of the Micra is replaced. A further 10,000 UK jobs could be lost at suppliers. This would have a significant impact on Nissan's stakeholders.

The Nissan Almeira and Primera will continue to be built in Sunderland, but the joint venture would allow the Micra to share major components with the Renault Clio and be produced much more cheaply in other countries in the European Union.

Source: adapted from OCR 2871, January 2002

Answer all questions.

1 State **two** possible examples of social costs that car manufacturing might create. *(3 marks)*

2 State the difference between 'private benefits' and 'social benefits'. *(2 marks)*

3 State the difference between 'private costs' and 'social costs'. *(2 marks)*

4 Analyse the possible stakeholder conflicts that could arise within Nissan UK. *(9 marks)*

5 Evaluate how the stakeholders in Nissan might be affected if the Micra is manufactured abroad. *(14 marks)*

(30 marks)

Business resources

A business requires a variety of resources to operate on a day-to-day basis and to succeed in reaching its objectives. **Business resources** can be defined as those factors that are absolutely essential for a business to operate. As well as the essential resources, there are other important factors. Some of these are generic (i.e. common to all businesses); others are more specific.

The running of a successful business is neither easy nor straightforward and there are certain personal qualities that are needed. This chapter considers these qualities and examines how success in business might be judged.

Essential business resources

The following resources are essential to any business.

Effective employees

A business that cannot obtain the necessary labour with the right skills and attitude will find it difficult to function successfully. Most businesses require employees with a variety of skills. When the correct employees have been recruited, they need to be properly trained and motivated in order for them to work effectively.

Effective managers

Managers help to ensure that a business is achieving its objectives. Effective managers are needed to coordinate the different areas of business activity — human resources, operations management, finance and marketing — so that the business runs smoothly.

In addition to their role as a coordinator, managers need to perform many other roles, such as motivating staff, planning, and reviewing progress. Managerial incompetence when dealing with stakeholders such as employees, the bank, suppliers and customers is one route to business failure.

Finance

 **EXAMINER'S VOICE**

If you are well acquainted with the issues concerning the importance of a business's resources, you will find it much easier to evaluate which factors might affect its success in a given situation.

Finance is needed for many reasons, including paying everyday bills and purchasing capital equipment such as machinery. A business with insufficient finance will find it hard to get properly started or to expand.

Cash flow is particularly important. This is dealt with in Chapter 31. For the moment it is sufficient to say that a business needs enough cash flowing into it in order to pay its bills. A business might be profitable, in the sense that it sells a product for a higher price than it costs to make or buy, but if customers pay on credit, it could still run into financial difficulty. This is because it will not have sufficient cash to pay its immediate debts.

Sources of finance are considered in Chapter 4.

What else does a business need to operate effectively?

As well as the above essential resources, any business would certainly benefit from the following.

A unique selling point

A business needs some way to make itself different from its competitors. A corner shop on a housing estate will be more expensive to buy from than a supermarket, but it has the 'selling point' that it is more convenient to go to if a customer only wants to buy a litre of milk or a newspaper. Other **unique selling points (USPs)** could be the standard of customer service, the help and advice offered, or the quality of the products on sale. It does not matter which are used as long as the business makes itself stand out from the competition.

Reliable suppliers

Suppliers that deliver the quantities of raw materials (or other inputs) needed, of the right quality, at a competitive price and at the correct time, are an extremely valuable asset. A reliable supplier allows a business to provide the right products to satisfy its consumers.

Loyal customers

A business needs customers in order to generate revenue and profit. Furthermore, it does not just want any customers; it wants customers who come back time after time, and who will recommend its products to others. A strategy to win (and keep) customers is essential.

Effective marketing

Effective marketing does not simply mean selling; it refers to all the activities involved in identifying customers and their needs, and then getting them to

KEY TERM

unique selling point (USP): the way a business makes itself different from its competitors

The USP of a corner shop is that it is more convenient than a supermarket if a customer only wants to buy a litre of milk or a newspaper

buy the product. A business has to produce the goods that customers want, at the price they are prepared to pay. It will also have to decide where to advertise and how to promote its products. In addition, if a business does not have its own shops, it will need a distribution system that ensures its products reach the retailers at the correct time.

Marketing is considered in depth in Chapters 20–29.

A clear business plan

A plan should detail not only the business's tactical and strategic objectives, but also who is responsible for reaching them, and the resources needed to achieve them. A proper plan, clearly communicated to employees, means that everyone in the business knows what they are expected to achieve — and how. Without a clear plan, a business is unlikely to be successful.

Figure 3.1
The requirements of a successful business

KEY TERM

business success: a measure of how well a business has achieved its objectives

Luck

To all the requirements for business success shown in Figure 3.1 may be added 'luck'. While a business cannot rely on luck alone, it cannot be denied that luck often plays a part in a business's success — or failure. For example, a particularly hot summer would benefit a newly established business selling ice cream. On the other hand, one of a business's most important employees may bump into an old friend who offers her a job at a hugely increased salary — a vital member of staff is therefore lost due to a lucky (for her) meeting.

A manager can try to maximise the effects of good luck and minimise the effects of bad luck, but luck, good or bad, cannot be ignored. It will certainly affect a business at some point in its existence.

> *e* **EXAMINER'S VOICE**
>
> The list of what a business needs is virtually endless. However, the way to score well in the examination is not to produce a long list of possible factors, but to evaluate which are the most important for the particular business in the case study.

Personal qualities needed to run a business

People setting up their own business need a variety of personal qualities, such as those shown in Figure 3.2.

Figure 3.2 The qualities of an entrepreneur

Energy and enthusiasm
These are required even for the aspects of running a business that are not enjoyable — laid-back pessimists are unlikely to succeed in business.

Self-belief and confidence
If people do not believe in themselves, who will?

Persistence and 'drive'
Success is very unlikely to come immediately. James Dyson, now a successful entrepreneur, had a hard time convincing his financial backers that his ideas had a future.

Leadership skills, such as motivation and communication
These are essential to achieve a committed, productive workforce.

What an entrepreneur needs

Ability to work under pressure, both alone and with others
Life in the early years of a business can be very difficult.

Ability to be comfortable with risk
Setting up a business is likely to involve a considerable personal financial risk and quite possibly a risk to health and family life as well.

Creativity and imagination
These are necessary for coming up with ideas and solutions to a variety of problems.

Reasons for business failure

Business failure can be ascribed to a variety of causes.

Failure to seek professional advice

Sometimes people running a newly established business are too ashamed to admit that they need help and may put off a meeting with a financial adviser at their bank until it is too late. Professional advice (e.g. on tax allowances or VAT regulations) can avoid expensive difficulties with the tax authorities at a later date.

Reluctance to use an accountant or a lawyer to avoid spending money can turn out to be a false economy

Lack of financial discipline

Failing to chase up money owed to the business can lead to poor cash flow (see Chapter 31) and is a common cause of failure. Another is not setting budgets (financial limits on how much can be spent), or not sticking to them, for each area of the firm, such as heating, lighting and advertising.

Other, less obvious, financial issues can cause problems, such as failing to ensure that the business is adequately insured against fire and theft.

Insufficient market research

Many people set up a business centred on their favourite hobby or interest. They assume that because they are enthusiastic about it, everyone one else will be too. This is known as being 'product orientated' and can be a bad mistake; a business must be orientated to the customer, not the product on sale. This requires the business to undertake **market research**.

Long before the business opens, crucial questions need to be asked. How big is the market? Is it growing or shrinking? What is the customer profile (in terms of age, sex, income level etc.)? Is demand seasonal? Are the products to be sold luxuries, demand for which may vary with the state of the economy, or necessities that will be bought on a regular basis?

Without clear answers to these sorts of questions, the business will not know how large the level of demand (and therefore its profit) is likely to be, who its customers actually are, or how best to target its products at them.

Inability to change

Markets change for all sorts of reasons: it may be that customer requirements change, the law alters, or there is an improvement in the technology that the business uses to make its products. If a business fails to adapt to changing market conditions and makes products that are out of line with consumer expectations, it will not succeed.

Problems for a newly established firm

In addition to those described above, a newly established firm faces a particular set of problems, such as:

- raising the necessary finance to pay for its day-to-day operations
- being able to pay competitive wages to attract the best staff
- convincing doubting customers that it can 'deliver'
- having to pay suppliers 'up front' (immediately) because there is no track record of successful payment

The survival of small businesses

In light of these difficulties, why do so many small businesses exist?

- The business may be just starting. It is relatively easy to set up a small business as a sole trader or partnership (see Chapter 5) due to the low initial costs. Few businesses start as large companies.
- The person (or people) running it may not want the business to grow. A larger business brings more problems. Those running a small business may not want any additional stress.
- The owner may prefer to be 'a big fish in a small pond' — that is, an important person whose business is well known and respected locally —

than 'a small fish in a large pond', where the business is simply one among many that compete nationally.

- A sole trader may enjoy the amount of control and power that he or she has over the business, which could be diminished if it grew larger by becoming a partnership.
- The business may offer a personal service, such as carpentry, tailoring or hairdressing. The owner may have a skill or talent that is not easily replicated.
- The market itself may be small, so the demand for the business's products will also be small.

How might a business judge whether it is successful?

It is tempting simply to say 'look at the amount of profit made'. It is certainly true that a large amount of profit usually indicates success, but suppose that the business has only been established recently. If so, it may not be making any profit at all. Perhaps its main objective is simply to survive its first year of trading — even if it makes a loss. In that case, if the business does survive then it has succeeded.

Small businesses may offer a personal service

Therefore, the most appropriate way to judge success is to compare the original objectives that were set for a particular time period with what has actually been achieved. These objectives should include target figures for profit (or losses) and will also be related to meeting the needs of the various stakeholders.

However, as shown in Chapter 2, not all stakeholders are necessarily going to be happy with how they have been treated. If shareholders have received a large dividend, they will consider that it has been a very successful year, whereas if employees have only had a small pay rise, they may not feel the same way.

Alternatively, if the employees at an airport that has built a new terminal receive a large pay rise as a result of the airport's growth, they may feel that their business is a successful one. On the other hand, the growth will have generated more social costs such as noise pollution, congestion and lower house prices. The residents in the local community may feel rather differently about this 'success'.

Other criteria for judging business success include:
- achieving a certain amount of revenue or volume of sales
- achieving a certain level of growth in the amount of revenue or sales
- increasing the business's market share
- improving customer loyalty — that is, repeat visits to the business, accompanied by sales

Further sources

www.shell-livewire.org — a (free) advice and information service for young people who want to start up and run their own business

In the case of a newly established business, particularly one that it is run by a person who used to work for someone else, the question might be approached from the perspective of their quality of life. Is he or she more stressed than before? Does running the business allow them sufficient family and leisure time? Are they 'happier' than before?

YOUR TURN

Case study

Time allowed: 40 minutes

Freshco UK

Freshco is a multinational US supermarket chain that has outlets in the UK, mainly in the north of England. In the late 1990s, the UK division performed well and throughout 2002/03 it opened over 30 new branches. In recent years, however, the company has found it hard to compete with better-known UK national stores such as Tesco and Sainsbury's. Profits have fallen and so has the company's share price. The board of Freshco UK has been reviewing the business's position and has announced what it calls 'a radical shake-up'. A spokesman for the company said:

We have always prided ourselves on looking after our customers and trying to use local suppliers. However, the market is very competitive and some of our stores are simply not profitable. We therefore intend to close down some of the smaller rural stores over the next 18 months. We will also introduce on-line purchasing. This will be a major benefit to all of our customers. Change may be painful, but it is necessary. The UK division of Freshco will emerge leaner and fitter. These changes will provide a secure base for benefiting our stakeholders in the future.

Answer all questions.

1 Freshco is a large multinational supermarket chain. Outline **two** reasons why so many small grocery retailers continue to exist in the UK despite the existence of large food retailers. *(4 marks)*

2 'Change may be painful, but it is necessary.' Outline **two** reasons why Freshco has had to change the way it operates. *(4 marks)*

3 Analyse how Freshco's UK stakeholders might be affected by the decision to close some of the smaller rural stores. *(9 marks)*

4 State **two** ways in which Freshco UK could judge its future success. *(2 marks)*

5 Evaluate the factors that are likely to determine the future success of Freshco UK. *(14 marks)*

(33 marks)

Finance

Businesses need money for a variety of reasons — for starting up, for everyday bill payments and for expansion, to name just three. When a business starts up, it needs money to buy buildings, machinery, raw materials and office equipment, ranging from essential pieces of capital equipment, such as computers, to everyday items like chairs and tables. Once it is established, it needs to finance its day-to-day running carefully.

The finance required for the day-to-day survival of a business is known as **working capital**. This is needed for a short period of time — possibly for only a few weeks or even days — and will not be raised in the same way as the finance required for a business's growth, which will be needed for a long period of time — possibly many years. How a business decides to finance each stage of its development is therefore extremely important.

 KEY TERM

working capital: short-term finance required for the day-to-day running of a business

 EXAMINER'S VOICE

Different sources of finance have different implications for a business, so it is important that the most appropriate method of finance is chosen for the purpose that the business has in mind. It is essential that you understand the advantages and disadvantages of each method of finance.

Apart from the owners' own funds, there is a variety of sources of finance available. These sources can be short-term, medium-term or long-term.

Short-term finance

Short-term finance (working capital) is needed for the day-to-day running of a business and is usually thought of as being for a period of up to 3 years. In order to understand short-term finance it is necessary to understand the concept of **cash flow** (see Chapter 31). It has already been noted in Chapter 3 that one of the most important factors determining whether a business succeeds is the ability to pay its bills. There must be a sufficient inflow of cash (revenue) to meet cash outflows (bills). If this is not the case, it has a cash-flow problem and so needs short-term finance to overcome this.

When considering the sources of short-term finance, an obvious one is a bank. All the commercial (high-street) banks offer various methods of finance for businesses.

KEY TERM

cash flow: a business needs sufficient inflows of cash to finance its day-to-day outgoings (e.g. wages and interest repayments); if cash receipts are insufficient, the business is said to have a cash-flow problem

Overdraft

There are two types of bank account: deposit accounts (also known as savings accounts), in which money deposited earns interest; and current accounts, which are used to make and receive payments. A cheque book is used with a current account.

A deposit account usually needs a period of notice before funds can be withdrawn, and is therefore not suitable for a business to use to make payments. With a current account, funds can be 'drawn' (i.e. taken out) whenever it is necessary. Current accounts therefore tend to earn less interest than savings accounts, and some pay no interest at all. When an overdraft is granted, no money is actually credited to the current account, but the business is allowed to run the account down to zero and then a further pre-arranged amount can be withdrawn — hence the term 'overdrawn'.

It is usual for a bank to permit a certain level of overdraft when a current account is opened. If a business wants a larger overdraft, it has to negotiate one, for which it may be charged an arrangement fee. If it fails to do this and simply tries to overdraw more than allowed, the bank may refuse to release the money and any cheques written will 'bounce' (i.e. not be paid). The business will then not be able to make its payments, which could lead it to have a poor reputation as a customer.

Interest on an overdraft is only paid on the amount actually overdrawn. If the overdraft that has been granted by the bank is for £2,000 and the business only uses £1,500 of it, the interest is only charged on this lower amount and not on the full amount of the overdraft. So if a business quickly returns its current account to a credit balance, it will not have to pay much interest.

An overdraft is therefore a safety net for a business; it should not be used for the purchase of capital items such as computers or photocopiers.

Loans are available from high-street banks

Loan

Another source of finance available from a bank is a loan. Short-term loans tend to be used to buy specific pieces of equipment or to purchase a particular consignment of raw materials in order to fulfil a contract.

A separate account (for the amount of the loan) is opened and the full amount is credited to the business's current account. When repayments are made, they are taken from the business's current account and paid into the loan account. This reduces the amount of the loan that is outstanding, and this

continues until the balance owing on the loan account falls to zero (i.e. the loan is repaid).

A loan is not a safety net in the way that an overdraft is. There is little point in a business borrowing money in the form of a loan and keeping it in its current account 'just in case anything happens', because this would mean paying interest on funds that it was not using.

There is another important difference between an overdraft and a loan. If a business exceeds its overdraft limit, the bank has the right to demand the whole amount back at once. This cannot happen with a loan. The loan is granted for a particular period of time and can only be demanded back by the bank if the business fails to pay the interest due.

If the business defaults on (fails to pay) its interest, the loan will take longer to pay off, and the amount on which interest is charged will be higher. It is usually possible for a business to arrange a reduction in the amount of interest payable (or even a 'payment holiday' when no payments are made) for a certain period of time. However, this does not mean that the business has been let off the money it owes; the interest payment is simply being deferred until a later date.

It is sometimes asked why a business would want to take out a loan and pay the full amount of interest when it could negotiate an overdraft and only pay for the amount of money actually used. The answer lies in the concept of an overdraft as a safety net.

An overdraft should not be used for the purchase of capital items such as vehicles or office equipment. Suppose a business plans to expand. It is granted an overdraft and uses it for these types of purchase. Assume that it does indeed sell a lot of extra products. However, if these are sold on credit, it will promptly run into a cash-flow problem and have to ask for an even greater overdraft. This will not look very financially responsible to the bank. If this extra overdraft is granted, it will be at a high rate of interest.

It is also likely that the amount of interest payable on an overdraft will be higher than the amount charged on a loan. A business therefore needs to use its short-term finance in the proper manner.

Factors influencing a bank's decision to lend

When deciding whether or not to lend, a bank will consider the following factors:
- what the finance is to be used for
- the company's past trading record, or the business proposal if it is a new firm
- the type of product being sold — is it a luxury purchase or one that consumers will always require?
- the business's current financial position, including existing debts. What does it already owe? Who has 'first call' on the firm's revenue?

- financial projections — revenue, profit, cash flow etc. This is where the preparation of a business plan is so essential.
- the nature of the market and forecasts of sales. Is the market growing or shrinking? At what rate?
- the role and experience of the business's managers. Are they 'steering' the firm in the right way, so that it will be profitable and generate the returns to repay any money borrowed?

KEY TERM

security: something that acts as assurance to a lender that it will get its money back if a business is unable to pay back money it has borrowed

In addition to these considerations, the bank will want to know what sort of **security** will be offered by the business: that is, what can be offered if the firm becomes unable to pay back the money borrowed. This may not be so important with a small overdraft or a loan, but it is when large sums of money are lent for long periods of time. The bank may want to take possession of the title deeds to the business's factory or office as security. These deeds are the documents that give legal ownership to a particular piece of land — the land that the factory or office is built upon. If the business fails to repay the loan, the bank — as holder of the deeds — is legally entitled to sell the factory or office in order to recover any amount outstanding on the loan.

Trade credit

This means making use of an opportunity offered to defer payment to a supplier. For example, a business called Soundrive makes high-quality audio equipment for luxury cars, some of which it sells to a company called Maximotors. It receives the majority of its components from a firm called Wireright. It assembles these components immediately into finished products, delivers them and receives payment 1 month later.

Wireright allows a 6-week period of trade credit to all its customers. Soundrive would therefore be foolish to pay for the components as soon as they are delivered. If it does not have to pay immediately, this means that it can wait until it receives payment from Maximotors and so use the funds it would have used to pay Wireright for other purposes in the meantime. Thus, Soundrive's use of trade credit is a form of short-term finance — one that does not incur any interest charges.

Figure 4.1 The use of trade credit means that Soundrive has £20,000 worth of finance to use, as necessary, for 2 weeks

Why would Wireright offer this sort of credit period? Surely it wants its money as soon as possible — after all, it has its own debts to pay. The answer is that it is common business practice and any firm not offering trade

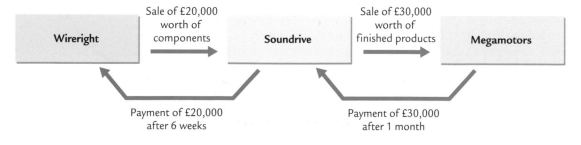

credit and insisting on immediate payment is likely to find itself at a considerable disadvantage when marketing its products. If trade credit is offered, a business should use it.

Factoring

This means a business selling its debts to raise finance. Debt often takes the form of an 'IOU'. With regard to the example above, assume that Soundrive is holding a signed invoice (bill) from one of its large customers called Megacars. In this document, Megacars agrees to pay £100,000 in 1 month's time for the audio equipment it has received. The problem is that Soundrive needs the money immediately to pay its employees and the interest on its bank loan. This debt can be sold to a factoring company. Specialist companies exist for this, although most banks offer factoring services.

The factoring company (factor) will offer a certain percentage of the debt to Soundrive (say, 90%) and will then legally own the debt. When the payment becomes due, Megacars will pay the factor and not Soundrive. The factoring of the debt makes little, if any, difference to Megacars, which will only pay what it owed anyway.

The advantage to Soundrive is that it gets most of the finance at once, instead of having to wait until the end of the month for it. On the other hand, the drawback is that it has lost a percentage of the money it is owed. Whether this is worth it depends on Soundrive's circumstances. It is not beneficial to lose 10% of revenue in this way every month. Soundrive should try to find some way of improving cash flow so that this is not necessary. However, if a

Figure 4.2 Factoring

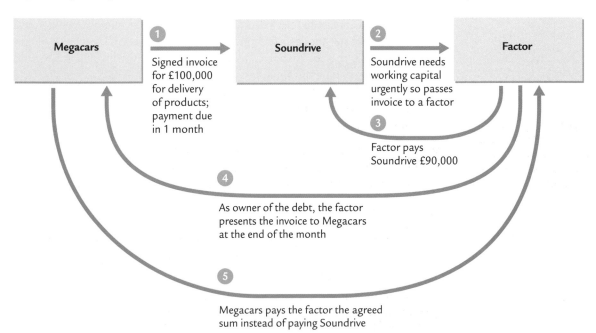

financial problem has arisen that is only expected to last for a short while, or, at worst, the need for cash means the difference between survival and closure, Soundrive's use of a factor is sensible.

Hire purchase

Hire purchase is a method of paying for an item in instalments over a period of months or years. As the name implies, while the payments are being made, the item is being hired by the business and does not actually become the business's property (i.e. is not actually 'purchased') until the last payment is made. Like all forms of credit, hire purchase has the advantage that a large sum of money does not have to be found all at once and the repayments can be spread over a period of time.

This method of finance can certainly help improve cash flow, but it means that at the end of the contract more money will have been paid out than if the business had paid cash in the first place.

Medium-term finance

Medium-term finance is normally thought of as being for between 3 years and 10 years. The most likely purposes for obtaining medium-term finance are:

- to replace expensive pieces of equipment that have broken down or become out of date
- to expand; if a business decides on the objective of growth, it will need larger premises, more equipment or more modern machinery
- to convert a business's persistent overdraft into a formal medium-term loan; the overdraft will then be cleared and, although a loan will have been created, this means that the overdraft can then achieve its proper purpose — as a safety net for cash-flow problems.

Various different forms of medium-term finance are available to a business.

Medium-term loan

As is the case with a short-term loan, an agreed amount is credited to the business's current account. For a medium-term loan (and, indeed, a long-term loan), the rate of interest charged by the bank is particularly important. Suppose that Soundrive wants a loan to finance some new technology in order to expand. The amount of interest payable on a medium-term loan depends on several factors:

- how much is borrowed
- how long the money is wanted for
- the security that is provided

Soundrive has the option to choose either a variable rate or a fixed rate loan. The former means that the amount of interest Soundrive pays varies with whatever decisions the Bank of England makes with regard to interest rates. A fixed rate loan has the advantage of certainty: if Soundrive takes out a fixed rate loan, then those running the business will know what the repayment

costs are going to be. This will make financial planning easier. Soundrive will not be 'thrown off course' by a rise in interest rates.

The disadvantage of a fixed rate loan is that, if rates fall, Soundrive still has to pay the rate that it has agreed to. It will therefore be paying more than if it were on a variable rate loan. It is usually possible to end the fixed rate agreement with the bank, but there is a penalty clause that could amount to several months' interest payments.

Hire purchase and leasing

Hire purchase, which has already been mentioned as a source of short-term finance, can also be considered as a method of medium-term finance. **Leasing** is similar in that it also allows payment to be made in instalments, thus spreading the cost over a number of years — although, as with hire purchase, this means that the total amount eventually paid will be (perhaps considerably) in excess of the cash price.

Leasing, however, differs from hire purchase in two important aspects. First, leasing an item is basically the same as renting it. This means that a business that leases something never actually owns it — unless, of course, the leasing company offers to sell it to the business when the agreement comes to an end.

If Soundrive wants a new network with specific facilities for computer-aided design and computer-aided manufacture, but cannot afford to pay for it all at once, it could contact a leasing company with the proposal to lease the equipment for 6 years. If the leasing company agrees, the equipment will be installed. Payments are made monthly but, unlike with hire purchase, the items leased do not become the property of Soundrive at the end of the 6 years.

The second way in which leasing differs from hire purchase is that, as the equipment is leased and not owned, if it breaks down, the leasing company must fix it at its own expense.

It may be part of the agreement that the leasing company updates Soundrive's computers and/or software. This would reduce the risk of the business getting left behind in technological terms. If this is the case, the lease will be more expensive.

Long-term finance

Long-term finance is usually thought of as finance for periods in excess of 10 years. This finance is for securing the resources for long-term growth. For the long term, a business essentially has the choice of raising finance by borrowing or through the issue of shares.

Long-term loans

Long-term loans are used for expensive pieces of machinery, the cost of which needs to be spread over a lengthy period of time — perhaps as long as 20 years.

CHAPTER 4   Finance

Loans for buildings are known as *mortgages* and can vary in duration between 20 years and 30 years, although they usually run for 25 years. The amount of finance involved is large and the bank will certainly require the title deeds of the land as security. As with the medium-term loan, it is possible for a business to opt for either a variable or a fixed rate mortgage. However, in the latter case, the rate would not be fixed for the whole length of the loan — 20 years plus is too far ahead for either the bank or the business to judge whether the rate fixed at the beginning would be beneficial or not. It is much more likely that the option to renew on a fixed rate basis will be offered every few years.

Debentures

These are a special type of long-term loan that is only available to a public limited company. There are two differences between debentures and other types of loan. First, the company does not borrow money from a bank in the usual way, but sells debentures to investors in order to raise finance. The debentures carry a fixed rate of interest which the company must pay to the debenture holders every year. Second, the debentures can be resold to someone else if the investor needs his/her money back before the debenture matures (is paid back). Debentures are sometimes called 'loan stocks' or just 'stocks' — as in the term 'stocks and shares'. Like other long-term loans, debentures are almost certainly secured on a specific asset of the company, so that if there are financial problems the debenture holders can force the company to sell the asset in order to get their money back.

The issue of shares

Share issue is also known as *equity finance*; when investors use the term 'equities', they are talking about shares. This type of finance is only available to a company (see Chapter 5).

In the case of a private company, there may be restrictions on the transfer of shares, and their value is not readily obvious because they are not traded in a market. With a public company, once shares are issued they are then traded on the **stock market** — the place where debentures and shares are bought and sold. Public companies are able to raise more capital than private limited companies, but in either case the shares are issued for ever — they are not like debentures or loans, which are paid back.

Shareholders are entitled to a dividend (a share of the company's profits), but it is not a legal requirement that a dividend is paid every year; theoretically, a company could retain all its profit. The shareholders cannot demand their money back in the way that a bank can if interest on a loan is not paid. However, this would not be very popular and would result in some interesting scenes with the directors at the annual general meeting. Moreover, once knowledge of the company's action became public, the share price would be bound to fall.

 TERM

stock market:
a market where shares and debentures are bought and sold; only public companies have their shares traded on the stock market

Module 2871

Only plcs can raise finance on the stock market

When a company wants to issue more shares, this is known as a *rights issue*. Existing shareholders are offered the opportunity ('right') to buy more shares at a price that is lower than the current market value. This makes the shares tempting to buy, and the shareholders know that control over the company is being kept among the same group of people as before.

EXAMINER'S VOICE

A common mistake among AS candidates is to assume that when shares are resold they are sold back to the company. This is not the case; they are sold to other investors. It should be apparent why. A company issues shares to raise large amounts of finance in order to purchase expensive buildings and equipment. If investors were entitled to sell their shares back to the company, it would either need to have a huge amount of cash constantly ready to hand (which would be earning no return) or have to sell the very equipment it has bought in order to pay them back.

Sale and leaseback

A business can raise finance by selling off an asset such as a building or a piece of land. This can raise a considerable amount of finance and is a sensible course of action if the asset is no longer needed.

Sale and leaseback is where the asset is sold but then leased back — usually for a long period of time. Soundrive, the audio business mentioned above, could sell off one of its factories and then agree to lease it back for 20 years. If it needs finance in order to fund an expansion, it can raise a large amount of finance in this way and has the knowledge that it can operate from exactly the same site as before for many years.

There are disadvantages. Soundrive no longer owns the asset it is leasing. When the lease expires, there is no guarantee that it will be renewed; the

business that owns the factory might want to sell it. Soundrive would then have to vacate the premises and go elsewhere. Furthermore, as is the case with all leasing, Soundrive must pay the leasing company for the next 20 years for using the very asset it owned previously.

Retained profit

Once a business has been operating profitably for several years, it is likely that some of the profit will be retained for the purpose of using in the future. When this has happened, the retained profit can be a useful source of finance that does not incur the business any debt.

Table 4.1 Sources of finance: a summary

Short-term	Medium-term	Long-term
Overdraft	Loan	Loan
Loan	Hire purchase	Sale of assets
Trade credit	Leasing	Sale and leaseback
Factoring	Retained profit	Retained profit
Hire purchase		Shares (if the business is a company)
		Debentures (if the business is a plc)

Other sources of finance

Government assistance

Government assistance does not come in the form of a 'no strings attached' bag of cash. It falls into two categories: assistance with obtaining a loan and regional aid.

The Small Firms Loan Guarantee scheme (SFLG)

A lender requires security to ensure that it will get its money back. But what happens if, despite the fact that there is a sound business proposal, a business has little security to offer? In the past, this could have made it hard to obtain finance. The idea behind the SFLG scheme, which began in 2003, is to enable small firms with little security to offer to obtain finance.

As the name implies, the SFLG is targeted at smaller businesses rather than established ones that are already financially secure. The finance is a loan *not* from the government but from a bank. The bank will obviously want to see the usual documents (e.g. cash-flow forecasts and business plans) and the actual decision whether to lend or not is left to the bank.

If the bank is satisfied with the proposal, the guarantee (security) for 75% of the loan comes from the government via the **Department of Trade and Industry (DTI)**.

Regional Development Assistance (RDA)

Government financial assistance is also available if the business is located, or is prepared to locate, in certain areas of the UK (see Figure 4.3). These are usually the areas where traditional industries (e.g. coal mining, steel making) have been in decline for a number of years. This decline often means that the

KEY TERM

Department of Trade and Industry (DTI): a government department that exists to help businesses improve their competitiveness and productivity

skills of the workforce are out of date and/or the infrastructure (e.g. transport links) is poor.

This aid is known as Regional Development Assistance. RDA is available for a business if it can demonstrate that, on receiving assistance, it will safeguard and create jobs or be helped to grow so that it can compete more effectively at home or abroad.

The assistance on offer includes *incentives* to locate in a particular area. These include:

- tax incentives, which lower the amount of tax a business has to pay
- sale of land or property to businesses at a discounted rate
- reduced rents for buildings and factories

In addition, there are *grants* to businesses for:

- investment in equipment — to improve competitiveness
- training or retraining their employees — to improve skills and productivity
- research and development into new products — to keep ahead of foreign competition

Whereas the SFLG is intended for small businesses, RDA assistance is available to larger, more established businesses.

Source: DTI

Depreciation

Over a period of time, some of a business's assets, such as a removal company's vans, will wear out. They become worth less each year; that is, they depreciate. Eventually, new ones will have to be bought. The Inland Revenue ('the taxman') permits the business to claim an allowance for this depreciation each year and to treat it as a cost to the business. Since profit equals revenue minus cost, any increase in cost will lower the firm's (pre-tax) profit. This seems a rather odd thing for a firm to want to do, but a lower profit will lower the amount of tax a business has to pay. It can therefore retain the amount 'saved' as a result of the depreciation allowance in order to purchase new equipment.

Figure 4.3 *Areas receiving Regional Development Assistance*

This is shown in Table 4.2. For simplicity, assume that the firm only pays two costs — wages and raw materials — and that the rate of tax is 25%. In example 1, it can be seen that with no allowance for depreciation the profit after tax is £75,000.

Assume that the allowance for depreciation is £10,000. In example 2, when depreciation is included, the profit after tax rises to £77,500.

Table 4.2 *Depreciation*

Example 1		Example 2	
Revenue	£200,000	Revenue	£200,000
Wages	£70,000	Wages	£70,000
Raw materials	£30,000	Raw materials	£30,000
		Depreciation	£10,000
Profit before tax	£100,000	Profit before tax	£90,000
Tax at 25%	£25,000	Tax at 25%	£22,500
Profit after tax	**£75,000**	Profit after tax	**£77,500**

KEY TERM

venture capital:
finance from individ-
uals or firms who lend
money to, or buy
shares in, small and
medium-sized
businesses that require
finance for starting up
or expansion

Venture capital and business angels

Venture capitalists are individuals or firms who lend money, known as **venture capital**, to small and medium-sized businesses that require finance for starting up or expansion. Venture capitalists often take a gamble in doing this because it is quite likely that the business requiring the funds has been refused finance by other lenders as the risk of failure is high. However, a high risk is associated with the expectation of a high reward. A venture capitalist might agree to provide a certain amount of finance in exchange for 20% of a new company's shares and might adopt a 'take it or leave it' approach. If the company accepts and does well, then in a few years the venture capitalist will be looking forward to large dividend payments and a substantial capital gain from the shares if it chooses to sell them.

Business angels are similar to venture capitalists, but they usually offer management advice as well. They can also bring knowledge of useful contacts, such as suppliers and potential customers, to a business.

The owner(s) of a small business need to evaluate carefully the use of this source of finance. An angel will require a financial return for its capital and time, and may insist on becoming actively involved in the running of the business in order to safeguard its investment. This may cause problems and conflict.

Internal and external sources of finance

Finance can also be classified according to whether it is internal or external.

If finance is raised internally, it does not increase the debts of the business. Internal sources include the funds available from the sale of any unwanted assets, from retained profit and from the use of trade credit. Internal sources are more likely to be available when a firm is well established.

External finance is provided by people or institutions outside the business in the form of loans, overdrafts, shares and debentures. The use of external sources of funding creates a debt that will require payment.

A business's choice of finance

There are advantages and disadvantages whatever methods of finance a business uses. The actual choice depends on several factors, as shown in Figure 4.4:

- **The type of business.** Sole traders and partnerships cannot issue shares and so are restricted in the types of finance available for growth.
- **The amount of control desired.** Becoming a partnership (or taking on a new partner if the business is already a partnership) will increase the capital available but reduce the control over decisions. In the case of a company, all shareholders have a vote (one per share), so becoming a company or issuing more shares will weaken control.

Figure 4.4
Factors influencing the choice of finance

Type of business

Length of time finance is needed for

Security

Factors influencing the choice of finance

Cash flow

Control

Existing debts

Internal versus external sources

- **Security.** A lack of security may mean that banks are unwilling to grant a loan, in which case some other form of finance must be found.
- **Internal funds.** If the firm has reserves of cash, should it use them for finance? On one hand, there will be no interest to pay; but on the other, once these funds are used, the firm has no financial cushion to fall back on. Another issue is whether a company should hold back some of the funds available for dividend payments in order to finance a project. If it is a public limited company, it needs to consider how the stock market is likely to react to such a decision. The share price will probably fall. A fall of a few pence does not matter, but a large drop would be a sign of concern that the wrong decision had been made, and might tempt another firm into making a takeover bid.
- **The length of time involved.** If equipment is purchased in order to expand the business, how long will it take to generate the funds to pay back the investment? If the answer is several years, short-term finance is not appropriate.
- **The current methods being used to finance the business.** Inappropriate financial management, such as poor cash-flow management or using an overdraft in the wrong way, will not impress a bank and will discourage it from lending.
- **Existing levels of debt.** If a business has already been granted several bank loans and then applies for another, the bank will think twice about authorising it because of the amount of interest that the business already has to pay. If yet another loan is allowed, the bank may wonder if the business will be able to repay all of them. If a company decides to try to raise the finance it wants via the issue of shares, it will find this difficult to do if it already has several loans. Potential investors will know that interest payments on the existing loans have to be met before any dividends are paid. If a lot of revenue is 'disappearing' into interest payments, this will reduce the amount of profit, and

Further sources

www.dti.gov.uk — information on the ways in which the government offers assistance to businesses

www.londonstockexchange.com — information about how the stock market works, share prices, company news etc.

dividends might be low as a result. This will make the proposed issue of shares unattractive to investors. For these reasons, a business has to be careful about obtaining too much finance in the way of loans.

Case study

Time allowed: 40 minutes

Problems for the partnership

Ron Eaves and Peter Slater run a small building firm (Eaves and Slater). The partnership was started during the economic boom at the end of the 1980s. Initially it was a carpentry and roofing business, but it now offers bricklaying and plumbing services as well. Tradesmen and labourers are hired as necessary.

Demand for building services is closely linked to the business cycle. Although the business has always coped with the variation in demand for its services, Ron feels it could be much more successful. He has recently been giving some thought to what they should be doing in the future to increase their income.

The administration of the firm is poor. There is no Deed of Partnership. Ron's wife works part-time doing some typing and filing when she can. Peter, who once attended evening classes in 'Basic Business Finance', is in charge of the accounts. He has been having problems keeping the accounts up to date. Last year he tried to obtain a large loan in order to finance a major carpentry contract for which Ron wanted the firm to apply. Their bank's small firms adviser was not impressed by the untidy and incomplete set of accounts that Peter showed him, and turned down the application.

Disagreement between the partners is now a major problem. Ron has, for the past year, felt that conditions are right for an expansion of the firm. They are having to turn down offers of work almost every week. He feels that in order to establish a secure basis for growth, the business should change its legal structure to a company. He has pointed out that, if this happened, the business would then have access to equity finance. He feels that at present the business is restricted in its ability to raise funds both internally and externally. He also feels they should move to larger premises. Peter, on the other hand, would prefer to maintain the partnership as it is.

What has made matters worse is that 4 months ago the town council invited estimates for a roofing repair contract for local primary schools. Ron did some rough calculations and sent in an estimate. He mentioned it vaguely to Peter at the time and they both forgot about it. Rather to their surprise, the council has accepted the estimate and wants the brothers to sign a contract within the next 2 weeks.

Peter thinks that the job is far too big for them and wants to know where they will get the money from to finance the materials and labour. Ron says that this is their chance to 'make it' and thinks that they should investigate the possibility of any financial assistance that might be available from the government. He is insisting that they sign the contract right away and that they can deal with their other problems immediately afterwards.

Source: amended from
OCR 2871, May 2002

Answer all questions.

1 Outline the difference between internal and external sources of finance. *(4 marks)*

2 State the difference between 'debt' and 'equity' finance. *(2 marks)*

3 Outline **two** differences between a loan and an overdraft. *(4 marks)*

4 Outline **two** features of the financial assistance available from the government. *(4 marks)*

5 'Their bank's small firms adviser was not impressed by the untidy and incomplete set of accounts that Peter showed him, and turned down the application.' Other than a clear, complete set of accounts, analyse the information that a bank will want to see before authorising a loan to a business such as Eaves and Slater. *(9 marks)*

6 Evaluate the sources of finance that Eaves and Slater could use for the council roofing repair contract. *(14 marks)*

(37 marks)

CHAPTER 5

The classification of businesses

This chapter deals with the different ways in which a business can be classified: by the nature of its output, by its legal structure and by its size. It contains the material needed to be able to understand and explain:

- the various stages of production in which businesses are involved
- the different legal structures businesses can have and how these affect the operation of a business
- why the government runs certain organisations and businesses
- how to judge the size of a business

The different stages of production

chain of production: stages that a product passes through until it reaches the final consumer

As products are made, they pass through what is known as the **chain of production**. For example, production of petrol starts with the extraction of crude oil from the ground, next the oil is refined, and then the petrol is distributed to garages, where it is sold to the final consumer. In some industries, one firm is involved in all stages of the chain, as shown in Figure 5.1.

Figure 5.1 Most petrol companies own their own oil fields, refineries and garages

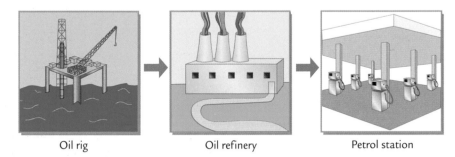

Oil rig   Oil refinery   Petrol station

In other industries, the businesses involved at each stage of the chain will be different. This textbook started out as part of a tree that was grown by one firm and quite possibly cut down by another. It was probably turned into wood pulp and then paper by another quite separate business. The paper was then printed with the text, which someone else had written, and made into a book, before being distributed (by yet another business) to a retailer where it was finally purchased by the consumer.

It does not matter whether one business or many are involved in the chain of production. What is important to note is that, as a product passes along

Business activity	Stage of production	Value of input (£)	Value added (£)	Value of output (£)
Timber is forested	Primary	0	500	500
Turned into wood pulp	Secondary	500	250	750
Turned into books	Secondary	750	1,000	1,750
Sold by the retailer	Tertiary	1,750	1,000	2,750

Table 5.1 Value is added by businesses along the chain of production

the chain, it has value added to it — in other words, it becomes worth more because of the business activity at each stage of the chain (see Table 5.1).

The actual amount of value added is the difference between the value (i.e. the cost) of the business's inputs used to produce a product, and the value of output — what the customer pays for it.

The total value of output (£2,750) is the sum of all of the values added at each stage.

The concept of value added is important because the greater the value added by a business, the greater the possibilities for stakeholders to benefit.

Business activity

This can be classified by the nature of output into three broad sectors.

Primary sector

Businesses in the primary sector are concerned with the extractive industries. These include farming, forestry, fishing and mining, as well as oil and gas extraction.

Secondary sector

Businesses in the secondary sector are concerned with manufacturing — that is, turning raw materials into semi-finished and finished products. The pressing of steel into a chassis, the production of an engine and then the final assembly of components into a complete car are examples of business activity in this sector. Secondary production also includes the construction industry — building houses, factories, office blocks and roads.

Tertiary sector

Businesses in the tertiary sector are concerned with the output of services. Services still count as production even if there is no actual finished product to see. They include a wide range of tertiary activities from retailing, banking and transportation, through the many services provided by the leisure industries, to the kinds of service provided by professionals such as teachers and doctors.

Extractive industries are examples of primary production

INGRAM

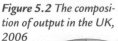

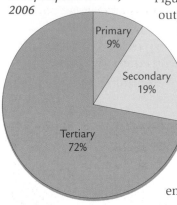

Figure 5.2 The composition of output in the UK, 2006

Deindustrialisation

Figure 5.2 shows the proportions of each sector in the output of the UK. A large tertiary sector is one of the features of an advanced economy. The decline in the level of secondary output and employment typical of advanced economies is referred to as **deindustrialisation**.

Types of business

Businesses can be classified by whether they are in the **private sector** or the **public sector** (see Figure 5.3). In the private sector, businesses are owned and run by individuals. These are referred to as 'private enterprise'. In the public sector, there are not many 'businesses' in the usual sense of the word. The term 'organisation' is more appropriate. In this sector, organisations are referred to as 'public enterprise' and are owned and run on behalf of the public by central or local government. Examples are the BBC, Railtrack and the National Health Service (NHS).

```
Private sector
  ├── Sole trader
  ├── Partnership
  └── Limited company
        ├── Private limited company (Ltd)
        └── Public limited company (plc)

Public sector
  ├── Central government owned
  └── Local government owned
```

*Figure 5.3
The private and public sectors*

The legal structure of a business is important because of the ways in which it influences the firm's operation. Legal structure is particularly important for the effects that it has on:

- ownership and control of the business
- responsibility for any debts
- sources of finance available
- the objectives pursued

Businesses in the private sector

When discussing businesses in the private sector, the term **entrepreneur** is often used. This is a French term which basically means 'a risk taker who sets up a business'. In order to produce output, the entrepreneur has to organise the business's resources and perform a variety of tasks, such as ensuring that customers remain loyal and creating a unique selling point (see Chapter 3). The entrepreneur risks his or her own money by going into business and organising these factors. In return for taking a risk, the entrepreneur hopes to get a reward — that is, make a profit. Generally speaking, the larger the risk taken, the greater the expected reward.

entrepreneur: a risk taker who sets up a business, organising the business's resources with the aim of making a profit

Although the original concept of the entrepreneur was developed in an age when most businesses were small and owned by one person, the term is still in common use. People such as Bill Gates and James Dyson, who come up with a new business idea or vision, are still referred to as entrepreneurs even though the businesses they run are definitely not small.

Sole trader

The sole trader (also known as the 'sole proprietor') is the simplest form of business organisation. The sole trader owns the business and makes all the decisions affecting it. This does not mean that the business has only one person working there; the sole trader could employ a number of people, but he or she is in overall control. The most important legal aspect of being a sole trader is that, as far as the law is concerned, the business and its owner are inseparable. The business does not exist in its own right — it is said to be 'unincorporated'.

James Dyson is a well-known entrepreneur

Advantages of being a sole trader

- There are few legal requirements when setting up as a sole trader, although some businesses may need a licence (e.g. to sell alcohol). It is therefore possible to start a business quite quickly and with relatively little capital.
- The sole trader does not have to consult with anyone and therefore making decisions (e.g. over the products on sale and the hours that the business will open) is quick and easy.
- A sole trader keeps all of the profit (after tax).
- As a sole trader cannot issue shares, he or she cannot be subject to a 'takeover' in the way that a public company can.
- Apart from having to provide information for income tax purposes, the financial state of the business can be kept private. This is not the case with a company, which has to publish its accounts.

Disdvantages of being a sole trader

- The sole trader is 'the business' and is fully responsible for all its debts. If the business runs into financial difficulty, the sole trader may be forced to sell his or her personal possessions (e.g. house or car) to pay the debts. This is known as unlimited liability.
- Sole traders have to be a 'Jack of all trades'; they must single-handedly perform all of the business's functions, such as marketing the products, controlling finance and motivating employees. No matter how talented a person is, it is unlikely that he or she

will be good at, or enjoy, all of these. Unfortunately, if any one of these is neglected or performed badly, the business is going to suffer.

- Successful businesses often want to grow. Capital for expansion can be hard to raise, which can limit the opportunities for growth.
- Sole traders can easily get overworked. This is especially true in the first years of the business's existence when the sole trader is likely to be working long hours to build up the customer base and reputation.
- Sole traders are usually small businesses. Larger firms may not wish to deal with them because they may feel that they do not have the expertise or ability to 'deliver' in the way that a larger business could.
- Since the sole trader is the business, if he or she dies, then legally the business comes to an end. There is no continuity.

Partnership

Whenever two or more people run a business together, as far as the law is concerned, they are partners. There does not have to be any formal documentation for a partnership to come into existence. Partnerships are common in the professions, such as solicitors, accountants and dentists.

Just as is the case with a sole trader, a partnership is not a legal entity in its own right. The partners are 'the business'. The law requires a minimum of two and a maximum of 20 partners.

It is good business practice for partners to draw up what is known as a Deed of Partnership. This is a legal document that governs the running of this type of business. It sets out and clarifies matters such as:

- how much money each partner is expected to contribute
- how much income each partner can draw (i.e. take) from the business
- the responsibilities and duties of each partner
- the arrangements to cover absence, sickness or holidays
- how decisions are to be made within the partnership
- the arrangements for taking on new partners
- the arrangements if the partnership is to be dissolved
- the arrangements for finance (e.g. will partners have separate or joint accounts?)

Dentists often form a partnership

If no deed exists, the business will be governed by the Partnership Act of 1890, which states that the responsibility for running the business and the distribution of profits and losses are to be shared equally among the partners.

Advantages of partnerships

- A partnership is easy to establish.
- Additional partners mean more capital. Expansion is therefore easier than it is for a sole trader.

- Work is shared and different partners with different skills can be employed.
- Partners can specialise in what they do best.
- Losses are shared.
- Partnerships, like sole traders, pay income tax, which means that the financial state of the business can be kept private.

Disdvantages of partnerships

- Partners, like sole traders, have unlimited liability. Furthermore, an individual partner is liable for any debts incurred by other partners even if he or she had no knowledge of the decisions that led to them. Partners may have limited liability if they simply contribute money and take no active part in running the business. These people are known as 'sleeping' partners. However, a partnership must have at least one partner with unlimited liability.
- Decision making is slower and there is the possibility of disagreement.
- The legal restriction on the maximum number of partners means that the business can still lack capital for expansion.
- Losses are shared but so are profits.
- There is no continuity.

Limited company

There are a number of important differences between companies and other types of business organisation:

- **Incorporation.** In law, sole traders and partnerships are unincorporated — that is, they do not exist separately from their owners. A company, on the other hand, is 'incorporated' — the business exists in its own right. Those who own the company (the shareholders) are not the same as those who run it for them (the directors).
- **Shares.** Companies can raise capital via the issue of shares, whereas sole traders and partnerships cannot. A 'share' is exactly what the term implies: buyers own a share of the company. They become one of its owners. Companies issue shares to raise money. Investors buy shares with two aims in mind: receiving a return on their money (which is known as a dividend) and making a capital gain — selling their shares for a higher price than they bought them at. The issue of shares was covered in Chapter 4.
- **Limited liability.** If a company goes into liquidation (has to cease trading) because of financial problems, its shareholders have limited liability. This means that the shareholders only lose their shares. This could mean the loss of a significant sum of money, but at least shareholders are not personally liable for the business's debts in the way that sole traders and partners are. The shareholders' liability is limited to the capital they have invested.

Private and public limited companies

There are two types of company: the private limited company and the public limited company. Private companies are often family businesses, where the advantages of being incorporated can be linked to the ability to keep control within a fairly small group of people.

Family businesses have a unique set of problems that set them aside from ordinary businesses:

- There might be rivalry between family members and quarrels over who is, or should be, in charge.
- Emotional factors might hinder decision making and affect the nature of the objectives that are being set.
- The perceptions of family members regarding fair treatment in terms of promotion, pay rises etc. can cause resentment.
- Poorly performing family members may not be disciplined when they should be.
- A shortage of 'new blood' from outside the business at management level can lead to a lack of ideas.
- Relationships can get strained as the boundaries between work and home become blurred.
- It is unusual to see a family business in the form of a public company.

Public companies are larger than private companies. Other differences are as follows:

- **The name.** A public company is a 'plc'. A private company's name must end with 'Limited' or 'Ltd'.
- **Where shares can be traded.** A plc can sell shares on the stock market. A private company cannot. A public company's shares can therefore be bought by anyone. In a private limited company, shares must be sold through private negotiation and cannot be advertised for sale to the public.
- **The possibility of being taken over.** As a plc's shares are available for anyone to buy, it can be quite legally taken over if an investor gains 51% of its shares. A private company can 'sell out' to an investor but cannot involuntarily be taken over.
- **The amount of share capital.** A plc is required to have a minimum share capital of £50,000. A private company has no minimum.
- **The way the company reports to shareholders.** A plc is required to include more detail in its annual publication to shareholders (the 'Report and Accounts'). In a private company, reporting to shareholders and the accounting procedures that the company has to use are less complicated.

The majority of large businesses in the UK are public limited companies

Private and public companies have a number of similarities too:

- **Directors.** Shareholders elect a board (a group) of directors to run the company on their behalf. In a private company, the directors may be the shareholders.
- **Information.** Shareholders must receive a copy of the company's Report and Accounts every year. They are also entitled to attend

the annual general meeting (AGM). At this meeting, they receive a report from the directors on the state of the company. This includes information on the company's finances. The shareholders are entitled to vote at meetings (e.g. in the election of directors) and to question the directors about the way the company is being run.

- **Voting.** Voting by shareholders is 'one vote per share', not 'one person, one vote'. This means that an individual or a relatively small group of people can own enough shares to outvote all the others. Theoretically, to do this a person or group would need 51% of the shares, but AGMs are often poorly attended and so it is possible to influence the business's decisions with a smaller percentage.

Advantages of companies

- The main advantage of a company is access to large amounts of capital through the ability to issue shares. This means that there are greater opportunities for growth.
- Limited liability for shareholders encourages people to invest in the company.
- Investors such as banks often regard companies as less risky than a sole traders or partnerships. This could mean better terms for borrowing money.
- Continuity — a company is a separate legal entity and so does not come to an end when the original owner(s) die. Unless a company has severe financial problems, it can exist for ever.

Disdvantages of companies

- Setting up a company can be expensive. In order for a business to be established as a company, two important legal documents need to be completed to protect the interests of shareholders. These are known as the Memorandum of Association and the Articles of Association.
- The Memorandum deals with the company's relationship with the outside world (whether it will be a private or a public company, the nature of the products it will sell etc.) The Articles deal with the internal running of the company (e.g. arrangements for the election and removal of directors). Completing these documents to the required standard means that establishing a company can be slower, more complicated and therefore more expensive than setting up as a sole trader or partnership.
- Running a company is more complicated than being a sole trader or partnership. Directors have certain legal responsibilities to the shareholders (e.g. holding the AGM, preparing the accounts in a certain way and publishing the Report and Accounts. This added complexity may mean that the company has to hire an accountant and a lawyer, which will be additional expense.
- Company accounts are not private. All company accounts, whether they are public limited companies or private limited companies, are on open access at Companies House. It is therefore difficult to keep the business's main financial details hidden from competitors.
- The danger of a takeover — in the case of a public company, the original owners could lose control if large blocks of shares are bought up by investors.
- Large companies can require complicated management structures. The more people there are to manage, the more difficult communication and coordination become.

e **EXAMINER'S VOICE**

Companies are different in their legal structure from sole traders and partnerships. This has important implications for how they raise finance, how they are run and how they report to stakeholders. It is therefore a mistake to refer to every business as 'a company'.

Limited liability partnerships (LLPs)

LLPs became legal in 2001. They combine some features of partnerships with some of those of limited companies. An LLP is a separate legal entity, so its owners have limited liability. The owners of an LLP are called members rather than partners.

Before 2001, if a group of people wanted limited liability (see p. 39) they had to form a company. The creation of LLPs means that it is possible to have the advantages of a partnership combined with limited liability. However, this limited liability comes at a price: LLPs, like private limited companies, are required to file their annual accounts at Companies House.

Franchises

A franchise is where a business with a well-known brand name (the franchiser) lets a person (the franchisee) or a group of people set up their own business using the brand. This is in exchange for an initial fee and continuing royalty payments (a certain percentage of turnover or profit) for as long as the franchise lasts.

A franchise is not a separate type of legal structure in itself. The liability for the person (or people) using the franchise depends on how the business was established. Franchisees have unlimited liability if they are in business as a

sole trader (or a partnership), but have limited liability if they have set up the franchise as a company.

Some of the best-known brand names operate some or all of their businesses as a franchise. McDonald's and Burger King are well known examples of franchises in the fast-food market, as is the Body Shop in the cosmetics market. However, franchisers can now be found in most sectors of the economy, from Chemdry for carpet cleaning, to Smart Cartridge for the recycling of printer cartridges.

Advantages for the *franchiser*

- The firm does not have to spend large amounts of money (quite possibly getting into debt) in order to expand.
- The products necessary for the franchise to operate are under the franchiser's direct control. This can mean high prices being charged to franchisees for supplies.
- Applicants to become franchisees are carefully selected for their suitability. Issuing franchises should therefore generate a continuous stream of revenue from franchisees determined to make their business succeed.

Advantages for the *franchisee*

- The franchisee is using a tried-and-tested brand name, so there is a greater chance of success than if they had gone into the same sort of business with their own brand.
- Specialist advice and training are available from the franchiser.

- The franchiser carries out market research and provides marketing support. Thus franchisees can spend more time actually selling products and making a profit for themselves.
- It may be easier to obtain finance from a bank because of these factors.

Disdvantages for the *franchisee*

- Supplies have to be bought from the franchiser, which may charge higher prices than those for similar products on the open market. This will lower profit margins.
- There will be continuing royalty payments (a certain percentage of turnover or profit) to the franchiser.
- The franchisee has less control over what it is selling, and how it sells it, than a person running his/her own business would usually have.
- The business cannot be sold without the franchiser's permission.
- A franchise is for a fixed period of time and is not automatically renewed.

Whether a franchise is an appropriate form of business for someone depends on factors such as how much time and money he/she is prepared to invest in the business, the expected rewards, and his/her attitude to risk taking.

The public sector

At central government level, money that has been raised through taxation is spent on essential services such as healthcare, education and pensions. At local government level, a range of services, including street lighting, a fire service, and refuse and recycling collection, must be provided for all residents. In addition to these, councils also provide libraries, parks and leisure centres.

The nature of the services being provided by public sector organisations means that their objectives are different from those of businesses in the private sector. The National Health Service is clearly not 'a business' in the usual sense of the word and is not expected to make a profit. The priority of most of the public sector is to provide a value-for-money service.

The fire service is financed by taxes paid to local government

However, there are likely to be certain similarities between an organisation in the private sector and one in the public sector: NHS managers may not have 'customers' in the sense that a business in the private sector has, but they are still expected to provide the highest quality of service possible. They are also expected to keep tight control on finances so as to eliminate wastage of scarce funds.

Privatisation

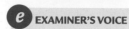 **EXAMINER'S VOICE**

Don't confuse the term 'public sector' with 'public company'. A public company is not the same as 'public enterprise'.

KEY TERMS

nationalisation: government taking ownership and control of a business or industry from private investors by buying up all its shares

privatisation: the process of selling state-owned industries to the private sector

Until the 1980s, the public sector was much larger than it is today. The government owned the industries providing services like gas, water and electricity as well as other important parts of the economy, such as the telephone network, the railways and the steel industry. Most of these industries had been **nationalised** (taken into the public sector via the compulsory purchase of their shares) by the Labour government in 1945. It was felt that ownership of the industries would give the government greater control over the economy. However, by the 1970s it was apparent that these industries were of little assistance in achieving control of the economy, and were overmanned and inefficient.

In the 1980s, Margaret Thatcher's governments decided that these industries should be **privatised**. The shares that the government owned were largely, or completely, sold and the businesses were returned to the private sector as public companies. This new approach was also felt at local level. Rather than employing their own workforce, councils had to allow private firms to compete to provide services such as refuse collection and street cleaning. Councils now have to ensure that local residents are getting the best value for their money, whoever is providing services for them.

Advantages of privatisation

Those who believe in privatisation claim that it offers the following advantages:

- **Efficiency will increase.** Privately run businesses have to keep costs down in order to survive. Nationalised industries have no such incentive because the government (or rather the taxpayer) will 'bail them out' if they are in financial trouble because of a failure to keep a grip on costs.
- **Competition between businesses is beneficial to the consumer.** Before privatisation, a person had to buy gas from the 'Gas Board'; now it can be bought from any supplier. The same logic applies to other services, such as electricity supply and rail travel. Competition leads to lower prices, more choice and better quality of service.

Disadvantages of privatisation

Critics of privatisation say the following:

- **The industries were sold off too cheaply.** The share prices usually rose quickly. The government (and therefore the public) lost out in terms of money that could have been raised.
- **Privately owned businesses are less socially responsible than nationalised ones.** When the government controlled an industry, it could tell those running it to try to take account of the social consequences of their actions — for example, when making people redundant or purchasing raw materials from UK suppliers. A private firm concerned with profit may not place much emphasis on these sorts of issues.

It is now widely accepted that the state should not provide services that the private sector can provide, as long as all consumers can benefit. There is little enthusiasm for state ownership of industries any more. Nevertheless, Railtrack, the public company that owned the railway tracks, was taken back into the public sector (and renamed Network Rail) when it ran into financial problems in 2002. It was simply too important to the economy to be allowed to collapse and disappear.

Network Rail is part of the public sector, whereas the train operating companies are part of the private sector

E-businesses

Most well-established businesses now use the internet as well as their usual outlets. The 'dot.com revolution', however, meant that a new type of business appeared that was said by some to require a completely different approach to trading. It is certainly true that some aspects of running an online business are different from those of a 'normal' firm. For example:

- the technology reduces the necessity to operate from a large, expensive building
- there is plenty of potential for cost savings in the way the operation is run; many e-businesses can be run from a person's home
- the business is convenient, as it is 'open' all day, every day

However, as well as opportunities, online trading brought new problems. For example:

- the technology must actually work!
- the payment system must be absolutely secure
- the website must be carefully designed to be user friendly
- time must be devoted to updating a website — it is not a one-off task
- awareness must be generated among a public that, initially at least, has no idea that the business exists
- once sales have been generated, the business must ensure that it has distributors who will get products to the customer on time
- not everyone has internet access and not everyone has a credit or debit card; this was overlooked by some e-businesses

E-businesses — a new type of organisation?

Even when established, poor publicity resulting, for example, from technological problems or a failure to deliver on time, can adversely affect an e-business very quickly. Most people involved in running an online business find that it is still 'a business', so factors like proper financing, reliable suppliers and motivated employees remain as important as ever.

How might the size of a business be judged?

A number of factors need to be taken into account when making a judgement about the size of a business.

Number of employees

Normally it would be expected that a 'large' business will employ a large number of employees. However, many factories are highly automated and capital intensive; they produce a lot of output, but do not employ a large number of people. There is also the problem of how to count part-time employees. In the UK, a business with fewer than 50 employees is regarded as small, and a business with more than 250 employees is large.

Number of factories, shops or offices

The more of these it has, the more the business will be perceived as 'large'. A similar criterion would be whether the business has factories, shops or offices in other countries — and if so, how many.

Many factories are highly automated

Turnover and profit levels

Turnover is the value of a business's sales. A high turnover is usually associated with a large business. However, a jeweller may only own one shop but still have a fairly large turnover. A turnover of less than £2 million is usually considered 'small', and one of more than £8 million is considered 'large'. In terms of profit, generally speaking, the higher the profit level, the larger the firm. Of course, a large firm might temporarily be having trading difficulties, so this measure may conflict with some of the others.

Stock market value

The value of a public company can be calculated by multiplying the current share price by the number of shares issued. The higher the figure, the larger the company is likely to be. There is, however, a significant drawback with this method: if the share price falls, it reduces the value of the company. This means that, on this measurement of size, the business has suddenly become smaller — even though a change in share price has no immediate impact on the number of factories, machines or employees. Since share prices can change daily, this method of estimating a business's size might be misleading.

Capital employed

Capital employed is the total value of a business's assets — its factories, machinery, offices etc. If the figure is high, it would be reasonable to assume that the business is large. However, as with a stock market valuation, prices, and therefore values, of factories and office blocks can rise or fall without any changes in the actual number owned. In addition, where the assets are located will affect their value. A factory unit in north London will be more valuable than a business of exactly the same type, in exactly the same sort of unit, in south Wales. On this measure, the London business would be 'larger'.

Further sources

www.franchisedirect.co.uk/directory — franchise opportunities available in the UK

YOUR TURN

Case study

Time allowed: 50 minutes

Boo.com

If there was one company that demonstrated the mania of the dot.com 'boom and bust' at the end of the twentieth century, it was online sportswear company boo.com. Boo became a textbook example of how not to run an e-business.

First, there was the technology. Boo thought it had hit on a great idea when its website allowed shoppers to view products from different angles. However, the pages took ages to load — and shoppers lost interest.

Second, it launched its business in more than 20 countries at the same time and spent vast sums buying and renting properties. The launch parties were wild and expensive, and they did little to attract the customers.

Finally, the control of its finances was relaxed, to say the least. The founders of the company liked to fly everywhere first class. The staff would regularly take deliveries of fruit and cake from local shops — all paid for by the company.

Boo's management seemed to forget that e-business is a business, and that traditional business theory and practice still apply — such as a clear business plan.

Having raised more than £100 million from investors in 1999, Boo collapsed in May 2000.

Source: amended from
OCR 2871, January 2003

Answer all questions.

1   Boo.com was a public limited company. State **two** ways in which a public limited company is different from a private limited company. *(2 marks)*

2   Boo was a company operating in the private sector. State **one** difference between the private sector and the public sector. *(2 marks)*

3   Analyse the methods that could be used to measure the size of a business such as boo.com. *(9 marks)*

4   Boo was an example of a business operating in the tertiary sector. Identify the other two sectors of economic activity and give an example of each. *(4 marks)*

5   Some high-street sportswear retailers are franchises. Evaluate the benefits of starting up this sort of business as a franchisee. *(14 marks)*

6   Boo.com was an online sportswear company. To what extent is running an e-company such as Boo different from running a high-street sportswear shop? *(14 marks)*

(45 marks)

CHAPTER 6

Objectives

A business needs some sort of target or sense of what it wants to achieve. To suggest that all businesses just want to make a profit is not enough; nor is it necessarily accurate. It may depend on what type of business is involved and how long it has been trading. Having a clear idea of its intentions is not only important in terms of providing a target, but it will also enable all who work within the business to be aware of where the business is hoping to go.

A company's intentions can be analysed in terms of its mission statement, its aims or goals, and its strategic and tactical objectives. These form a *hierarchy of objectives*, as shown in Figure 6.1.

Figure 6.1 *A company's mission statement, goals and objectives*

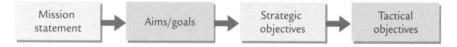

The mission statements

A mission statement gives a general idea of what the business is about and its purpose. Examples are given in Figure 6.2. The statement is intended to appeal to employees and customers alike. It is a qualitative statement, which contains no specific elements. The mission statement can be used as a form of marketing.

Figure 6.2 *Mission statements: Unilever and Cadbury Schweppes*

> **Unilever**
> '…the highest standards of corporate behaviour towards everyone we work with, the communities we touch, and the environment on which we have an impact…'
>
> **Cadbury Schweppes**
> 'Our core purpose is working together to create brands people love.'

Aims/goals

Aims or goals are more specific than a mission statement, but they are sometimes confusingly used as alternative terms for the main objectives of a business. The principal aims of most businesses include:

- **survival.** For a new business, the most important aim is survival, especially if the new business is trying to compete with well-established companies.
- **breaking even.** It is not likely that a business will be profitable straight away. There are many costs to cover, especially those of the premises and

all the fixtures (fixed costs or overheads — see Chapter 32). Therefore, it is more realistic to set a target of breaking even within a given time period (see Chapter 34).

- **share of the market/growth.** Much depends on the type of business and the market in which it operates. Capturing a larger share of the market not only increases sales with all the benefits that follow, but also puts the business in a position from which it can try to dominate the market.
- **profit.** This is a longer-term goal than survival. The ability to make a profit depends on the type of products or services offered by the business and the amount of competition in the marketplace.

Cadbury Schweppes states that its main aims are to:
- deliver top-quartile shareowner returns
- profitably double its global confectionery share
- profitably maintain and grow its regional beverages share
- develop best-in-class capabilities
- grow as a company admired internally and externally

Objectives

Companies seek to achieve their main aims or goals by setting various specific objectives. Setting objectives provides:
- a greater sense of direction for the business
- a possible motivational force for all employees
- an aid to controlling existing and future operations within the business

Objectives are of two kinds: strategic and tactical.

Strategic objectives

In order to achieve its main aims, a business adopts a plan that contains several strategic objectives. For example, the business might have the aim of achieving a 10% growth in sales within 3 years. To reach this goal, the business may decide that its strategic objectives are:
- to increase productivity within the business in order to reduce costs and thereby increase sales via lower prices
- to sell its products in new markets

However, before deciding on the most appropriate strategic objectives, the business might undertake a SWOT analysis (see Chapter 19). This will help the business to decide the best way forward in order to achieve its aims.

Tactical objectives

These are the short-term objectives necessary to achieve the business's strategic objectives. They are likely to be concerned with the day-to-day activities of the business. If the company's aim is to achieve 10% growth in sales and its strategic objective is to sell its goods in new markets, the tactical objectives will concentrate on how this is to be achieved. For example, the business, might want to advertise and merchandise its products within a chosen area within

KEY TERMS

strategic objectives: how a business plans to achieve its aims or goals; often a long-term approach

tactical objectives: the day-to-day (short-term) objectives needed to ensure the strategic objectives are achieved

6 months. It might also decide that the best way of achieving the strategic objective is to reduce its prices in these new markets.

In October 2003, Cadbury Schweppes set its strategic objectives for the period 2004–07 (see Table 6.1). Each objective has two 'priorities', which might be considered to be its tactical objectives. The strategic objectives are unlikely to change from year to year, but the priorities will.

Table 6.1
Strategic objectives:
Cadbury Schweppes

Strategic objectives for 2004–07	Priorities for 2005
1 Deliver superior shareowner performance	**1** Deliver annual contract **2** Execute 'Fuel for Growth' and focus on free cash flow
2 Profitably and significantly increase global confectionery share	**3** Invest, innovate and execute **4** Execute 'Smart Variety'
3 Profitably secure and grow regional beverages share	**5** Invest, innovate and execute **6** Strengthen non-CSDs and RTM
4 Ensure our capabilities are best in class	**7** Roll-out Building Commercial capabilities **8** Refine supply chain disciplines
5 Reinforce reputation with employees and society	**9** Motivate, develop and reward our people **10** Continue high corporate and social responsibility standards

Note: for an explanation of the terms used, see Cadbury Schweppes, Report and Accounts, 2004.

Setting objectives

A useful set of criteria for setting objectives is SMART. According to these criteria, objectives should be:

- **Specific.** It is important that everyone understands what the target is.
- **Measurable.** Normally, the objective statement should contain some kind of measurement to ensure that success or failure can be ascertained.
- **Agreed.** Agreement between different departments makes it more likely that objectives will be achieved. In practice, not only might different departments within a single business set different objectives, but some of these objectives might be conflicting. The marketing department may want to achieve an increase in sales of 10% and therefore decide to run a larger advertising campaign. Meanwhile, the finance department may want to achieve cuts in costs of 5% and therefore want to restrict the spending of other departments. To be successful, all departments need to work together in setting objectives. It is also useful for stakeholders, such as employers and workers, to agree on the firm's objectives. In practice, the stakeholders of the business have different needs and therefore often have different objectives (see Chapter 2).
- **Realistic.** It is important to be realistic when setting objectives, in order to avoid employees becoming demotivated. How would you feel if you were set the objective of gaining an A grade for all your subjects? What objectives are realistic will vary according to the type of business. A large multinational plc will have as one of its major objectives achieving a certain

level of profit in a certain timescale. This is because it has shareholders to satisfy. On the other hand, a new business that is owned and run by one person will want eventually to make a profit, but in the short term will be more concerned with survival.

- **Time-bound.** Often there is a timetable specifying the period over which an objective is to be achieved. A time constraint aids measurement and tends to focus people.

Constraints

Once objectives have been set, it is not just a question of sitting back and waiting. The circumstances in which the business operates (the business environment) may hinder progress, and in some situations may require a complete change in direction.

Constraints on a business can either be internal or external. *Internal constraints* include:

- a lack of finance to meet the chosen objectives
- poor communication within the business
- a conflict of interests between departments within the business
- an industrial dispute with the workforce

External constraints include:

- changes in the law that affect the operation of the business
- the state of the economy
- the behaviour of competitors
- the opinions and behaviour of external stakeholders

Changing objectives

Over time, as circumstances change, businesses may need to adapt their objectives. In particular, a firm's tactical objectives might alter, depending on priorities and circumstances, in order to achieve both the implementation of the strategic plan and the firm's main goals.

An industrial dispute is an example of an internal constraint on a business

However, only in extreme circumstances will the strategic plan have to be changed. Following the attack of 11 September 2001 and the suicide bombings in London in 2005, companies in the travel industry had to adapt their plans. For some businesses, it even led to a change in their strategic objectives, such as their sales targets, as these were no longer realistic.

A business may have a plan in place to deal with such circumstances — this is known as its *contingency plan*. Airlines have plans to counter any event that is outside their control. For example, during British Airways' dispute with the catering company Gate Gourmet, contingency plans were quickly put in place to cope with feeding large numbers of passengers.

Further sources	
www.shell.com	**www.cadburyschweppes.com**
www.unilever.com	**www.tt100.biz** — Michelin Tyres

YOUR TURN

Questions

Time allowed: 30 minutes

All of the following are reasonable objectives for a business to set:
- to survive in the market during the next 12 months
- to make a minimum of £10,000 in the next financial year
- to capture at least a 20% share of the market by 2010

1 State why the statements above are all examples of objectives. *(2 marks)*

2 Suggest when each of the above would be an appropriate objective. *(4 marks)*

3 Explain reasons why a business may need to change its objectives. *(4 marks)*

4 A business wanted to increase its profits and therefore decided to cut its costs by buying supplies from abroad. Evaluate the appropriateness of its objectives from the stakeholders' point of view. *(14 marks)*

(24 marks)

Group task

Different stakeholders of a business have different objectives. Using one business of your choice, select at least five stakeholders and show how they have differing objectives.

OR

Internal and external constraints affect the ability of a business to meet its objectives. Using one business of your choice, select one internal and one external constraint and suggest how the business might be affected.

CHAPTER 7

The market

To analyse how markets operate and what the effects of any change in a market are on a business, it is necessary to look at some basic **microeconomics**. Microeconomics is the study of individual consumers, businesses and markets, rather than the behaviour of the economy as a whole.

What is a 'market'? People tend to think of a market as a collection of stalls in a town centre with lots of traders selling fruit, vegetables and other products. This certainly is an example, but in economic terms a market is *any situation where buyers and sellers are in contact in order to establish a price*. They do not have to be face-to-face to buy and sell. The foreign currency market, for example, is not a market where people are standing around with piles of notes and coins in one large building; it exists in the interaction of buyers and sellers in many different financial institutions all over the world. The important point is that this interaction establishes a price. In any market, price is something that affects all the businesses trading within it.

KEY TERM

microeconomics: the study of individual consumers, businesses and markets

In a market, the price of the product is established by buyers and sellers

TOPFOTO

How is market price relevant to a business?

The market price is important to a business for two reasons:
- **All businesses have competitors.** No firm can charge a price that is too far out of line with the market price for the sort of product that it is selling. Even large, powerful firms have competitors. Although there is no such thing as *the* market price, in the sense of a single price for a product, there is a *price range* in a market at which consumers are prepared to buy. A business tries, through advertising, to stress how good its product is, but even so, if its

price is very different from the going market price, it will be hard to sell many products. Similarly, if one firm's price is much lower than others in the market, consumers may feel that something is wrong with the product.

■ **Market price affects a business's mark-up.** Mark-up is basically profit. It is the difference between the cost of producing an item and the price at which it is sold. If the market price *rises*, so does the mark-up, and this is a signal to businesses selling in that market to try to supply more because it is now more profitable to do so. If market price *falls*, a business must lower its costs or else it will have to accept a lower mark-up and make less profit per item. The same would apply if a business's costs rose. A business cannot automatically pass on cost increases (e.g. from a rise in raw material prices) to consumers by putting up the price. Therefore, a business is, to a large extent, disciplined into keeping costs down by the market price.

How is market price determined?

In order to answer this question, it is necessary to look at what are often referred to as 'market forces' — demand and supply.

Demand

When economists talk about 'demand', they are not talking about what people would buy if they had an unlimited amount of money. They are talking about *effective demand*, which means the quantity that people in a particular market actually can and will purchase at each price.

Table 7.1 Demand schedule for soft drinks

Price (£)	Quantity demanded
0.50	1,000
0.75	800
1.00	600
1.25	400
1.50	200

Generally speaking, if the market price is low, more people will purchase the product, and vice versa. Of course, there are exceptions to this: if someone saw a car or a mobile phone on sale at a quarter of its normal price, they might think that there was something wrong and therefore not buy it.

Suppose that there is a small grocer's shop situated on a housing estate, which sells cans of soft drink. Table 7.1 shows the quantities of cans that consumers in the market (in this case, the people living on the estate) would buy at various prices.

Figure 7.1 shows this information graphically. *Quantity is always put on the x-axis and price is always put on the y-axis. A change in price moves a consumer up or down the demand curve.*

At £1.25 consumers would buy 400 cans, but if the price fell to 75p, demand would increase to 800 cans. The curve slopes down from left to right.

Note that, although the line in Figure 7.1 is a straight line, it is still referred to as a 'demand curve'; in other situations it may have a curved shape.

Figure 7.1 *Demand curve for soft drinks*

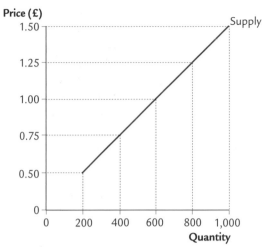

Figure 7.2 *Supply curve for soft drinks*

Supply

Supply refers to the quantities that are offered for sale by businesses at each price. Whereas the demand curve looks at the behaviour of consumers when price changes, the supply curve looks at price from the point of view of the business. *If market price rises, businesses will try to supply more because they can make more profit.* This is shown for the grocer's supply of soft drinks in Table 7.2.

The terms 'cost' and 'price' should not be confused. If the market price of a can of soft drink rises and the cost to the shop of buying the cans from the supplier stays the same (or rises by a smaller amount than the price increase), it will be more profitable for the shop to supply.

Figure 7.2 shows the quantities supplied at the various prices. Once again, *quantity is put on the x-axis and price is put on the y-axis. A change in price moves a business's supply plans up or down its supply curve.*

At £1.25, for example, the shop will supply 800 cans, but if price falls to 75p, supply will become less profitable and will be reduced to 400 cans.

Equilibrium price

The price at which the consumers' demand coincides with what businesses are prepared to supply is known as **equilibrium** price. In Figure 7.3 it can be seen that this can only occur at one price — £1.

 KEY TERM

equilibrium: the situation in a market when demand is equal to supply

Table 7.2 *Supply schedule for soft drinks*

Price (£)	Quantity supplied
0.50	200
0.75	400
1.00	600
1.25	800
1.50	1,000

Figure 7.3
Equilibrium price

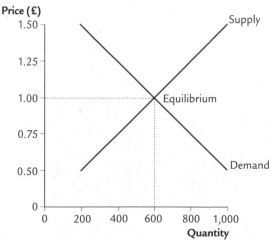

At the price of £1, the demand for soft drinks is equal to the supply of soft drinks. In this situation, consumers are able to buy everything that they want to buy; they are satisfied with the situation. So is the business, because at this price there are no unsold stocks of cans in the shop. When this is the case, *the market is in equilibrium*.

In any market, price is always moving towards equilibrium: in other words, it changes until both businesses and consumers are satisfied.

How is equilibrium established?

At first sight, this situation seems rather unlikely to occur. A business would like a high price for its products but consumers would like a low price. What happens if the plans of consumers and businesses do not coincide?

Suppose that the shop is trying to sell at a price that is quite high, say £1.25. If Tables 7.1 and 7.2 are put together, as in Table 7.3, it is obvious that demand and supply are not in equilibrium at this price: 400 cans are demanded, but the firm is trying to supply 800.

However, this situation would not last for long. Where demand in the market is less than supply (and therefore there are unsold stocks of goods), this is known as a situation of *excess supply*. This is not something that businesses want because it means they have incurred costs making products (or, in the case of a shop, buying them from a supplier), but are not making any profit because they cannot sell them.

Price (£)	Quantity demanded	Quantity supplied
0.50	1,000	200
0.75	800	400
1.00	600	600
1.25	**400**	**800**
1.50	200	1,000

Table 7.3 Excess supply

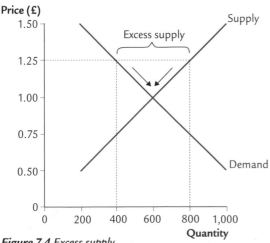

Figure 7.4 Excess supply

This means that if the price being charged in the market is too high, businesses have to lower their prices if they want to sell their goods. The fall in price encourages consumers to buy more. Price is pushed down towards equilibrium, as shown in Figure 7.4.

On the other hand, the price being charged may be particularly low, say 75p. Table 7.4 shows that, at a price of 75p, the firm is less keen to supply than it was at £1.25, but consumers certainly want to buy. In this situation, consumers are prepared to buy 800 cans, but firms are prepared to supply only 400.

In this instance there is *excess demand* — that is, more demand than supply. With people trying to buy more of the product than is on sale, the price rises. This encourages businesses to supply more because they are able to make more profit. In this way, excess demand pushes prices up towards equilibrium, as shown in Figure 7.5.

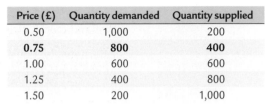

Both businesses and consumers 'read' the price in the market.

- Businesses respond to price changes by adjusting their supply plans — increasing or lowering output in order to maximise their profit.
- Consumers respond to price changes by increasing or decreasing demand so that they always buy the quantity they require. They will not buy products that they feel are too expensive.

These actions mean that market price moves towards equilibrium. At equilibrium, both parties are satisfied; there is no excess supply and no excess demand.

Once equilibrium has been established, it does not mean that it stays at this point for ever. If the conditions that influence consumers' demand change, a new demand curve is created because the market situation is now different. The same applies to businesses. If the conditions under which they supply change, a new supply curve is created.

Price (£)	Quantity demanded	Quantity supplied
0.50	1,000	200
0.75	**800**	**400**
1.00	600	600
1.25	400	800
1.50	200	1,000

Table 7.4 Excess demand

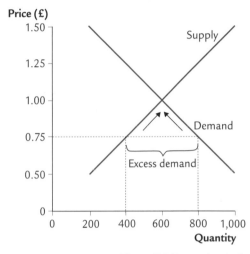

Figure 7.5 Excess demand

What are the factors that determine demand?

Demand is determined by the following factors.

Price

The higher the price, the lower the quantity demanded, and vice versa. Figure 7.1 showed that *a change in price moves a consumer along an existing demand curve*.

If changes in other factors occur, a new demand curve will be created because the conditions under which consumers buy will have changed, and they will demand more or less of the product at every price.

Income

An increase in income leads to an increase in demand for most goods; economists call these *normal goods*. Figure 7.6 shows a rise in quantity demanded from 600 to 1,000, but this does not happen because of a fall in price — which has stayed the same at £1. The increase in demand has come about because of a change in another factor affecting demand — in this case, a rise in income.

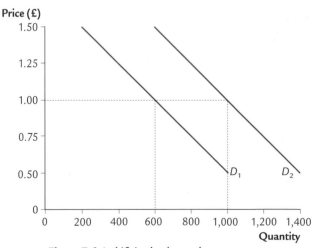

Figure 7.6 A shift in the demand curve

This change has created a new demand curve, D_2, to the right of the old demand curve, D_1. More is now being demanded at every price level.

Alternatively, consider a fall in income. This will cause less to be demanded at every price level. At a price of £1, the quantity demanded will fall from 1,000 to 600.

Not all goods are 'normal'. There are some goods whose demand goes down when income rises. These goods are known as *inferior goods*. Products with names like 'value', 'budget' or 'discount' are inferior goods. This does not mean that there is anything wrong with them; it just means that there are other, similar goods of better quality. As their income rises, people tend to buy fewer inferior goods.

It is by no means a disadvantage for a business to produce or sell inferior goods. Most supermarkets supply both normal goods and low-budget goods that might be regarded as inferior. This enables the business to cater for two different sections of the market: those on a high income and those on a low income. Furthermore, in a recession, the demand for inferior goods will almost certainly rise, whereas the demand for better-quality goods will probably fall.

Wealth
Wealth is not the same as income. Wealth is the combined value of savings, shares owned, your house (if owned) etc. This last factor is important: there is evidence that when house prices rise, people feel wealthier even though they have not had an increase in income. They therefore feel confident about spending more. A business needs to be aware of consumer confidence and to consider how demand might be affected if this confidence changes.

Advertising, promotional offers and public relations
Television advertisements, 'two for the price of one' offers, and the sponsorship of sports teams all affect demand. That is the reason why firms spend so much money on them. A successful promotional campaign shifts the demand curve to the right, as was shown in Figure 7.6.

Taste and fashion
Some fashionable products, such as certain brands of clothes, or iPods, are seen as 'in' and some consumers regard these products as essential for their lifestyle.

Demographic changes
A larger population means more spending. Apart from considering the total population, businesses need to be aware of other demographic changes as well. These include:

- any shift in the *age structure* of the population, because young people tend to buy different products from older people
- a change in the *gender ratio*, because men buy different products from women

Government action

A campaign by the government — for example, to encourage a healthier lifestyle — will alter patterns of consumption. A 'keep fit' campaign by the government will affect the demand for both healthy and unhealthy food.

The price of other goods

As far as the price of other goods is concerned, two terms are important: substitutes and complements.

Substitutes

A **substitute** is a product that can be used instead of another one because it performs the same sort of function: for example, apples and pears are substitutes, as are electricity and gas for heating a home.

 KEY TERM

substitute: an alternative product that serves the same function

Consider apples and pears. What would happen if the price of pears stayed the same but the price of a substitute, such as apples, went up? If the price of apples rose, this would not only decrease the demand for apples, but also increase the demand for pears. This is shown in Figure 7.7.

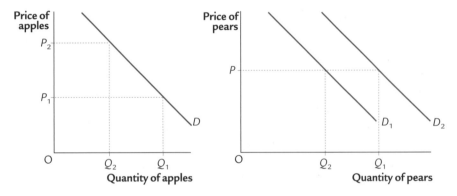

Figure 7.7 Substitutes

An increase in the price of apples reduces the demand for apples. This is shown as a movement along the demand curve for apples from Q_1 to Q_2. As pears are a substitute for apples, there is a shift in the demand curve for pears. A new demand curve for pears is established because the conditions of demand for them have changed. The demand for pears increases to Q_2 not because the price of pears has gone down, but because the price of a substitute (apples) has gone up.

How quickly will this occur? The changes in demand might happen quite fast; consumers who enjoy eating fruit and do not mind whether they buy apples or pears are likely to react to the price change the next time they go shopping. But will the same thing happen with the other example — gas and electric heating? The answer to this is no. If the price of gas rises, it is not easy for households to switch their heating systems to the now relatively cheaper electricity. They would probably wait until their gas system broke down or wore out — which could be several years.

Apples and pears are examples of *close substitutes*; they are very similar products. However, not all substitutes are close. Consider travelling to work by car or by bus. Millions of people use their cars every day to drive to work. What might happen if the price of petrol rose? This happened in 2005 following Hurricane Katrina. Logically, people should start to look for a cheaper alternative, such as bus travel. However, is waiting at a bus stop, having to queue, then stopping and starting throughout the journey really a close substitute for driving in the comfort of your own car? The answer might well be no. It could take a very large rise in the price of petrol to make commuters abandon their cars and start demanding journeys by bus.

The relevance of this to a business is twofold:

- When considering any likely changes in the demand for its product that are caused by a change in the price of a substitute, a business needs to make a judgement on how close the substitute is.
- It also needs to make a judgement on whether the price change in the substitute will be short-term or long-term. Is it a temporary 'one-off', or has a price war started?

Brand names are used to distinguish a product from its substitutes

 TERM

complement: a product that is used, and is therefore bought, in conjunction with another

Complements

Complements are products that are in *joint demand*: that is, when one product is bought, so is the other

CD players and CDs show this relationship. If the price of CD players falls, there will be an increase not only in the demand for CD players — because they are cheaper — but also in the demand for CDs, because more people now own the players. This is shown in Figure 7.8.

Figure 7.8 Complements

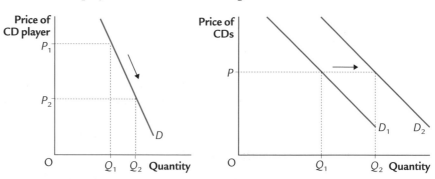

The fall in the price of CD players moves consumers along the existing demand curve for these. The rise in the demand for CDs does not result from a fall in the price of CDs — their price is still at P. It is because CDs are a complement to CD players, which are now cheaper. The opposite would apply if the price of CD players rose.

A business can use the relationship between complements to maximise its revenue and profit over a period of time. A printer for a PC might be fairly low priced, say £85, but the ink cartridges that have to be used with it are likely to be quite expensive, say £20. The low price of the initial printer tempts consumers to buy, but they are 'forced' to purchase the expensive complementary product thereafter.

The revenue from a football match comes not only from ticket sales but from sales of all the complementary products as well

The reverse is also true. Suppose a car manufacturer puts up its prices because it thinks that the effect on demand will be small. Even if it is correct, in the future, fewer spare parts, such as radiators, brakes and bulbs, will be sold. A business must therefore exercise caution when increasing the price of a product, as it may find that it decreases the demand for any complements that it sells as well.

What are the factors that determine supply?

Supply is determined by the following factors.

Price

The relationship between price and supply is the opposite to that of price and demand. When prices are low, businesses supply less because it is less profitable to do so. Conversely, the higher the price, the more a business will try to supply. Figure 7.2 showed what happens when price changes. *A change in price moves a business along an existing supply curve.*

If changes in other factors occur, a new supply curve will be created because the conditions under which businesses supply will have changed, and they will supply more or less of the product at every price.

Costs

A fall in costs will cause supply to rise. Imagine a very simple situation in which the owner of a gravel pit employs people to dig gravel for him using spades. When he bought the gravel pit, he was given a free supply of spades as part of a special offer. This means that if he takes on extra workers there will be no increase in equipment costs.

Suppose the owner of this pit has a budget of £100 per week for labour. If the wage of his workers is £20 per week, he will employ five of them. If the wage falls to £10, he will employ ten workers and will be able to supply more gravel to market. Conversely, if the workers' wages rise to £30, he will only be able to employ three people and therefore the amount he can supply will fall.

Now consider a more normal situation — a business producing furniture. Exactly the same reasoning as above would apply to the cost of any raw materials, such as wood or plastic. If the price of one of these falls, the firm will be able to supply more from its budget for raw materials. *The same amount of money will now buy more raw materials because their cost has gone down.*

Figure 7.9 Effect of changes in costs on supply

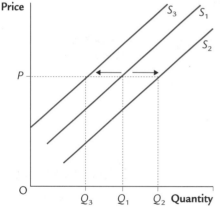

Similarly, if the rate of interest goes down, the firm's cost of borrowing will fall, so it will have more money available to employ workers and buy raw materials. It can therefore supply more.

In both of these situations, the supply curve will shift to the right — more will now be supplied at all prices. This is shown in Figure 7.9 as a movement of the supply curve from S_1 to S_2.

Conversely, if a business's costs rise (e.g. if there is an increase in wages), it will supply less. This will shift the supply curve to the left. Less will now be supplied at all prices. This is shown in Figure 7.9 as a shift in the supply curve from S_1 to S_3.

Taxes and subsidies

A tax

The government may put a tax on a product in order to raise revenue, but it might also want to discourage the consumption of certain products, such as cigarettes and alcohol, because it believes them to be harmful. How will a tax on a product affect a business's supply? It has exactly the same effect as an increase in costs — it shifts the supply curve to the left. This is because for every unit of the product sold, the business will have to pay a certain amount of tax to the government.

If the tax is £1 per unit and the firm sells 1,000 units a week, this means a rise in costs of £52,000 per year. This increase in costs means that the firm will supply less.

Any government legislation that lays down minimum standards, such as the minimum wage or health and safety laws, will have the same effect on a product as the imposition of a tax. As minimum standards increase costs, they will reduce supply. In Figure 7.9, the supply curve will shift to S_3.

A subsidy

Alternatively, the government might want to encourage the supply of certain products, such as organic fertiliser, because it believes them to be beneficial. One way to do this would be to offer a **subsidy** to any business supplying this product. A subsidy is a payment from the government to the business for every unit supplied. This will have the opposite effect to a tax.

The government might decide that for every bag of organic fertiliser supplied, a business will receive a subsidy of £1. Suppose, as in the previous example, that the business supplies 1,000 bags per week: this would mean an increase in annual income of £52,000. This payment has exactly the same effect as a fall in the business's costs — the product is now cheaper to produce. The effect would be to increase the supply of organic fertiliser. In Figure 7.9, the supply curve would shift from S_1 to S_2.

The price of other products

This is sometimes known as *competitive supply*. Consider a business that supplies tinned foods, shown in Figure 7.10. A fall in the price of baked beans from P_1 to P_2 makes it less profitable to supply them (so supply falls to Q_2) and more profitable to supply some other commodity — say, tins of spaghetti. The supply of canned spaghetti rises to Q_2.

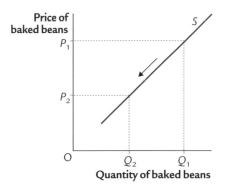
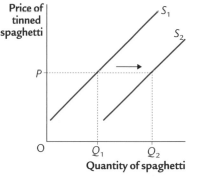

Figure 7.10
Competitive supply

The weather

The weather is a very important determinant of supply for agricultural products. A prolonged period of rain or drought may cause a bad harvest, which will shift the supply curve to the left. Good conditions may produce a large yield and this will shift the supply curve to the right.

Putting it all together

A change in demand

First consider the effect of a change in demand on the equilibrium price and quantity of a product.

Figure 7.11 shows the market for PCs. Suppose that there is an increase in consumers' spending caused by an income tax cut. The initial equilibrium (E_1) is at price P_1 with quantity Q_1 being demanded and supplied. The rise in disposable income shifts the demand curve to the right. The result is a new equilibrium (E_2) at P_2 and Q_2 — with a higher quantity now being demanded and supplied at a higher price.

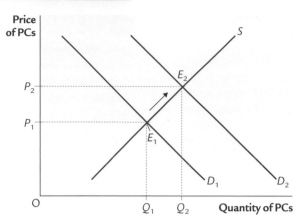

Figure 7.11
Effect of an increase in demand on price and quantity

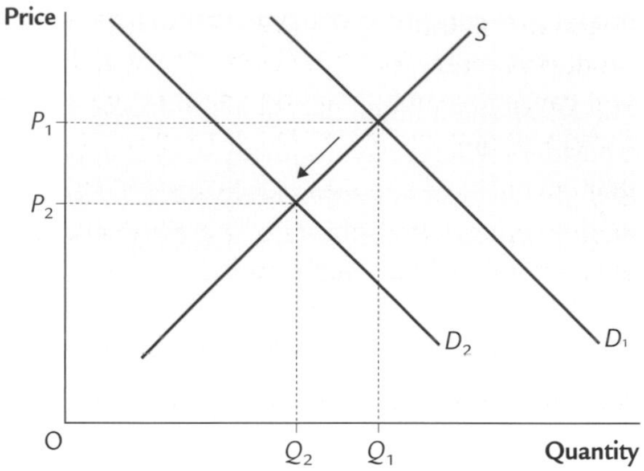

Figure 7.12
Effect of a fall in demand on price and quantity

Exactly the same result would occur following a change in any determinant of demand that caused a rightward shift of the demand curve.

Figure 7.12 shows the opposite. Consider the market for mobile phones. Suppose that a piece of scientific research proves that mobiles really are dangerous to health. The demand for mobile phones will change. There will be a shift of the demand curve to the left. A new equilibrium will be reached where a lower quantity is demanded and supplied at a lower price.

Exactly the same result would occur following a change in any determinant of demand that caused a leftward shift of the demand curve.

A change in supply

Now consider what happens when supply shifts and there is a movement along an existing demand curve.

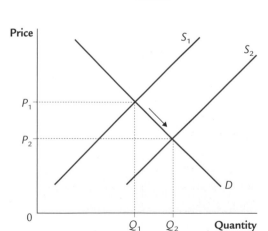

Figure 7.13 *Effect of an increase in supply on price and quantity*

Figure 7.13 shows the market for cornflakes. Suppose that the cost of corn to the manufacturer of breakfast cereal falls. Any fall in the cost of a raw material input will shift the supply curve to the right and cause an increased quantity to be bought at a lower price.

Exactly the same result would occur following a change in any determinant of supply that caused a rightward shift of the supply curve.

Figure 7.14 shows the market for bread. Assume that bakery workers throughout the country

Module 2871

negotiate a large pay rise. This will increase production costs for all bakeries. These rising costs will cause the supply curve to shift to the left. Less bread will now be demanded at a higher price.

Exactly the same result would occur following a change in any determinant of supply that caused a leftward shift of the supply curve.

Elasticity of demand and supply

Price elasticity of demand shows how responsive demand is to a change in price. *Price elasticity of supply* shows how responsive supply is to a change in price.

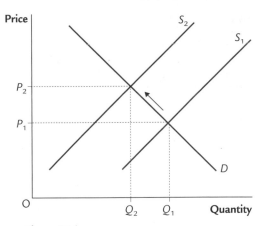

Figure 7.14
Effect of a decrease in supply on price and quantity

The demand and supply curves included so far in this chapter have been shown as sloping at about 45 degrees. Economists would say that these curves are quite **elastic**. In other words, they are quite *responsive to a change in price*. This is not always the case. Sometimes demand and supply are very *unresponsive* to price, in which case we say they are **inelastic**.

> ℮ **EXAMINER'S VOICE**
>
> A detailed knowledge of elasticity is not required for Module 2871. It is dealt with in detail in Chapter 27. Nevertheless, in this module a degree of understanding will certainly help strengthen your analysis of the effects of a price change on a business.

Elasticity of demand

If an economist says that a demand curve is quite inelastic, this means that the curve is quite steep and that demand will not change very much when price changes. This is shown in Figure 7.15.

If demand for a product is price inelastic, it means that when price rises (in this case, from P_1 to P_2), the quantity demanded falls, but not by a proportional amount. In this situation, a business can put the price of its product up and there will not be a large fall in demand. The firm's revenue (price multiplied by quantity) will rise because area OP_2BQ_2 is larger than area OP_1AQ_1. On the other hand, a price cut from P_2 to P_1 only generates a small increase in demand and the business's revenue actually falls because OP_1AQ_1 is smaller than area OP_2BQ_2.

'Flatter' demand curves are said to be elastic. If a product has elastic demand, this means that a rise in price will generate a large fall in demand and revenue will decrease. In Figure 7.16, OP_2BQ_2 is smaller than OP_1AQ_1. On the other hand, if there were a fall in price, the

KEY TERMS

elastic: where the change in demand or supply that results from a price change is greater than the change in price that caused it

inelastic: where the change in demand or supply that results from a price change is less than the change in price that caused it

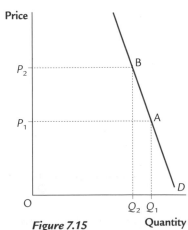

Figure 7.15
Inelastic demand curve

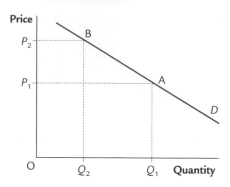

Figure 7.16 *Elastic demand curve*

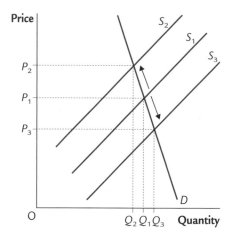

Figure 7.17 *Effect of a change in supply on a product with inelastic demand*

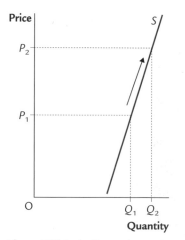

Figure 7.18 *Inelastic supply curve*

opposite would apply. Lowering price will increase revenue because OP_1AQ_1 is larger than OP_2BQ_2.

Elasticity is important because of the effect on market price. If demand is inelastic, the effect of a change in supply can be quite dramatic, as shown in Figure 7.17.

The demand for petrol is a good example. If garages run short of fuel, there is a distinct lack of substitutes for motorists to use and so petrol prices will rise sharply when the supply curve shifts from S_1 to S_2. If the supply of petrol rises due to lower production costs (S_3), there will be the opposite effect.

What makes demand elastic or inelastic?
If a business has few substitutes for its products, then if the price of the product rises, demand is likely to be inelastic as consumers cannot switch to another product. Where there are many alternatives, demand will be elastic as consumers will be able to switch to a substitute if price rises.

Another factor is the cost of buying the product in proportion to the consumer's income. For example, a 50% rise in the price of a can of baked beans will not affect demand as much as a 50% rise in the price of a product such as a car.

Elasticity of supply
In Figure 7.18 it can be seen that when price rises quite a lot (from P_1 to P_2), supply does not increase by very much (only from Q_1 to Q_2); it is inelastic.

As with demand, when a supply curve is 'flatter', it is said to be elastic. This means that a rise in price will generate a large rise in the quantity supplied, and vice versa. This is shown in Figure 7.19, where a relatively small price rise from P_1 to P_2 results in a larger increase in quantity demanded from Q_1 to Q_2.

The elasticity of supply is important in a market because if it is quite inelastic, there will be a relatively steep rise in price when demand increases. In Figure 7.20, when demand increases from Q_1 to Q_2, price increases quite steeply from P_1 to P_2.

This was demonstrated during the BSE crisis of the 1990s. The demand for beef fell dramatically and the demand for substitutes, such as chicken, went up very quickly. As the supply of chicken could not respond quickly, its market price increased considerably in a short period of time.

A fall in demand from Q_1 to Q_3 would have the opposite effect — a large drop in price.

What makes supply elastic or inelastic?

If the firm is in the primary sector (e.g. mining, forestry or agriculture), it is not going to be easy to increase supply very quickly.

Alternatively, the problem may be with labour. A business may not be able to get enough employees with the right skills. Either of these factors will hinder the ability to increase supply.

A business needs to be aware of the elasticity of demand and supply for its products in order to evaluate the likely effects of any change in price.

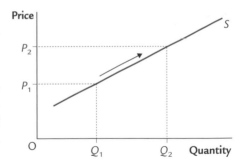

Figure 7.19 Elastic supply curve

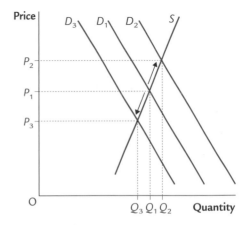

Figure 7.20 Effect of a change in demand on a product with inelastic supply

The supply of many raw materials is inelastic

YOUR TURN

Case study

Time allowed: 35 minutes

Jam at James's

James Porter was made redundant, aged 35, and decided to start his own business with his redundancy payment. Playing guitar was something that had been his hobby since his teenage years and he had often wondered whether he would ever have the nerve to start up a music shop specialising in guitars and amplifiers.

He knew from experience that the town lacked a specialist music shop and all the musicians he talked to were very enthusiastic. As a result of this encouragement, James made a rough estimate of customer numbers, then he considered the factors likely to affect his ability to supply products to his customers. Finally, he decided it would be worth taking the risk.

James knew that it was necessary to draw up a business plan and to set clear objectives if he wanted to succeed. He used the Business Start Up pack from his bank as the basis for his plan. He found it quite straightforward and was able to obtain a loan of £25,000. This loan, along with his redundancy money, provided sufficient finance to buy the fixtures and stock for the new shop.

Jam at James's opened for business in a rented unit at the start of May. He had two part-time casual 'employees' (who were musician friends of his) to help out, whom he paid 'cash in hand'.

As his friends had predicted, there was a great deal of interest in the new shop — at least to start with.

However, by the following February, trade had slowed considerably and the future did not look as promising as it had only a few months ago. Customers often only bought one item at a time. 'If only I could get them to buy more than one thing at a time!' James thought. He now had only one person helping him out in the shop — and that was for only a few hours a day. 'Running a business in practice isn't as easy as it seemed on paper,' he thought sadly. He was 'his own boss', he reflected, but he certainly had less income than when he was an employee.

He wondered if increasing the price of his amplifiers would boost the business's revenue and give him a bit more spending money.

Source: amended from
OCR 2871, June 2003

Answer all questions.

1 Amplifiers are a complementary product to guitars. Other than amplifiers, state **two** complementary products that James could sell with his guitars. *(2 marks)*

2 'He wondered if increasing the price of his amplifiers would boost the business's revenue and give him a bit more spending money.' Analyse how this might affect his business. *(9 marks)*

3 Outline **two** factors likely to affect James's ability to supply products to his customers. *(4 marks)*

4 State **two** ways in which the government might have an economic effect on James's business. *(2 marks)*

5 Other than through the government, evaluate the economic factors that are likely to influence the demand for James's products. *(14 marks)*

(31 marks)

CHAPTER 8

The nature of economic activity

The economy is a major influence on all types of business; indeed, it could be argued that it is the most important influence. Chapter 7 dealt with micro-economics — the study of individual markets, firms and consumers; this chapter deals with **macroeconomics** — the study of the whole economy.

Anyone who says that economics is irrelevant to their life is definitely wrong! The main groups involved in the operation of the economy are highly inter-connected and a business can find its situation considerably changed by eco-nomic events, such as a fall in consumer spending or a change in the exchange rate. These economic events may force the business to change how it operates, in ways that might not be positive for some of the business's stakeholders.

Consider a UK firm that has been exporting sports equipment to a large retailer in Germany. The German retailer subsequently finds that it can buy equipment of the same sort of design and quality from a new supplier in Poland at a much more competitive price. The German retailer therefore does not renew its contract with the UK business.

The emergence of this new low-cost supplier will make the UK business's life very difficult and it may have to make some of its employees redundant. Thus, an employee who thought he had a reasonably secure job in a business selling to a growing area of the leisure market suddenly finds his life turned upside down by economic events entirely outside his own control. How is it, he may ask, that the Polish firm can produce these products so much more cheaply than his firm can? Furthermore, what action could his firm take in order to avoid the job losses?

What is meant by 'the economy'?

The **economy** is not a single entity. It refers to the collective behaviour of a number of different groups. These are:

- all the different *businesses* in the UK, ranging from sole traders to multi-national companies
- people acting as both *employees* of businesses and *consumers* of their products
- the *government*, which sets the economic framework within which businesses have to operate, and is also a major provider of many goods and services which it finances through taxation and borrowing

> **KEY TERM**
>
> **macroeconomics:** the study and analysis of the behaviour of the whole economy

> **KEY TERM**
>
> **economy:** collective behaviour of a number of different groups — businesses, people as employees and consumers, and the government

e **EXAMINER'S VOICE**

Although a clear understanding of macroeconomic issues is essential, examiners are not looking for highly detailed and technical explanations of how the economy works. What is much more important is for you to be able to analyse how the economic environment affects the behaviour of businesses.

In addition to these, any study of the economy must also take into account the UK's trading relationship with other countries, especially the European Union (EU).

The economy is dynamic; it changes all the time. People become unemployed, then find jobs; some people retrain to gain new skills and others retire. Some firms close down or get bigger; others start up. The government also changes in terms of what it does in the economy. Until the 1980s, the government owned whole industries, such as coal, steel, water and electricity. The economy is very different now from how it was 50 or even 20 years ago. Businesses have to adapt to the changing nature of the economic environment in which they operate.

The nature of economics

Economics is not a science in the way that chemistry and physics are. Whereas scientists can conduct laboratory experiments using the same conditions time and time again, the economist's 'laboratory' never stays the same. The economy, as already noted, is dynamic. This means that the effects of a particular policy at any one time may be different from the effects that occurred previously from the same policy.

Consider a cut in the rate of income tax. Lowering the rate of tax to increase spending on the grounds that it was successful in a similar situation 10 years ago may not be a sensible policy today. The economy will have changed since then: many of the businesses within it will be different, consumer spending patterns will be different, and the UK's trading position with other countries will also have changed. Comparing the economy today with the economy 10 years ago is not comparing like with like.

In addition, although economists would agree that a cut in the rate of income tax will increase consumer spending, the *extent* of the increase in spending might be the subject of considerable disagreement. Will it be a lot or a little? When will it happen — within 6 months, a year, or longer?

It is important to approach macroeconomics in a structured way. The analysis of how the economy influences businesses can be divided into the following five clear steps:

1 Explaining what is meant by the term 'economic activity'.
2 Identifying the economic variables (i.e. factors) that affect economic activity. These two steps are dealt with in the remainder of this chapter.
3 Analysing what can cause the variables to change. This involves an understanding of an important concept known as the *economic cycle*. This is dealt with in Chapter 9.
4 Explaining what the government's macroeconomic objectives are likely to be, since *what* objectives it is trying to achieve and *how* it is trying to achieve them will have a major effect on businesses. This is dealt with in Chapter 10.

5 Explaining what the government and/or the Bank of England might do as a result of any change in the variables. Economic policy is dealt with in Chapter 11.

What is 'economic activity'?

'**Economic activity**' refers to the production of goods and services. In Chapter 5 it was noted that production can be primary, secondary or tertiary. Therefore, the level of economic activity refers to output in all of these sectors (see Figure 8.1).

A term often used when discussing economic activity is **gross domestic product**. This is usually shortened to GDP. It means the total output of all goods and services produced — usually in a year. 'Gross' in this case means total, and 'domestic' means within that particular country, in this case the UK.

This is distinct from *gross national product* (GNP), which is GDP plus the output of any UK businesses operating abroad. Another term that is used to discuss economic activity is *national income*. Any of these terms can be used to describe economic activity, but GDP is the most commonly used measure.

Usually, a high level of economic activity (i.e. rising GDP) is beneficial for all. It means that there is likely to be a high level of employment, since if the demand for products is rising, firms will need to employ more people in order to produce them. Jobs are also more likely to be secure when GDP is rising and this, coupled with increasing incomes, means that people's spending power will increase.

KEY TERMS

economic activity: the level of output in all sectors of the economy — primary, secondary and tertiary

gross domestic product: the total value of all of the economy's output (in a year)

Businesses too will benefit: if spending is rising, there will be more demand for products and (assuming that their costs are not rising too much) profits will also rise. This is good for the business's stakeholders. It also means that more money is available, which can be used for further expansion and development.

The government should also benefit from rising GDP, since high levels of spending and output caused by the rise in economic activity mean more tax revenue from people and businesses. This can then be used for spending in socially desirable areas such as the health service and education. Alternatively, the government could use this extra tax revenue for tax cuts. Both these measures will be popular and may help to get the government re-elected.

Conversely, a fall in GDP is not normally welcomed by wage earners, consumers, businesses or the government.

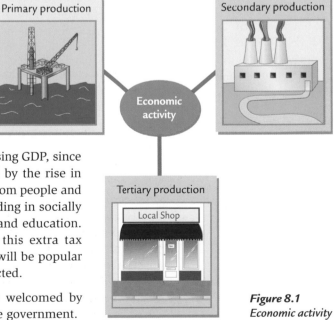

Figure 8.1
Economic activity

Factors that affect economic activity

The simplest way to analyse how the whole economy operates is to divide it into two groups: households and firms. In the households group, people go to work and earn income. There is therefore a flow of income from firms to households as payment for the work done.

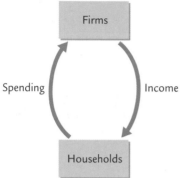

Figure 8.2 *The circular flow of income*

Most of this income will promptly be spent and therefore there is a flow of income in the opposite direction from households to firms. Economists call this *consumption*. Of course, economists are not saying that people spend their income at the same firm at which they work, although this could be true in some cases — for example, if someone worked in a supermarket. They are saying that businesses in the economy pay their employees and then receive income back when people, acting as consumers rather than employees, spend it. Figure 8.2 shows this diagrammatically.

The **circular flow of income** begins with the flow of income that households have earned being spent on goods and services. This spending then enables firms to acquire the money they need to finance the next round of production.

Consider a starting position where the level of economic activity is quite high and GDP has been rising. If consumption spending by households is sufficient to buy the whole output produced by businesses, firms will be very pleased because they will have made a profit and will not have unsold stocks of goods. Firms will continue to employ the same number of people and may even think of expanding output.

However, this situation may not occur automatically because some of the income earned by households is not going to be spent. This means that businesses run the risk of not having all their output purchased by consumers. If this happens, they will have unsold goods that will not earn them any profit.

There are three reasons why all the income earned by households in the UK will not go directly to UK firms:

- **Taxes.** The government takes a proportion of income through taxes.
- **Savings.** Whatever remains after tax from an employee's wages is known as *disposable income* and people may decide to save some of this. Any income saved is obviously not spent.
- **Imports.** Some income left after taxation and saving does not get spent on products made in the UK, even though they might have been bought from UK retailers. Products that are made abroad and purchased by UK households are known as **imports**. When income is spent on products that are imported, there is a flow of income to foreign, rather than UK, firms.

These three reasons mean that there are **leakages** from the circular flow of income, which is why UK businesses do not receive back all the income

KEY TERMS

circular flow of income: the (continuous) flow of income from firms to households as payment for work, and from households to firms as payment for products

imports: purchase of goods from abroad

leakages: income that 'leaks away' from the economy and so does not get passed back to UK firms from households; this comprises taxes, savings and imports

that they have paid out to their employees. The diagram of the circular flow of income in the economy, including leakages, looks like Figure 8.3.

There are, however, a number of **injections** of income into the economy, which help to offset the leakages. These injections do not arise from UK consumers; they come from elsewhere. They are:

- **Government spending.** The government is a big spender in the UK on services such as schools, hospitals and defence. Many billions of pounds that firms receive from the sale of their goods and services come not from household consumers, but from central and local government.
- **Exports.** Consumers abroad will buy goods from the UK. The sales of products made by UK businesses to other countries are known as **exports**. The products go abroad, but income flows into UK businesses in payment.
- **Investment.** Investment (also known as *capital spending*) by businesses is very important. It involves businesses buying products such as new buildings, machinery and improved technology, in order to make themselves more competitive and productive in the future. Notice that when economists talk about investment, they are not talking about the firm depositing money in a bank. That action would represent saving, which has the opposite effect on the economy to investing. Saving reduces total spending, while investment increases it.

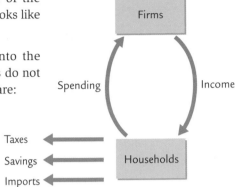

Figure 8.3 The circular flow of income, including leakages

KEY TERMS

injections: income coming into the UK economy that does not come from UK households; this comprises investment, government spending and exports

exports: sale of goods to other countries by UK businesses

investment: purchase of capital equipment and/or buildings by businesses

We can now amend the circular flow of income to show both leakages and injections, as in Figure 8.4.

In summary, the circular flow of income is a continuous process. People are earning and being taxed, saving and spending (sometimes on imports) all the time. Businesses are continuously employing and therefore paying people income. They are also exporting products abroad and investing in capital equipment. The government takes in tax revenue and spends it.

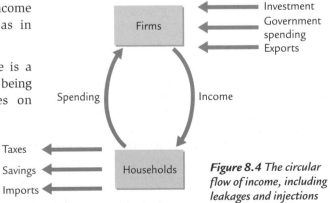

Figure 8.4 The circular flow of income, including leakages and injections

What happens to economic activity when the variables change?

Even though the circular flow of income never stops flowing, this does not mean that the level of economic activity stays the same. When one of the variables changes, the level of economic activity is likely to change as a result. In reality, several variables are likely to be changing at the same time and what actually happens to the economy depends on whether a change in one variable is offset by another.

Assume that a newspaper report states that 'imports rose by £10 billion last month'. Imports are a leakage from the circular flow and so economic activity could be expected to fall. However, it may be the case that, over the same period of time, businesses have invested £10 billion. In this case (since investment is an injection), the net effect on income, and therefore the level of activity, in the economy will be nil.

Take the statement 'investment has risen by £5 billion'. Investment is beneficial (the economy needs modern factories) and it should increase the level of activity. Suppose, however, that at the same time households had decided to save £5 billion more than before. This leakage from the circular flow would offset the injection of income from investment. Furthermore, if the rise in saving was in fact greater than £5 billion, then, despite the rise in investment, the level of economic activity would fall.

This shows that when considering any news about the state of the economy, those running businesses need to consider what is happening to all the relevant variables. When reading headline statements in the press, they must ask themselves 'Yes, but what else has happened?' before passing a judgement on the likely effects of a change.

What happens to economic activity if leakages do not equal injections?

The total amount of leakages from the economy in any given period of time is highly unlikely to be the exactly the same as the total amount of injections.

- *If total leakages are greater than total injections, the level of economic activity will fall.* This means that some businesses will experience a drop in the demand for their products, may make employees redundant, will invest less (as they are not very optimistic about the future) or may even close down.
- *If total injections are greater than total leakages, the level of economic activity will rise.* This means that demand will rise and firms will take on more employees and invest more. However, rising injections of income may mean that spending is increasing too fast, and that businesses cannot

meet the rising demand for their products. The result will be that prices will start to rise rapidly and this can be very damaging for the economy (see Chapter 10).

In reality, small differences between leakages and injections do not matter much. Economic policy is not concerned with trying to balance them to the last pound — or even the last billion pounds. Economic policy is about creating a stable macroeconomic environment within which businesses can succeed. The government and the Bank of England are trying to prevent the potentially damaging effects of either a huge rise or a huge fall in GDP. Their policies to achieve this can have significant effects on businesses, as you will see in Chapter 11.

Further sources

www.hm-treasury.gov.uk — macroeconomic data and information about current government economic policy; the site includes a powerful search facility for all sorts of economic/business issues

www.whystudyeconomics.ac.uk — information about the nature of economics and advice on how to study it

---

YOUR TURN

Questions
Time allowed: 20 minutes

1   State the difference between GDP and GNP. *(2 marks)*

2   State what is meant by 'the level of economic activity'. *(2 marks)*

3   Outline the difference between imports and exports. *(4 marks)*

4   Outline the difference between saving and investment. *(4 marks)*

5   Analyse the importance of the circular flow of income to a business. *(9 marks)*

(21 marks)

CHAPTER 9

The economic cycle

An understanding of the concept of the economic cycle is important because it makes possible an analysis of the macroeconomic variables that affect a particular business. It was seen in Chapter 8 how these variables are represented in the circular flow of income, which is reproduced in Figure 9.1. The economic cycle is likely to affect all these variables, both the injections and the leakages.

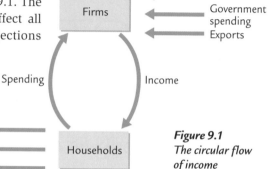

Figure 9.1
The circular flow of income

 KEY TERM

economic cycle: rises and falls in economic activity; these follow a pattern that can be identified as boom, recession, slump and recovery

What is the economic cycle?

The **economic cycle** refers to the changes that occur in the level of economic activity over a period of time. It is also known as the *business cycle* or the *trade cycle*.

Economic activity in industrialised countries tends to proceed in cycles. Sometimes gross domestic product (GDP) is rising and sometimes it is falling. A period of economic prosperity is followed by a period of slower or falling economic activity. Then, after a time, this gives way to a rise in GDP and the cycle starts again.

The economic cycle is usually represented by the graph in Figure 9.2. The trend (i.e. the general direction) in GDP is upwards, but the actual level of economic activity does not follow the smooth path of the trend.

What happens at each stage of the cycle?

Boom

In this stage of the cycle, there is a high level of employment and consumption, and therefore a high demand for products. Businesses are profitable and feeling confident about future sales. This may encourage them to invest in new plant and machinery, which, in turn, leads to further rises in GDP. The boom eventually reaches a peak and GDP will not rise any further in that particular cycle.

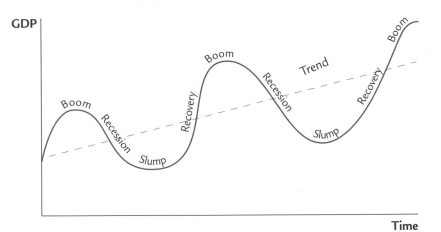

Figure 9.2 *The economic cycle is divided into four stages*

Recession

A recession is defined as *two successive quarterly falls in GDP*: in other words, output falls for two consecutive 3-month periods. In a recession, sales are falling and so business confidence about future consumer demand in some sectors is low. Initially, this may only happen in markets for luxury products, such as new cars and foreign holidays. This causes a fall in investment in those industries, since no business wants to invest in equipment and buildings that are going to be underused.

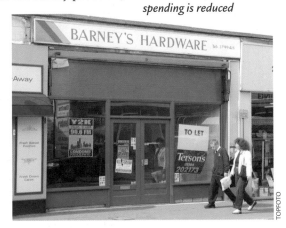

In a recession, consumer spending is reduced

The affected businesses make employees redundant, and this increased unemployment reduces consumer spending. This lowers demand and profits in other sectors of the economy, which is likely to depress investment even further. The government and the Bank of England need to act before a recession becomes too serious — otherwise business confidence will collapse, which could lead to a slump.

Slump

The symptoms of a slump (also known as a *trough* or a *depression*) are similar to those of a recession, except that they are more serious and widespread. In a depression, almost all the economy is affected, not just a few sectors. This leads to high levels of unemployment in many different industries, low business confidence, low levels of consumer spending, low levels of investment and low profits for businesses.

Recovery

In the recovery phase of the cycle, economic activity rises. Consumers start spending again and demand increases. Business confidence starts to increase as profits rise. Firms take on more employees, and higher employment in turn increases consumer spending. This is how the upturn in economic activity gets under way. This eventually leads on to the next boom.

The time taken to complete a cycle can vary, as can the length of each particular phase. Obviously, it would be better for businesses if recessions were as brief, and booms as long, as possible.

How might a business evaluate where the economy is in the economic cycle?

A business needs to know where the economy is in the cycle in order to plan ahead and make decisions about output, employment and marketing. Much of this can be done through *desk research* (see Chapter 23). Several sources of data should be used; a business should not rely on just one. Possible sources of data include:

- output/sales trends from the business's own plant(s)/shop(s)
- national/regional/local output and sales levels in the business's own sector
- national/regional/local employment levels
- national/regional/local spending levels
- national/regional/local sales levels
- professional journals/reviews of the economy, such as the Bank of England's Inflation Report
- news coming from managers' or directors' contacts with other (local/regional/national) firms about the state of their business

Why does the economic cycle exist?

There are many different views as to why the economic cycle exists. Figure 9.3 shows the economic cycle again, but this time includes an explanation for the various changes in GDP at each stage of the cycle.

There are other explanations for the cycle. Some theories look at technological change and how it can increase GDP but also make employees redundant. Other theories look at changes in stock levels and the effect of businesses becoming either more pessimistic or optimistic about the future; their views on how much stock they need to hold will obviously affect their suppliers' output and employment decisions. Another possible cause is a 'shock' from an event such as 9/11 or Hurricane Katrina, which devastated much of the Gulf of Mexico and its oil production in 2005.

Whatever the cause, the cycle exists and is a major influence on a business.

Effect of the economic cycle on the macroeconomic variables

In order to examine the effects of the economic cycle on businesses, it is first necessary to consider briefly how the macroeconomic variables themselves are affected as the economy moves through the cycle.

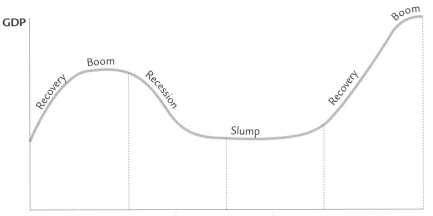

Figure 9.3
Reasons for the economic cycle

The high level of spending means that total demand in the economy exceeds supply. This starts to cause demand-pull inflation.

The boom in spending may suck in a large volume of imports. This will worsen the UK's trading position.

To counter these effects, the Bank of England puts up interest rates which slows down spending.

The government may also cut back on its level of spending.

As spending falls, some sectors of the economy start to experience a fall in the demand for their products.

These businesses then begin to lay off employees.

Spending falls further.

Businesses are highly interdependent, so these falls in spending multiply across the economy, causing even larger falls in consumption.

As a result, many businesses postpone investment in new plant and equipment.

The Bank of England will probably cut interest rates, as inflation is not likely to be a threat at this stage of the cycle.

The government may also stimulate demand by its own spending.

Businesses eventually have to undertake investment in the upkeep of buildings and machinery if they are to keep trading at all.

These three actions cause spending to rise.

Output and employment also start to grow — and the cycle begins again.

Consumption

Consumption depends mainly on *income*. The higher the level of employment, and therefore income, in the economy, the higher will be the level of consumption. The position of the economy in the cycle is therefore the major determinant of consumer demand for a business's products. Of course, in a recession or slump, consumers can still borrow money to spend.

An important additional determinant of consumption is the availability of credit

Investment

 KEY TERM

investment: purchase of capital equipment and/or buildings by businesses

Businesses will always undertake a certain amount of **investment**, whatever the level of economic activity. There will always be a need to replace equipment that has worn out, and to keep up with competitors. However, a large amount of investment is

related to GDP. If GDP is falling and a recession is predicted, businesses are unlikely to build new factories or install the latest technology. The reverse is also true: if GDP is rising, businesses will feel more confident about future sales and will invest in order to meet the demand that is coming.

Government spending

Government spending is also known as *public spending*. It is important not to confuse 'public spending' with 'spending by the public', which is consumption spending.

Government spending can be used as a tool to stimulate or reduce the level of economic activity. As government spending is an injection into the circular flow of income, any rise in it will increase the level of economic activity, while any reduction will slow it down. This is known as *fiscal policy* (see Chapter 11) and is of considerable relevance to the economic cycle.

> **KEY TERM**
>
> **public spending:** spending by central and local government for the public's benefit, either on essential services or to change the level of economic activity

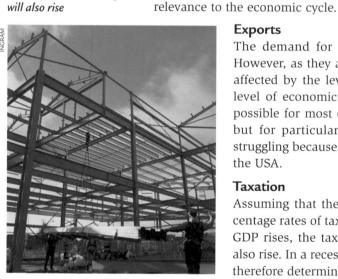

When spending rises, business investment in buildings and machinery will also rise

INGRAM

Exports

The demand for exports is partly affected by their price. However, as they are goods that are sold abroad, they are not affected by the level of GDP in the UK; they depend on the level of economic activity in other countries. It is therefore possible for most of the UK economy to be doing quite well, but for particular businesses dependent on exports to be struggling because of a recession in, say, continental Europe or the USA.

Taxation

Assuming that the government makes no change to the percentage rates of tax that people and businesses have to pay, as GDP rises, the tax revenue collected by the government will also rise. In a recession, the reverse will be true. Tax revenue is therefore determined to a large extent by the economic cycle.

Saving

Higher levels of *income* are generally associated with higher levels of saving in the economy. Two other factors also affect saving:

- **The rate of interest.** For many people, this is unlikely to be the major factor affecting saving. If a person is earning the minimum wage and interest rates rise, this is unlikely to generate much more saving because of their relatively low income. On the other hand, if a person's income doubles as a result of finding a new job, this might increase the amount saved.
- **Expectations of the future.** If people feel that they are about to lose their jobs, they may try to save more money. However, if people are confident about the security of their jobs, they may see little point in saving.

Module 2871

Imports

A rise in the level of economic activity is associated with an increase in the amount of imports. This is for two reasons:

- As spending rises, some of it will go on goods that have been produced in other countries.
- As businesses increase output to meet rises in demand, they will need more raw materials and capital equipment. Some of these will have to be imported.

How does the economic cycle affect businesses?

Not all firms in the economy are affected in the same way by changes in economic activity caused by the economic cycle. Consider the following examples.

A business selling PCs

How might this firm be affected in a recession? To what extent are PCs essential for everyday life? If they are considered necessary, there may be little effect at all on demand. Presumably, though, some people who are worried about losing their job will now cancel their planned purchase of a PC. Others will stick with the one they have rather than upgrade. Demand is therefore likely to fall.

However, even if the market for PCs to be used at home suffers a fall in demand, PCs are often provided for people at work. To what extent will businesses cancel purchases or put off upgrading? If businesses continue to buy PCs in large quantities, the effect of the recession on the firm selling them will not be so severe.

A business selling mobile phones

Mobile phones have quickly changed from being a luxury item to a necessity for some people. If there is a recession in the UK, to what extent will sales be affected? This could be an even more difficult question to answer than the one concerning PCs. This is because the groups who buy mobile phones are different.

The firm may find that demand from young people, who use mobile phones partly as a fashion statement, will be largely unaffected. This is because these consumers see them as essential for their lifestyle. They will almost certainly continue to buy the latest models. A business selling mobile phones would need to consider demographics very carefully. If the proportion of younger people in the population is relatively small, the fact that they continue to buy mobile phones may not offset the decline in purchases (and upgrades) among other age groups.

A supermarket chain

If the economy moves into recession, will there be any change in demand for a supermarket's products? On the face of it, the answer is no, since people must eat in order to live. They also require other household goods, such as washing powder. However, if incomes are falling, there is likely to be an increased demand for 'budget' or 'value' products, so the supermarket will need to start stocking more of these if it is to meet consumer requirements. New suppliers may have to be found for some of these products. At the same time, the business may alter its advertising and promotional policies to reflect the change. Both these factors will involve additional expense.

e **EXAMINER'S VOICE**

Questions in the examination will centre around one specific business, not all the businesses in the economy. Therefore, you will need to apply your knowledge of the economic cycle and its effects to a particular firm.

Further sources

www.statistics.gov.uk
— data on the macroeconomic variables, the overall state of the UK economy and the different regions and sectors

Summary

Businesses are, to a large extent, at the mercy of the state of the economy, but that does not mean that they can and should do nothing when the level of economic activity changes. The likely effect of a recession on a business depends on how it chooses to respond. How firms should respond is not part of Module 2871, but you need to be able to use your knowledge of economics to evaluate what strategies are appropriate for businesses to adopt. This is essential knowledge for the rest of the AS course.

YOUR TURN

Case study

Time allowed: 35 minutes

A. A. Alarm Systems

Alan Armstrong runs a small private company that installs alarm systems to households and businesses. He decided to start his own business, having worked for 10 years as an engineer for one of the major installation companies in the region.

He founded A. A. Alarms in 2003 and business has grown steadily. He won a major contract with a large house-building business early on and his good workmanship here earned him a reputation that has since generated a steady stream of customers.

He now employs three other people.

Alan, however, was slightly puzzled by the economic reports in his morning newspaper that seemed to be contradictory. One article discussed the government's intention to press on with more housing developments in several parts of the country — which included Alan's. Reading this pleased him and made him feel optimistic about the future. But another article stated that although there had been a rise in GDP over the past 6 months, it was less than had been predicted by the government. This, the article said, meant that the increase in consumers' income and spending had also not been as large as expected. Alan was not so pleased with this.

He was also not pleased when one of his employees, Nick, told him that morning that he was handing in his notice in order to work for a new alarm installer that had just started up in the area. Nick told Alan that the new company was offering installations at up to 20% less than A. A. Alarms, so he felt that his job would be more secure and that the prospects were better.

Alan decided to do some careful planning. He had been thinking about investing in some new technology that would be a major help to him and his engineers when diagnosing faults in a system. Now he was not so sure. He thought it would be best to start planning by establishing just where the UK was on the economic cycle.

Answer all questions.

1 Outline **one** effect on of an increase in consumers' income on A. A. Alarms. *(4 marks)*

2 State **two** ways in which Alan could assess the state of the economy. *(2 marks)*

3 State **two** ways in which the government might benefit from a rise in GDP. *(2 marks)*

4 Outline **two** factors that could influence Alan's decision to invest in some new technology. *(4 marks)*

5 **Other than** through decisions about investment, evaluate how the economic cycle might affect A. A. Alarms. *(14 marks)*

(26 marks)

CHAPTER 10

The macroeconomic objectives of government

Most economists would agree that a government has four **macroeconomic** objectives:

- **A low and stable rate of inflation.** The current government has set a target of 2% a year for the rate at which prices in the economy should increase.
- **A high level of employment.** As many people as possible should be in work.
- **Economic growth.** There should be an increase in the amount of goods and services produced in the economy each year.
- **A balance of payments equilibrium.** The value of the payments that the UK makes for imports should be similar to the value of the income it earns from exports.

A textbook from 30 years ago might have said 'another possible objective is a fairer distribution of income and wealth'. Since then the gap between those at the top of the income distribution and those at the bottom has become wider, so what has happened to this objective?

The government *is* still interested in the distribution of income and wealth, but policies to tackle inequality are now different from those of the past. Previously, money was taken in tax from the relatively wealthy and distributed in the form of various benefits to the less well off. This was sometimes called the 'Robin Hood' approach. Although, of course, the relatively poor still receive benefits, the emphasis now is on the government providing opportunities for people to improve their employment prospects. Unemployment benefit has been replaced by a Jobseeker's Allowance to reflect this. The government tries to improve people's ability to find jobs — and therefore earn more income via their own efforts — through policies on education and skills training, and by creating the right conditions in the economy for people to set up their own businesses and run them successfully.

These right conditions involve achieving as many of the four objectives as possible. When these objectives are not being met, it creates problems for the economy and therefore for businesses. This chapter considers these problems and why the achievement of the macroeconomic objectives is so important if businesses are to succeed.

KEY TERM

macroeconomics: study and analysis of the behaviour of the whole economy

A low and stable rate of inflation

People often say that inflation means rising prices, but this is only partly correct. At any one time, some prices in the economy will be rising but some will be falling. It would therefore be more accurate to say that **inflation** is *a persistent general tendency for prices to rise*. A high rate of inflation is bad for the economy and therefore bad for businesses.

Inflation makes UK exports uncompetitive. As a result of **globalisation**, identical products (e.g. the same model of car, brand of clothes, can of soft drink) can be made more or less anywhere in the world. If the UK has a rate of inflation that is higher than those in other countries, the price of UK exports will rise, making them less attractive to consumers abroad. A fall in the level of exports will mean less income for businesses, which could affect employment.

Inflation can also affect investment. Multinational companies look to produce in the cheapest possible location. This means that when they invest in a new plant, they choose the country with the lowest rate of inflation. They do not want to locate in a country where the price of labour and raw material inputs is rising sharply because this would make their products uncompetitive.

Inflation creates uncertainty. Managers dislike uncertainty about what the return on an investment will be. It is one thing to estimate that the profits from an investment will be £100,000 a year for the next 10 years, but if inflation is running out of control, how much will this be worth **in real terms**: in other words, what quantity of products will this sum of money actually buy? Low inflation allows businesses to plan their investments with some degree of certainty about their return and so encourages investment.

In summary, inflation is bad for businesses because:
- it makes UK businesses uncompetitive internationally
- it can lead to unemployment
- it creates uncertainty, which can deter investment

A high level of employment

The government wants a low level of unemployment for three reasons:
- **Unemployment is a waste of human resources.** If the unemployed were at work producing goods and services, society as a whole would have more goods and services to enjoy. People would have a higher standard of living.
- **Unemployment is bad for the individual.** Unemployment is often associated with social problems such as vandalism and drug abuse. The lack of a job can also be damaging to a person's self-esteem.
- **Unemployment is bad for society as a whole.** The problems associated with drugs and vandalism have to be paid for. In addition, benefits have to be paid to those with no job. 'Society' has to pay, in the sense that this

 KEY TERMS

inflation: persistent general tendency of prices in the economy to rise

globalisation: ability of multinational companies to purchase inputs, make products and sell them, all over the world

in real terms: adjusted for the effects of price rises

EXAMINER'S VOICE

When inflation falls, this does not mean that prices have gone down; it just means that the rate of increase in prices has fallen.

money could be spent in other, more productive areas, such as education and health.

Unemployment is bad for the individual and society

In summary, unemployment is bad for businesses because:

- it means lower levels of spending and therefore lower demand for businesses' products
- it can lead to social problems, which have to be paid for

Economic growth

KEY TERM

economic growth: an increase in the volume of goods and services produced each year

The benefit of **economic growth** is that, if more goods and services are produced, people have a higher standard of living. Over the past 30 years or so this objective has changed slightly. It is not just a continuous growth of goods and services that is desired; the growth should be *sustainable*. In other words, where possible, growth should come from the use of renewable resources, and damage to the environment resulting from growth should be minimised. Moreover, the needs of future generations should be considered. Issues such as the ozone layer and global warming have put this sharply into focus.

Sustainable growth has become much more important in recent years

HOLE IN THE OZONE LAYER GETTING BIGGER

GLOBAL WARMING ON THE INCREASE

5,000 SPECIES THREATENED BY POLLUTION

In summary, a lack of growth is bad for businesses because:

- it causes unemployment and so reduces the demand for businesses' products
- it means that people's standard of living (and therefore spending) is not increasing as fast as it could be

A balance of payments equilibrium

'Balance of payments' is the term used to describe the financial records of the UK's trade with the rest of the world. For example, someone who stays in a hotel abroad makes a payment to the hotel, which is recorded as an *outflow* of income from the UK. If a UK company operating abroad sends its profits back to the UK, these are recorded as an *inflow* of money.

The balance of payments is about the measurement of all these types of inflows and outflows, but the most important component of the balance of payments is known as the **balance of trade**. This is the record of all the UK's **imports** and **exports**. It is this figure that is usually used in the news.

 TERMS

balance of trade: difference between the value of exports and imports — if exports exceed imports, there is a balance of trade surplus; if imports exceed exports, there is a balance of trade deficit

imports: purchase by UK businesses and consumers of products made abroad

exports: sale of products from UK businesses abroad

An excess of imports over exports is known as a *trade deficit*; an example is shown in part (a) of Figure 10.1. An excess of exports over imports is known as a *trade surplus*; an example is shown in part (b).

Why is the balance of trade important? If people spend more than thay receive in income, at first their savings will be run down and then, if the pattern of earning and spending continues, they will have to borrow. It is the same principle for a country if it continuously imports more than it exports. All countries have balance of trade deficits from time to time, but a prolonged deficit causes problems because the imported goods have to be paid for somehow. It is important that the UK exports sufficient products to 'pay its way' internationally.

(a) Trade deficit

| Imports £80bn | Trade deficit £30bn |
| | Exports £50bn |

(b) Trade surplus

| Trade surplus £30bn | Exports £80bn |
| Imports £50bn | |

Figure 10.1
Balance of trade

In summary, a trade deficit is bad for businesses because:
- UK businesses are losing out on sales to foreign firms because of imports, and this will cause unemployment
- UK businesses are not earning sufficient revenue from exports to pay for the country's volume of imports

Why do these problems occur?

The problems of inflation, unemployment, balance of trade deficits and low economic growth have to be tackled if businesses and the society they operate within are to prosper. In order to do this, it is necessary to establish their causes.

Labour £10	Selling price £25
Interest £5	
Raw materials £5	
Mark-up £5	

Labour £10	Selling price £28
Interest £5	
Raw materials £8	
Mark-up £5	

***Figure 10.2** Effect of a rise in costs on selling price*

What causes inflation?

Why do prices rise? The answer is deceptively simple — because businesses put them up. There are two main reasons for this:

- **A rise in costs.** The price of any product is made up of the total cost of all the inputs that go into it, such as labour, raw materials and interest rate charges, plus an amount for profit put on top — the mark-up. If any of the input costs rise, it is likely that the firm will put up prices in order to maintain the same mark up. In the example shown in Figure 10.2, if the cost of raw materials rises from £5 to £8 per unit, the business is likely to try to increase the selling price from £25 to £28 in order to make the same amount of profit. When rising costs force UK businesses to increase their prices, this is known as *cost-push inflation*.
- **The level of demand in the economy.** If total demand in the economy exceeds supply, this will cause prices to rise. If a business's telephones are ringing constantly with customers asking for more products, managers will feel confident about putting up prices without there being any adverse effects on demand. Where there is too much demand and not enough supply, there is said to be *demand-pull inflation*.

What causes unemployment?

Some people choose not to work and try to exist on benefits; these people are said to be *voluntarily unemployed*. There is also *seasonal unemployment*, which means that some employees (e.g. in the hotel or agricultural sectors) tend to be unemployed at certain times of the year. Finally, there are always people moving from job to job; when people are between jobs, this is known as *frictional unemployment*. Economists tend not to worry too much about these types of unemployment because they are usually short term. Other causes of unemployment can be much more serious because the problems are longer term:

INGRAM

- **A slowdown in the level of economic activity.** This causes the demand for products and thus the demand for workers who produce those goods to fall. This type of unemployment is known as *demand deficient (or cyclical) unemployment* (see Chapter 9).
- **Wages are too high.** High wages create more spending and so help prevent demand-deficient unemployment. However, if they rise too high, this will cause businesses to lay off workers and/or try to replace them with machines. This type of unemployment is known as *real wage unemployment*. Of course 'too high' is a matter of opinion; workers will view wage rates rather differently from the businesses that pay them.
- **A decline in certain types of industry.** When industries decline, workers have to try to find jobs in the expanding sectors of the economy. This is not always easy because they may not have the right skills. If someone has been a coal miner for 30 years, he

cannot easily find work in one of the new, fast-growing labour markets of the economy, such as designing software games for children. If unemployment results from a change in the whole structure of output in the economy, this is known as *structural unemployment*. The traditional industries that made Britain 'great' during the Industrial Revolution, such as coal, steel, shipbuilding and textiles, declined rapidly after the Second World War.

What causes a poor rate of growth?

Several causes of a low growth rate may be suggested:

- **A lack of investment.** If businesses do not invest, they will lack modern factories with the most up-to-date capital equipment with which to compete with businesses in other countries. This could mean that UK goods are priced uncompetitively and/or are of lower quality than those made abroad, so consumers will not buy them.
- **Laws may hinder business activity.** If the UK's legal framework (sometimes called 'red tape') is tougher on businesses than other countries this will deter entrepreneurs and may also put off inward investment into the UK from foreign firms.
- **The workforce may lack skills and qualifications.** If so, the UK will not have a highly productive workforce capable of producing high-quality products.

What causes a balance of trade deficit?

A trade deficit for the UK means that it is importing more than it is exporting. The causes are twofold:

- **Imported products are cheaper or of better quality than those produced in the UK.** If this is the case, it is not surprising that UK consumers buy them.
- **UK businesses are not selling sufficient quantities of goods that consumers in other countries want.** This could be because the design or quality is poor and/or their prices are high. Sometimes it is the exchange rate that makes UK exports expensive abroad. There is often little that UK businesses can do about this problem, which is considered further in Chapter 12.

Further sources

http://eh.net/hmit — to find out the purchasing power of money in different years — for example, to buy the equivalent of £1,000 worth of goods bought during the Second World War, you would need around £29,000 today

YOUR TURN

Case study
Time allowed: 25 minutes

Greenland Electrical

Greenland Electrical Ltd (GEL) was established in 2002. It is a small company producing motors, pumps and other components for washing machines. The design of the components means that the washing machines that they are used in are very efficient in terms of water and power use. The company employs 30 people, most of whom belong to a trade union.

The chief executive, Rory Palmer, is the person who came up with the ideas in the first place and who established the firm. This proved very difficult to do because he had little previous experience of running a business. He had a lot of trouble raising sufficient finance to get started and even now cash flow is often a problem. The company does not make the whole washing machine — it sells its products to two established manufacturers.

The use of Greenland's technology means that the final selling price of the machines is higher than ordinary models, but as they are targeted at the middle and higher income groups this has, so far, not been a problem. GEL's two customers have been very effective in their advertising and sales have been growing. Rory was, however, concerned when he heard a news bulletin warning about a possible rise in the rate of inflation. He was also alarmed that some economists were talking about the possibility of a rise in unemployment as well.

Answer all questions.

1 State the **four** macroeconomic objectives of a government. *(4 marks)*

2 State what is meant by the term 'standard of living'. *(2 marks)*

3 Analyse how rising inflation might affect GEL. *(9 marks)*

4 Analyse how rising unemployment might affect GEL. *(9 marks)*

(24 marks)

Module 2871

Economic policy and its effect on businesses

KEY TERMS

Bank of England: the central bank in the UK; as banker to the government and other banks, it conducts monetary policy and is not involved in personal banking

monetary policy: manipulation of the level of demand in the economy using the rate of interest.

Monetary Policy Committee (MPC): committee of the Bank of England that meets once a month to decide whether to change the rate of interest

Economic policy is conducted in three ways: through *monetary policy*, *fiscal policy* and the *exchange rate*. All of these can be used to influence the economy. To speak of the government controlling the economy would be wrong; a better phrase might be 'steering it in the right direction'.

The government cannot alter the behaviour of people and firms simply by *telling* them what to do, so it has to use economic policy to try to alter their behaviour. The economic policy or policies that are used depend on what economic objective(s) the government or the **Bank of England** is trying to achieve (see Chapter 10).

Monetary policy

Monetary policy is concerned with manipulating the level of demand in the economy through the rate of interest. 'Rate of interest' has two different meanings:

- To borrowers it is the *cost of borrowing* — that is, what has to be paid back to the lender.
- To savers it is the *reward for saving* — that is, the return on their money.

When interest rates change, they all move in the same direction: when rates rise for savers, they also rise for borrowers.

Until 1997, monetary policy was decided by the chancellor of the exchequer and then put into effect by the Bank of England. One of the first actions taken by the chancellor of the exchequer, Gordon Brown, when Labour came to power in 1997 was to make the Bank of England independent and hand control of monetary policy to the bank's **Monetary Policy Committee (MPC)**. The MPC is a panel of experts from the financial and business world, which meets once a month to decide whether to change the rate of interest. Although the government owns the Bank of England, the MPC is entirely independent.

When monetary policy was in the government's hands, there was always the temptation to use the rate of interest for political purposes. For example, a government might lower the rate of

Gordon Brown granted the Bank of England control of monetary policy in 1997

interest before a general election in order to induce a feel-good factor, even if the economy was at the wrong place on the economic cycle for this to be the appropriate policy. If the level of demand was already rising too fast, a *rise* in interest rates would have been the correct policy.

As a result of this, when interest rates were eventually raised, they would have had to go higher than would have been necessary had the government acted economically rather than politically in the first place — and high rates can be damaging to businesses.

Virtually all economists now agree that giving the Bank of England control of interest rates was a good decision; governments can no longer meddle with the economy for political reasons.

What is the Bank of England trying to achieve?

The Bank of England is responsible for meeting the government's target for the rate of inflation in the UK economy. This is currently 2%. A low and stable rate of inflation is beneficial to businesses (see Chapter 10).

The bank does look at factors such as the level of unemployment and output when assessing the level of demand (and therefore the possibility of inflation exceeding the target), but low inflation is its priority.

How does monetary policy work?

The rate of interest is essentially the *price of money*. The price of something affects its demand, and therefore the demand for money responds to changes in the rate of interest.

If the Bank of England wants consumers and businesses to spend less, it raises the rate of interest. Figure 11.1 shows that if the rate is increased from r_1 to r_2, this will discourage borrowing and spending. The demand for money will fall from Q_1 to Q_2. It may also encourage some people who have surplus cash to save. The opposite would apply if the bank cut the rate to r_1.

Figure 11.1
The demand for money

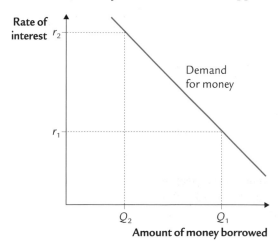

Rate of interest

To quote from the Bank of England's website:

> Monetary policy operates by influencing the cost of money. The Bank sets an interest rate that affects the whole pattern of rates set by the commercial banks for their savers and borrowers. This, in turn, affects spending and output in the economy, and eventually costs and prices.

Therefore, if the Bank of England wants to slow down the economy and control inflation by lowering consumer spending and business investment, it puts up the rate of interest. If it wants to encourage people to spend and businesses to expand, it lowers the rate of interest.

Effects of a rise in the rate of interest on businesses

A rise in the rate of interest is likely to have the following effects.

Investment will fall

Businesses are more likely to make do with older, less efficient machinery and hardware because the cost of borrowing money to replace them has risen. This will have a knock-on effect on their suppliers. In addition, businesses know that a rise in interest rates will slow down consumer spending — this will make it even less attractive to invest.

A fall in investment will slow down the level of economic activity, and if the fall in investment is severe enough, it may cause a recession (see Chapter 9).

Consumer spending will fall

As the interest payable on mortgages, loans and credit cards increases, spending on other products will fall. The demand for luxury items, which are often bought on credit, will fall.

It is often said that when rates rise, people save more. This, however, ignores the reality of the effect of a rate rise on a typical household with, say, £2,000 in savings and a mortgage of £100,000.

Using these figures, let us consider this point in more detail. First, we make some assumptions to simplify the analysis, as shown in Table 11.1.

The Smiths have a disposable income of £1,500 per month.	+£1,500
The household has £2,000 saved in the bank, earning 3% interest. This means that the interest paid to them is £60 per year, or £5 per month.	+£5
The rate of interest on the family's £100,000 mortgage is 6%. This makes the monthly interest charge £500 (£6,000/12). The household also has to make a capital repayment of £400 each month towards the money it owes. The total monthly repayment is therefore £900.	−£900
The household's total monthly income available for spending is: £1,500 + £5 − £900 = £605	**£605**

Table 11.1 The Smiths' family budget with a 3% interest rate

Assume that rates rise by 1% and stay up for a whole year. Many people would say that consumer spending will fall because households like the Smiths will save more. The effect is right, but the analysis of why it occurs is wrong.

CHAPTER 11   Economic policy and its effect on businesses

Table 11.2 shows what happens to the Smiths' finances when the rate rises.

Table 11.2 The Smiths' family budget with a 4% interest rate

Assume that disposable income is still £1,500. Employees do ask for higher wages when interest rates rise, but even if granted this will not happen at once.	+£1,500
At the bank the £2,000 savings now receives interest at 4%. This means a yearly return of £80. The monthly interest paid increases from £5 to £6.67 (£80/12).	+£6.67
As the rate of interest is now 7%. Repayments on the mortgage go up to £7,000 a year. This means a monthly interest repayment of £583 (£7,000/12). Add on the £400 capital repayment and that is a total of £983.	–£983
This means that income left for consumption is now £523.67. The Smith household is worse off by over £80. £1,500 + £6.67 – £983 = £523.67	£523.67

Some people (probably those with no mortgages or other loans) can save more when the interest rate rises, but for the 20 million or so people like the Smiths with various loan debts, this is unlikely to be possible. The main reason for the fall in consumer demand when interest rates rise is the *rise in borrowing costs*, not an increase in saving.

Conversely, a cut in the interest rate will raise consumer spending, not so much because it is no longer worth saving, but because of the effect on consumers like the Smiths of having to pay less on their loans.

A rise in the interest rate will also slow down the rate of growth of house prices. When this happens, there is a *wealth effect*. As people see that the value of their property is no longer rising (and it may even be falling), they feel less confident about spending and this reduces demand.

The exchange rate is likely to rise

When UK interest rates rise, the pound becomes a more attractive currency to invest in and the increased demand for sterling causes the exchange rate to rise. This means that any business selling abroad will find that its exports become more expensive to foreign customers. It also means that imports become cheaper. This will be good if a business uses imported raw materials, but not so good if it is competing with foreign imports of a finished product (see Chapter 12).

Effects of a fall in the rate of interest on businesses

A fall in the rate of interest is likely to have the following effects.

Investment will increase

A lot of investment is made with borrowed money. Any fall in the rate of interest means that it is now cheaper for businesses to borrow money to finance expansion and capital spending. They will therefore increase their purchases of new buildings, machinery and technology.

Any investment will raise the level of economic activity and this means more spending by consumers and a further boost to GDP. The installation of

Module 2871

modern plant and equipment will also help UK businesses to be more competitive internationally.

Consumer spending will increase

Anyone with a mortgage (or any other type of loan) will now pay less interest and so their purchases of other goods and services are likely to rise — although not all businesses will be affected in the same way. For example, a travel agent is more likely to expect an increase in demand as a result of a fall in interest rates than a baker. When it comes to spending on credit, consumers will now be prepared to borrow to buy consumer durables such as cars, DVDs and washing machines.

The exchange rate is likely to fall

How this occurs and the precise effects on businesses are explained in Chapter 12. For the moment, it is sufficient to say that a fall in the exchange rate makes UK exports cheaper abroad, so any business that sells abroad will find that its exports become more attractive. It also means that imports become more expensive. This causes an unwelcome rise in costs if a business has to buy raw materials from abroad. On the other hand, a fall in exchange rates will benefit any UK firms that are competing with foreign imports.

If interest rates are cut, consumer spending is likely to rise

How quickly do changes in interest rates take effect?

The Bank of England works on a timescale of around 18 months — that is how long it takes for changes in interest rates to have their full effect on investment and consumption. Suppose that the bank increases the interest rate. Although some investment planned for the future will be cancelled or postponed, many projects will already be under way. Once the construction of a factory has been started, it has to be completed.

Consumers also take time to react. Spending patterns do not change overnight and for millions of people it could be many months before their behaviour adjusts to the fact that they have less to spend. This is partly because there is a strong element of 'keeping up with the neighbours' when buying goods such as cars and mobile phones. For quite a long time, people may run down their savings to maintain levels of spending.

This time lag is not necessarily a disadvantage to the Bank of England. When it puts up interest rates, what it is hoping for is that the slowdown in economic activity is gradual rather than sudden — it wants a 'soft landing' rather than a recession. The bank hopes that as demand slows down, businesses will try to lower their costs and hence the prices they charge to their customers. If price rises slow down, that is precisely what the bank is trying to achieve in terms of its inflation target.

Similarly, when interest rates are cut, the Bank of England is hoping for a steady, sustained increase in output, which will encourage long-term prosperity in the economy, rather than a burst of inflationary growth that has to be swiftly curbed by rate rises.

Fiscal policy

Fiscal policy is conducted through taxation and government spending. It is controlled by the government through the chancellor of the exchequer — the member of the cabinet responsible for the government's finances. The chancellor works closely with the Treasury, which is the ministry responsible for helping to determine and implement the government's economic policy.

Fiscal policy affects the level of demand in the economy and so has a significant impact on businesses. In order to evaluate what is likely to happen to the demand for its products, a business needs to analyse **the Budget**. The Budget is the occasion (usually in April) when the chancellor states how much the government intends to spend in the next year and how this spending will be financed.

Taxation

There are two types of tax: *direct* and *indirect*.

Direct taxes

Direct taxes are taken directly from:

- a person's income when they work. This is called *income tax*.
- a business when it makes a profit. The type of tax paid by a business depends on its legal status: sole traders and those in a partnership pay *income tax*, whereas a company (private or public) pays *corporation tax*.

There is another direct deduction from a person's income called *national insurance*. This is taken as a contribution towards the state pension and treatment under the National Health Service. It may not be called national insurance *tax*, but it is deducted by law directly from a person's income and so can be treated as a direct tax. A business also has to pay a certain amount of national insurance for every employee. The more employees a business has on its payroll, the more it has to pay. For this reason, national insurance paid by a business is sometimes called a *payroll tax*.

There is also direct taxation at local level. Households pay *council tax* to the local authority for services such as refuse collection, street cleaning and the fire service. Businesses have to pay the *business rate* to help fund the same services. This local authority taxation on a business is in addition to any national insurance payments and taxes that are paid to central government.

Indirect taxes

These taxes are not paid when a person or business earns money, but when they *spend* it; that is why they are 'indirect'. Most products have *value added tax (VAT)* put on them. This means that a percentage of the selling price is paid to the government as a tax. VAT is currently 17.5%.

On many goods there is another indirect tax as well as VAT. The government puts *excise duty* on certain products. This duty is a fixed amount of tax on each item rather than a percentage rate, but the effect is the same: it makes the product more expensive and raises revenue for the government. Examples include car tax (the proper name of which is *vehicle excise duty*), tobacco, alcohol and petrol.

The government taxes businesses and people (see Figure 11.2) in order to:

- raise revenue
- affect the level of economic activity
- influence the pattern of expenditure

Raising revenue

The government plays a major role in the economy and the amount it spends amounts to around 40% of GDP. Much of this spending comes from tax revenue.

Affecting the level of economic activity

In the years following the Second World War, the government often tried to manipulate the economy to achieve full employment and low inflation through tax and expenditure changes. However, the idea that this can be done with any precision is no longer popular; experience shows that the policy may have the wrong effect. This is because there are *time lags* before the effects occur. This means that when the effects eventually come through, the economy may have moved on to a situation in which the policy is no longer appropriate. For example, if taxes are cut to avoid a recession, by the time the extra spending starts to happen the economy may already be recovering strongly — which is likely to have the unintended consequence of a rise in inflation.

Nevertheless, the principle of using tax and expenditure changes to 'nudge the economy in the right direction' is still accepted. Lower taxation should encourage spending by consumers and businesses, which will boost the level of economic activity. On the other hand, if too much demand is causing inflation and/or too many imports, the government could increase tax rates, which will reduce spending.

Influencing the pattern of expenditure

The government tries to encourage certain kinds of behaviour and discourage others. Lower rates of tax are placed on products that the government is trying to encourage people to buy — for example, unleaded petrol has a lower rate of tax than leaded. Taxes are put on products that can be harmful, such as cigarettes and alcohol, in order to discourage their use.

Other[1] (£65bn)   Business rates (£20bn)
Council tax (£21bn)   VAT (£74bn)
Corporation tax (£42bn)
Excise duties (£40bn)
Income tax (£136bn)   National insurance (£84bn)

[1] Other sources include capital taxes, stamp duties, vehicle excise duties and some other tax and non-tax receipts (e.g. interest and dividends).

Source: HM Treasury

Figure 11.2 *Sources of UK tax revenue, 2005/06*

Indirect taxes are put on products that the government wants to dissuade people from buying

Public spending

The government intervenes in the economy through **public spending** (see Figure 11.3). It does so for three main purposes.

To provide essential services that the private sector is unlikely to offer

A business would not usually want to supply services such as a police force, a fire service or street lighting, as these are unlikely to make a profit. This means that central or local government has to provide them. Other examples are healthcare and pensions. It is likely that many people will fail to realise how important these are (and therefore will not save any money to pay for them) until it is too late — that is, when they become ill or old. This means that the government has to do it for them by taxing people and providing the services when they need them. These goods are known as **merit goods**.

Merit goods are important for UK businesses. Some of these services are, of course, provided by the private sector. However if, for example, education were left completely up to people to buy privately, they might not buy 'enough' education for their children. This would not be good for an economy whose businesses need an educated workforce. The same argument applies to healthcare. The economy needs a healthy workforce because healthier workers are more productive. If the government thinks that people are not getting enough of these sorts of products for businesses to function effectively, it will increase its spending on them.

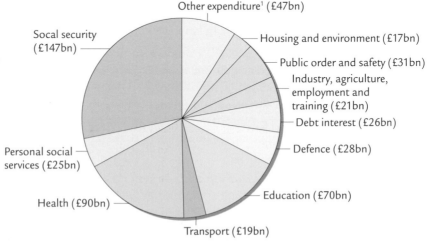

Other expenditure[1] (£47bn)

Social security (£147bn)

Housing and environment (£17bn)

Public order and safety (£31bn)

Industry, agriculture, employment and training (£21bn)

Debt interest (£26bn)

Defence (£28bn)

Education (£70bn)

Transport (£19bn)

Health (£90bn)

Personal social services (£25bn)

Figure 11.3 Where taxpayers' money is spent, 2005/06

[1] Other expenditure includes spending on: general public services; recreation, culture, media and sport; international cooperation and development; public service pensions; spending yet to be allocated and accounting adjustments.

Source: HM Treasury

To influence the level of demand in the economy

The government can influence the level of demand by its own spending as well as through taxation. If the amount of government spending rises, this will increase the level of economic activity. The reverse is also true.

To assist certain regions in the UK

As seen in Chapter 4, the government targets some of its spending (Regional Development Assistance) at specific regions of the country where industry has been in decline for a number of years. This is known as **regional policy** and some of the funds for this assistance come from the European Union.

Some areas of the UK suffer from much higher levels of unemployment than others, while the more prosperous regions get overcrowded, creating congestion and pollution as well as pressure on facilities such as schools and hospitals. As well as preventing this, the aims of Regional Development Assistance are to:

- safeguard jobs in order to support communities
- encourage new businesses into the area and create jobs
- improve people's skills to make them more employable and productive
- minimise the loss of tax revenue to the Treasury — unemployment causes government spending on benefits to increase
- encourage investment and so boost the local economy
- help firms survive and/or grow, so they can compete more effectively abroad and also domestically against imported products
- help tackle *social exclusion* — this is where people (particularly young people) feel that they have little chance of participating in society and so turn to crime, vandalism and drugs; creating job opportunities will help prevent this

The amount of assistance given to a business depends on the extent to which it will help meet these aims. A project that creates a lot of jobs that are likely to be permanent will receive more assistance than one that creates a few jobs that may only be short term. As well as finance for businesses, funds are available to local authorities for urban renewal and infrastructure improvement, so that an area can be made more attractive to businesses.

The multiplier

Put simply, the **multiplier** means that if businesses experience a change in the demand for their products, this will have a knock-on (multiplier) effect on the businesses that supply them. The multiplier is a very useful concept not only for analysing the effects of fiscal policy, but also for considering other changes in economic activity.

A cut in income tax will increase the demand for cars made in the UK and this increase in demand will cause a multiplier effect (see Figure 11.4). Car manufacturers will order more of all sorts of components from their suppliers — everything from brake shoes to bumpers, seats to CD players, and windscreens to wheels.

 KEY TERM

regional policy: government economic measures to try to encourage businesses into regions of the country where economic activity is low

KEY TERM

multiplier: the effect of changes in economic activity in one sector on other sectors; if one business experiences a rise or fall in demand for its products, this has a knock-on effect on businesses supplying it

Figure 11.4
Multiplier effect of
a cut in income tax

A cut in income tax will increase the demand for cars

This will increase the demand for car components

Bumpers This will increase the demand for plastic and metal

Seats This will increase the demand for springs, fabric etc.

In-car CD player This will increase the demand for electrical components, speakers etc.

In turn this will increase employment in the businesses making these products

Income is being created at each stage of the process. This causes a rise in spending, and therefore employment is multiplied across the economy. The same would apply if there were an increase in UK exports of aircraft engines, for example. This would have a multiplier effect on the businesses that supply the exporter. Quite a small rise in spending in one or two industries can quickly generate increased demand for products elsewhere.

The multiplier also operates in reverse. A fall in demand will cause spending to fall, which in turn has a multiplier effect across the economy. Any government putting up taxes to raise more revenue or cutting public spending must consider the multiplier effects of such a policy.

The multiplier also helps to explain why the closure of a large business such as a steelworks, car plant or shipyard can be so devastating. Not only does the area lose a major source of employment, but in addition, all the smaller firms that depend on the large business suddenly find themselves with vastly reduced order books. This is why there was so much concern about the closure of the Rover car plant in 2005.

As unemployment rises, there is less spending in the local shops on consumer items such as televisions, clothes and carpets. When the multiplier 'goes into reverse' nationally, for whatever reason, unless action is taken by the government or the Bank of England, a full-scale depression might occur.

The multiplier helps to explain why the closure of a large business such as a car plant can be so devastating

Further sources

www.dti.gov.uk/regional — part of the Department of Trade and Industry website that gives information and data on regional policy and other government assistance for businesses

www.thebankofengland.co.uk — what the Bank of England does, and how monetary and exchange rate policies operate

www.hm-treasury.gov.uk — a good source of economic data and other useful information about current economic policy

YOUR TURN

Case study   Time allowed: 40 minutes

McAvoys Ltd

The aquaculture industry in Scotland, of which salmon farming is a part, has developed significantly over the last 30 years. Salmon farming is mainly undertaken in the sea-lochs of the West Coast, Orkney and the Shetland isles.

Multinational companies dominate the salmon farming industry in Scotland, whereas it is more usual to find small companies in the trout and shellfish industries. McAvoys Ltd is, however, one of the few smaller UK companies. It has carved a niche market for itself by supplying organically farmed salmon. The cofounders, Jamie and Ben McAvoy, farm from a sea-loch on the West Coast. They inherited the area from

their grandfather and as a result have a relatively small amount of debt outstanding to their bank.

Although the demand for salmon has continued to rise, the competition has intensified considerably. Producers from Chile and Norway dominate world salmon farming. Chile, in particular, has a cost advantage that Scottish producers find hard to match.

The West Coast is not always well served in terms of infrastructure and the farm is quite isolated — even though, as part of its regional policy, the government has designated much of this region of Scotland as a Development Area.

As a result of organic production requirements, the individual fish are more expensive to produce than on an ordinary farm. The brothers, however, decided from the outset to compete not on price but on quality. There are clear benefits to the organic approach and this is most apparent in the premium price that McAvoys Ltd can charge. The 'Scottishness' of the McAvoys' brand name that they have established has served them well and the brothers feel that the business has been a success. In 2006, McAvoys began to export salmon to three countries in the EU.

Source: amended from OCR Module 2871, June 2005

Answer all questions.

1 State **one** difference between fiscal policy and monetary policy *(2 marks)*

2 McAvoys has to pay a variety of taxes to the government. Analyse the likely effects of this taxation on McAvoys. *(9 marks)*

3 As part of its regional policy, the government has designated much of the West Coast of Scotland as a Development Area. Outline **two** likely reasons for the government offering support for businesses in this area of Scotland. *(4 marks)*

4 Evaluate how a change in the rate of interest might affect McAvoys. *(14 marks)*

(29 marks)

CHAPTER 12

The exchange rate

The UK trades with many different countries and these countries use different currencies. It is therefore important to understand the nature and effects of the exchange rate.

The **exchange rate** is the value of the pound in terms of another currency. When people travel abroad, they usually take an interest in how much foreign currency each pound will buy, and how many pounds they are likely to get for any currency brought back. It is exactly the same for UK businesses.

The exchange rate can have a number of different effects on a business, which can significantly affect its operation. Before these are examined it is necessary to consider how the exchange rate is determined. It is not 'fixed' by the government, although the government can try to influence it. Currencies are traded in a market — in this case, the **foreign exchange market**. This market is global: wherever banks and other financial institutions trade currencies, they are part of the foreign exchange market.

KEY TERMS

exchange rate: the value of the pound in terms of another currency

foreign exchange market: the market for currency, which is not in a single location but exists globally whenever buyers and sellers deal

How is the exchange rate determined?

As in any market, the price (in this case the 'price' of the pound, i.e. the rate of exchange) is determined by the interaction of demand and supply.

What determines the demand for pounds?

The demand for pounds on the foreign exchange market is determined by several factors, as shown in Figure 12.1.

Foreign investment in the UK
Any foreign business wishing to build a factory or office in the UK will have to use its currency to demand pounds in order to pay the UK construction companies.

Desire of foreign customers to buy UK exports
If a UK firm sells clothes to a business in Germany, it would want to be paid in pounds, not euros. This is because it does not want to go to the trouble and expense of exchanging euros into pounds. The German retailer must therefore use euros to demand pounds in order to pay the UK exporter. Similarly, German tourists coming to the UK would go to their bank and use euros to demand pounds.

'Hot money' flows into the UK
Hot money is money that flows from country to country in search of the highest possible rate of interest. If UK interest rates are higher than those in other countries, foreign banks will use their surplus foreign currency to demand pounds, which they will then deposit in UK banks. Hot money is dealt with in more detail later in this chapter.

Figure 12.1 Determinants of the demand for pounds

What determines the supply of pounds?

The supply of pounds on to the foreign exchange market is determined by the factors shown in Figure 12.2.

UK investment abroad
If a UK business wants to start trading in eastern Europe and decides to build a factory in Russia, the land that it is buying will have to be paid for in roubles (the Russian currency), as will all the construction workers and suppliers of equipment. The business therefore supplies pounds and demands roubles.

Desire of UK residents and businesses to buy imports
If a UK business buys a product from the USA, the US business does not want to be paid in pounds. So the UK business has to supply pounds to its bank and demands dollars in exchange with which to make the payment.

Supply of pounds

'Hot money' flows going abroad
If UK banks have funds to spare and think that the rate of interest in the USA, for example, is attractive, they will supply pounds and demand dollars. They will then deposit those dollars in US banks, where they can get a better return.

Figure 12.2 *Determinants of the supply of pounds*

The interaction of the demand for and supply of pounds establishes the exchange rate, as shown in Figure 12.3.

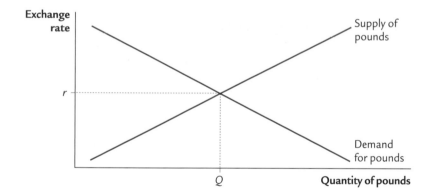

Figure 12.3 *Determination of the exchange rate*

What are the effects on a business if the rate of exchange changes?

Assume that there are 1.5 euros to the pound. This means that:

- for every £1 supplied, a business will get €1.5
- for every €1.5 supplied, a business will get £1

Consider an Italian pizza producer that sells a box of 20 'Mama Mia' pizzas' for €100. A restaurant in London imports them from Italy. This transaction is shown in Figure 12.4.

Module 2871

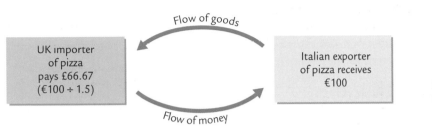

Figure 12.4 Cost to the UK importer of pizza

Just down the road from the London restaurant is a business that sells fountain pens. It sells a box of five for £100. A lot of its business is in the EU. A stationery shop in Italy buys these for its more exclusive customers. This transaction is shown in Figure 12.5.

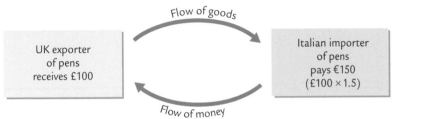

Figure 12.5 Cost to the Italian importer of fountain pens

What happens if the exchange rate rises?

Assume the rate is now £1 = €2. This means that the pound is now stronger — that is, it buys more foreign currency than before. Both of the two businesses will be affected, as shown in Figures 12.6 and 12.7.

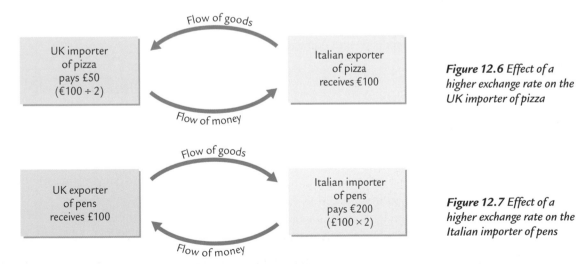

Figure 12.6 Effect of a higher exchange rate on the UK importer of pizza

Figure 12.7 Effect of a higher exchange rate on the Italian importer of pens

The effect of a rise in the exchange rate is to make imports cheaper, but exports more expensive.

What happens if the exchange rate falls?

Assume that the rate is now £1 = €1. The pound is now weaker: that is, it buys less foreign currency than before. Once again, both businesses will be affected, as shown in Figures 12.8 and 12.9.

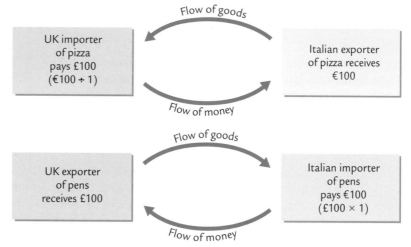

Figure 12.8 *Effect of a lower exchange rate on the UK importer of pizza*

Figure 12.9 *Effect of a lower exchange rate on the Italian importer of pens*

The effect of a fall in the exchange rate is to make imports more expensive, but exports cheaper.

The interaction of the supply and demand for pounds causes the rate of exchange to change on a daily basis. Unless there is some factor that is out of the ordinary, such as 9/11, a war or an unexpected change of government, these daily changes are minor. This is just as well as the changes in costs and prices caused by sudden large changes in the rate of exchange can be very destabilising and damaging to a business.

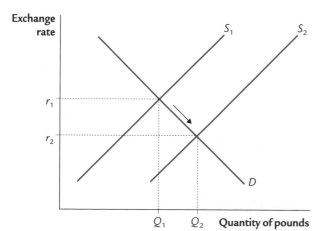

Figure 12.10
Effect of the Bank of England selling pounds

The Bank of England and the exchange rate

The Bank of England undertakes what are sometimes called 'smoothing operations'. It buys and sells currency whenever it is thought necessary in order to stop ('smooth out') potentially damaging changes in the exchange rate. However, it certainly does not seek to bring about large changes on a regular basis. For example, if the bank thought the rate was slightly too high, it would sell (supply) pounds and buy foreign currency or gold. This is shown in Figure 12.10; the sale of pounds lowers the exchange rate from r_1 to r_2.

Module 2871

Alternatively, if it thinks the rate is too low, the bank will buy (demand) pounds using reserves of foreign currency or gold to do so.

The Bank of England can also use flows of 'hot money' to alter the rate of exchange.

Hot money

Rises in the rate of interest affect the exchange rate via flows of **hot money**. It is important to understand this relationship because hot money is a major determinant of the exchange rate. Consider the following: someone receives £100 as a birthday present and decides to save it rather than spend it. Naturally, he/she will look for the bank or building society that offers the best rate of interest.

Exactly the same principle applies to international finance: international banks are looking for the best rate of interest for their money. Suppose there is a Japanese investment bank in Tokyo and that interest rates are 2% in Japan while UK banks are offering 5%. If the Japanese bank has some surplus funds, it will transfer them to the UK because the return is better. However, it will have to change its yen into pounds first. This increased demand for pounds will raise the price of pounds — that is, the exchange rate.

So, if the Bank of England wants the exchange rate to rise, instead of buying pounds itself (using foreign currency or gold), it can put up the rate of interest. This will encourage inflow of hot money into the UK to take advantage of the higher returns. This will shift the demand curve in Figure 12.11 from D_1 to D_2 and raise the exchange rate to r_2.

Alternatively, if the bank wants the rate of exchange to fall, it can lower the rate of interest. This makes deposits of money in the UK less attractive and the rate of exchange will fall.

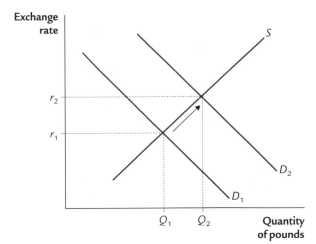

Figure 12.11
Using hot money to raise the exchange rate

The exchange rate as a tool of economic policy

What is the Bank of England trying to achieve when it intervenes? Apart from smoothing out temporary fluctuations, the bank may intervene for other reasons.

Inflation

Raising the rate of exchange can be a useful part of an anti-inflationary policy. Imports become cheaper, which lowers the cost of raw materials bought from abroad. This means that UK businesses can keep costs, and therefore prices, down.

In addition, an increase in the value of the pound means that the price of UK exports rises. The prices charged by any UK businesses exporting now appear uncompetitive, and they must try to cut their prices if they want to continue to export. This means they will have to keep control of wages and other costs. This will help to lower the rate of inflation.

Economic growth

Lowering the rate of exchange can help to increase economic activity. A lower rate makes UK exports cheaper, which is useful if the UK is not exporting enough. A fall in the rate helps boost exports and in doing so creates employment and economic growth.

Unfortunately, a lower rate may cause *imported inflation*, as any raw materials purchased from other countries will become more expensive.

Are all businesses affected in the same way by changes in the exchange rate?

The answer is 'no'. Consider the following three examples.

A UK business that exports but does not import
If the rate rises

Consider the business mentioned earlier that exports pens to Italy. It sells boxes of pens at £100. The original rate of exchange is £1 = €1.5, so the euro price of the pens is €150. Assume the exchange rate rises to £1 = €2. This means that the selling price has gone up in terms of what foreign countries must now pay: the price is now €200. This may make the product uncompetitive compared with pens produced in other countries. So why does the UK firm not lower its selling price to £75, which would put the euro price back down to where it was before at €150?

A price reduction of £25 per box of pens is quite substantial. If it wanted to keep profits per box of pens at the same level, the company would have to lower costs by £25 per box. However, it may not be able to find a cheaper supplier of the components that go into the pens, and its employees are unlikely to take a pay cut.

If the costs of production are £70 and the pens now sell at £75, this means a profit of only £5 per box. Worse still, if the total cost of making the pack in the first place was £80, the business will now make a loss if it sells them abroad.

The business is now faced with the issues of:
- selling fewer pens abroad because the foreign exchange price has risen
- trying to sell more pens in the UK to make up for reduced sales abroad
- trying to offset the rise in the exchange rate by lowering costs and therefore the selling price
- selling at a loss abroad because it is taking a long-term view of its relationship with its Italian customers (but how long can it keep this up for?)

If the rate falls

A fall in the exchange rate means that the foreign currency price falls, although the price in pounds is still £100 per box. The business is now faced with the issues of:

- increasing the profit per box (i.e. deciding whether it could raise the selling price in pounds) — if the rate fell to £1 = €1, the selling price could be raised to £150; this would be equivalent to €150 — the same euro price as before
- leaving the price unchanged at £100 (which is now equivalent to €100) and hoping the Italian importer will buy more because they are now cheaper

A UK business that imports but does not export

If the rate rises

UK firms that do not export products will not be affected by the higher foreign currency price of exports. An example of this would be a hairdresser.

However, even if they do not export, many businesses will import raw materials or components. For example, a hairdresser might import shampoo and conditioner from Spain. If the pound rises, these imported products will become cheaper. What will the owner of the salon do? If her costs have fallen by 5%, she is now faced with the issues of:

- passing this saving on to her customers in the form of a price cut, if she feels that this will generate a lot of extra business
- taking a larger profit margin, if she decides that she has enough customers already and wants to take advantage of the cost reduction

If the rate falls

A fall in the exchange rate means that the cost of the imported shampoo and conditioner rises. The business's owner is now faced with the issues of:

- passing the cost increase on to her customers — will this be possible or will they go elsewhere?
- absorbing the increase in costs, accepting lower profits — this may be likely if the situation is not expected to last very long

In both of these instances, if the shampoo and conditioner costs were only a small percentage of total costs of the business, the impact of the rate change would not be very significant. If they were a large part of total costs, the impact would be greater.

A UK business that both imports and exports

Consider a business that imports various components in order to make tractors. It assembles them into finished tractors, which it then exports. If the exchange rate changes, whether it is 'good' or not depends on the relative magnitude of the two effects.

If the rate rises

Imported components are now cheaper, but this good news may be offset by bad news in the form of the

higher foreign currency selling price of the product. Fewer finished tractors may be sold abroad.

If the rate falls

Exports are now cheaper and so, theoretically, more tractors should be sold abroad. However, the fall in the rate will mean that the imported parts that the business uses have become more expensive. This could mean a rise in the final selling price, and this bad news may offset the good news.

Summary

In conclusion, there will not be an exchange rate that is satisfactory for all UK businesses; it depends on their circumstances. The various effects of changes in the exchange rate are summarised in Table 12.1.

Table 12.1 Summary of the effects of a change in the exchange rate

Rise in exchange rate	Fall in exchange rate
The pound will buy more foreign currency than before	The pound will buy less foreign currency than before
UK exports become more expensive	UK exports become cheaper
Imports into the UK become cheaper	Imports into the UK become more expensive

e **EXAMINER'S VOICE**

You will not be asked to perform any calculations involving a change in the exchange rate. However, if you want to gain marks for evaluation, you will need to be able to form a judgement on the extent to which a particular business may be affected.

The extent of the effect(s) depends on:

■ the amount of goods exported. With the tractor business above, if exports were only 5% of the business's total sales, it might not be too concerned about a rise in the rate. However, if 50% of its sales were abroad, this would be much more significant.

■ the value of the components imported. If these are a small proportion of its total costs, it will not be badly affected by a fall in the rate.

■ whether any cost increases caused by a fall in the rate can be easily 'passed on' to customers

■ whether the rate change is large or small

■ whether any rate change is expected to be temporary or permanent

Can a business avoid the effects of a change in the exchange rate?

There is a way for a business to shield itself from exchange rate fluctuations. Just as a business can opt for a fixed rate loan from a bank, it is possible to sign a contract to buy foreign currency in advance of when it is actually required. The rate will be fixed at the agreed figure. The business will then be certain of what it has to pay or what it will receive. However, the bank will charge a fee for this *future trading*, and this will be a further cost to a

business. Managers must assess the risk of any rate changes and their impact, and in the light of this decide whether it is worth signing up to the fixed rate.

Further sources

www.thebankofengland.co.uk — what the bank does and how exchange rate policy operates

www.x-rates.com — one of many websites that offer foreign exchange services; it is useful for explaining why currency values change, and offers a conversion table and the ability to plot rate changes over time in virtually any currency

YOUR TURN

Questions   Time allowed: 35 minutes

1 Outline **one** difference between the rate of interest and the rate of exchange.   *(4 marks)*

2 State what is meant by the term 'hot money'.   *(2 marks)*

3 Analyse the factors that affect the rate of exchange.   *(9 marks)*

4 Two businesses exist side by side on an industrial estate. One is a bakery specialising in quality bread rolls and loaves that it sells mainly to local restaurants. It imports all its flour from France. The other is a manufacturer of hi-tech vehicle tracking equipment for road haulage firms. It exports 40% of its output to the USA. Evaluate the extent to which these businesses would be affected by a rise in the exchange rate.   *(14 marks)*

(29 marks)

CHAPTER 13

The European Union

The European Union (EU) is a group of 25 countries that aim collectively to improve the standard of living of their citizens. This is achieved by:

- creating a large market where businesses can compete, prosper and, in doing so, benefit their stakeholders
- generating economic and political stability
- achieving balanced economic growth across all of Europe
- protecting all EU citizens' rights via a common framework of law

Membership of the EU has a significant effect on UK businesses.

Free trade and the single market

A thriving business community improves standards of living and promotes growth. One of the major goals of the EU is to create a large market where member states can trade freely. That is what 'single market' means: countries can trade freely with a common (i.e. single) set of regulations and rules on the movement of goods, people and finance, rather than having different regulations for each country.

KEY TERMS

free trade: trade without tariffs or quotas being imposed when products are traded

single market: a market in which there is a single (i.e. common) set of laws and regulations relating to the movement of products, people and money; all businesses in the single market have to abide by these

Figure 13.1
Member countries of the European Union

Module 2871

This single market can help to make trade easier, and so businesses can sell more. This creates more wealth and jobs. The problem is that trade is not always free.

Trade barriers

Countries sometimes import more than they export (see Chapter 10). Many people think that the solution to this is straightforward: they say that a country in this position should restrict the number of imports allowed in. This is known as imposing a *quota*. Another way to solve the problem would be to put a tax on goods entering the country from abroad. This would make imports more expensive and home-produced goods relatively cheap. This tax is known as a *tariff*.

The problem with these actions is that other countries will retaliate. This can result in a quota and tariff trade war that is damaging to businesses in all the countries concerned. Quotas and tariffs are *trade barriers* and using them could mean that businesses in all countries that trade abroad end up selling less.

The removal of trade barriers

One aim of the single market is to remove these trade barriers between member states. However, goods entering the EU from outside (e.g. from the USA or Japan) face a barrier called the *common external tariff* (CET), but it is thought that the negative effects of any retaliation are outweighed by the benefits for members of trading within the single market. Furthermore, many businesses outside the EU are encouraged to build their own factories in EU countries in order to avoid the CET. This *inward investment* creates employment in the EU.

Another example of the removal of trade barriers is the *harmonisation* (i.e. adopting a similar set) of specifications, safety standards and testing requirements for products. Before the single market came into being (on 1 January 1993), these were different in each EU country. This meant that a UK business that sold electrical components and was thinking of starting to export them faced considerable duplication of work. Moreover, different standards in different counties meant that it was expensive — perhaps impossible — for some businesses to comply with all of them, and in some cases they did not even bother to try to trade. Now, a single set of rules makes trade easier and has opened up a larger market.

Labour market barriers are also being removed through, for example, the harmonisation of qualifications needed to do a certain job. Previously, a professional person might have needed a qualification gained in a specific country to be allowed to work there. Now, individuals with the appropriate qualification (e.g. doctors, teachers and social

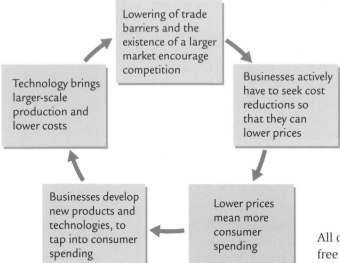

Figure 13.2 Benefits of free trade within the EU

workers) have the right to work in any EU country, not just the one in which they were trained. In this way, people can improve their own lives and the lives of others in the country to which they move.

Finally, restrictions on moving money around within the EU have been abolished. This is helping to encourage investment in profitable opportunities, and promoting competition in the financial world. It should give both borrowers and savers a better deal.

All of these measures encourage free trade, and free trade brings competition. Competition is good because it brings down prices, drives up quality and improves customer service. Any business that does not strive to improve in these areas will find its customers taken by those who do.

The single market is intended to create the sort of virtuous circle shown in Figure 13.2. The hope is that the circle will continually repeat itself, with competition in the single market ensuring that the best businesses and their stakeholders prosper.

Critics point out that this is all very well, but there is a huge burden of EU laws and regulations that distract businesses by taking up a huge amount of management time to ensure compliance.

What are the implications of trading in the EU for a UK business?

A business does not just start selling in Europe. There is an almost endless list of implications. Some of the most important are as follows:

- Someone in a senior position in the business must be put in charge of analysing the strengths, weaknesses, opportunities and threats in the proposed EU markets. They need to conduct and update market research, which takes up a lot of time and other resources.
- Employees in the business have to be fluent in different languages and have an understanding of the culture of other countries. This requirement applies not just to senior executives but also to staff at all levels.
- It is not only competition for customers that has to be considered. With the free movement of workers, businesses offering the best employment package attract the best staff. This is particularly true

for young graduates, who are very mobile. Recruitment policies have to be reviewed.

■ Businesses have to comply with the common requirements on specifications, standards and labelling if they want to trade. This can be costly.

■ Marketing policies need to be adapted, and links established with a reliable distributor, bank and, probably, lawyer abroad.

■ Competition is not all one way. EU firms can take UK businesses' customers away. UK firms must fight to be efficient, concentrating on their strengths and maximising opportunities arising from their competitors' weaknesses.

■ A business operating in other countries can gain *economies of scale* (see Chapter 45). These are the advantages in terms of lower unit costs that come from large-scale production. Lower costs per item mean a larger profit margin.

■ Selling in other EU countries can increase a UK business's stability. It no longer has all its eggs in one basket.

■ Customers in Europe may insist on paying UK businesses in euros, since that is the currency they use with all other European firms. If this is the case, the UK business has to bear the cost of exchanging the money into pounds.

The euro

The **euro** came into existence because it made no sense to have a single market with over ten different currencies operating in it. So, in 1999, most of the member countries gave up their individual currencies and adopted the euro as a common currency. The UK did not join the euro, but it is clearly still an important economic issue both for the UK as a whole and for its businesses.

The single currency began on 1 January 1999

Advantages to UK businesses of joining the euro
Adoption of the euro would offer UK firms a number of advantages.

It would encourage trade
UK businesses would no longer have to pay commission for buying or selling euros. Anyone who has been on holiday abroad recently will have had to pay commission to buy currency and travellers' cheques. Although this will probably have amounted to only a few pounds, they might still have felt quite annoyed. For a UK business buying from, and selling to, EU countries, the commission may be quite considerable. This extra cost might discourage some businesses from exporting, and so reduce trade.

Prices would be more transparent
Different currencies make it difficult for firms to compare prices. The euro enables businesses to compare prices of raw materials and components from other EU countries quickly. Finding the best deal is a lot easier.

KEY TERM

euro: the single currency that came into being in most EU countries on 1 January 1999

KEY TERMS

eurozone: the collective name for countries that have adopted the euro as their single currency

European Central Bank (ECB): the central bank that sets interest rates for the whole of the eurozone

There would be less uncertainty over costs and profits

Changing exchange rates cause uncertainty. Before the euro, it was possible for member countries' exchange rates with each other to fall, making imported raw materials more expensive. This caused lower profit margins for firms having to buy them. Alternatively, the rate could increase, making the price of exports rise, which deterred some foreign customers from buying. If the UK adopted the euro, this would not happen, which should help UK businesses feel more confident of success when trading with other EU countries.

Disadvantages to UK businesses of joining the euro

Membership of the euro presents some problems too.

Loss of control over monetary policy

Decisions on interest rates are made by the **European Central Bank (ECB)**. This could cause problems if not all economies in the EU are at the same stage of the economic cycle. Suppose that the UK joined the euro at a time when the UK economy was in a mild recession, while the rest of the EU was booming. The correct policy for the ECB to adopt would be to increase the rate of interest. This, however, would mean that economic activity in the UK would slow down even more — and it might even provoke a slump. This situation would clearly not be beneficial to UK businesses. Joining the euro could mean UK businesses suffering for the good of the others.

The rate of interest set by the ECB may not suit all members of the eurozone

'Outer' countries may get left behind

Economic activity in a country is often concentrated around its capital and a few of its other important cities. Sometimes the regions 'get left behind' — that is why governments have a regional policy (see Chapters 4 and 11). Exactly the same argument applies to the EU as a whole. Some people think that economic power, prosperity and decision making will become centred on the leading member countries — especially France and Germany. Businesses in other countries could suffer unless they received considerable financial assistance. Where, it is often asked, will the funds for this assistance come from? One source could be increased taxation on UK businesses. This would be an unwelcome burden.

At what exchange rate should the pound join the euro?

This is potentially the most significant problem. If the UK joins the single currency, on an agreed day, all pounds will be converted to euros. Suppose that, for a long time, the rate of exchange has been €1.5 to the pound. Now, as the day for joining approaches, the pound rises so that it is worth €3. Is this the correct rate?

At first sight, it would be a good idea to have as many euros to the pound as possible on the day of joining. If there were €3 to the pound, then a pound would have a lot of purchasing power in the rest of the EU; imports would be very cheap. This would be good for UK consumers, but bad for UK businesses because they might not be able to compete with the flood of cheap imports. However, the reverse of this would mean that businesses in other EU countries would have to supply €3 instead of €1.5 for every product that previously cost a pound. This would make UK products very expensive — and so all exporting firms would suffer. This could lead to unemployment.

Alternatively, if the pound fell in value to €1 just before the date for joining, this would make exports cheaper but would make imports from the rest of the EU, including raw materials, a lot more expensive, since £1 would only buy €1. This could also lead to inflation and unemployment.

Joining the euro would be a one-off: it would not be a reversible decision. It is therefore extremely important that the correct rate is agreed before the UK joins. It is essential that the pound is not locked in to a rate that is permanently damaging to businesses. However, there is little agreement on what the 'correct' rate actually is.

 EXAMINER'S VOICE

There is no clear answer to the question of whether joining the euro is appropriate for UK businesses or not. It depends on an individual business's circumstances.

Further sources

www.cbi.nl — website of the 'employers' organisation', the Confederation of British Industry (CBI); it has a useful 'export readiness checker', featuring an excellent list of issues for a UK business considering exporting for the first time

www.ecb.int — for the European Central Bank and the euro; it contains useful EU economic statistics

www.eurofound.eu.int — trends in EU consumer spending and living standards

YOUR TURN

Case study

Time allowed: 25 minutes

Tony's Plastics

Tony Walker is the majority shareholder and chairman of a business producing goods made out of recycled plastic. The business was established 6 years ago and has proved very successful.

The products that Tony's factory makes are not of high quality but are low cost and easy to produce. They are also cheap for consumers to buy, but despite this, there is quite a large profit margin on them.

The main items that the business sells are plastic cutlery, coat hangers and clothes pegs. The fact that the colours of these products can vary is not a disadvantage to Tony and can actually be turned into an advantage when selling products such as 'children's party packs' of cutlery and cups.

Two years ago, Tony led the business through a successful diversification into making plastic carrier bags for shops. It is quite straightforward to change

the logo on these and this has proved to be a growing market. Tony's business is reliable and competitive with a very good reputation. He now thinks that with his business expertise and experience he should start to export some of these products to countries in the eurozone. He has called a board meeting today because there are a number of issues that he wants to discuss and clarify.

Answer all questions.

1   State **two** aims of the EU.   *(2 marks)*

2   Outline, using examples, what is meant by the term 'trade barriers'.   *(4 marks)*

3   Discuss the implications of Tony's decision to start exporting to countries in the EU.   *(14 marks)*

(20 marks)

CHAPTER 14

Technology

KEY TERM

technology: application of practical or mechanical sciences to industry or commerce, as a means of improving efficiency

This chapter considers the importance of **technology** to businesses. The pace of technological change is such that no business can afford to ignore it. A failure to keep up with technological developments may mean a loss of competitiveness.

Technology includes a wide range of innovations that enable a business to produce goods of a higher quality and in a more efficient manner. If a business can improve the efficiency of its production process, it may be able to reduce its unit costs and thereby become more competitive. This resulting efficiency provides the business with the opportunity either to increase profits or to pass on any savings in the cost of production to the consumer.

Many electrical and electronic consumer goods have fallen in price, partly as a result of technology. More of these goods are now on the market and in our homes. Technological progress has raised the standard of living for all of us. No home of 20 years ago would have had products such as a PC, digital camera, mobile phone, plasma TV, DVD or MP3 player, but many homes now have some or all of these products.

Technological progress in the three sectors of production

We will now consider how technology has advanced in the three sectors of production we introduced in Chapter 5.

Primary sector
In the primary sector, extractive technology has transformed the way in which raw materials are collected, from the now old technology of a combine harvester to the latest technology used to find and extract oil.

Secondary sector
Use of computer-aided design (CAD) and manufacture (CAM) is well established and helps to reduce the lead time for the manufacturing of many products. The use of virtual sites within the design process enables designers to view their creations prior to producing prototypes, and in some cases such prototypes are no longer needed. Technology continues to advance in car production, with a greater emphasis on safety. There are now parking sensors and external sensors that warn a driver when their car drifts out of lane or provide a warning that the car in front is too close. Technology to combat

speed cameras is selling well, as are GPS satellite navigation ('sat-nav') systems that direct the driver to a given location by voice instructions and/or visual display units.

Information technology has increased the level of control over the production process, improved the stocking of raw materials and enabled the implementation of sophisticated quality control methods. The role of technology in enabling a business to reduce its unit costs may also be vital if it is to remain competitive.

Such is the demand for flights that airline manufacturers have responded in differing ways. Boeing has developed a plane with a longer non-stop capability, whereas Airbus has developed the A380, which was unveiled in 2005 and should be in service before the end of the 2006. The A380 will probably be configured to carry about 550 passengers, but will have the capability to carry 850. The technology to enable such a vast plane to take off and fly has meant the design of a new range of Rolls-Royce engines. Even within the plane, technology has been used. Intelligent lighting helps lessen the effects of jet lag by assimilating the right time of day throughout the length of the journey. Such technological developments will, however, bring not only benefits but also additional problems. The existing infrastructure (airport terminals and some runways) may need altering in order to facilitate such a large plane.

Tertiary sector

The retail industry has been transformed by technological change. Electronic point of sale (EPOS) systems have greatly improved the efficiency of distribution and delivery.

The use of virtual sites has transformed the estate agency sector. Potential house buyers can 'visit' houses for sale and view each room, thus saving the need to go there in person. Only a few that catch the buyer's eye on the screen need to be visited. Similarly, designs for a new kitchen or bathroom can now be viewed in virtual reality to enhance the decision-making process. This kind of technology has saved retailers valuable time and therefore costs.

> **KEY TERM**
>
> **hot-desking:** the sharing of an office space by several employees who each use it at a different time or on a different day

The ability to transfer data electronically has allowed industry and those employed in it to be more mobile. The need to sit in the office has been reduced, which has led to enormous savings and the development of **hot-desking**. Training can now take place internally via e-learning, which negates the need for expensive travel and off-the-job training. This, in turn, provides the business with further cost savings.

Opportunities and threats from new technology

New technology presents businesses with a variety of possible benefits, and also confronts them with several potential problems.

Opportunities

The opportunities provided by technological developments are as follows:

- In a competitive market, ensuring that costs are kept to a minimum is very important. Using technology such as computers enables the production process to be more streamlined, therefore reducing costs. A reduction in costs may allow a business either to spend more on marketing and offering a higher specification, or to reduce the price of the product and improve its competitiveness.

- Technology allows for a shorter lead time — that is, it reduces the time taken from the conception of a new product to the completion of its production. Having a shorter lead time enables a business to be more competitive. It allows the business to be first onto the market and therefore to be seen as an innovator. The business will also be able to satisfy demand quicker and therefore have a competitive edge.

- Technology can improve the quality of the product. For example, computers and robots can be used to ensure that a consistently high standard of work is achieved, therefore reducing the number of rejects or returns to the business.

EXAMINER'S VOICE

Technology does not always mean that employees will be made redundant. Employment opportunities often arise as a result of technological progress. Losses in one sector of the economy may also be replaced by more jobs in another sector. For example, the banking sector now has fewer people employed at branches around the country, but due to advances in technology, many more are now employed in call centres in order to meet the demand for tele-banking. Moreover, if a business fails to keep up with technology, this may lead to a loss of competitiveness and result in job losses as a consequence of falling demand for its products.

Threats

Potential problems of new technology are as follows:

- Technological progress relies heavily on research, which can be very expensive, and there is no guarantee of success. The dilemma for any business is whether to wait and see what its competitors do and then try to imitate, or to initiate progress by attempting to be a market leader. Each may bring its own problems. Being seen as an innovator may, in the short term, be good for the business as a competitive advantage may be gained. However, those that copy a new development will not have incurred the same research and development costs and will therefore be able to produce a similar product much more cheaply. On the other hand, if a business does not undertake technological innovation, it may be left behind.

- New technology might lead to a loss of employment. If there is a possibility of job losses as a result of technological changes, the employees, or their union representatives, might resist them. A redundancy package might need to be negotiated, which will be an additional cost to the employer. The morale of the employees might also suffer as a result of the fear of redundancies and changing work practices.

- New technology may require employees to retrain, which will place additional costs on the business. In some cases, the new technology may involve fewer skills and therefore employees might suffer in terms of motivation, as they become machine minders.

- A major difficulty for many businesses is whether or not to invest in the latest technology. The pace of change is now very rapid, with improved versions and new developments occurring all the time. The problem facing a business is not only 'when to buy' but also 'which to buy'. Waiting for the next improved version may lead to a loss of competitiveness. However, buying too early may mean that competitors buy a much improved version of the required equipment at a later date.

e EXAMINER'S VOICE

It is important to consider both the positive effects of new technology and the possible short-term negative effects that may arise. In handling case studies, you need to show how technology affects the business and how that business may react to changing technology.

Technology will be welcomed by some and feared by others. The stakeholders of a business undertaking technological change will have differing views. Depending upon the exact wording of the exam question, referring to how each stakeholder is affected, and to what extent, will help you gain the higher-order marks.

YOUR TURN

Questions   Time allowed: 40 minutes

1 State **three** ways in which technology can help a business.   *(3 marks)*

2 Explain how technology may reduce costs.   *(6 marks)*

3 Explain **one** of the disadvantages of introducing new technology into a business.   *(4 marks)*

4 Discuss the consequences of new technology for either a supermarket or a car assembly line.   *(9 lines)*

5 Evaluate the likely implications of technological change for the stakeholders of a business.   *(14 lines)*

                                                                          (36 marks)

Case study

Time allowed: 45 minutes

iPods

iPods are the latest fashion accessory in the modern music world. CDs, audio cassettes and vinyl may be destined for the recycling bin!

Digital cameras have been around for a few years now; however, their usage has expanded into new fields. Putting music and photographs together, Apple Computers Inc. has launched the special thicker and more expensive version of the iPod music player. This iPod not only plays music, but stores and displays digital photos as well.

'We're not standing still,' states Steve Jobs, chief executive of Apple. 'But such innovation brings its own problems. The competition is intense — Dell, Sony, Virgin Electronics and Samsung, to name but a few.'

Consequently, Apple must decide whether to wait and see how the competitors respond or license its technology while it is still ahead. History is not on the side of innovators such as Apple. Many a pioneer of technology has seen its early domination wither rapidly. Nintendo in games consoles and Apple in PCs are classic examples. Rivals are quick to copy and usually at a lower price. The rivals are able to produce at a lower price because they have not had to spend the same amount of money on research. Nevertheless, iPod is holding its own for the moment.

Source: adapted from articles by P. Burrows and J. Greene, *Business Week*, 8 November 2004

Answer all questions.

1 Discuss how technology may affect Apple's stakeholders. *(14 marks)*

2 Explain the problems of being an innovative business such as Apple. *(6 marks)*

3 Outline the likely human resources management implications of introducing new technology in a business such as Apple. *(4 marks)*

4 Evaluate how factors other than technology may affect the operation of Apple. *(14 marks)*

(38 marks)

CHAPTER 15

Social demographics

KEY TERMS

demographics: the structure of the population in terms of number, sex, age and ethnic origin

birth rate: the number of births per thousand of population

death rate: the number of deaths per thousand of population

Demographics is the study of population structure. This structure includes age, gender and ethnic origin. Changes in the structure of the population are taking place all the time. Changes in the birth and death rates in the UK, along with migration and emigration, alter both the numbers and the age range of the population.

Business is concerned with any change in the population, whether it is the number of people or the age range, as these will affect demand for goods. If there is a falling **birth rate**, demand for baby products will decrease. Similarly, if there is a fall in the **death rate**, there will be more demand for retirement and nursing homes. Businesses monitor changes in the population to enable them to predict demand over time.

Size and structure of the UK population

The size of the UK population is rising, and the percentage of older people in the population is rising dramatically, as shown in Figure 15.1. This is due to both a fall in the death rate and a fall in the birth rate. Medical science has contributed much to the increased life expectancy of the population. As life expectancy continues to rise (see Figure 15.2), this means not only that there are more people in the UK, but also that they are living longer and will therefore demand more goods and services.

Figure 15.1 UK population by age and sex, 2001 and 2032 (projected)

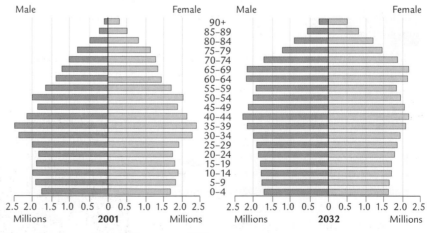

Source: Government Actuary's Department, 2002

Figure 15.1 shows that the number of people over 50 is due to increase significantly. In addition, the number of younger people, especially in the

30–39 age group is falling. Although the UK's population is ageing less rapidly than those of many other EU member states, it is still doing so at a concerning rate.

Implications of social demographics for business

Changing demographics affect businesses in two principal ways: through changing demand and changing employment patterns.

Changing demand

Businesses need to satisfy the demands of consumers, whoever they are. As the average age of the population rises (see Figure 15.2),

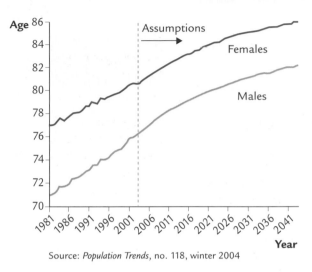

Source: *Population Trends*, no. 118, winter 2004

Figure 15.2 *Life expectancy, 1981–2043*

together with the number of people of retirement age, businesses need to provide the goods and services for this ageing population. More homes for the elderly will be needed. There has already been a massive growth in the number of nursing homes built by the private sector, to cash in on this developing market. The so-called 'grey needs' have led to a surge of products and services just for retired people.

As the proportion of the population over 65 increases, the burden on the working population to support them increases as well. This may lead to increases in taxation in order to provide essential services for the elderly. As a result of this, the working population may have less disposable income, which will affect their ability to demand goods and services. The pension problem is highly significant in terms of the burden on the workforce. Ensuring there is sufficient money available to pay for the retired has become headline news.

David Smith, Economics Editor of the *Sunday Times*, quoted Professor Nick Bosanquet, who stated: 'The next half century is likely to see an unprecedented transfer of wealth from the younger to the older generation.' The professor spoke of the results of a study by Reform, which suggested there would be an 'Ipod' generation: 'insecure, pressured, over-taxed and debt-ridden'. The report suggested that the ageing population would mean younger people having to support an increasing number of pensioners, and claimed that any additional spending on the health service would benefit older people disproportionately (*Sunday Times*, 21 July 2005).

It may be coincidental, but the initial surge in the demand for cruises was thought to be caused by the ageing population wanting a specific type of holiday. Similarly, the growth in cafés and restaurants at garden centres has been attributed to the ageing population wanting to spend more time in such places.

Another demographic change that has taken place since the Second World War concerns the ethnic balance in the UK. With an increase in the number of immigrants during this period, the demand for goods and services has changed to reflect the diversity of cultural and ethnic needs. The multiplicity of food now available mirrors the widening dietary requirements of the cultural mix throughout the country.

Changing employment patterns

Finding suitable employees among a workforce with a smaller proportion of younger people is problematic for many employers. Good workers in some areas are already hard to find when the economy is buoyant. This has led several employers to rethink their strategies with regard to taking on new staff.

B&Q was one of the first retail outlets to advertise openly for older employees

B&Q was one of the first retail outlets to advertise openly for older employees. It realised that as the number of people of retirement age was growing and, at the same time, there was a willingness and ability among some older people to work beyond the official retirement age, there was an untapped source of reliable labour waiting to be used. Many of these people had all the required skills and experience, and would therefore need less training, thereby reducing the costs of employing them.

Further sources
www.statistics.gov.uk
Population Trends (HMSO, 2004)
Social Trends (HMSO, 2005)

YOUR TURN

Questions

Time allowed: 25 minutes

 EXAMINER'S VOICE

> Whenever you are studying figures, ensure you are clear as to the values, such as millions, or, in this case, thousands. Note also the age spans in tables; they will not always be the same and therefore you will need to take care when analysing such data. You should also check how accurate the data are.

1 Table 15.1 gives UK population figures for 2003. Use the table to construct a demographic chart. *(4 marks)*

2 Explain the likely implications of these figures for a business of your choice. *(5 marks)*

3 Analyse how a rise in the number of people from the rest of the European Union settling in the UK might affect the demand for particular products. *(9 marks)*

(18 marks)

Table 15.1 UK population by age group, 2003 (000s)

Age group	Population
All ages	49,856
Under 1	575
1–4	2,273
5–14	6,300
15–24	6,304
25–34	6,843
35–44	7,643
45–59	9,533
60–64	2,438
65–74	4,159
75–84	2,852
85–89	596
90+	340
Under 16	9,804

Source: *Population Trends*, no. 118, winter 2004, Table 1.4

Case study

Time allowed: 30 minutes

Saga this and Saga that!

According to the statistics issued by National Statistics in 2002, there are nearly 20 million people (19.8) aged 50 and over within the UK. This represents a 24% increase since 1961 when there were 16 million in this category. The projections for 2031 are expected to show a further increase of 37%, when there will be approximately 27 million aged 50 and over. The causes of this population ageing are primarily a sustained low birth rate and a further decline in the death rate. The latter is probably the most important factor, especially as technology in medicine continues to save lives and prolong the life expectancy of the UK population.

As a consequence, the structure of the UK's population has led to many forecasters predicting a huge shift in the demand for thousands of products and services, from holidays to household goods. Saga, founded in the 1950s by Sid De Haan, was

originally seen as a holiday agent, but today the range of its services has escalated significantly. In 2000, Saga even launched its own local radio station.

The number of Saga members has also risen significantly, reflecting the increase in potential members. The expenditure patterns of Saga members may surprise many.

The nation's over-50s currently have 30% more disposable income than those under 50 and the research shows they are not afraid to spend it. Nearly a third (31%) of the over-50s questioned, if given the opportunity, would prefer to spend £20,000 on holidays and travelling, compared with only 8% who stated that they would leave the money for inheritance, suggesting that this generation are 'living it up' and leaving the kids to earn for themselves.

Given the opportunity, over a third of the over-50s surveyed would consider spending their high level of disposable income on purchasing goods over the internet (34%), downloading music (19%) or buying a fast car or motorbike (17%). Nearly 40% of over-50s enjoy texting friends, a quarter currently enjoy the buzz of playing computer games and nearly a third would like to improve their fitness levels by joining a gym.

Source: 'Empty nesters fly the nest in pursuit of adventure', Saga press release, 21 July 2005, **www.saga.co.uk**.

Answer all questions.

1 State **two** reasons for the decline in the death rate in the UK. *(2 marks)*

2 Explain how the fall in the birth rate may affect those in employment. *(4 marks)*

3 Evaluate the likely effects on the demand for goods and services resulting from the ageing population. *(14 marks)*

(20 marks)

CHAPTER 16

Businesses and the law

The law is a very important aspect of the business environment. It can be quite difficult for a business — particularly a small one — to keep up with all the legal changes that take place. Nevertheless, it has to be done; in the event of a business doing something illegal, it is no defence for a director or manager to say that they were not aware of the law. In addition, where necessary, employees have to be informed of, and trained in changes in, the laws affecting their business.

Types of law

There are two different types of law in the UK.

Civil law

Civil law is concerned with the rules that govern the relations between businesses and/or people, such as employment rights and consumer rights. A breach of civil law does not make a business or person a criminal. If the civil court's decision goes against a business or person, they are not fined or imprisoned but have to pay damages. Damages are a payment to compensate the injured party (business or person) for any loss or injury, and to restore them to the position that they would have been in had the law not been broken.

Criminal law

Criminal law defines the actions that the state has decided are wrong and the punishment that will result from these actions. In a criminal court, if a business or person is found guilty, the result can be a fine or imprisonment. Because of this, the 'burden' (standard) of proof is higher in a criminal court. The court has to be convinced 'beyond reasonable doubt' (i.e. certain) that the defendant is guilty, whereas in a civil court the case is decided on 'the balance of probabilities' — that is, 'it is more likely than not' that one party is correct.

Why have laws?

The law aims to make individuals and businesses behave in a responsible way. Laws define the kind of behaviour that is unacceptable. Without laws a business could:

- dismiss employees at a moment's notice for any reason, with no explanation
- provide dangerous and unhealthy working conditions that might lead to the injury or death of employees
- change the amount of money it had agreed to pay to a supplier for a particular delivery
- pollute and destroy the environment

KEY TERMS

civil law: legislation governing the relations between businesses and/or people (e.g. employment and consumer rights)

criminal law: legislation defining the actions that the state has decided are wrong (e.g. theft and deliberately misleading others) and the punishment that will result from these actions

Similarly, employees could:

■ turn up for work whenever they liked, completely disregarding the hours they had agreed to work
■ remove products from their place of work and use facilities such as telephones or photocopiers for their own purposes
■ ignore instructions about work from their managers

A civilised society simply could not operate in this manner; there needs to be a framework for the protection of rights. Laws mean that there are legal minimum standards that must be adhered to by all businesses. If laws are to be effective, they have to be enforced. That is why the state provides the judicial system.

For the AS course, it is important to know about legislation that falls into three areas:

■ laws governing the relationship between one business and another
■ laws governing the ways a business treats its employees
■ laws governing the way a business treats its consumers

KEY TERM

contract: legally binding agreement between two or more parties

 **EXAMINER'S VOICE**

You do not need to know about the laws that affect businesses in great depth on this module, but you do need to be able to identify the main pieces of legislation that affect a business. You also need to be aware of the implications of complying (and not complying) with the law.

INGRAM

It is against the law for one party to change the terms of the contract without the other's agreement

Laws governing the relationship between businesses

Contract law

A **contract** is a legally binding agreement between two or more parties. Most business relationships are of a contractual nature, so contract law sets out the basic framework of rights and obligations. A contract may be an offer to supply something at a particular time and/or of a particular quality.

The breach (breaking) of a contract is a breach of the civil law and the aggrieved party (i.e. the person or business who has been wronged) can recover damages. Suppose a business selling frozen desserts has signed a contract to deliver £10,000 worth of ice cream to a supermarket in 1 month's time. Its ability to do this depends on the ingredients being delivered 1 week before by its own supplier. Suppose that the supplier fails to deliver the ingredients. This means that the dessert business is unable to make the product and unable to deliver to the supermarket. Naturally, the supermarket does not pay because the goods never arrived. The dessert business would be able to sue its supplier for damages — that is, for the revenue lost as a result.

Competition law

Consumers benefit in terms of price and quality when businesses compete against each other for customers. In the UK the *Competition Act* (*2000*) made it illegal for businesses to restrict competition. This could occur in various ways:

- a relationship between businesses aiming to restrict supply
- businesses conspiring together to keep up prices (known as a *cartel*)
- a business charging an artificially low price in order to destroy a competitor — or to deter any new entrants into the market
- a business forcing its distributors to stock all its products under the threat that otherwise they will not get supplied at all

The two organisations that try to ensure UK businesses comply with the Act are the Office of Fair Trading (OFT) and the Competition Commission. They also consider whether a merger between two businesses is likely to result in any sort of anti-competitive behaviour. The OFT has a special 'cartel-busting squad', with wide-ranging powers of entry into business premises to look for evidence. It is now a criminal offence to obstruct their investigation and actions such as shredding important documents can result in a prison sentence. For breaches of the Act a business can be fined up to 10% of its turnover.

Data protection

A business, even a small one, needs to keep all sorts of records on employees and customers. However, under the *Data Protection Act (1984)*, a business is not allowed to disclose whatever information it likes, whenever it likes, to other businesses, organisations or individuals — even though it might be profitable to do so. The Act is designed to prevent harm resulting from the misuse of any data that a business holds. Information about a customer's credit record or an employee's sickness or disciplinary record could easily be misused, particularly if the information has become outdated. The Act tries to balance the need for a business to process essential information with the right to privacy.

There is a legal obligation on a business to protect the security of its data

In the past, a lot of the data that a business held were kept in filing cabinets and were accessible only to senior members of staff. With computers, data can be collected, viewed, altered and passed on very easily (often without leaving a clearly identifiable trace), so it is important that safeguards are in place. This has cost implications.

All users of personal data must register with the Data Protection Registrar. This entry must detail the nature of the data and the purposes for which they are held, as well listing the parties to whom the data may be made available.

It is a criminal offence to hold unregistered data and breaches of the following principles can also lead to prosecution:

- Data shall only be kept for the specified purposes.
- Individuals are entitled to reasonable access to the data.

The Act was updated in 1988 to include paper-based data-recording systems.

Laws governing the treatment of employees

Contracts of employment

A contract of employment is an agreement between a business and an employee under which each of them has certain obligations. As soon as someone starts work, a contract comes into existence. It does not need to be in writing; it could be oral or 'implied'. The implied terms of a contract are those that are so obvious they do not need to be explicitly agreed, such as duties on employers to pay wages and to take reasonable care of employees. In return, employees must 'render service' (work properly) and obey lawful and reasonable instructions.

If a business employs someone for a month or more, then within 2 months of starting work the employee must be given a 'written statement of employment particulars'. This is a document setting out the main aspects of a person's employment. The sort of information in a statement would be: the hours of work (including overtime or shift work), pay, sickness entitlement, pension scheme details and the period of notice required. It is not in itself a contract, although it covers most of the particulars in the contract.

The existence of a contract and a written statement of employment particulars means that both the business and the employee are clear about their rights and responsibilities.

Prevention of discrimination

Discrimination occurs when an employer treats one person less favourably than another without any justification. This discrimination can occur in various ways: when employing someone, when promoting someone, or when allowing them access to training courses. Several acts have been passed to tackle discrimination.

Disability Discrimination Act (1995)

This Act came into force to try to end the discrimination that many disabled people had to face as employees at work, and also as consumers when accessing the services of a business. The disabilities may be mental, physical or sensory — that is, they include people who are partially sighted or deaf. The Act makes it illegal for any business with 15 or more employees to treat its disabled employees, or potential employees, any differently from others.

In terms of access to facilities and services, a business has to make 'reasonable adjustments' to the way products and services are delivered so

that disabled people can use them. The adjustments can be physical, such as making changes to buildings by adding ramps and handrails, or they can be procedural — for example, a retailer having a member of staff who, as part of his/her duties, is always on hand to help a disabled person.

The implications of this for a business are as follows:
- There needs to be a clear policy on how services are to be provided to disabled people.
- This policy needs to be communicated clearly to all staff.
- The policy needs to be reviewed and monitored. The Act makes it clear that tackling disability discrimination is not a 'one-off', but a continuing duty for a business.
- Staff should be trained in a disabled person's rights and the way that disabled people are to be treated.

e EXAMINER'S VOICE

If you can detail these sorts of implications when answering a question, you will be producing an analytical answer that will put you well on the way to a good grade.

Sex Discrimination Act (1975) and Race Relations Act (1976)

These laws are similar to the Disability Discrimination Act. A business is breaking the law if it refuses to employ or promote a person on the grounds of race or sex. Similarly, it is illegal to draw up an advertisement for a job that specifies that the business will only employ a person from a particular racial group, or of a particuar gender. There are limited exceptions to this — for example, if a swimming pool has separate changing rooms for men and women, it would be legal to advertise for, say, a female changing room attendant.

Equal Pay Act (1970)

This Act aims to prevent discrimination in terms of pay and other benefits. It states that if the work being done by someone 'is the same or broadly similar' to work being done by another person, their rate of pay and other terms of employment should be the same.

The minimum wage

This measure, which came into effect in 1999, lays down the minimum level of pay to which all employees in the UK (except those under 18) are entitled. It does not matter if the employee is part time or full time. If employees are paid on a piece rate (a certain amount for each item produced), the business has to ensure that enough items can be made for the employee to earn at least the minimum wage.

Health and safety

The *Health and Safety at Work Act (1974)* was an important piece of legislation when it was introduced and it has been extended since its introduction to take account of new issues and hazards. These include repetitive strain injury and possible damage to the eyes from working on visual display units — hazards that people were not fully aware of or which did not exist when the original Act was passed.

Not only do businesses have 'a duty to take reasonable care' of employees, but criminal law lays down minimum safety requirements. There is a positive obligation to create a safe and healthy working environment, and breaches of the law can lead to criminal prosecution as well as civil proceedings for compensation.

The provisions of the Act relate to:
- the place of work
- the system of work
- the working environment
- any machinery used
- the use and storage of substances
- employees

The implications for a business are as follows:
- It must ensure that its buildings are safe. Entry to them and exit from them must also be safe.
- It must coordinate the whole system of work so that it is safe.
- It must ensure that the temperature in the working environment is within certain limits, that the atmosphere is safe to breath, that the floors are safe to walk along and so on.
- It must fit guards onto machinery to prevent accidents. Employees must be provided with the correct safety equipment (and clothing) and trained to use it.
- It must provide training in any hazards associated with the work, such as the lifting of loads and the handling of dangerous substances. A business that failed to provide any training 'because it was common sense for employees not to lift heavy loads' would not have a legal defence if employees injured themselves.
- It must have a written safety policy, making clear who is responsible for safety issues. This policy must be communicated clearly to employees.

The Act also places a duty on employees to comply with the Act. Employees must comply with lawful instructions relating to safety matters. For instance, an employee who was trained and told to use lifting equipment could not sue the business for an injury to his back if he ignored the instructions. Tampering with safety equipment (e.g. letting off a fire extinguisher for malicious purposes or 'in fun') is a serious matter and one for which an employee can be dismissed immediately.

The Act says that a business must comply 'so far as reasonably practicable'. A business may argue that it cannot afford to comply with the Act down to the last detail, on the basis that the expense is not 'reasonably practicable'. If an accident occurred and the business was prosecuted, the court would decide whether it was 'reasonably practicable' or not.

The Health and Safety Executive (HSE) is the organisation responsible for regulating risks to health and safety at work. If a breach of the Act is

serious enough or there is repeated disregard for the law, the HSE can close a business down.

Termination of employment

It is important to be clear about the difference between dismissal and redundancy.

Dismissal

A business must have a valid reason to dismiss someone; an employee cannot get the sack without a valid reason. Fair dismissal would be for:

- misconduct (e.g. theft, being drunk or taking drugs at work, fighting, or a major breach of health and safety law)
- incapacity (e.g. being too ill to work at all or taking time off work when genuinely ill on a regular basis)
- incompetence (e.g. repeated inability to do the work required, or a major incident such as losing the business a valuable customer)

Redundancy

An employee is not made redundant because he or she has done anything wrong. Redundancy arises from a situation where the job that used to be performed no longer exists, so the employee is surplus to requirements. This might arise because a particular job is mechanised or where a section or all of a factory or office is closed down. Employees made redundant are entitled by law to a redundancy payment that varies according to how long they have worked for the firm. It is, of course, open to a business to pay them more than this.

Laws governing consumer protection

Sale of Goods Act (1979)

This was an important Act when it was introduced and still is, although like the Health and Safety Act of 1974 it has since been extended — especially by the *Consumer Protection Act (1987)*.

Under the Sale of Goods Act, all goods must be:

- of 'satisfactory quality' (i.e. the product must not be damaged or defective)
- 'as described' — this applies not only to advertisements but also to any explanations given by a shop assistant
- 'fit for the purpose for which they were intended'

If any of these conditions is not met, a business must provide consumers with a replacement or their money back. A business cannot avoid the law by saying that it has a policy not to accept returned goods. The Act also imposes a duty on a business to ensure that its products are safe to use.

In addition to these civil laws, there are a number of criminal laws.

Trade Descriptions Act (1968)

A consumer cannot be expected to understand everything about a product.

This Act is to prevent consumers from being intentionally misled when they buy. It states that any description of the goods on sale must not be false or misleading. The Act refers to all types of description — sign, advertisement or verbal.

Weights and Measures Act (1985)

It is an offence to give 'short measures' or an incorrect indication of the amount of a product on sale. If a product is labelled as containing 1 litre, that is what it should contain.

Unsolicited Goods Act (1971)

It is illegal to demand payment for services that have not been ordered. If a publishing business delivers a quantity of books that have not been ordered to someone's house, and then demands payment for them, the firm is breaking the law.

The Trading Standards Authority is a public body that investigates breaches of consumer laws. It also assists consumers in taking a business to court if the business refuses to comply with its legal obligations.

EU laws

Some laws affecting UK businesses originate in the European Union (EU). Many of these come from the EU's Social Charter, which is a charter of rights for employees concerning areas such as working conditions, wages and consultation of the workforce. UK businesses have to adhere to these EU laws just as if they had originated from the UK parliament. There are two types of EU law:

- *Regulations* have to be adopted and applied in a certain way.
- *Directives* must also be applied as law, but it is up to the individual member country to decide how to implement them.

Working Time Directive

The Working Time Directive is an example of an EU law. It became part of UK law in 1998. A business must not allow an employee to work more than 48 hours per week on average. The directive is partly aimed at reducing the UK's culture of long working hours. There are also provisions relating to an employee's entitlement to rest breaks and the pattern of shifts that can be worked. Employees can sign away their legal rights to these if they wish, but if a business dismisses a person for refusing to do so, this constitutes unfair dismissal. Some employees (such as the police) are exempt from the directive.

What happens if a business breaks the law?

Alleged breaches of *employment law* are heard in an **Employment Tribunal**. This is a special sort of court that deals with employees' claims of unfair dismissal, discrimination, breach of contract and victimisation by their

KEY TERM

Employment Tribunal: a special sort of court that only deals with employment-related issues (e.g. victimisation by an employer, unfair dismissal and discrimination)

employer. If the tribunal rules in favour of the employee, it will order the business to pay the employee compensation for what has occurred.

For alleged breaches of *criminal law*, the business will be prosecuted in the criminal courts — either a magistrates' court for minor offences or the Crown Court, where the penalties are more severe, for serious offences. If found guilty, a business can be fined and/or those responsible for the breach may be imprisoned. Any alleged breach of the *civil law* will be heard in the County Court, where the business can be sued for damages.

If a business fails, or refuses, to pay damages or compensation, the firm or person that is owed the money can apply to the County Court for payment to be enforced. County Court judgements against a business can generate a lot of bad publicity and the hearing will be expensive. Furthermore, an adverse County Court judgement can affect a business's ability to obtain credit.

Benefits to a business of complying with the law

Compliance with the law offers the following potential benefits to a business:

- It should be able to avoid fines, claims for compensation, and bad publicity, which might deter potential employees and customers.
- Health and safety is an area where there is likely to be close agreement between managers and employees. Therefore, a properly constructed, implemented and monitored safety policy should result in fewer accidents. This could result in better relations between managers and employees in other areas of the business.
- If a business treats any employees badly, it will not get the best out of them. It is to be hoped that where a firm adopts practices to avoid discrimination, this will benefit all employees.
- There are over 8 million people in the UK with disabilities; good treatment will hopefully encourage these customers to return.

Further sources
www.hse.gov.uk — the Health and Safety Executive website, which offers advice on improving workplace health and safety, and outlines the benefits to businesses of a healthy and safe working environment
www.businesslink.gov.uk/regulationupdates — information on new and changing regulations affecting UK businesses
www.disability.gov.uk — information for businesses on how to meet their legal obligations on disabled rights
www.employmenttribunals.gov.uk — the employment tribunal system in the UK
www.opsi.gov.uk/acts.htm — Acts of Parliament at a glance
www.oft.gov.uk and **www.competition-commission.org.uk** — information about consumer protection and the regulation of anti-competitive behaviour

YOUR TURN

Case study

Time allowed: 45 minutes

Discountec

Mrs Richardson bought a new washing machine from her local branch of Discountec plc, a well-known national chain of shops selling electrical consumer goods. The first time she used it there was a strong smell of burning. As soon as she became aware of this, she switched it off, but it then flooded water all over her new carpet, which had cost £2,000. The flooding meant that she had to get a plumber, who charged her £75 for an emergency call-out.

When she went back to the store, she was not in a very good mood. This was worsened by the fact that at the entrance she tripped over some bricks that some workmen had left scattered around, and cut her ankle. It looked to her as if they were building some sort of ramp for the disabled to access the store, but neither any workmen nor any 'work in progress' signs were anywhere to be seen.

When she eventually got to see the manager, he demanded to know who had installed the machine. She replied that it was her son, 'who was not an expert but knew how to connect two taps'. On hearing this, the manager refused to accept any responsibility, saying that her son must have plumbed it in wrongly and broken it. Then he suggested that Mrs Richardson contact the manufacturer and take the matter up with it. She refused to do this, and as their discussion was becoming noisy, he agreed to replace it 'as a goodwill gesture from an ethical company', but said that was all he was prepared to do. Mrs Richardson said that if this was the case then she would take the business to court and sue it under the Sale of Goods Act. The manager replied that 'she could do what she liked' and in an aggressive tone asked if she knew how much it was going to cost her 'when she lost the case'.

Answer all questions.

1 In terms of business studies, state how 'ethics' are different from 'the law'. *(2 marks)*

2 Outline **two** differences between civil law and criminal law. *(4 marks)*

3 Discuss whether Mrs Richardson would be wise to sue Discountec plc under the Sale of Goods Act. *(14 marks)*

4 Evaluate the legal influences, other than the Sale of Goods Act, that are likely to affect the operation of a branch of Discountec plc. *(14 marks)*

(34 marks)

Module 2871

CHAPTER 17

The role of the state

The state or government plays a significant role in the UK. There are few activities that we as individuals undertake that are not affected by the government. Its involvement in the economy is an *external influence* on all businesses. Whether the government is acting as a consumer, supplier or regulator, business will be affected.

What services the government decides to supply, where to buy the goods it requires and which laws are passed are all *political* decisions. All these decisions are based on the beliefs of the politicians who are part of the government. It was a political decision not to help MG Rover early in 2005, just as it was a political decision to send troops to Iraq.

Not everyone will like all the government's decisions. Taxation is not popular with most people, for instance, although it is necessary for financing essential services such as health and education. The level of taxation and how much is spent on various areas of the economy is also a political decision. A business has to respond to such decisions in order to satisfy its stakeholders and meet its objectives.

This chapter addresses the four principal roles of government identified in Figure 17.1: consumer, supplier, economic regulator and legal regulator.

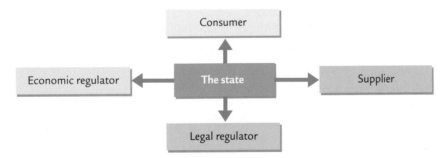

Figure 17.1
The roles of the state

The state as consumer

The government consumes goods in order to provide services for the country. Whenever the government wants to improve the roads, it employs a company to do the work. All government departments consume vast quantities of paper, which is supplied by paper manufacturers. Hospitals require supplies of drugs from pharmaceutical manufacturers.

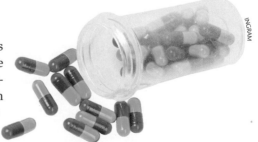

The state as supplier

The government supplies many services for the benefit of the community. These include:

- healthcare
- education
- regional aid
- the armed forces
- roads
- social services (e.g. sickness benefits, Jobseeker's Allowance)

Many of these services are not provided at all by the private sector, or are only provided for a small minority of people. Many of them are essential for the wellbeing of the population, and are referred to as *merit goods* (see Chapter 11). The government provides these services to ensure that all members of the population have at least a minimum standard of living.

The state as economic regulator

The government is responsible for the country's economic wellbeing. It attempts to meet the main objectives of low inflation, high employment, a balanced level of international trade and sufficient economic growth (see Chapter 10). Various economic weapons are used to influence the economy.

The government is responsible for raising revenue (via taxation) to meet the needs of the country and control the level of economic activity (see Chapter 11).

The state as legal regulator

The government introduces laws (legislation) to protect individuals and businesses from being treated improperly. The range of laws and regulatory bodies is extensive, affecting all our lives on a daily basis.

There are laws and regulatory bodies protecting:
- consumers — consumer protection laws
- employees — recruitment and unfair dismissal laws
- businesses — competition law

These were explained in detail in Chapter 16.

The government has set up regulators to control the large corporations that run the trains, provide our water (Ofwat) and supply telephone lines (Oftel).

Other responsibilities

The government is also concerned about its *social responsibilities*. What is beneficial for a business may not be seen as beneficial for society. Smoking is a case in point. British American Tobacco (BAT) manufactures cigarettes and provides employment for many people and dividends to its shareholders. However, the consequences of smoking are well known and put a burden on

EXAMINER'S VOICE

The government is *not* responsible for interest rates in the UK. This is a common mistake made by students. The setting of interest rates is the responsibility of the Bank of England's Monetary Policy Committee.

INGRAM

the health service. Business is also affected because of the number of days lost due to ill health.

Business for Social Responsibility (BSR) helps firms to raise their awareness of the ethical, environmental and social aspects of business. However, the government does not just rely on business taking a responsible attitude. For example, concern has grown over the type of advertising that is aimed at children, especially for food. This has arisen because of the growing number of children who are obese (overweight). The House of Commons Health Committee has suggested that the economic cost of obesity to the country is £6.6–7.0 billion a year. In 2004, Ofcom, the regulator for television and radio, was asked by the Department of Health to tighten the controls on the advertising of food aimed at children. In 2005, a government White Paper, 'Choosing Health', suggested the modification of food advertisements.

HEMERA TECHNOLOGIES

As a member of the EU, the UK is subject to additional regulations. There are regulations affecting the operation of the economy, which includes the amount of tax a country can put on goods bought from abroad (customs or import duties), how many goods can be bought from various countries outside the EU (quotas), and a wide range of laws affecting the design of goods. The European Patent Office protects the designs and trade marks of businesses' products and services.

Further sources

www.timesonline.co. uk/debate — opening hours

www.dti.gov.uk — Department of Trade and Industry

YOUR TURN

Questions
Time allowed: 20 minutes

ℯ EXAMINER'S VOICE

1 State **two** examples of how the government is a consumer. *(2 marks)*

2 State **two** examples of how the government attempts to protect the consumer. *(2 marks)*

3 Explain how obesity may cost £6.6–7.0 billion a year. *(4 marks)*

4 Apart from through legislation, analyse how the government affects the activities of business. *(9 marks)*

(17 marks)

With only 20 minutes to answer these questions, it is important to note the marks available. There is no need to spend a lot of time on the first two questions because both ask you to 'state'. Therefore, they do not require any explanation.

Case study
Time allowed: 25 minutes

Compensation for those left waiting

The pictures on our televisions of hundreds of passengers waiting to find out if and when their flight will take off are now common place. It appears that every August, some dispute breaks out and consequently passengers are left stranded. The odd voucher to get a drink while waiting in the departure lounge, often for several hours, was seen by the European Union as no longer acceptable.

The EU has therefore introduced a new regulation, allowing airline passengers to claim compensation for delayed flights (see Table 17.1). The regulation, which came into force in February 2005, will have a significant effect on the airline companies.

The regulation applies to all airlines departing from airports in EU member states. Compensation is to be paid even when the delay is due to a factor outside the airline's control. However, the airline is exempt from paying if it can prove that the delay is due to extraordinary circumstances, which could not have been avoided, or to technical problems with planes.

Distance of cancelled flight	Compensation	Plus
Up to 1,500 km	£173	Free meals and drinks and two phone calls during long delays
1,500–3,500 km	£277	Hotel room if delay continues overnight
Over 3,500 km	£416	Hotel room if delay continues overnight

Table 17.1 *Compensation for flight cancellations*

Answer all questions.

1 State whom this EU regulation is trying to protect. *(1 mark)*

2 Explain how the introduction of this regulation might increase prices. *(4 marks)*

3 Evaluate whether airline passengers will benefit from the introduction of the regulation. *(14 marks)*

(19 marks)

Group task

The introduction of extended licensing hours, enabling alcohol to be served 24 hours a day, has been controversial.

Prepare a presentation showing how the various stakeholders will be affected.

OR

Evaluate how the changes in the licensing law concerning opening hours will affect the businesses in your local area.

CHAPTER 18

Environment

Environmental issues are another example of external factors that affect the working of a business. Damage to the environment — which may be described as a **social cost**, an **external cost** or a **negative externality** — is moving ever higher up the agenda for both politicians and the general public alike. Consequently, businesses cannot afford to ignore the problem.

The environment is not just an issue for the UK economy. Throughout the world the demand for energy resources has serious environmental repercussions. China now consumes 12.1% of the world's energy resources — second only to the USA. Since its own oil reserves are modest, China remains reliant on coal, which causes huge environmental damage.

The type of cars people drive has been targeted by an alliance of environmental groups. In January 2005, they staged protests in an attempt to shame drivers of 4 × 4 vehicles into buying smaller cars that consume less fuel and emit less pollution. According to an article by Ben Webster in *The Times* (8 January 2005), some Range Rover models produce 389 grams of carbon dioxide per kilometre — double the rate of a Ford Mondeo. However, sales of 4 × 4 vehicles increased by 12.8% in 2004 to more than double the number sold a decade ago.

The increasing use of cars and planes has added considerably to air pollution from emissions. According to an article by Sarah-Kate Templeton in *The Times* (21 August 2005), even those of us who are trying to stay fit by cycling to work face an increased risk of heart disease. Dr D. Newby of the British Heart Foundation stated: 'Cycling through congested traffic exposes the cyclist to high levels of air pollution, especially as the exercise of cycling increases breathing and the individual's exposure.'

KEY TERMS

social cost (also called **external cost** or **negative externality**): cost of an activity to society as a whole

e EXAMINER'S VOICE

The environment is a highly controversial topic and you should avoid the use of emotive language and political dogma. It is better to put forward a balanced view highlighting both the positives and the negatives of a business that may or may not be responsible for a particular form of pollution. Marks are awarded for the way in which you write your points and *not* for any particular viewpoint.

Environmental issues and their consequences

Air pollution

Our air continues to be polluted by a wide range of industrial processes. The power stations that generate our electricity and the incinerators that burn some of our rubbish are, according to experts, a major cause of air pollution. But as we have seen, it is not only industry that is responsible: cars and planes used by consumers are another major source of air pollution.

The rise in air pollution seems to be having a serious effect on our climate. Even in the UK, weather conditions appear to be becoming more extreme, with more frequent winds of greater intensity and rainfall in greater quantities that causes flooding. Researchers have found that without a sharp reduction in greenhouse emissions, sea levels could rise far more than the 2–3 feet already expected by 2100. One consequence of this is that London will need to build another barrier across the Thames if regular flooding is to be avoided.

The Environment Agency is responsible for monitoring the amount of air pollution caused by industry.

Noise pollution

Living close to either a motorway or an airport means a considerable amount of noise pollution. The value of houses tends to be lower as a consequence of their proximity to either of these. Expensive anti-noise measures have been fitted to houses close to the runways of some airports (e.g. triple glazing), while large fences have been erected on motorways to deaden the constant noise. Such measures add to the expense of the transport system but are essential if the social costs are to be tolerable.

River or sea pollution

Water can be contaminated by waste from industry. Chemical plants have, in the past, been guilty of causing environmental damage by careless disposal of toxic waste (e.g. without sufficient treatment). Oil has been spilt into the seas around the world on a regular basis. Some of the spills have been due to accidents as ships have run aground. The consequences of these accidents are significant. Oil spills are expensive to clear up and the damage to wildlife and the land is enormous. Money spent clearing up such spills could be spent providing more hospitals or new schools.

Land pollution

The scarring of land by quarrying or mining is a form of pollution, as is the damage done to areas of rainforest by deforestation. Brazil has continued to fell millions of its hardwood trees, leaving the land bare, as there are no trees to hold the soil in place. Once the land is reduced to a barren state, nothing can be grown on it and a valuable resource has been lost.

Congestion

Traffic congestion is an environmental issue because cars in traffic jams are still using petrol and therefore polluting the atmosphere. In addition, such traffic often leads to a call for more roads to be built, which erodes the amount of land available for other uses.

Government measures

Sustainable development

The government has introduced the Sustainable Development Strategy, which aims to deliver a better quality of life for everyone. This requires action to preserve and improve the quality of the environment. The strategy includes:

- a reduction in vehicle excise duty for cars with low emissions
- an increase in the standard rate of landfill tax (a charge for disposing of waste, which is related to the amount disposed)
- tax allowances for industry that invests in environmentally friendly technology
- encouragement of recycling schemes operated by local government — many households now have additional bins and containers for bottles, plastic waste and paper

Transport

The European Union's Transport Committee is contemplating a project aimed at moving freight off the roads of Europe and onto rail. According to an article by Ari Schwartz in *European Voice* (28–31 August 2005), 'Stephan de Rynck, a spokesman for Jacques Barrot, the commissioner for transport, said that numerous EU studies had shown that switching from road to rail provided a plethora of [i.e. many] social and environmental benefits.'

The UK government has allowed local authorities to introduce road congestion charges. In London, an initial congestion charge of £5 was imposed each time a vehicle entered the congestion zone. Although traffic fell by up to 15%, the charge was increased in 2005 to £8 per vehicle. Professor David Begg, who advises the government on road issues, stated that the London congestion charge would have to be increased to £15 per vehicle before it would have a significant effect on the levels of traffic.

Environmental management

'Environmental Stewardship' is a new agri-environmental scheme launched in August 2005, which provides finance to farmers in England who deliver 'effective environmental management on their land'. This is described in detail in an online *Environmental Stewardship* booklet.

Waste management

Following publication of its report entitled *Waste Not, Want Not*, the Department for Environment, Food and Rural Affairs (DEFRA) has introduced its Waste Management Programme, which sets targets for the disposal of waste.

- By 2010, the amount of biodegradable waste that is landfilled is to be 75% of the 1995 quantity.
- By 2013, the amount is to be down to 50% of the 1995 figure.

Climate change

The government has introduced the climate change levy, which is a tax on the use of energy in industry and commerce.

The Kyoto Treaty of 1997 committed the world's industrialised nations to reducing emissions of greenhouse gases, such as carbon dioxide, by about 5% below the 1990 levels within 10 years. Unfortunately, however, the USA refused to sign the treaty. It is hoped that a revised version of the treaty will be in place by 2008.

Alternative sources of energy

The government has invested some money in the development of alternative sources of energy. The number of wind farms has escalated in the last few years, but they have encountered resistance from local residents who object to them because they are unsightly. At present, wind farms only generate a single-figure percentage of the UK's total energy production.

Wind farms do not create greenhouse gases, but they only generate a small amount of the UK's total energy production

Pressure group activity

Environmental damage may not only be expensive for businesses to reduce, but may bring unwanted publicity. Pressure groups such as Greenpeace and Friends of the Earth exist in order to highlight environmental issues. Negative publicity can affect sales or damage the image of a business.

Business has had to respond to the demand for environmental issues to be addressed. Car manufacturers have responded by meeting the changing demand for cars. Consumers, due in part to the rising costs of petrol and diesel, and increasing environmental concerns, have been switching to smaller, more fuel-efficient vehicles.

According to the chief executive of the Society of Motor Manufacturers and Traders, 10 years ago small cars such as the Ford Fiesta and the Vauxhall Corsa constituted 27% of the overall market. Today that proportion has increased to nearly 33%.

Further sources

www.defra.gov.uk

www.greenpeace.org.uk

www.unilever.com

www.shell.com

YOUR TURN

Questions

Time allowed: 25 minutes

1 Give **two** alternative terms for 'social cost'. *(2 marks)*

2 State **two** social costs of building another runway at an existing airport. *(2 marks)*

3 Explain who bears the social costs incurred after an additional runway is built. *(4 marks)*

4 State **one** way in which the UK government is trying to reduce environmental damage. *(1 mark)*

5 What are the likely costs of trying to improve the environment? *(4 marks)*

6 Explain why it may be difficult for a government to increase taxes on cars and petrol in order to reduce pollution from car emissions. *(5 marks)*

(18 marks)

Case study

Time allowed: 20 minutes

Jet stream changes its course and sends our weather wild

Forest fires, droughts and floods have hit Europe. While Switzerland, Romania and Bulgaria have suffered from devastating floods, Spain and Portugal have been without water and as a consequence have had difficulty in coping

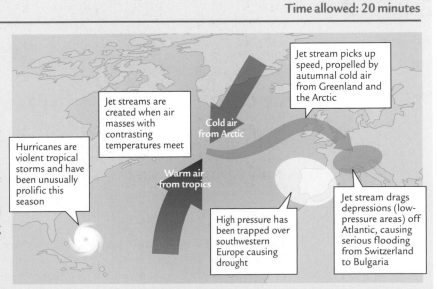

Jet streams are created when air masses with contrasting temperatures meet

Jet stream picks up speed, propelled by autumnal cold air from Greenland and the Arctic

Cold air from Arctic

Hurricanes are violent tropical storms and have been unusually prolific this season

Warm air from tropics

High pressure has been trapped over southwestern Europe causing drought

Jet stream drags depressions (low-pressure areas) off Atlantic, causing serious flooding from Switzerland to Bulgaria

***Figure 18.1** The strange summer of 2005*

with the forest fires that have been ignited. People have lost their lives and up to 140,000 hectares of land have been destroyed. England has not escaped freak conditions, with Birmingham suffering a hurricane in August 2005, which left many homeless.

Source: adapted from an article by Paul Simons and Tosin Sulaiman, *The Times*, 27 August 2005

Answer all questions.

1 State **two** possible causes of pollution. *(2 marks)*

2 Using the evidence in Figure 18.1, explain how a business may benefit from the adverse weather conditions. *(4 marks)*

3 Analyse the likely effects of the changing weather on consumers in the UK. *(9 marks)*

(15 marks)

CHAPTER 19

Ethics and corporate social responsibility

Virtually every topic in the news has an ethical element: human and animal rights, genetically modified crops, medicine, warfare — the list is almost endless. Ethics can be a major external influence on a business.

This chapter ends with an explanation of how to carry out a SWOT analysis to complete this section on influences on business.

What is ethical behaviour?

If someone is asked what they understand by **ethical behaviour**, they are likely to reply: 'doing the right thing', 'being honest', 'listening to one's conscience' and so on. Ethics are often defined as 'a moral code of conduct', so these comments are certainly valid. In this chapter, *ethical* behaviour is defined as 'behaviour that is right' and *unethical* behaviour as 'behaviour that is wrong'.

However, what constitutes ethical or unethical behaviour is often a matter of opinion — 'right' or 'wrong' according to whom? The 'right' course of action might, in practice, be hard to identify and might not exist at all. Ethics are a matter of degree; a matter of what someone is personally comfortable with.

Furthermore, *unethical* actions are not the same as *illegal* actions. Laws lay down what businesses *must* do; they are minimum standards to be adhered to. If a business meets a minimum standard and chooses to do no more (even though it could and/or most people would think it should), this is not illegal.

Some examples of a business acting *unethically* could be:

- paying only the minimum wage, or cutting spending on health and safety down to the legal minimum, when the business is very profitable
- holding down wages and other benefits to 'ordinary' employees, while senior managers and directors are awarded lavish remuneration packages
- exploiting people or natural resources in developing countries, where laws protecting employees (e.g. health and safety) or

KEY TERM

ethical behaviour: actions that businesses or people take because they believe them to be 'right'

Many occupations, for example in medicine and law, involve the study of ethics as part of the training

INGRAM

the environment (e.g. the disposal of hazardous waste) are less stringent than, for example, in the EU
- delaying payment of invoices to suppliers as long as possible in order to improve cash flow
- selective publication of financial data or research findings, which could mislead investors, customers or others
- selling weapons to countries with a history of poor human rights

None of these actions is illegal and there might be disagreement over whether they are unethical. Let's take the last example: weapons are made to maim and kill others. The justification for a UK business selling them is that it keeps UK workers in employment. Furthermore, it is also usually stated that a condition of the sale is that they will only be used for defensive purposes — not for internal repression of dissidents or for offensive actions against other countries. However, the arms trade can be rather different in practice; weapons can, and do, find their way into the wrong hands.

Employees could also act unethically. For example:
- using the business's resources (e.g. telephones, computers, postage and photocopying facilities) for their own purposes
- deliberately overstating expense claims for mileage, food or hotel bills
- 'throwing a sickie' or, when given permission to attend a medical appointment, claiming that the doctor was running late and taking the whole morning off work

---

e EXAMINER'S VOICE

Although, most of the time, ethical issues can be ambiguous, one ethical statement that does seem to cross national boundaries and contexts is 'treat others as you would like to be treated yourself'. This is something to be borne in mind when answering any question involving the consideration of ethics as an influence on a business.

What are the benefits to a business of acting ethically?

There are some people who belittle the potential benefits of treating stakeholders ethically, but it is a fact that that many people will not buy products from, or work for, a business that behaves in an unethical manner.

Employees

Ethical treatment of employees in matters such as health and safety, pay, conditions of work and service (holidays, pensions etc.) is likely to result in more commitment from employees and higher productivity. An ethical firm may also be more attractive to potential employees. Research has shown that young people are particularly concerned about 'green' issues, and an ethical approach might be an important factor affecting their choice of employment.

This is particularly true at graduate level. Suppose that a very talented graduate has received three offers to start work as a management trainee. If pay and conditions are similar in all three firms, an ethical approach to business might prove to be the deciding factor in which offer to accept.

Suppliers

The obvious way to treat suppliers ethically is to offer prompt payment for goods and services. This will improve their cash flow and make them more likely to supply the business in the future.

While all businesses should be trying to reduce their supply costs, achieving this by forcing a succession of price cuts on smaller and weaker suppliers via a 'take it or leave it' approach is not ethical. Building a good relationship based on ethical principles with a supplier can be useful if raw materials or other supplies are needed urgently.

The local community

A business could act ethically by 'putting something back' into the community through sponsorship of sports teams, arts groups or other local initiatives. Another way is to try to buy as many products from local suppliers as possible, thus helping to boost the local economy. This will generate favourable publicity and, quite possibly, sales at local level. It may also assist with the recruitment and retention of staff.

A business can support its local community by sponsoring local sports teams

Other benefits

An ethical approach can be used for *marketing purposes*. The business's ethical stance can be used as part of advertising and promotion — for many consumers, this is a deciding factor in whether to buy or not. It is also quite often the case that a large business, keen to show its ethical credentials, will demand that its suppliers also behave in an ethical manner. An ethical code of conduct might be requested from a supplier before any deal is signed. In 2005 the publisher Random House UK adopted a 'forest-friendly' policy. This means that its suppliers have to use either recycled paper or paper made from wood grown in a sustainable forest. Suppliers acting in an ethical way can use this to help win sales contracts.

In 2004, BT announced a plan to obtain all its energy needs from renewable sources. BT has long maintained an ethical stance in the community and this could be seen as a continuation of that policy. This approach might persuade other businesses, which are keen to demonstrate how 'green' they are, to use BT instead of another company. A similar point can be made about *investors*. Suppose that an investment bank decides that the telecommunications market is where it intends to invest as part of its strategy for the next year. Its research shows that the risks and returns from the various companies in that sector are roughly the same. The fact that one company has an ethical approach might be the deciding factor in where the investment finally ends up.

Finally, it should be mentioned that an ethical approach to running a business might occur not because of the likely benefits, but simply because those who own and/or run it think that it is the right thing to do; it accords with what they believe in and how they view the world.

Corporate social responsibility

Allied to ethics is the notion of **corporate social responsibility** (often shortened to CSR). 'Acting responsibly' and 'acting ethically' are two sides of the same coin; the government provides the legal framework within which businesses should operate, but CSR refers to the actions that a firm *voluntarily* takes to benefit society.

CSR would include:

- purchasing raw material inputs from sustainable sources, preferably from local businesses
- when redundancies are necessary, seeking to minimise the effects of these job losses on the workforce and the community
- minimising environmental damage by doing more than simply meeting legal pollution controls
- insisting that suppliers have an ethical code of conduct that is adhered to, so that a socially responsible approach is in place all the way down the supply chain

CSR in less economically developed countries might include health facilities and educational provision for employees' families

McDonald's, for example, has spent a lot of money promoting itself as a socially responsible company.

Corporate social responsibility in less economically developed countries

In less economically developed countries, Western multinational firms have often attracted a lot of criticism — and in some cases, rightly so — but CSR in poor countries can bring major benefits. Factories need clean water and sanitation. A business might provide these at its own expense or at least contribute towards them, rather than simply demand that they are in place before it will consider building a factory. It might also improve the local infrastructure; good roads are needed so that raw materials can be moved in and finished products moved out more easily.

In these ways, the socially responsible business is fulfilling roles and functions (albeit locally) that the less economically developed country's government has not been able, or has failed, to perform.

Problems with the stakeholder approach

The approach considered so far is known as the **stakeholder approach** (see Chapter 2). But acting in a socially responsible, ethical manner does not automatically ensure that all stakeholders are satisfied. An obvious example is that paying employees more in order to be ethical could mean a fall in profits and a reduction in dividends for shareholders and/or less funding for community initiatives. There are likely to be losers as well as winners with an ethical approach — in the short term, at least.

Eventually, a business must decide to whom it is ultimately responsible. Should business decisions always involve a balance between the stakeholders? Even if this is the case, sooner or later a business will have to evaluate which are the most important.

Alternatively, should the directors take the view that the shareholders, who after all elected them and to whom they will be answerable at the annual general meeting, always come first? This view is known as the **shareholder approach**. This approach regards trying to meet the needs of several different stakeholder groups as an unnecessary distraction for managers and directors. In the USA, the shareholder approach is common.

Some US businesses regard making a profit, by producing products that their customers want, and paying their taxes on time, as their only responsibilities to society. Giving to charitable causes or getting involved in the community, in the way that many UK firms do, would make some US managers uneasy. This is because if their business gained any benefit in the form of increased sales from these community actions, it would taint the act of giving. It could be argued that this is the more ethical approach.

The costs of an ethical approach

Adopting an ethical approach is not just a matter of printing 'XYZ plc is a socially responsible company' on the firm's letterheads. Some issues for consideration are as follows:

- Some sort of stakeholder survey will have to be conducted into how the various parties currently see the firm in terms of its ethical behaviour and what they would expect from it in the future. This will involve a financial cost.
- Directors and managers must decide how the approach is to be implemented, and then monitored once it is in place. If those running the business are serious about its responsibilities, this is going to take time and resources that could be spent on other matters.
- Employees may need to be trained, in which case others may be needed to cover their absence (at extra cost).
- There may be costs in finding and negotiating ethical contracts with suppliers that comply with the company's requirements.

- Buying products from a variety of different local suppliers may mean that bulk discounts are not possible and so costs are higher.
- Share prices of a public company may fall in the short run if it 'goes ethical', due to fears of reduced dividends because funds are now being channelled differently. A fall in its share price is psychologically bad for a company: it is a sign that 'the market' does not like what is happening. It also makes it more vulnerable to investors buying large blocks of shares cheaply, which might lead to a takeover.

Obviously, a business hopes that once the ethical approach is up and running, the benefits will outweigh the costs. If they do not, there is another issue to be faced — does the firm give up or try harder?

Do businesses really believe in corporate social responsibility?

There is a lot of debate about whether businesses, especially those that generate a lot of publicity about their social responsibility, actually believe in what they are doing. Is it simply a marketing ploy? Some people argue that it doesn't really matter: if people in less economically developed countries are now being paid a decent wage for picking fruit or sewing clothes, does it really matter whether those who own and run the business truly believe that what they are doing is right? Others say it does matter because this goes to the heart of what ethics are about — wanting and believing it is right to act in a manner that benefits others.

One fact is clear: a half-hearted approach to ethics, or treating CSR as a gimmick, is likely to backfire in terms of poor publicity if the firm is caught acting in an unethical way. Such publicity can spread very quickly and will be used by consumer groups to draw attention to the business's failings, which will almost certainly impact on sales.

Furthermore, if directors and managers really do not believe in the concept but are merely trying to use it for marketing purposes, their actions are not likely to bring about the desired results. Those who truly believe in something are more likely to carry out their tasks with enthusiasm and will ensure that others are working towards the same goals. If it is all a sham, the other employees in the organisation will, sooner or later, realise this and divert their effort to the issues that senior managers are really interested in.

SWOT analysis

A SWOT analysis is a technique that a firm uses to assess the internal (**s**trengths and **w**eaknesses) and external (**o**pportunities and **t**hreats) factors related to aspects of its business activity. It is often presented as a two-by-two grid (see Figure 19.1).

Internal factors

First the firm considers its current strengths and weaknesses. Managers within the firm make a list of the aspects of business activity that could be considered to be strengths of the business and at the same time draw up a list of the current weaknesses. The firm can then focus on making the strengths more of a feature while trying to reduce the impact of the weaknesses.

External factors

The firm then tries to identify the possible external opportunities that might present themselves to it in the near future. It is important to try to consider how the firm might be able to grasp those oppor-tunities. At the same time, the firm also tries to establish possible threats that are posed to it by its external environment. These may include the problems of competition, the changing nature of the market and so on.

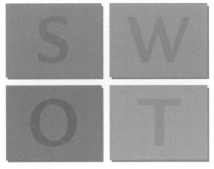

Figure 19.1
SWOT analysis

Uses of SWOT analysis

A SWOT analysis can be carried out by an individual department within a firm or by a firm as a whole. For example, a marketing department might assess the current market conditions and the quality of its current marketing strategies. These can then be considered in relation to the future. What might happen? How might the competition react? What is happening in the wider market?

The whole analysis can be used as a forward-looking tool. The managers can consider how effective the business is in respect of the environment in which it operates and adjust their strategies and tactics as appropriate (see Chapter 6).

Further sources

www.ibe.org.uk — the Institute of Business Ethics, covering business ethics in principle and practice

www.ethicaltrade.org — the Ethical Trading initiative

www.smile.co.uk — ethical banking; Smile is part of the Cooperative Bank

---

YOUR TURN

Case study
Time allowed: 45 minutes

Big Mac's makeover: too much to swallow?

McDonald's has often been accused of acting in an unethical manner. Critics say its activities damage the environment. They say that rainforest land has been destroyed and local people displaced in order to establish ranches to provide the ingredients for burgers.

Criticism is not restricted to McDonald's activities in less economically developed countries. In the developed countries where most of the products are sold, there have also been allegations of unethical behaviour. Among the allegations are that, although it is a profitable company, McDonald's pays relatively low wages and discourages the formation of unions. Another allegation is that every year McDonald's uses thousands of tonnes of unnecessary packaging that is not only a waste of resources but also ends up littering the streets.

Perhaps the most publicised and best-known criticism is that McDonald's knowingly produces food that, being high in fat, salt and sugar, and low in fibre and vitamins, is very unhealthy and a risk to the health of its customers. If true, what could be a clearer example of unethical behaviour?

McDonald's, of course, has always vigorously disputed these claims and the latest weapon in its war against this last criticism is a complete makeover of its product range. Now there's not a greasy burger in sight. These days McDonald's is for ladies who lunch; the fast-food giant now features attractive, sophisticated, thirty-something women in its adverts.

There are also wholesome-sounding educational ads on children's television 'using songs to help children learn about eating smart and being active'. So is McDonald's much publicised conversion to sport and mineral water a desperate rearguard action against bad PR? Or is it a ruse to get more punters to the burger counter? 'Not at all,' says Amanda Pierce, McDonald's spokeswoman in the UK. 'There's a heck of a lot of variety in the menu now. We have to recognise that our customers' tastes and expectations have changed.'

This is certainly true, but although McDonald's may be one of the most successful brands in history, it has had to be rebranded. In the USA, where the proportion of overweight adults has soared to about 65%, many of the fast-food industry's biggest companies are fending off lawsuits from large-waisted former customers. The industry has been reviewing portion sizes and reviewing ingredients. McDonald's is no different. It has been encouraging customers to exercise and is sponsoring the Olympic Games and the England football team.

McDonald's has so far managed to avoid obesity lawsuits in the USA by appealing to common sense. 'Nobody is forced to eat at McDonald's,' said one judge in a recent verdict. 'It is not the place of the law to protect people from their own excesses.'

Source: adapted from the *Observer*, 8 August 2004

Answer all questions.

1 State **two** ways in which the employees of McDonald's could behave in an unethical manner. *(2 marks)*

2 Outline the difference between the 'stakeholder approach' and the 'shareholder approach' to running a business. *(4 marks)*

3 Analyse the likely objectives behind the 'complete makeover' of McDonald's product range. *(9 marks)*

4 McDonald's has made its product range healthier, promotes involvement in sport, and supports a number of community initiatives. To what extent might the stakeholders of McDonald's benefit from running the business in an ethical manner? *(14 marks)*

(29 marks)

Group task

Time allowed: 35 minutes

Read the following examples of ethical considerations. Within your group, see if you can reach an agreement on the issues raised. Be prepared to report back to the class as a whole.

1 Criminal convictions

Would a firm want to be associated with someone who has a criminal conviction for dishonesty? The answer is likely to be 'certainly not!' But are things this straightforward? Perhaps a better question is: *should* a firm want to be associated with someone with this sort of criminal record?'

Let us take the case of Tecwen Whittock. The facts are that he was found guilty of coughing during questions in the television game show *Who Wants to Be a Millionaire?* in order to assist Major Charles Ingram to select the right answers and claim the £1 million jackpot. He was fined £10,000 and given a suspended prison sentence for conspiracy. After this happened, he got his own website, which used this fact as publicity and proclaimed that he was available for lectures and after-dinner speeches.

One newspaper report stated that Whittock had been approached by a firm selling cough sweets. Firms are free to use whom they like to advertise and promote their products, so is this sort of thing unethical? Whittock has, after all, been found guilty, has been sentenced and has now 'paid the price'.

Would the use of Whittock in any manner by a business be 'a bit of harmless fun' and/or 'a bit of a joke', or is this unethical and something we should be concerned about?

2 Using the business's time for personal reasons

Suppose an employee on an assembly line deliberately and repeatedly comes back from his tea break 10 minutes late because he likes to read the football news in the paper. This will almost certainly be a disciplinary offence. Now consider a white-collar employee at the same firm who does a lot of work online. He spends 10 minutes a day on the internet looking at websites devoted to his favourite bands and football club.

Is this the same 'offence'?

3 Theft

If an employee deliberately takes a 50p bar of chocolate from the business's canteen without paying for it, this is theft — in fact, it could be considered 'theft from an employer', which is even more serious. This is fairly clear cut. However, suppose instead of stealing chocolate she makes a 50p phone call using the phone on her desk, and makes no attempt to pay for it. The firm has lost out just as it did with the chocolate.

Is this also a case of theft? Is there a difference?

Suppose she was arranging a service for her car. This is not likely to be a valid reason for running up the firm's phone bill. However, suppose that the previous night her son had been ill. The next morning she had to decide whether to go to work or not. Suppose she decided that she would; she did not want to let her clients and colleagues down. She left her son with his grandmother but was worried about how he was getting on and so she phoned.

Does this now make the phone call ethically acceptable?

Could she justify her action by saying that she was so worried that she couldn't concentrate on her work properly until she knew her son was okay?

If your answer is 'of course this is all right', consider some recent cases in the USA where people with pets but no children have been taking time off to look after them when they are ill. They argue that if parents can have time off to look after children, they are justified in taking time off to look after their animals. They are being honest, they say, in not pretending that they themselves are ill. The reason they are not at work is that their pet is ill.

Is it ethical to take time off from work for this reason? Are the firms they work for ethically justified in disciplining them if they think such behaviour is unacceptable?

4 Taking a 'sickie'

Consider a workplace situation where teamwork is the norm. An employee says to himself, 'If I was on my summer holiday, my colleagues in the department would be doing my job. They can cope without me for just one day'. He therefore telephones in 'sick' when he is not.

Does the fact that the company can manage without the employee make his absence less unethical?

5 Life or death?

Suppose you see a television programme that has an interview with an entrepreneur in a less economically developed country who owns a number of factories there. The conditions of pay and work are shown to be far worse than those in the UK. There is little health and safety provision and trade unions are banned. The reporter points this out to the entrepreneur and he replies, 'This is all true. But you are looking at this with Western eyes. These people may be being treated badly by your standards, but if they were not in those factories, they would have starved. They would be dead. I am keeping them alive'.

Is the business acting ethically or not?

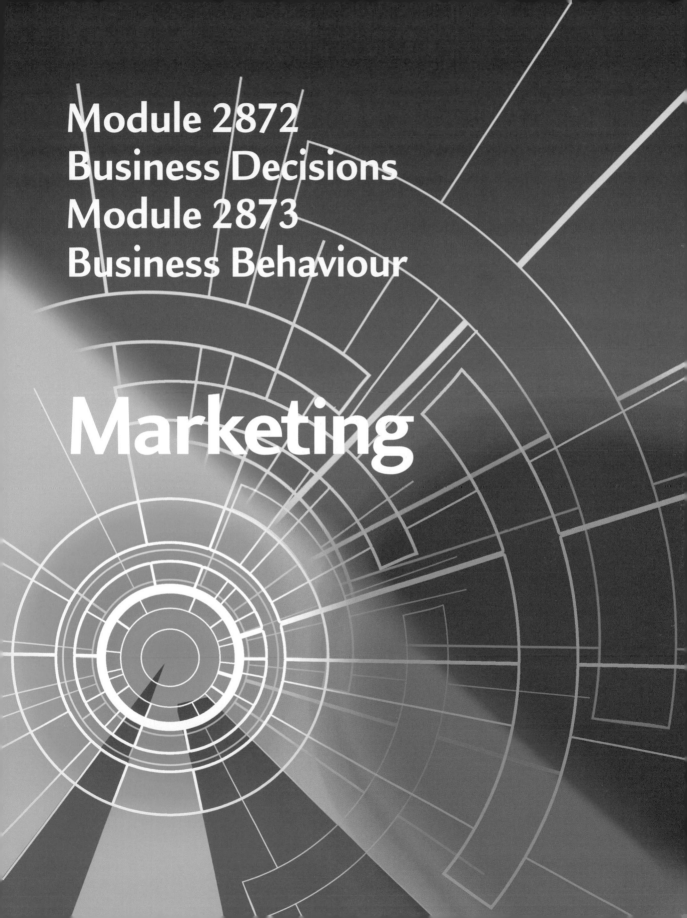

Module 2872
Business Decisions
Module 2873
Business Behaviour

Marketing

CHAPTER 20

Marketing

What is **marketing**? There are many definitions, including: 'satisfying customers', 'making money', 'selling things' and 'promoting goods and services'. Elements of all of these form the basis of marketing. An accepted definition usually comprises:

- identifying customer demand
- satisfying customer demand
- making a profit

It is important to remember that marketing consists of all these elements. It is not enough to focus on any one of them.

Marketing should not be seen in isolation from other functional areas of the business; nor can it ignore the external environment within which business operates.

Marketing is often studied through the consideration of four elements known as the *marketing mix*. Briefly, these are aspects of *product*, *price*, *promotion* and *place*. They are introduced in Chapter 21 and covered in full in Chapters 25 to 29.

The significance of marketing

Business is about providing something that someone wants to buy. The specific functions of marketing assist businesses in the process of achieving their objectives.

Closer consideration of the three bullet points above shows the significance of marketing.

Identifying customer demand

All producers of goods and services must take the time to establish exactly what their customers and potential customers want. It may be possible to produce a fantastic product, to promote it really effectively and to have it on sale at an extremely low price. But if no one wants it, an awful lot of money is wasted. How firms try to find out their customers' needs is called *market research*; this is considered in Chapter 23.

Satisfying customer demand

Firms must respond to the information gained when they carried out their market research. This process involves combining the various elements of marketing (i.e. the *marketing mix*) into a *strategy*. The aim of this strategy is

KEY TERM

marketing: a process that attempts to identify customer demand, and then satisfy it, at a profit

to match supply with demand. The firm must ask whether it can provide what customers actually want. If not, can the firm produce something that it can then convince the customers that they want?

Making a profit

Most firms have the desire for some kind of profit as a stated objective. Even those organisations that do not view profit as a primary aim usually need to avoid making a loss on their activities.

Customer versus product orientation

The focus of marketing tends to place the customer at the heart of the process. Firms have traditionally employed two approaches:

- **Customer orientation.** This allows customers to determine what they need. It is then up to businesses to enter the market to try to provide this effectively. Improvements in communication and changes in lifestyles have led to the average consumer being more aware of the market and the products in it. Increased desire for products and services in the leisure industry has led to a massive increase in the variety of those services. For example, the rise in demand for worldwide travel has increased the number of organisations willing to provide holidays such as cruises.
- **Product orientation.** This approach tends to involve firms developing and producing products in the hope that they can encourage customers to buy them. Technologically advanced producers strive to push the boundaries by producing new, high-quality gadgets that appeal to certain customers. These customers need some convincing that the new product is 'the future', but positive innovation is often well rewarded.

All organisations must judge whether they are able to provide what the market wants or whether they should develop their idea and use their skills in marketing to 'create' demand in the market, in the way that very good marketing has developed the demand for MP3 players.

The reality, in many cases, is that each business needs to adapt to the particular market in which it operates. This may involve being both customer and product orientated at different times.

The relationship between marketing and other functions

The marketing function is only one aspect of the day-to-day operation of a business. The AS Business Studies course focuses on four main areas:

- accounting and finance
- marketing
- people (human resources management, or HRM)
- production (operations management)

KEY TERMS

customer orientation: where a firm considers what the market wants before trying to produce it

product orientation: where a firm produces a product and then tries to convince the public that they need it

These functional areas must work together to increase the chances of achieving the stated objectives of the business. The principal roles of each function are listed in Figure 20.1.

Figure 20.1 Principal roles of each business function

Accounting and finance
- records financial transactions
- monitors cash and profit
- aids planning
- budgetary control of the business

Marketing
- determines what the market wants
- develops a strategy to coordinate price, product, promotion and distribution (i.e. the marketing mix)

Business functions

People (HRM)
- anticipates future labour requirements
- considers the skills mix of the workforce
- recruitment/selection/dismissal
- training of existing and new staff
- motivation of workforce

Production (operations management)
- determines the size of the production unit
- manages stock
- maintains quality
- maintains efficiency
- produces goods

Conflicts may arise between marketing and each of the other business functions for a number of reasons:

- **Accounting and finance.** One of the key aims of the finance department is to control costs. This may conflict with the marketing function because one of the key aspects of marketing is promotion. Promotion is relatively expensive and is unlikely to generate an obvious return. Market research is another important role of marketing, and many important spending decisions are made on the strength of its findings. Again, market research can be quite costly and offers few guarantees as to its validity.

- **People (HRM).** Marketing aims to create demand. Increased demand leads to a need to employ staff and/or to ask existing staff to work longer (entailing overtime pay). On the other hand, the failure of marketing to generate sufficient demand can lead to a reduction in staffing requirements. HRM departments generally prefer stability, while the aim of marketing is to stimulate change.

- **Production (operations management).** It is vital for marketing and production to work closely together. Production sometimes takes the view that it is what generates the profit, while marketing simply spends the money

IKON/CADMIUM

made. This is clearly simplistic, but it highlights the problems that can exist in coordinating the two functions. In a customer-orientated situation, there is a need to involve the production function in all aspects of the market research process. Marketing cannot promise what production cannot deliver. In a product-orientated situation, the cooperation probably needs to be even closer. The production department must be able to convince the marketing function that what is being developed is saleable. Marketing staff must be convinced so that they can go on to convince the market about the value of the newly developed idea.

A marketing manager makes decisions for the good of the marketing department. Other stakeholders have their own priorities and objectives. It is the art of good management to be able to coordinate and control all areas working together. Conflict is more likely when a business is struggling. At this time, the marketing manager may argue that increased spending is the key to survival, but the finance manager will clearly have a different view. Other sources of conflict may be more day-to-day issues.

e EXAMINER'S VOICE

Exam questions are set to test your understanding of a particular aspect of business studies. Remind yourself of the need to take into account the possible views of others when providing your answers. The marketing manager needs to be aware of how a particular situation looks from the perspective of other departments. In the questions that test the higher skill of evaluation, if you are able to recognise that there could be a way of handling the question from a different perspective, it might be a route to higher marks.

Further sources

www.marketingsurvivalkit.com   **www.revisionguru.co.uk/business**   **www.jusbiz.org/resources**

YOUR TURN

Questions   Time allowed: 25 minutes

1 State **three** aspects that make up the function of marketing.   *(3 marks)*

2 State and then explain the importance of marketing in a business.   *(4 marks)*

3 Explain the difference between customer and product orientation.   *(4 marks)*

4 Using a business that you are familiar with, explain **two** reasons why it might be described as market oriented.   *(4 marks)*

5 Analyse why your own school or college might consider marketing important.   *(9 marks)*

                                                                               (24 marks)

Case study 1

Time allowed: 30 minutes

Levi 501 jeans

Boxing Day 1985 saw the first showing on UK television of an advert for Levi 501 jeans. The advert itself was set in a laundrette in the 1950s and featured the classic Marvin Gaye hit, 'I heard it through the grapevine'. The sight of model Nick Kamen stripped down to his white boxer shorts while waiting for his jeans to be washed is one that changed, almost overnight, the flagging fortunes of the Levi brand. At the time, Levi's had been losing out to all sorts of other fashionable brands and its jeans were seen as the sort worn by people's dads.

This advertisement kicked off a series of classic retro 1950s-style ads, which increased the sales of Levi 501 jeans by 800%. Eventually the promotion had to be stopped because the company was unable to produce enough jeans to meet the new demand.

Demand for boxer shorts also increased dramatically, as did demand for the re-released version of the hit single. The advert reached no. 6 in a recent UK poll of 'The Greatest TV Ads'.

Answer all questions.

1 What does the Levi 501 example suggest about the importance of marketing? *(8 marks)*

2 Why was market research unable to anticipate the massive increase in demand? *(5 marks)*

3 Evaluate the problems created by the increase in demand on the other functional areas within Levi. *(9 marks)*

4 To what extent is the Levi example product or customer orientation? *(8 marks)*

(30 marks)

Case study 2

Time allowed: 20 minutes

'To infinity and beyond' — the tale of a space ranger

Toy Story, the animated movie from Pixar, was a huge hit in the cinema following its release in 1995. Toys from the movie became very sought after. Parents went to desperate measures to secure a Buzz Lightyear doll. The rights to produce toys from the film were sold to a small independent Canadian manufacturer that simply could not cope with the demand. Why? Because all of the major toy manufacturers turned down the chance to make *Toy Story* merchandise, as they felt the movie would never catch on. US retailers only ordered a paltry 60,000 Buzz Lightyear dolls in the year of the film's release, a source of much heartbreak among children that Christmas! Now, 9 million sales later, it is easy to see to what extent the market was miscalculated at that time.

Answer all questions.

1 To what extent is marketing at fault in the miscalculation of the production requirements for the Buzz Lightyear doll? *(9 marks)*

2 Is this case an example of customer or market orientation? Explain why. *(7 marks)*

(16 marks)

Group task

Divide yourselves into groups of four. You are the managers of an organisation that has developed mobile technology that makes it possible to switch on the central heating, dishwasher, washing machine and other electrical appliances without needing to be at home. Allocate the roles of marketing manager, personnel manager, production manager and finance manager among your group. Determine:

- the issues that might affect your department
- the possible areas of conflict
- how these might be overcome

Now repeat the exercise for a snacks manufacturer that has developed a new flavour of crisp following extensive market research.

What do you notice about the issues discussed in each example?

CHAPTER 21

Marketing objectives and strategy

Objectives set the targets for all organisations. A *strategy* is a plan devised to achieve these objectives. This chapter considers the different types of objective devised by a marketing department and how they might be achieved. It also looks at how strategic plans are developed, and how marketing behaviour reflects the objectives, the resources available and the characteristics of the customer. Firms must also consider the financial constraints that they face in trying to achieve their objectives.

Marketing objectives

Marketing objectives should be devised so that a clear strategy to achieve them can be followed. All objectives set by individual departments or functional areas must be in line with the overall objectives of the firm. Chapter 20 highlighted the possible areas of conflict that might exist between departments. Another possible area of conflict is between the objectives of one department and those of the firm as a whole.

The objectives of the marketing department form part of the hierarchy of objectives for the whole firm (see Figure 21.1), introduced in Chapter 6.

All parts of the hierarchy are designed to support each other. The day-to-day aims assist the business in complying with its overall mission statement.

The *strategic objectives* that relate specifically to marketing include:

- increasing sales
- increasing market share
- increasing product awareness
- gaining a unique selling point

Tactical objectives can be categorised using the marketing mix (see Figure 21.2).

Product objectives

- to launch new products
- to update and improve products
- to improve after-sales service
- to improve product packaging
- to extend the life of the products

KEY TERM

marketing objectives: desired outcomes of a marketing plan or the marketing function

Mission statement
(e.g. to become the biggest seller in the market)

Strategic objectives
(e.g. to increase sales by 10% in 12 months)

Department or function objectives
(e.g. to launch the new product successfully in the next 6 months)

Tactical objectives
(e.g. to set targets for sales staff)

Day-to-day aims
(e.g. to manage customer accounts and deal with problems)

Figure 21.1
The hierarchy of objectives

Price objectives
- to remain competitive
- to reduce prices while maintaining returns
- to develop new pricing strategies (e.g. psychological pricing)

Promotion objectives
- to maintain brand awareness
- to increase brand loyalty
- to develop memorable advertising
- to widen the range of promotion options

Place objectives
- to increase product availability
- to improve product delivery times

Other objectives may also stem from market research activities — for example, improving the quality of information gathering. Most of the stated objectives can be worked on without fear of conflict with other objectives of the firm. However, conflict between objectives can arise. For example, a price decrease may make it difficult to increase expenditure on promotion.

Marketing strategy

Marketing strategy needs to be devised to achieve the objectives described above. Again, this can be described in terms of the marketing mix (see Figure 21.2).

Product strategy
Chapter 25 considers aspects of product strategy in terms of the product life cycle, product positioning and the Boston matrix. More specific strategies relating to product objectives will also be followed. The need to update and improve the product range is obvious. Firms should carry out ongoing market research to ensure that they stay in touch with the wishes of their customers. Monitoring after-sales service is particularly important in some markets. Marketing departments must work closely with production and research and development (R&D) to ensure that new products in demand can be produced effectively.

Price strategy
Chapter 26 considers aspects of pricing strategy. Every decision to change a price should be taken as part of an overall strategic plan. Pricing strategies are many and varied. Any desire to remain competitive is likely to be reflected in a price-based strategy.

Promotion strategy
Chapter 28 considers many aspects of promotion in detail. Strategic aspects of promotion involve concerted efforts to raise the profile of products using a variety of promotional activities. An advertising

> **KEY TERM**
>
> **marketing strategy:** a plan to achieve stated marketing objectives

Figure 21.2 Elements of marketing strategy

campaign for a product is often run at the same time as some other promotion activity, such as a competition or free gift idea.

Place or distribution strategy

Chapter 29 considers aspects of distribution. Most specific strategies are concerned with choice of retail outlets and the impact this has on other aspects of the marketing strategy.

Market research strategy

An additional element of marketing strategy is *market research strategies*. Chapter 23 consider aspects of this. The gathering of information is vital and strategies are concerned with effective research methods and the validity of the data.

KEY TERMS

tactics: day-to-day decisions that are taken to manage the firm and to help fulfil its overall strategy

resources: physical items needed to assist in the achievement of the company's objectives

e EXAMINER'S VOICE

At AS, you are unlikely to be asked to write about a whole marketing strategy. You do, however, need to be aware of the different aspects of a strategy and to relate these to the objectives set by the firm. Learn about the importance of planning and always relate your answers to the specific business given in the case. Two businesses will rarely respond to a situation in the same way. Be prepared to argue your chosen course of action.

Determine/consider
the objectives

↓

Examine current position
(SWOT — see Chapter 19)

↓

Consider external factors

↓

Develop the strategy

↓

Plan the implementation
of the strategy
(resources required etc.)

↓

Strategy implementation

↓

Strategy review/evaluation
throughout

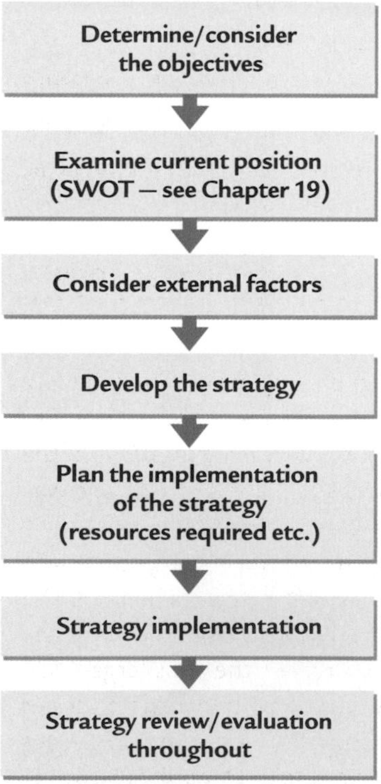

Figure 21.3 A strategic approach

A strategic approach

The individual strategies described above are often combined into an overall, coordinated approach. A strategic approach to decision making is considered in more detail at A2. At AS, it is important to be aware of the general part played by strategic thinking in the whole function of marketing.

Strategic thinking involves looking at the wider picture. A distinction is usually made between strategies and **tactics**. All strategic thinking includes some form of constant review. A typical approach is set out in Figure 21.3.

At each stage of review, it should be possible to adjust and learn from the decisions made and the actions taken. As the strategy is being implemented, it may be necessary to change aspects of it. It must be remembered that any strategy is following objectives set by a variety of different stakeholders. A marketing strategy must take these issues and any changes in the external environment into account. Such changes can be quite significant and very difficult to predict.

Another important factor to consider is the strategy's resource requirements. Planning the **resources** can be crucial in ensuring the success of a marketing strategy. Coordination of different resources (e.g. finance, staffing) in relation to the company's objectives and the overall plan will enhance the likely success of the strategy.

Overall, the development of an effective marketing strategy is vital in achieving a range of objectives set by most firms. Most organisations desire increases in sales, profits or market share. The need to be different and to establish a **unique selling point (USP)** sits high on the agenda of many organisations. Coordination and being mindful of external factors are crucial.

> **KEY TERM**
>
> **unique selling point (USP):** a feature that differentiates a business's product from those supplied by its competitors

Further sources

www.businesslink.gov.uk   **www.thetimes100.co.uk**

YOUR TURN

Questions   Time allowed: 35 minutes

1 State **three** marketing objectives.   *(3 marks)*

2 Explain the difference between a marketing strategy and marketing tactics.   *(4 marks)*

3 Give an example of a product that has a 'unique selling point'.   *(2 marks)*

4 Discuss why it is important for Cadbury to have a clearly defined marketing strategy.   *(6 marks)*

5 Analyse **two** specific resources that would be needed by Sony in the marketing of PlayStation 3.   *(6 marks)*

6 Evaluate the success of the marketing strategies of easyJet and Marks and Spencer.   *(8 marks)*

(29 marks)

Case study   Time allowed: 35 minutes

Confetti.co.uk

Confetti.co.uk is the UK's most popular online wedding site. The firm arranges all aspects of weddings and provides a variety of products and services for other special occasions. This includes honeymoons, invitations, cakes, entertainment and wedding venues. Since its launch it has enjoyed continual growth, well outstripping most other online retailers. When Steve Abbis, former marketing manager at Argos, became head of marketing at Confetti, he took on the responsibility of all online content, website design, and offline marketing and promotion at the retail outlets in London, Leeds and Birmingham. One of the first areas Steve set about developing was the affiliate marketing programme.

Affiliate marketing is using other websites, called affiliates, to market the company's products. Amazon.com, the bookseller, created the first large-scale affiliate program and hundreds of other companies have followed its example. Affiliates receive a fee for each hit registered via their website.

HEMERA TECHNOLOGIES

The aims and objectives set were:

- to increase sales revenue from affiliate marketing by 200%
- to improve search engine marketing results through affiliate marketing
- to develop a more strategic approach by making better use of seasonal sales opportunities
- to avoid an increase in the budget (cost savings in other aspects of the strategy needed to be made)

Steve's approach was to view affiliate marketing as more than a simple sales generator. The other companies must be given incentives to promote Confetti.

Since Steve was appointed, the number of affiliate companies has increased from 217 to 445, with sales increasing by 400%. Confetti is reversing the impact of seasonality and the future looks even healthier. The organisation is predicted to grow stronger in the coming months with further use of e-commerce working from an increasing base.

Answer all questions.

1 Assess the objectives set by Confetti as it experiences rapid growth. *(5 marks)*

2 Using the case material, assess the concept of a unique selling point. *(4 marks)*

3 Evaluate the importance of each of the aspects of the marketing mix in achieving the objectives set by Confetti. *(8 marks)*

4 Develop and justify an alternative promotion strategy that Confetti could use to achieve the objectives set. *(8 marks)*

5 Explain why it is important to 'cost' when planning marketing strategies. *(4 marks)*

(29 marks)

Group task

Imagine that you have just established a business providing alternative lunches for the staff and students in your school or college. As a group, make a list of the possible marketing objectives that you might set. Do all these objectives stem from a desire to make a large profit?

In small groups, present a marketing strategy based on the objectives that you set.

Discuss how the objectives and the strategy are likely to differ from those set by a well-known company such as Pret a Manger.

CHAPTER 22

Market segmentation, market share and market growth

All firms are aware of what they are selling. The most successful businesses are even more aware of their customers. This chapter considers the way firms are able to target their customers by understanding market segmentation. It shows how types of segmentation can assist the development of marketing strategies such as niche marketing and product differentiation. It also considers the importance of understanding the concepts of market share and market growth.

Market segmentation

Market segmentation involves trying to identify specific groups from within a larger market, which can be targeted with promotion campaigns in a different way from other groups, or from the market as a whole. Segmentation allows a firm to offer its products in a specific version that differentiates it from other versions of the same product. A specific version can also satisfy demand in a niche market, as will be shown below.

Market research (see Chapter 23) attempts to gather a range of information about the market, the customers, competition and so on. This information can be used to build a picture of individual customers who can then be grouped together into market segments.

Segmentation is important because it allows a firm to target its marketing effort towards those customers who have similar interests. Very few firms are involved in mass-market selling. The need to identify and target is therefore crucial in reducing costs and making the marketing effort more effective. Gaps in the market can be identified and niche markets can be found.

Types of market segmentation

Businesses use a variety of ways of splitting the market, including those considered here.

Geographical

This involves splitting the market according to the areas in which people live. This is quite common, as there are several differences in the way people in

KEY TERM

market segmentation: breaking down a large market into subgroups or sections, that are likely to respond to products in different ways

different parts of the country view products. For example, sales of sterilised milk are significantly higher in the Midlands than in other parts of the country.

Lifestyle

This is where individuals are grouped on the basis of their interests and hobbies, and how these impact on the products they desire. For example, the demand for takeaway meals has increased among certain consumer groups. Consumers are also categorised according to their leisure activities.

Age

This is one of the more obvious methods of market segmentation. Firms often produce a variety of versions of their products, which appeal to specific age groups. One of the fastest-growing brands is Saga. Saga provides products and services for the over-55s, and is a strong player in a number of markets.

Gender

Many products are produced specifically for a particular sex. For some types of product this is obvious, but products available to both genders can be specifically tailored through choice of packaging or individual styling to target a particular sex. For example, perfume is sold to both men and women, but the approach to selling is quite different.

Social class

Social class is identified by categorising individuals according to their occupations. While this can be a good guide, income and products purchased are not always in direct relation. A typical social class listing uses six groups:

- **A** Upper class/upper-middle class — professional, higher managerial (e.g. company directors, lawyers, accountants)
- **B** Middle class — other professional, middle management, senior administrative (e.g. teachers, nurses)
- **C1** Lower-middle class — junior management, skilled non-manual workers (e.g. police, clerical staff)
- **C2** Skilled working class — trained (trade) skilled workers (e.g. technicians, plumbers, electricians)
- **D** Working class — unskilled manual workers, semi-skilled workers (e.g. labourers, farm workers)
- **E** Unskilled/unemployed — those on state benefit (e.g. pensioners, unemployed)

Residence

This is a popular form of segmentation, which attempts to consider potential customers based on the type of housing in which they live. The ACORN approach (A Classification Of Residential Neighbourhoods) allows firms to target those living in flats or apartments in a different way from those living in large, detached houses. While this is similar to geographical segmentation, the focus is on types of housing. It is argued that much can be gained from an understanding of the type of housing that customers live in.

Behaviour

This involves segmentation on the basis of people's spending patterns. Specific groups tend to behave in a certain way on particular days. It is quite common for a local garden store to run a discount day to attract its older customers, who are more likely to frequent the store on that day. Particular offers targeted at that group also feature more prominently on those days.

Summary

Segmentation is vital to firms that need to focus their products and their marketing efforts on a specific group of customers. Consideration of the marketing mix in later chapters will demonstrate the need to target marketing activities closely to the needs of customers. One of the main aims of segmentation is to enhance the development of specific marketing strategies. Some of these will be considered in other chapters, but two are developed here.

Niche marketing

Niche marketing is essentially about targeting a business's marketing efforts to a specific market segment. The alternative to niche marketing is **mass marketing**. In mass marketing, a business attempts to reach the entire market with a single product idea, such as Coca-Cola.

Niche marketing is an option for firms in markets where segmentation allows them to break down a large market into smaller, characteristic groups that can be targeted separately. Niche marketing has the main advantage of there being fewer competitors. Unless another firm has decided to target the same niche, it may be possible to exploit economies of scale in that small market.

The main disadvantage of selling to a niche market is related to size. Smaller markets often have less potential to make a large profit. Another issue could be over-reliance on a single, small market. If this market changes and demand falls, it could be very bad for the business. Another problem is that success in a niche market encourages others to enter it. This can limit the company's success in the future.

Examples of firms currently operating in niche markets are Rolls-Royce in the luxury car market and Equestrian Tourism, which provides equestrian holidays.

KEY TERMS

niche marketing: targeting a clear and identifiable segment of the market

mass marketing: selling into a market containing many products that are similar

KEY TERM

product differentiation: where producers alter specific features of their product to make it seem different from the products of other firms

Product differentiation

Another strategy that firms try to employ is **product differentiation**. This involves firms attempting to encourage consumers to see their products in a different way from other brands in the market. Possibly the best example of this is the perceived difference between Pepsi and Coca-Cola. Some consumers will only drink one of the brands, although many are happy to consume either and are unable to tell the difference.

Some firms try to create tangible differences between products as a means of targeting specific market segments. Some models of car feature in more than one market. A sporty version of the Ford Focus car (Zetec) sits in the same showroom as the luxury (Ghia) and basic (Finesse) versions. In other cases, firms use a variety of promotion strategies to develop a belief among consumers that the products are different. Segmentation is again important in establishing the promotion focus.

The main advantage of product differentiation is the ability to target products, achieve higher sales, and possibly charge a higher price. Branded sportswear firms achieve very high profit margins by developing loyalty among customers who are prepared to pay premiums to continue their affiliation to that product range.

> **e EXAMINER'S VOICE**
>
> Market segmentation is a popular topic with examiners. In a case study, try to establish the market and how, or if, it could be segmented. Look at the nature of a market. How big is it? Has it changed? Whom is the company selling to? Whom could it sell to? The answers to these questions will ensure that you have a greater understanding of the case study.

KEY TERM

market share: the proportion of total market sales accounted for by an individual firm

Market share

Market share is the proportion or percentage of the total market that a particular firm has managed to achieve. The total market can be measured in two ways:
- by sales value — using sales revenue
- by sales volume — using the number of actual units sold

The two methods can give quite different results and it is important to compare like with like. For example, if you compare sales of Ford Fiestas with sales of Lotus Elises, there would be quite a difference depending on which of the two calculations you used.

The formula for calculating market share is:

$$\text{market share} = \frac{\text{sales value (or volume) of one product line or brand}}{\text{total sales value (or volume) in the whole market}} \times 100$$

For example, we can calculate the market share of restaurant A in the total number of Chinese takeaways sold in the town each week as follows:

sold by restaurant A　　　　　　 = 450
total sold in the town (per week) = 4,500

market share　　　　　 $= \dfrac{450}{4,500} \times 100 = 10\%$

The 10% market share may be quite acceptable, but it would serve as a target to improve on in the future.

The calculation of market share allows a firm to assess its performance in a variety of markets. It is a good way of measuring success because it compares the performance of the business directly with that of all its competitors. The greater its market share, the greater the power that a firm may have in the market.

One factor to consider is the way that the size of the overall market is calculated. The definition of a market is crucial to the calculation. Market share is only useful if the overall market can be determined and measured. It is often more useful to measure one small part of a greater market and then calculate share based on that. For example, it is more useful to the product manager for the Renault Clio to calculate the share of the Clio in the small car market than its share in the market for all cars sold. In the restaurant calculation above, if the total market had been defined as all takeaway meals rather than Chinese takeaways, the final result might have been very small and of little use for analysis.

ⓔ EXAMINER'S VOICE

Be careful when dealing with market share calculations. Ensure that you have determined the specific market and the correct figures. The percentage calculation tends to confuse many candidates. Practice makes perfect!

Market growth

Although it is useful to have an appreciation of market share, it must also be remembered that an increase in the overall market size — **market growth** — can have a dramatic impact on product success.

Firms try hard to develop products that are in a growing market, but the changing size of a market is largely beyond the direct control of an individual firm. It must try to react to or even pre-empt situations when market growth might occur. A number of factors might influence growth in the market:

KEY TERM

market growth: an increase in sales in the total market

- **The nature of the product.** Some products experience higher growth at certain stages of their life cycle than others. The market for mobile phones has grown, then slowed down, then grown again.
- **Changes in tastes and fashions.** These clearly affect market growth in the clothing industry, but other products also go in and out of fashion. For example, the market for home improvements has changed over time.
- **Standard of living.** The market for certain goods increases in line with increases in the overall wealth of the nation. Economic growth and upturns in the trade cycle have similar impacts (see Chapter 9).
- **Social and demographic changes.** Increases in sales in the leisure industry stem from lifestyle changes. The market for electrical products (e.g. high-definition televisions) will increase in line with greater leisure time.

Changes in market growth can be calculated by measuring the size of a market in one time period and comparing it with the same market in a different time period. For example:

sales in the total market (2005) = 2,000,000 units
sales in the same market (2006) = 2,200,000 units

The market has increased in size by 200,000 units.

$$\text{market growth} = \frac{200,000}{2,000,000} \times 100 = 10\%$$

Comparing market share and market growth

Many firms consider it useful to make comparisons between changes in market share and changes in the overall size of the market. The Boston matrix (see Chapter 25) considers changing marketing strategy in terms of market share and market growth.

One key issue is the difficulty of trying to measure both market share and the size of the market. Gathering accurate data can be very tricky, and data are more easily collated in some markets than others. Market conditions also change over time and these changing variables can make comparisons difficult. Classifying specific markets can be a particular problem. Comparing like with like when it comes to measuring a small subsection of a large market is very difficult.

Further sources
www.betterproductdesign.net/guide
www.marketsegmentation.co.uk
www.academyofmarketing.info

Overall, a greater understanding of market share and market growth will be of some use to firms in a variety of different markets. Success in business is often related to the ability of the organisation to predict accurately. Greater knowledge of the market could make all the difference.

YOUR TURN

Questions

1 Giving an example, define the term 'market segment'. *(3 marks)*

2 Analyse the advantages for organisations such as Sony in identifying and targeting specific market segments. *(6 marks)*

3 Explain the difference between niche marketing and mass marketing. *(4 marks)*

4 Calculate the market share of a firm that has sold 30,000 units out of a total market of 900,000 units. *(2 marks)*

5 If total sales in that market increase to 1,080,000 units, calculate the percentage increase in the size of the market. *(3 marks)*

6 Evaluate the importance to Tesco of increasing market share. *(8 marks)*

(26 marks)

Case study

The market for soft drinks

Coca-Cola and PepsiCo saw their shares of the US soft drinks market decline in 2004, in a report that ranks the top ten US makers of carbonated soft drinks (CSD). Coca-Cola, the industry leader, saw its market share drop by 0.9% to 43.1%. PepsiCo (no. 2) saw a drop of 0.1% to 31.7%. Coca-Cola's case volume dipped 1% to 4.4 billion, while PepsiCo had 3.2 billion cases with a gain of 0.4%, according to annual rankings by Beverage Digest/Maxwell, a New York-based data service that tracks soft drinks sales. As for individual brands, Coke had a 17.9% market share, down 0.7%. Pepsi ranked no. 2 with an 11.5% market share and a 0.4% dip. Cadbury Schweppes and Cott, the leading producer of private-label CSDs, increased their shares of the $65.9 billion market. Cadbury Schweppes is the no. 4 CSD producer, followed by Cott, National Beverage, Big Red, Red Bull, Hansen Natural, Monarch and Rockstar. The overall industry grew 1% in 2004.

Together, the top three companies — Coca-Cola, PepsiCo and Cadbury Schweppes — accounted for about 90% of industry volume, the report said. There were some changes in the top ten brands in 2004. Diet Dr Pepper re-entered the rankings at no. 9. Sprite dropped down one place to no. 6, Diet Pepsi moved ahead of Sprite into the no. 5 spot. And for the first time since the tracking began in 1985, 7UP dropped out of the top ten brands. Coke Classic holds the no. 1 spot with 17.9% market share, followed by Pepsi at 11.5%. Both saw slight dips in market share of 0.7% and 0.4% respectively. Sales volumes for both were also down — by 3% for Coke and 2.5% for Pepsi. Diet Coke holds the no. 3 position, followed by Mountain Dew (Pepsi), Diet Pepsi, Sprite (Coke), Dr Pepper (Cadbury), CF Diet Coke, Diet Dr Pepper and Sierra Mist (Pepsi).

In 2004, the retail value of the soft drinks industry overall grew by 3.25% to $65.9 billion, up from $63.8 billion in 2003, as prices increased faster than volume.

Source: adapted from **www.mind-advertising.com**

Answer all questions.

1   According to the case material, 'the overall industry grew 1% in 2004' and 'the retail value...grew by 3.25%'. Explain this difference.   *(4 marks)*

2   Calculate the retail sales of Coke Classic in 2004.   *(3 marks)*

3   Using examples from the case, explain how the drinks manufacturers try to use product differentiation.   *(5 marks)*

4   Analyse the advantages that Pepsi and Coca-Cola have in operating in a mass market.   *(6 marks)*

5   Evaluate the importance of market share and market growth to either Pepsi or Coca-Cola.   *(8 marks)*

   (26 marks)

Group task

Look at the market for cars. Each group should take one of the following market segments and develop a marketing strategy for it:

- small cars (e.g. Renault Clio, Ford Fiesta, Nissan Micra)
- medium family cars (e.g. Peugeot 307, Citroën Picasso, Renault Scenic)
- larger family cars (e.g. Ford Mondeo, Peugeot 407, Citroën C4)
- luxury cars (e.g. BMW 5 series, Mercedes C class)

List other categories or segments that car producers could use to segment the market, such as by gender (the Peugeot 206 is generally purchased more by female customers than by males).

CHAPTER 23

Market research

This chapter considers aspects of market research, focusing on sources and methods of data collection. The distinction is made between quantitative and qualitative data. A further distinction is made between field and desk research and between primary and secondary data. How to determine the most effective and appropriate methods of market research is also considered.

KEY TERM

market research: gathering information to help understand the market in which firms operate

What is market research and why is it done?

Market research is a collective term to describe different ways of gathering information. Popular theory suggests that there are four reasons why market research might be carried out.

To describe the market
This involves:
- exploring trends
- comparing market performance
- establishing market share
- finding out who the customers are

To explain the market
Firms might want to know:
- why market share has fallen
- whether a price reduction worked
- whether customers prefer their products or those of the competition
- how good a promotion campaign was

To predict changes in the market
It might be useful to find out:
- what customers will do if the company raises prices
- the effect of introducing a new model on existing sales
- the likely impact of increased competition
- the possible future impact on market share

To explore future customer reaction
A firm might use market research to:
- explore customers' reaction to new ideas
- find the target price
- establish the most appropriate retail outlets
- discover the best methods of promoting a new product

Put simply, the process of gathering information aims to achieve a more effective approach to decision making.

EXAMINER'S VOICE

When you suggest ideas about market research, you must always consider the resources that the firm has available. What you suggest must be appropriate to that business in that situation at that time.

Types of information

Information can be categorised in two different ways, according to whether it is:

- quantitative or qualitative data
- primary data gathered by field research or secondary data gathered by desk research

Quantitative and qualitative data

Quantitative data

Quantitative data are collected in such a way as to allow numerical analysis of the results. The quantitative approach works best when there are a lot of data and statistical conclusions need to be drawn. It is useful when trying to describe the market — for example, '48% of our customers are male'. The sample size used in the research (see Chapter 24) can have a dramatic impact on the use of quantitative data, but such information is good when considering trends, however small the sample size. The use of numerical data has the disadvantage that it is not possible to assess genuine opinion because it concentrates on numbers, not reasons. To achieve this, it is usually necessary to gather qualitative data.

Qualitative data

Qualitative data tend to be gathered from a smaller number of people using a variety of methods. The focus is more on opinions and the information gathered is often difficult to quantify. There is a tendency to ask more open-ended questions, which allow the respondent to offer a variety of answers. The main advantage of qualitative data for a business is that it is possible to study the information obtained and to use it to explain customer behaviour. This can enhance decision making.

Primary and secondary data

Field research to gather primary data

Field research is the gathering of **primary data** using a variety of methods. Primary data are obtained specifically for the purpose of analysis by a particular firm. Therefore, the data will have specific significance to this firm.

There are several methods of gathering primary data. These include the following:

- **Observation.** This is exactly as it seems: observing customer behaviour, watching shoppers in action, monitoring how long people spend doing certain things as they consider spending their money, and so on. Observation can be time consuming, but it can generate very specific and useful information about the behaviour of particular groups.
- **Experimentation.** This involves trialling ideas and testing out products and services in certain areas or with particular groups. Test marketing and product trialling can be very effective at establishing whether a full-scale

KEY TERMS

quantitative data: information gathered that can be analysed in a numerical way

qualitative data: information containing a wide variety of types of responses

KEY TERMS

field research: gathering original data for a specific purpose

primary data: data gathered by field research

campaign would be successful. The information gathered from a test or experimental idea can be invaluable.

- **Interviews.** This is a popular approach used by many organisations to focus on a small number of individuals who are able to give detailed and precise information about their views on all aspects of a product or service. A good interviewer will allow respondents to talk at length without constricting them with a formal set of questions or a script that must be followed.
- **Surveys.** The use of questionnaires to ask a series of pre-set questions to a large group of people can be an effective way to gather a lot of quantitative data. The traditional survey is a good method of standardising responses into groups, which allows for effective analysis of the data. Survey information can be gathered in a number of ways, such as via the post, on the telephone or face-to-face. Each method has advantages and disadvantages, and is often combined with some sort of selling or promotional activity.

Whichever method of primary data collection is used, it is important to establish the objectives of the research before decisions about how to collect the data are finalised. The nature of the research will help to determine the chosen method. Face-to-face surveys allow the interviewer to explain questions fully and to deal with any issues that a respondent might have. Telephone or postal surveys are less good in this respect, but are more useful for obtaining answers to direct questions. Issues of cost and analysis time are further considerations.

Desk research to gather secondary data

Desk research involves the manipulation of **secondary data**, which have been gathered for some other purpose. The information may be obtained from a variety of sources both inside and outside the organisation.

Internal data

Internal data include the following:

- **Sales figures.** These provide accurate results from previous time periods. Past trends and results can be monitored and used to establish possible patterns of behaviour.
- **Previous survey results.** The use of past surveys will depend on how long ago the surveys were carried out. There may be some relevance in using survey data from a previous batch of market research.
- **Customer data.** Firms can gather large quantities of general data about their customers using a variety of methods. For example, retail organisations use loyalty cards, which can monitor the spending patterns of customers at particular times of the day, on certain days of the week and so on.

External data

Sources of **external data** include the following:

- **Government statistics.** The government collects data from a variety of

KEY TERMS

desk research: gathering information that has been collected for some other purpose

secondary data: data gathered by desk research

internal data: information gathered inside the organisation

external data: information gathered outside the organisation

sources for many different purposes. These include useful data about changes in population, local and national trends, and different industries.

- **Competitors.** Firms can gain useful information by looking at the websites of their competitors, accessing their published accounts, getting hold of their sales brochures and so on.
- **Market research organisations.** Several firms exist to provide market research data covering a wide spectrum of information. Organisations such as Mintel continually gather data, which they then sell to firms trying to increase their understanding of the markets in which they operate.
- **The internet.** This has become a popular way for small firms, in particular, to find out issues that may be relevant to them.
- **Trade publications.** These can provide a wealth of relevant information related to specific industries.
- **Newspapers and magazines.** Most quality newspapers carry business pages and supplements that often feature particular industries.
- **Libraries.** Libraries run by the local authority and major university libraries can be useful sources of general data.

What is the most effective method of market research?

The advantages and disadvantages of primary and secondary data are set out in Table 23.1.

Table 23.1 Advantages and disadvantages of primary and secondary data

	Primary data	Secondary data
Advantages	■ Relevant ■ Up-to-date ■ Specific information	■ Information already available ■ Can be cheaper to collect
Disadvantages	■ Can be expensive to collect ■ Can be time consuming	■ Could be out-dated ■ Available to everyone ■ Not specific

The decision to use a particular method of gathering data should relate to the objectives of the research and the reason for needing the data. Market research does not guarantee success. There is no certainty that the information gathered will be accurate. Research information may be biased due to a poor method being used. It is also not possible to rely on those being interviewed giving honest or accurate answers all the time. However careful a firm might be in ensuring that the research is carried out in an effective way, if people fail to give honest responses, the value of the research can be brought into question.

The effectiveness of market research is considered further in Chapter 24.

Further sources

www.marketresearchontheweb.com   www.taforum.org   www.marketresearch.com

YOUR TURN

Questions   Time allowed: 30 minutes

1   Define the terms 'primary data' and 'field research', and distinguish between them.   *(5 marks)*

2   Give **three** examples of secondary data that a firm wanting to assess demand for fizzy drinks might collect.   *(3 marks)*

3   Give **three** reasons why a firm might use field research rather than desk research.   *(3 marks)*

4   Explain why a postal survey may be more effective than a telephone survey.   *(4 marks)*

5   Explain why a firm might wish to use observation as a means of collecting data.   *(4 marks)*

6   Discuss the most appropriate ways of gathering data for a firm that needs to research the local market for beauty salons.   *(9 marks)*

(28 marks)

Case study   Time allowed: 30 minutes

French Connection

Last week's 69% plunge in pre-tax profits at French Connection was more than just a symptom of the wider retail slump. The company also posted a 9% fall in UK like-for-like sales a day after discount retailer Primark reported a 12% sales increase. Sales at Next fell too, but only by 3%. The crisis at French Connection is laid bare for all to see.

After the advertising industry's doyen, Trevor Beattie, created the fcuk brand in 1997, punters flocked to buy the company's goods. Two years later, profits had risen by 32% and fcuk expanded into everything from alcoholic drinks (fcuk spirit) to men and women's toiletries.

The brand thrived on stoking controversy. But sex does not sell like it used to. 'The fcuk brand was a brilliant idea,' says Lorna Hall, features editor of fashion industry magazine *Drapers*. 'But they have hung on to it too long, to the point where it is not fashionable any more.'

It was a *Drapers* straw poll in 2004 that first showed the fcuk rot had set in. The survey of French Connection's all-important wholesalers found that many thought fcuk to be 'tired' and 'tacky', with one commenting that it was 'time to move on'.

Soon afterwards, French Connection distanced itself from the fcuk name, without abolishing the brand. Plans for lower-key branding emerged in July 2004, and the following month the fcuk moniker was dropped from a £3 million advertising campaign.

Hall likens French Connection's problem to that of Burberry, whose unwanted 'Check and Chav' moniker stuck long after it abandoned check clothing. 'French Connection will still have to fight that kind of perception even though it has moved away from fcuk,' she says. French Connection head of PR, Lorna Perrin, says: 'Fcuk is interchangeable with French Connection as the company's name and so will continue to exist and be used. Branding on the recent autumn/winter collections has been significantly reduced and used in a softer manner — the logo is now used to offer more subtle branding. Fashions have changed and we have moved on, too.'

Perrin is tight-lipped about future campaign plans. But wholesalers and the media are all eager to know where French Connection will go next.

While the French Connection/fcuk brand accounts for around 85% of the company's global turnover, the group also owns designer label Nicole Farhi, mail-order women's fashion range TOAST and 'fashion basics' range Great Plains.

The trouble is that, for many, French Connection does not stand out as a premium clothing company. 'I think French Connection's problem is simply down to prices,' says Iroquois head of fashion, Jo Reynolds. 'For many people, shopping is a pastime. They are not looking for an investment when they want a quick purchase. Competition on the high street is fierce from shops such as Zara, River Island, New Look and H&M, which have increased their level of quality while retaining competitive price points.'

Source: adapted from **www.fashionunited.co.uk** and **www.smh.com.au**

Answer all questions.

1 To what extent do you feel that French Connection carried out market research in the development of the fcuk brand? *(6 marks)*

2 Why do you think that French Connection relied heavily on the research carried out by *Drapers*? *(6 marks)*

3 Analyse the possible use of focus groups in gathering information for French Connection. *(6 marks)*

4 Evaluate the possible uses of field research to a firm in a competitive market, such as French Connection. *(9 marks)*

(27 marks)

Group task

Time allowed: 30 minutes

In groups, prepare a market research plan for an individual looking to open a new fish and chip shop in your local town or village. In putting together your plan, have different groups working on the following:

- primary data
- secondary data
- quantitative data
- qualitative data

Present these to the other groups and carefully monitor the overlap between the required data.

In developing the overall plan, try to consider factors such as timescale and cost.

CHAPTER 24

Sampling

Chapter 23 explained that primary research involves the gathering of data. The decision about whom to ask and how many people to ask is a vital component in the success of the research.

Sampling is a process that enables an organisation carrying out market research to gather information from a small, but still representative, section of the targeted population. This chapter looks at a variety of sampling methods.

Organisations spend large sums of money on the basis of the research carried out, so it is a good idea to try to ask the right people. The assessment of whether you are asking the right people is what sampling is largely concerned with.

KEY TERM

sampling: asking a smaller, representative group in the hope of finding out the opinions of a larger group

Why do firms sample?

The simple answer to this question is *cost*. Market research can be very expensive, and without the option of effective sampling, the cost would be multiplied still further.

Time is another important consideration. When an organisation carries out market research, it does so because it needs information. It often needs this information quickly, so it needs to try to minimise the time between gathering the information and processing it.

Sampling reduces the cost of the research and the time spent processing the data. The real skill of sampling is ensuring that the people asked are representative of other people's views. Opinion polling of voting intentions at the time of national elections tends to rely on a sample size of less than 2,000 people. These polls are usually accurate to within 2–3%. Skilled polling organisations are expert at ensuring that any research is carried out effectively.

> **EXAMINER'S VOICE**
>
> When answering questions about sampling and sampling methods, there is a tendency for students to extend their answer to include wider aspects of market research. This often wastes time and leads to answers losing their focus.

Sampling methods

There are many sampling methods that organisations will use from time to time. The six methods discussed here are not an exhaustive list, but they include the majority of approaches that organisations tend to use.

CHAPTER 24 Sampling

KEY TERMS

random sampling: where everyone in the population has an equal chance of being included in the survey

population: the total number of people who could be included in a particular survey

quota sampling: where the number and characteristics of people surveyed are deliberately matched to the actual population

Random sampling

Random sampling involves selecting people in such a way that everyone in the total population has an equal chance of being selected.

It is important at this stage to define the idea of a **population**. A population may not be everyone in a particular country or even everyone on the planet. In many cases, when you consider whom you may wish to ask, there are clear boundaries. For example, if you are keen to gain the views of the workforce in a particular organisation, the total population is simply the entire workforce. A random sample would involve ensuring that each worker had an equal chance of being involved in the research. To achieve this, it would be necessary to plan very carefully. Drawing lots or using random numbers is possible, but to be genuinely random, the equal chance criterion must be applied. A common approach involves using every nth person. Even this method may not be random, given that the order in which the data are presented influences the selection.

Where the population is larger, the chances of using a random sample are smaller. Many organisations that carry out research — and, indeed, many students doing coursework involving sampling — will argue that their sample is random. The reality is that the research is more likely to be based on a convenience sample (see p. 187).

Quota sampling

Quota sampling attempts to select the individuals in the survey in relation to the characteristics of the overall market or population.

For example, in trying to consider the views of those at a school concerning the school catering, it may be useful to break the students down into different sections, such as those in years 7 and 8, those in years 9, 10 and 11, and those in the sixth form. Staff views are also considered important. Table 24.1 represents such a school and the final column shows the number that would need to be included in each group to match the population of the school to those who need to be surveyed.

Table 24.1 Quota sampling for a school

	Number in each group	Percentage of the total population	Number of each group in a sample of 50
Years 7 and 8	300	30	15
Years 9, 10 and 11	400	40	20
Sixth form	200	20	10
Teaching staff	60	6	3
Non-teaching staff	40	4	2
Total	**1,000**	**100**	**50**

Attention to detail is crucial. When the survey is carried out, the important consideration is to ensure that all categories are asked in the exact proportions

shown — for example, if three teachers have already been included, no more should be asked. You must, at the same time, ensure that all 20 in the years 9/10/11 category are included. More importantly, it does not matter what other characteristics these 20 may have — any 20 respondents can be included as long as they are from years 9, 10 or 11.

Stratified sampling

This is used when there is a need to survey only a specific group of people with specific characteristics related to a specific product or service. For example, research about a product sold exclusively to men over the age of 50 should only really question that age group and gender. Within the selected group, it may then be possible to use either a random or quota sampling technique to determine the actual respondents. This approach is often then considered to be either stratified random sampling or stratified quota sampling.

Cluster sampling

This is used when it is difficult to gather information on the entire population and where it is known that the required information could be gathered from one section or group in the hope that this smaller group is representative of the whole population. In a general election, political commentators are always striving to find the electoral constituency that is representative of the country as a whole. This is a cluster approach. From the chosen cluster, a further sampling technique (e.g. random sampling) could then be used.

Systematic sampling

This is the attempt to apply some form of scientific or formulaic approach to the selection of respondents, such as choosing every hundredth person in a list. How the list is drawn up will determine how valid this method is.

Convenience sampling

This is probably the most frequently used method of choosing individuals to be involved in data collection. Organisations will often try to use a more 'scientific' approach and will even make this a stated aim of the research. The reality is that corners are often cut and, in a bid to save time and money, elements of convenience sampling are used. The approach generally involves the interviewer selecting from a group of people who might vaguely fit the desired type of respondent, but actually asking people to be involved who are ready to do so quickly and cheaply. An example might be research done in a busy shopping street. You may have carried out research for a GCSE assignment. There were probably strong elements of convenience in the approach you adopted (e.g. asking friends).

Which sampling method should be chosen?

Each method of sampling has advantages and disadvantages. The actual choice probably depends most on the need for accuracy, the time available and the research budget. No method has any guarantee that the 'right' people will be chosen and that those chosen will therefore fully represent the actual

KEY TERMS

stratified sampling: where the population is divided into smaller groups, which are the ones most likely to be interested in the product being researched

cluster sampling: where a particular group is included, hopefully reflecting the views of the whole population, when information about the population is incomplete

systematic sampling: where a set formula is used (e.g. every tenth person) to select the people in the research

convenience sampling: where any non-scientific method is used to help the speed of response and to lower the cost

population. Anyone carrying out research must consider carefully the use to which the information will be put and how important the decisions that will then be taken are.

> **e** EXAMINER'S VOICE
>
> Examination questions on sampling are quite rare. Much of the knowledge is implied in other topics, and the issue of sampling should be included when considering market research as a whole. If you are asked about which sampling method a particular firm might use, it is important to focus on the need for and importance of the information being gathered. Remember the different methods, but also be aware of what often happens in reality. Very specific conditions must be in place for a firm genuinely to use either random or quota sampling.

Sample size

Along with any decision about whom to ask and how best to ask them is the crucial consideration of how many people to involve in the actual survey. It is generally true that the larger the **sample size**, the more likely it is to be representative of the whole population and therefore the more accurate the sampling should be. The more people who are asked, the less likely it is that extreme and/or unrepresentative views will be included in the results.

What is the ideal sample size?

The ideal sample size depends on a variety of issues. Carrying out research is expensive and each response gathered has a cost in terms of interview time and in terms of result analysis time. Each additional response increases the time needed to complete the overall research. This is a particular issue if it is necessary to process the information quickly.

Clearly the size of the sample should relate closely to the size of the specific population. Remind yourself of what is meant by 'population' in this context. If you are interested in the views of the workforce in a particular department of 20, it may be appropriate to interview everyone. A sample of 10 of those may or may not reveal the responses you need. A sample size of 1,000 in a large population will tend to be enough to reduce the level of biased responses. You may wish to break down these 1,000 responses into other identifiable groups. The size of these groups should also be large enough to analyse effectively.

The aim in assessing the ideal sample size is to reduce the potential for bias in the results. A researcher must be confident that all has been done to eliminate as much bias as possible.

> **KEY** TERM
>
> **sample size:** the number chosen to be included in the research

Further sources

www.nao.org.uk/publications/samplingguide.pdf   www.nationalarchives.gov.uk/recordsmanagement

www.learnmarketing.net

YOUR TURN

Questions

Time allowed: 25 minutes

1 Define the term 'sampling'. *(3 marks)*

2 Using an example, define the differences between quota and stratified sampling. *(4 marks)*

3 Explain why a quota sample is likely to be more costly than a convenience sample. *(4 marks)*

4 Explain why a sample intended to be random is often systematic or convenience. *(4 marks)*

5 Discuss the optimum size of a survey when finding out:
  a views on a possible new flavour of crisps
  b opinions of the teaching staff in your school *(8 marks)*

(23 marks)

Case study

Time allowed: 35 minutes

Local authority services

In 2004, a local authority in the north of England used a market research organisation to carry out its annual survey of citizens in the local area. The survey was conducted to determine views on services run by the local authority. The research organisation carried out the survey in two distinct ways.

First, a telephone survey of 600 households took place. The first question tried to determine whether there was an adequate number of households with children. A key objective of the survey was to obtain views on education provision and it was felt necessary to include respondents who had direct and recent experience. To ensure a degree of randomness in relation to the person actually spoken to, it was decided to ask the adult in the household who had had the most recent birthday.

The second aspect of the survey was a postal questionnaire. This contained 47 questions. A total of 1,500 surveys were mailed, 23 were returned for non-delivery and a further 12 were sent back with notes saying that the addressee had moved. Therefore, 1,465 questionnaires were actually delivered. After the mailing, 197 completed questionnaires were returned (response rate: 13.4%).

Sampling methodology was under scrutiny and the local authority was concerned about the un-representative nature of the research.

Answer all questions.

1 To what extent is the telephone survey likely to produce the results that the local authority needs? *(8 marks)*

2 Analyse whether the low response rate to the postal questionnaire increases the likelihood that the results are biased. *(8 marks)*

3 Would it have helped the survey results if the numbers included in the telephone survey and/or the postal questionnaire had been increased? *(5 marks)*

4 With a full discussion of sampling methodology, suggest a better way of finding out the required information. *(9 marks)*

(30 marks)

Case study 2

Time allowed: 35 minutes

Young Enterprise

A local school Young Enterprise company decided to carry out some research into whether it would be better to produce letter-headed notepaper or a calendar of school sports teams.

Anna Salman, the marketing director, felt that it would be a good idea to provide high-quality notepaper. She thought that research among the teaching staff, fellow pupils and their parents would help to determine whether there would be enough demand.

She suggested getting a pupil and staff list from the school office. Selecting every tenth person from the list in each case would help to predict overall demand.

Robert Timms, however, thought that the calendar would work better. He realised that it was likely to have less overall demand, but he felt it would be much easier to target sales to interested customers. His research idea was only to survey the players from the various teams who would actually feature in the team photographs.

Anna and Robert both decided to proceed with their research and agreed to present their findings at the next Young Enterprise meeting in 2 weeks' time.

Answer all questions.

1 What type of sampling method do you think that (a) Anna and (b) Robert might actually be using? Explain why. *(6 marks)*

2 In the survey carried out by Anna, using every tenth person will give her 90 responses. Discuss whether you feel this is enough, about right or too many. *(8 marks)*

3 Evaluate which approach to sampling is likely to be more representative of the 'population'. *(8 marks)*

4 Discuss the other factors that might be considered in judging the effectiveness of the sampling method selected. *(8 marks)*

(30 marks)

Group task

Divide into groups of four. Conduct a debate, with each member of the group arguing in favour of either random, quota, stratified or convenience sampling as the preferred method for a school wanting to find out the views of people using:

- the dining hall for lunch
- the tuck shop
- the sports hall

Agree on the best method. What do you notice about the method in each case?

CHAPTER 25

Products

The term 'product' can be used by firms and others to represent both a physical product and a service. A good product is one that customers are interested in. A product-orientated firm will make a product in the hope that it can be sold. A market-orientated firm will respond to the wishes of consumers. In each case, it is important to consider what characteristics of a product or service are likely to be successful. This chapter also looks at marketing models. These models help to analyse the market position of the firm and to enhance future marketing strategies.

Product is only one aspect of the marketing mix, but many would argue that it is the most important factor. No one will buy what he or she does not want. It requires really good marketing to be able to sell a product that has no obvious demand. Products that have great demand for a short period of time are often heavily promoted, with producers really convincing customers that they 'need' the product. Such 'must have' products have included bottled water, ice cubes and pro-biotic yoghurt.

What makes a good product?

A number of factors must come together to guarantee the success of a product. Some organisations use a process of **value analysis**, which considers product success based on three criteria:

- *function* — can the product do what it is meant to do?
- *aesthetics* — does it look as the consumer would want it to?
- *economic production* — can it be produced and sold at a profit?

Function

When consumers buy a product, there is an expectation that the product will satisfy some aspect of demand. Function relates to the actual achievement of that satisfaction in terms of the expectations of the consumer. For example, if you purchase a television set, you hope that it will receive television pictures. A 'good' product will do exactly as it claims it will, or come as close to the expectations of the consumer as possible. When a consumer buys an expensive television set, he/she expects it to do more than an average-price one: to offer more in the way of functions (e.g. wide screen, plasma screen, surround sound). The consumer's level of expectation tends to rise with the price.

Aesthetics

This refers to the 'look' of the product (e.g. shape, colour, design, style or size). As with function, the consumer has certain expectations about how a product should look. This expectation is based on current trends and fashions.

> **KEY TERM**
>
> **value analysis:** a process that firms carry out to assess the attributes of their product in relation to what is likely to be successful

Producers are often very good at creating a fashion and many consumers are keen to keep up with the current trend. Continuing with the example of television sets, they have changed dramatically in appearance over many years. Consider also the shape and size of mobile phones.

Economic production

Most organisations desire profit. A good product will generate a profit for its producers. There seems little point in producing a product that customers desire, that looks good, that has all the functions that consumers want and more, but that fails to provide a return for the producer.

Using value analysis

Many firms use the value analysis framework to assess their product range and to ensure that they are providing good products where possible. A firm manufacturing washing machines, for example, will be keen to assess its products by considering the colours, functions, shapes and specifications of machines in its range.

Marketing models

Two marketing models in common usage are the product life cycle and the product portfolio.

Product life cycle

There is a generally accepted view that all products have a finite life in the marketplace. But comparisons in the chocolate market show some variation: Kit Kat is still fully available and has been near the top of the chocolate chart since its launch in 1935; the Aztec bar was launched to coincide with the 1970 football World Cup, but was withdrawn in the late 1980s; and more recently, Willy Wonka chocolate bars were launched to coincide with the blockbuster film. Are all these products really following a similar path?

The theory of the **product life cycle** assumes that all products follow a similar set of characteristics in relation to their pattern of sales. This does not suggest that all products sell the same, but that they all go through a series of stages in their life, as shown in Figure 25.1.

Stage 1: Introduction
During the introduction phase, the product is initially presented to the marketplace, having been thoroughly researched and developed. Sales are often slow at first, with the firm needing to promote the product heavily to create awareness and develop demand.

Stage 2: Growth
The growth phase is where sales really take off, following additional promotion pushes from the firm. This is the 'make or break' period for the firm and a high proportion of products fail to make it to this point. Moving the product

KEY TERM

product life cycle: a marketing model that assesses the pattern of sales over time, in which four stages represent different aspects of the product's life

beyond this point is crucial to having a long-term, successful product.

Stage 3: Maturity

Maturity is the phase that all producers strive to reach with their products. During maturity, profits tend to be maximised and the level of promotion activity can usually be reduced. The Kit Kat chocolate bar has been in the maturity stage of its life cycle for many years. Sales may vary from the smooth curve depicted in Figure 25.1, but the general trend is one of fairly steady and constant sales over an increasing period of time.

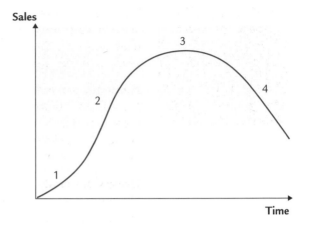

Stage 4: Decline

This point is reached as sales drop. Firms often determine when they want a product to decline, intending to replace it with a newer version. In other cases, the product simply loses favour with the public and there becomes little economic reason to keep it on sale.

Figure 25.1
The product life cycle

The classic shape of the product life cycle tends to fit in with most products. Some products have very short lives even though they still follow the four stages. Other products, such as Mars Bars, have been around for many years with no sign of reaching the decline stage.

Uses of the product life cycle

The main reason why any organisation would consider the product life cycle is to enable it to assess the nature of its marketing requirements. Organisations need to consider the marketing strategy required for each of their products and this will change depending on how long that product has been in the marketplace.

All firms should monitor sales, since a greater understanding of the pattern of sales allows firms to assess where in the product life cycle an item is, and therefore what strategy is appropriate for each part of the marketing mix. This is shown in Table 25.1.

The maturity stage remains crucial and many firms try to extend this phase to enhance profitability. The use of **extension strategies** in the maturity phase is common. These include special offers and developing new uses for the product.

The product life cycle is only useful if the business uses it to assess when changes need to be made to the products in its range. Decisions about when to replace a product can be assisted by considering the pattern of sales over time.

KEY TERM

extension strategies: methods used to extend the maturity phase of the product life cycle

Stage	Product	Price	Promotion	Place
1 Introduction	Fine tuning of the product requirements	Assessing price: possible skimming or penetration strategy	Creating awareness	Establishing a position in the marketplace
2 Growth	Slight improvements to the product	Depending on previous strategy, establishing the 'normal' price	Real push on advertising; consumers must be convinced	Widening the availability of the product
3 Maturity	Consolidation; the firm should now know why the product sells and should try to find new uses for it	Possible special offers to lengthen this stage	Regular, 'reminder' promotions to keep the product in the public eye	Continuing to look for enhanced ways of making the product available
4 Decline	Little change; allow the product to die at minimal cost	Possible price reductions to dispose of old stock	Rapid reduction in promotion activities; special deals to 'kill off' the product	Allowing the product to 'die'

Table 25.1 Implications of the product life cycle for marketing

KEY TERMS

product portfolio analysis: a way of examining the existing products of a firm

Boston matrix: a marketing model that assesses individual products in terms of their market share compared with the growth in the market in which they operate

Product portfolio analysis

Product portfolio analysis allows a firm to assess the current position of its products. There are many methods of carrying out product portfolio analysis. In the simplest method, a business lists its products together with their good and bad points.

The most famous form of product portfolio analysis was developed by a firm of marketing consultants called the Boston Consulting Group. They called their method of analysis the **Boston matrix**.

The matrix is a comparison between the market share of a particular product and the state of the overall market measured in terms of growth. Most students tend to remember the matrix because of the labels given to particular parts of the grid, as shown in Figure 25.2.

In the model, a product is placed into one of the boxes to allow the firm to analyse its position in relation to other products in the same market. The actual values of market share and market growth are often difficult to quantify, and it is important to bear in mind the characteristics of particular markets. For example, the market for chocolate bars, which contains a large number of individual brands, would need to be analysed in a different way from the market for cola fizzy drinks, where Pepsi and Coca-Cola have over 95% of the market.

Figure 25.2 The Boston matrix

	High market share	Low market share
High market growth	RISING STAR	PROBLEM CHILD
Low market growth	CASH COW	DOG

Uses of the Boston matrix

As with the product life cycle, the Boston matrix is useful in helping a firm to assess the nature of its marketing

requirements. In each segment, it is likely that a different course of action is required, as described in Table 25.2.

Table 25.2 Implications of the Boston matrix for marketing

Segment	Possible course of action
Rising star	The firm must be aware of the overall market. The market is fast growing and competition will be strong. Promotion will be important, as will price monitoring.
Cash cow	The market is slow growing but this product is a 'leader'. It is vital that it stays as market leader and has much to lose if it relinquishes its position. Reminder advertising will be used and possibly extension strategies (e.g. changing price) when required.
Problem child	The overall market offers tremendous opportunities, but this product is struggling to make an impact. The product needs financial support to turn it into a cash cow or rising star. Rewards are high and a real marketing push should be made to gain a foothold in the market. A product relaunch is a popular approach used for such products.
Dog	Decision time for many firms. There is little appeal in keeping products in this category and the decline of such products may be a feature of wider market factors. A product out of favour in the market as a whole is unlikely to be demanded in the future. Firms have tried a variety of marketing strategies to revive the fortunes of such products, with varying degrees of success.

e EXAMINER'S VOICE

Always discuss products in the Boston matrix in terms of their share of a particular market. Consider also the rate of growth of that market. Learn what the terms stand for and what is actually going on, rather than just the terms themselves; and don't confuse them.

Summary

Marketing models such as the product life cycle and the Boston matrix are useful tools in assessing the current performance of a firm's product range and they both help in the planning of future marketing strategies. They are considered in more detail, along with other models, in the A2 part of the course.

e EXAMINER'S VOICE

Analysing products is important. In examination questions, you are much more likely to have to use the information rather than simply to draw the product life cycle or the Boston matrix. The questions will almost always be of the 'so what does this all mean?' type. Be specific to your particular question and your particular product. The models are trying to cover all situations. Your own question will be about one firm or one product that has its own particular characteristics.

Further sources

www.marketingteacher.com/Lessons/exercise_boston%20matrix.htm

www.market-modelling.co.uk/MATRIX/MATRIX_Step08_1.htm

www.managing-innovation.com/innovation/files/t06.pdf

YOUR TURN

Questions

Time allowed: 25 minutes

1 Using the value analysis approach, list the **three** factors that determine whether a product is a 'good' product. *(3 marks)*

2 List the **four** stages of the product life cycle. *(4 marks)*

3 Suggest **four** courses of action open to a firm making breakfast cereal to extend the life of the product. *(4 marks)*

4 Explain how Freeview digital boxes for television reception fit into the Boston matrix analysis. *(4 marks)*

5 Analyse the product position of the Sony PlayStation products (PSOne, PS2 and PSP). Evaluate the product strategy for Sony games consoles. *(9 marks)*

(24 marks)

Case study

Time allowed: 40 minutes

The market for mobile phones

Mobile phone technology continues to offer consumers great choice in terms of the range of services and the style of phones and packages available. One 'great new revolution' in mobile technology was meant to be the use of video on the move. However, promises of watching goals as they are scored and news as it happens failed to ignite the market and mobile operators have spent considerably less effort marketing their mobile video services than they did with MMS (multimedia messaging service). Case studies show how operators across the globe have rolled out understated ad campaigns for mobile video.

Even the launch of 3, the world's first predominantly 3G carrier, has been relatively muted. After an initial fanfare advertising its mobile video services in the UK, for example, 3 pulled back and started to focus on low call rates and cheap phone prices instead.

Operators have been at a loss as to how to market mobile video, falling back on value for money as a selling point. The case studies show how operators such as T-Mobile, Vodafone and O_2 have tried to convince consumers that mobile video is a 'must have' by focusing on some core advertising images. In particular, ad campaigns have focused on child/parent relationships and on scenes of friends in two different places at once. There

has been hardly any advertising of mobile video in a business environment.

Compared with MMS campaigns in 2002, ads for mobile video in 2003 have seemed weak and lacking in direction. Operators have even reused old MMS ads and converted them to mobile video campaigns, suggesting that budget restraints were high on the agenda.

Answer all questions.

1 To what extent did 3 make a mistake in launching the video services in the way that it did. *(5 marks)*

2 Analyse the fortunes of T-Mobile and 3 in the market for mobile phones. *(6 marks)*

3 Discuss the importance of 3 producing a good product. Use value analysis to assist your discussion. *(9 marks)*

4 How might knowledge of the product life cycle assist 3 in its push for higher sales? *(6 marks)*

5 Evaluate which segment of the Boston matrix 3 is currently in and develop a strategy for improving its performance. *(9 marks)*

(35 marks)

Group task

Make a list of ten different chocolate bars and consider their current position in the marketplace in terms of the product life cycle and the Boston matrix.

Focus on two chocolate bars at different stages or in different segments and, in pairs, present a strategy to the group for their improvement. Highlight the options available to the firm and reflect on how the use of the models helped you to reach your conclusions. Be prepared to be critical of the use of the models if necessary.

CHAPTER 26

Price

Price is often considered to be the most important aspect of ensuring that a product sells. 'Sell it cheap and people will buy it' is a common view. However, although determining the 'correct' price to attach to a given product is a crucial factor, it must be considered in line with the other aspects of the marketing mix. This chapter focuses on different *pricing strategies*, giving guidance on how to determine the best price for a product.

Significance of price

Price is one aspect of the marketing mix. Consumers often have a pre-conceived idea about price and what they expect to pay for almost everything they purchase. As with all aspects of the marketing mix, if the price charged is too high, or even too low, in the eyes of the consumer, it can seriously jeopardise the success of the product. A lower price is not the answer to every marketing problem. Few consumers buy the cheapest product on the market. What price does is to give the customer the chance to judge 'value for money'. Price is also an indication of quality for some consumers.

What determines price?

Firms consider several factors when deciding on the 'best' price to charge for a product.

- **Price elasticity.** This is the effect on demand of a change in price, which is dealt with fully in Chapter 27.
- **Demand.** This is concerned with how many consumers want the product. The greater the demand, the higher the price that firms can generally charge for their products.
- **Product quality.** This is difficult to quantify. Quality is often *perceived* and this makes it difficult to 'improve'. In general, the higher the perceived quality, the higher the price.
- **Pricing strategy.** The price charged is often part of an overall strategic plan to ensure that the full range of products on offer reflects current market conditions and what is agreed as being best for those products at that time. **Pricing strategies** aim to achieve long-term objectives, while **pricing tactics** are for the short term.

Chapter 25 considered how the different aspects of the marketing mix are likely to change in response to the position of the product in the marketplace and in terms of its own life. Very different pricing methods are applied to new products than to products at a later stage in the product life cycle.

KEY TERMS

pricing strategies: the means by which pricing objectives are achieved

pricing tactics: short-term adjustments to a price to achieve a particular response

Pricing methods and strategies

A number of different approaches are used. The OCR specification requires understanding of:

- cost-plus pricing
- contribution pricing
- price discrimination
- promotional pricing
- psychological pricing
- price skimming
- penetration pricing
- loss leading
- predatory pricing

Cost-plus pricing

Cost-plus pricing uses costs as a means of setting the price. There is often considerable confusion between cost and price. Cost relates to production and selling expenses. The price is what is then charged to the customer. The price clearly needs to be greater than the cost to allow for a profit to be made. A process of adding to the cost either by an actual value or, more often, by a percentage is undertaken. This is often referred to as *mark-up pricing* and forms the basis of many pricing strategies.

For example, let us assume that the costs involved in a particular product are £1.50. If a 200% mark-up or target profit is then added to the cost to determine the price, the final price will be:

£1.50 + 200% (£3.00) = £4.50

This is shown in Figure 26.1.

Cost-plus pricing is an effective way of ensuring that a profit is made, assuming that all products are sold at the correct price.

> **EXAMINER'S VOICE**
>
> With any cost/price calculation, it is vital to show all your working. These are popular questions with examiners and they cause problems for many candidates. Not showing your working is a certain way of scoring no marks if you make a single mistake.

 KEY TERM

cost-plus pricing: adding a certain amount to the cost of a product to determine the price

Figure 26.1
Cost-plus pricing

Contribution pricing

In **contribution pricing**, the price is set to ensure that the direct (variable) costs of making a product are covered along with an additional amount that helps to cover the other costs (fixed costs or overheads). It works well when the fixed costs or overheads are difficult to allocate to a particular product. Multiproduct firms use contribution pricing as a form of cost-plus pricing.

For example, let us assume that the direct cost of making a tin of baked beans is calculated to be 7p. If the firm sells these tins for 15p to the supermarket, each tin is making an 8p contribution to the overheads of the factory where the tins of beans are produced. The same factory will also be making many

KEY TERM

contribution pricing: setting a price to cover at least the direct costs

other tinned products and it would be almost impossible to allocate the total overheads on a per tin basis.

Contribution pricing is an effective way of setting a price based on the costs of producing a product that are clearly identifiable.

Price discrimination

Price discrimination means charging a higher price to some customers for what is essentially the same product or service. This can happen because the customer is willing to pay a premium price for that product or service at a specific time or to suit a specific need that they have. The system works well in the transport industry, where different prices are charged to different customers based on the time of travel, how early they book and the type of customer (their age). This often has little to do with the quality of service provided.

For example, travelling from Wolverhampton to London on an inter-city train can cost anything from £17 to £172 return. These prices reflect the nature of the customer and the issue of peak/off-peak pricing. Similarly, cinemas charge different prices for evening showings of films and matinee showings.

Firms must determine whether they are able to use price discrimination in their particular industry. This method is clearly far more applicable to the service sector than to manufacturing.

Promotional pricing

Promotional pricing can take a variety of forms, including the *loss leader*, where a product is sold at a very low price for a short period to attract customers to a specific outlet or range of products (see p. 201). It can also form part of a wider promotional strategy using special offers. Promotional pricing is most often used for short periods of time. Supermarkets do this to great effect. The positioning of the special offers in the store can encourage greater sales of other, higher-priced items.

Psychological pricing

Psychological pricing attempts to convince the consumers that they are paying significantly less for a product than is actually the case. For example, a price may be set at £9.99 rather than £10.00. The customer is paying less than £10, making the product seem psychologically much cheaper.

Price skimming

Price skimming is used when products are first introduced to the market. It involves charging a higher price than would normally be expected, to assist in the recovery of development costs. The products often have specific appeal

to certain groups of customers who are keen to be among the first to buy. Consider the price of DVD recorders. When Phillips introduced the first DVD recorder to the market, it retailed at £1,399.00.

Compare that price with those charged today. A price skimming policy is only likely to last as long as the market (and competition) will allow.

Penetration pricing

Penetration pricing is also used when a product is introduced, but is the opposite approach to price skimming. A deliberately low price is set to attract customers to the market. New magazines often have a 'trial' price to encourage people to buy them, in the hope that they will continue to buy when the price rises. The aim is to gain market share quickly, to develop a degree of brand loyalty and then to raise the price slowly to reach the desired position.

Loss leading

Loss leading is selling one or more products at a loss to encourage sales of other products at the same time. The technique is used frequently by supermarkets, which often have a number of goods on sale at very low prices to encourage customers into the store. The costs are recovered by selling other product lines at slightly higher prices than normal.

Predatory pricing

Predatory pricing, which is often referred to as *destroyer pricing*, involves setting prices very low in a highly competitive market to attempt to force out the competition. When the market is less competitive, prices can be raised to maximise the profit potential. Large firms are able to use predatory pricing in a bid to eliminate competition from smaller firms. Small firms find this very hard to deal with.

Selecting the most appropriate method

A pricing strategy involves making decisions on pricing methods to achieve the long-term objectives of a business. Price is one aspect of the marketing mix and the best method of pricing products must take into account how price fits in with changes to the product, the product position, the promotion strategy, where the product is sold and the level of competition.

An individual product may be priced using a variety of different methods and approaches. These different prices will relate to many factors and could be subject to fairly regular changes.

Customers are generally more aware of retail prices today than they have ever been before. Similarly, because businesses use price as a major marketing weapon, it is vital for them to be aware of price changes in their market.

Supermarkets operate in a highly competitive situation and are continually trying to achieve the right balance of price and quality of service. The recent success of Tesco is based on product availability, customer service and accessibility as much as on price. The very low-price supermarkets, such as ALDI and Lidl, are not as successful as Tesco, suggesting that price is not necessarily the most important factor in achieving sales.

 KEY TERMS

penetration pricing: setting a low price for a new product

loss leading: selling one or more products at a loss to encourage sales of other products at the same time

predatory pricing: setting low prices to force out the competition in the market

> **e** **EXAMINER'S VOICE**
>
> The case study approach, often used in examinations, requires candidates to assess a particular situation. The prices used by the firm in the case will often need to be considered and analysed effectively. Try to determine which pricing strategies or tactics are being used and think of possible changes that could be made. Examiners frequently ask candidates to calculate prices and this must be practised.

Further sources

www.is4profit.com/businessadvice/product-pricing/index.htm

www.businesslink.gov.uk/bdotg/action/detail?type=resources&itemId=1074300216

www.bizhelp24.com/marketing/cost_based_pricing_2.shtml

YOUR TURN

Questions

Time allowed: 30 minutes

1 State **three** factors that influence the price of fish and chips. *(3 marks)*

2 Calculate the price charged to the customer if a firm adds a 300% mark-up to a product costing £12. *(4 marks)*

3 Explain why a product retailing at £99.99 is likely to be more appealing than one selling at a price of £100. *(4 marks)*

4 Analyse which method of pricing is most likely to be successful to a firm selling:
   a a plasma television set
   b remaining seats on an aircraft *(8 marks)*

5 Evaluate the most appropriate method of pricing for a self-employed builder. *(8 marks)*

(27 marks)

Case study

Time allowed: 35 minutes

It's war: ASDA cuts prices by £100m

The vicious price war between supermarkets is boiling up with ASDA unveiling more than £100 million of price cuts this week and rival Tesco expected to hit back within days.

'Tesco and ASDA are raising the ante and it's going to have a ripple effect on the whole market,' said Richard Hyman, chairman of retail research group Verdict. 'Price competition has been relatively

benign in recent years, but when something like this happens, you can see things are getting tough. Sainsbury's and Morrisons are going to be hugely hurt by this. They haven't got the luxury of room for manoeuvre to hit back.'

ASDA's latest price cuts on 1,000 products from clothing to cakes brings the total price reductions at the second-largest supermarket to £231 million this year.

Last month, ASDA, whose advertising is led by TV celebrity Sharon Osbourne, slashed the price of its George jeans from £4 to £3 a pair. Tesco quickly followed with cuts to its 'Value' range of denims.

Morrisons, which delivered another profits warning last month as it still struggles with the integration of the Safeway chain, could find it hard to respond. The Bradford-based chain has little by way of high-margin non-food products to allow it to soften the impact of a price-led campaign.

Source: adapted from *Financial Mail on Sunday*, 3 April 2005

Answer all questions.

1 Identify and explain the different pricing strategies being used by supermarkets from the evidence in the case study. *(6 marks)*

2 To what extent do you think that ASDA is using cost-plus as an approach to pricing its George jeans? *(6 marks)*

3 Explain how price is being used in line with the other factors of marketing as part of the overall campaign for ASDA. *(8 marks)*

4 Evaluate why it is likely that ASDA and Tesco are more likely to survive a price war than Sainsbury's or Morrisons. *(10 marks)*

(30 marks)

Group task

In small groups, carry out some research on the following products and services. Assess the reasons why different prices are charged and present your results to the other groups in your class.

- In your local neighbourhood, research the prices charged for different services available in hairdressing salons.
- Try to find out how many different prices are charged for a small drink of Coca-Cola (glass or can). You may wish to think about the different situations in which the drink can be purchased.
- Compare different ways of travelling to London from Newcastle. Is there any pattern to the prices charged?
- Compare the prices charged for tins of baked beans in different supermarkets or other stores.

CHAPTER 27

Elasticity of demand

As discussed in Chapters 7 and 26, one of the factors that determines the price charged by a firm for a product or service is how demand is likely to change. There are several reasons why changes in demand might take place, but it would clearly be very useful to any firm to have some idea about the likely extent of any particular change.

The concept of elasticity of demand is concerned with the degree to which changes in demand occur when prices are changed. This chapter considers the nature of the calculation and the use to which such information could be put. It starts with some consideration of basic pricing theory (supply and demand). It also discusses other types of **elasticity**.

Theory of pricing

Microeconomic theory (see Chapter 7) suggests that it is possible to plot the amount of demand that all consumers are likely to show at each level of possible price for a particular product or service. In simple terms, **demand theory** states that the higher the price, the less those consumers would demand. We can plot a demand curve showing that the quantity demanded increases as the price falls (see Figure 27.1).

The slope of the demand curve is an indication of the possible reaction of demand to changes in price. A steep demand curve indicates that the quantity demanded changes relatively little when price changes, while a flatter curve indicates that the quantity demanded changes quite substantially in response to a price change.

Economists also argue that suppliers of goods and services are likely to want to supply more if the price is rising — this is known as **supply theory**.

KEY TERMS

elasticity: a measurement of the relative change in one variable when another is changed

demand theory: higher prices generally lead to lower demand for goods and services

supply theory: a firm is prepared to supply more products as their price is increased

Figure 27.1 Demand curve

Figure 27.2 Supply curve

The relationship between supply and price is therefore likely to follow the pattern shown in Figure 27.2. The quantity of goods supplied clearly increases as price rises because suppliers are likely to make more profit with a higher price.

If we put the demand and supply curves on the same chart, as in Figure 27.3, it is possible to establish the price at which the quantity demanded equals the quantity supplied. This is usually referred to as the **equilibrium price** and is shown as X on Figure 27.3.

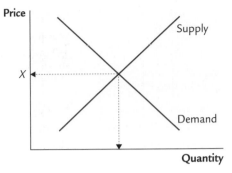

Figure 27.3 Equilibrium

The theory of demand and supply helps us to consider how a price might be determined. The main problem is trying to find out the information that enables a firm to put this kind of diagram together. Can any firm actually establish what all its customers are prepared to pay for particular items?

KEY TERM

equilibrium price: the price at which quantity demanded and quantity supplied are equal

Price elasticity of demand

Price elasticity of demand is a measure of what might happen to the demand for a product or service if a firm decides to change the price. The theory of demand and supply shows that, for the vast majority of goods, when price increases, the quantity demanded is likely to fall. Elasticity measures the extent of that impact and also considers the effect on revenue.

The calculation

The actual measure of price elasticity of demand compares the percentage change in the quantity demanded with the percentage price change that brought it about. The formula is:

$$\text{price elasticity of demand} = \frac{\text{percentage change in quantity demanded}}{\text{percentage change in price}}$$

Calculating a percentage change can be quite tricky and you should practise the technique. Looking at the top part of the equation:

$$\text{percentage change in quantity demanded} = \frac{\text{change in demand (the actual number)}}{\text{original demand}} \times 100$$

For example, if the quantity demanded falls from 10,000 units to 8,000 units:

change in demand $= 10,000 - 8,000 = 2,000$

original demand $= 10,000$

percentage change in quantity demanded $= \dfrac{2,000}{10,000} \times 100 = 20\%$

Demand has fallen by 20%.

To obtain figures for the price change, the formula is similar:

$$\text{percentage change in price} = \frac{\text{change in price}}{\text{original price}} \times 100$$

For example, if the price per unit increased from £2.00 to £2.20:

change in price = £2.20 − £2.00 = £0.20
original price = £2.00
percentage change in price = $\frac{0.20}{2.00} \times 100 = 10\%$

The price was increased by 10%.

Putting the results of these two calculations together enables us to calculate the price elasticity of demand:

percentage change in quantity demanded = 20%
percentage change in price = 10%
price elasticity of demand (PED) = $\frac{20\%}{10\%} = 2$

The value is greater than 1. This shows that the change in demand is greater than the change in price in relative terms. A relatively small change in price has led to a more dramatic change in demand. In this situation, demand is said to be **elastic**.

A different example will show the contrasting situation. If a price increase from £3.00 to £3.30 causes the quantity demanded to fall from 20,000 units to 19,000 units:

percentage change in quantity demanded = $\frac{1,000}{20,000} \times 100 = 5\%$

percentage change in price = $\frac{£0.30}{£3.00} \times 100 = 10\%$

price elasticity of demand = $\frac{5\%}{10\%} = 0.5$

The relatively large change in price has led to a smaller change in demand. This time the result is less than 1 and demand is said to be **inelastic**.

EXAMINER'S VOICE

The calculation of a percentage change will keep on occurring in this course and the skill is really worth practising.

KEY TERMS

elastic demand: where a change in price causes a greater proportionate change in demand

inelastic demand: where a change in price causes a smaller proportionate change in demand

Vegetables normally have low elasticity of demand

INGRAM

EXAMINER'S VOICE

Make sure that you use the formula the right way up. In most questions, you are given the price change first. You must remember to put this on the bottom of the equation. As with all calculations, examiners will use the own-figure rule. If you make an error, you can still get most of the available marks by showing your working.

The examples given so far have related to price increases. If we now take a product where the price changes from £1.00 to £0.95, causing the quantity demanded to increase from 100,000 units to 115,000 units, the elasticity calculation is as follows:

$$PED = \frac{\dfrac{15,000}{100,000} \times 100}{\dfrac{£0.05}{£1.00} \times 100} = \frac{15\%}{5\%} = 3$$

The result is greater than 1 and demand for the product is therefore considered to be *elastic*. The small change in price has led to a much greater change in demand.

A final example completes the possibilities. If the price of a product falls from £2.00 to £1.80, causing the quantity demanded to increase from 80,000 units to 84,000, then:

$$PED = \frac{\dfrac{4,000}{80,000} \times 100}{\dfrac{£0.20}{£2.00} \times 100} = \frac{5\%}{10\%} = 0.5$$

The result is less than 1 and demand for this product is therefore *inelastic*. A relatively large change in price has led to a smaller change in demand.

It is possible for the percentage change in quantity demanded and the percentage change in price to be the same. In this case, price elasticity of demand is 1 and this is known as *unitary elasticity*.

How useful is price elasticity of demand to businesses?

If a firm is able to establish whether demand for a particular product is elastic or inelastic, it may be able to judge whether price changes are likely to be appropriate. From the elasticity calculations, it is possible to assess whether a price change will be a good or bad idea in terms of the relative impact on price and quantity demanded. It is also possible to establish what the impact will be on revenue gained.

In terms of revenue, we can draw the conclusions presented in Table 27.1. Unfortunately, it is not possible to reach any conclusions about changes to *profit* because demand elasticity does not take costs into account.

Change in price	Elasticity	Impact on sales revenue
Price increases	Elastic demand (demand changes more than price)	Overall revenue falls
Price increases	Inelastic demand (price changes more than demand)	Overall revenue rises
Price decreases	Elastic demand (demand changes more than price)	Overall revenue rises
Price decreases	Inelastic demand (price changes more than demand)	Overall revenue falls

Table 27.1 Effect of price elasticity of demand on sales revenue

Elasticity is particularly useful when firms plan special promotional campaigns involving price reductions. There is little point in choosing a price-led marketing campaign if the anticipated outcome is likely to be poor — that is, if the product has inelastic demand.

Factors affecting price elasticity of demand

A number of factors have an impact on elasticity, and different products in different markets show quite different patterns.

The factors that influence the level of elasticity include:

- **customer knowledge.** The more aware that customers are of other products in the market, the more likely it is that they will be able to switch to them. The internet makes customers much more aware of what is available in any given market.
- **brand loyalty.** Many customers are loyal to a particular brand or product and will remain so even if its price increases.
- **availability of substitute products.** If there is little or no competition, it becomes very tricky to switch. For example, there is only one brand of cola available in Burger King.
- **ability to switch to other products.** Many firms make it difficult to change from their product (e.g. mobile phone companies that tie customers into long-term contracts) and this reduces elasticity.
- **uniqueness of the product.** If a product (e.g. Dyson washing machine) is very different from possible competitors, this makes it difficult to switch in response to a price change.

Other kinds of elasticity

The AS course requires understanding of the concept of price elasticity of demand. You might, however, find it useful to be aware that the concept of elasticity can be further developed to analyse the impact of other factors on demand. Two quite common calculations that have much to commend them in the area of marketing are *income elasticity of demand* and *advertising elasticity of demand*.

Income elasticity of demand

Income elasticity of demand calculates the change in demand for a particular product that follows a change in income. The formula is:

$$\text{income elasticity of demand} = \frac{\text{percentage change in quantity demanded}}{\text{percentage change in income}}$$

Understanding the likely impact on demand of changes in overall incomes is useful for product development.

Advertising elasticity of demand

Advertising elasticity of demand calculates the change in demand that follows the implementation of an advertising campaign. The formula is:

$$\text{advertising elasticity of demand} = \frac{\text{percentage change in quantity demanded}}{\text{percentage change in advertising}}$$

This allows a firm to assess the likely success of an advertising campaign.

Although it is not necessary to have a full understanding of the above techniques, they may help you to assess what elasticity is trying to show — the effect of a change in one variable on some other variable.

> ### *e* EXAMINER'S VOICE
>
> Elasticity is a theoretically useful concept for most organisations. It is also a popular topic area for examiners to set questions on. You must practise the technique and look back at recent papers to see how it is being tested. Remember that this topic is rarely tested just for the sake of it. There will usually be a follow-up question where you will be required to demonstrate your understanding.

YOUR TURN

Questions

Time allowed: 25 minutes

1 Explain why supply theory suggests that producers are more likely to want to sell more at higher prices. *(4 marks)*

2 Using Table 27.1, explain the relationship between price changes and revenue. *(4 marks)*

3 a Calculate price elasticity of demand when price rises by 10% and demand falls from 50,000 units to 40,000 units. *(4 marks)*
  b Is demand elastic or inelastic in this case? *(1 mark)*
  c Discuss the likely impact on revenue and profit of the calculation in part **a**. *(4 marks)*

4 Discuss the factors that might influence price elasticity of demand for McDonald's Quarter Pounders. *(8 marks)*

(25 marks)

Case study

Time allowed: 30 minutes

Jan Potter runs a local independent convenience store selling a wide range of everyday items. She has studied business and is aware of the concept of elasticity. She fully understands that a variety of factors impact on demand, but that for everyday products, changes in price (special offers etc.) have varying degrees of impact. She decides to test the idea of elasticity out by monitoring the changing pattern of sales for three products: milk, Heinz baked beans, and egg mayonnaise pre-packed sandwiches.

She discovered the pattern of sales shown in Table 27.2. She calculates the elasticity of demand and attempts to explain to her staff how useful the information is when planning future price changes.

Product	Weekly sales before 10% price rise	Weekly sales after 10% price rise
Milk	130 cartons	128 cartons
Baked beans	26 tins	13 tins
Sandwich	10 packs	8 packs

Table 27.2
Sales before and after a price rise

Answer all questions.

1 Calculate the price elasticity of demand for the three products in her test. *(6 marks)*

2 Determine whether the products are elastic or inelastic. *(3 marks)*

3 Assess the factors, other than price changes, that may be affecting the results shown. *(8 marks)*

4 Discuss the usefulness of elasticity in helping to assess the pricing policy for Jan's business. *(8 marks)*

(25 marks)

Group task

In small groups, consider the extent to which price changes influence demand. Encourage everyone in the group to present an example of a product that they have purchased more of when its price has fallen, or less of when its price has risen. Which products are not affected by changes made to the price?

Assess the extent to which elasticity is having an impact. Argue the case either in favour of or against using elasticity for the following products:

- cigarettes
- used cars
- digital radios
- free-range eggs

CHAPTER 28

Promotion

Many people think that promotion is the only aspect of marketing and selling that really matters; and some people would define marketing as **advertising**. The reality is that advertising is only one small part of the function of promotion, which is itself only one aspect of marketing. This chapter considers different types of promotion, making the distinction between above-the-line and below-the-line forms. Consideration is also given to the factors that determine the most appropriate method of promotion to use in a given situation.

KEY TERM

advertising: communication that tries to inform potential customers about products and persuade them to purchase

What is promotion?

Promotion is the process of communicating with customers. This communication can take several forms and goes beyond just passing on a message.

- *Informative promotion* attempts to pass on information about the products and services provided. This can take many forms and is largely concerned with creating greater awareness. The first adverts aired by e-bay focused on making possible viewers aware of the e-bay concept. Banks tend to promote their services in an informative way.
- Persuasive *promotion* attempts to encourage the purchase of particular goods or services using a variety of techniques designed to illustrate the product in the best possible light. For example, advertisements for the Peugeot 407 Coupé highlighted aspects of the car's style and performance.

Methods of promotion

Promotion can take place in a variety of ways, and different methods are often used together as part of an overall promotional campaign. A distinction is usually made between above-the-line and below-the-line methods of promotion.

Above-the-line promotion uses mass media to reach a wide audience, some of whom will be targets for the products being promoted. It does not enable a firm to focus on a specific target audience.

Below-the-line promotion is targeted at specific potential customers and a firm therefore has slightly more control when using this approach.

KEY TERMS

above-the-line promotion: use of mass media to promote to a wide audience rather than a specific target market

below-the-line promotion: promotion targeted more directly at likely customers

Above-the-line methods

Television advertising

When asked to give a method of promotion, most people would answer 'television'. It is the highest-profile method of promotion and is often the most memorable. Many mass-market consumer goods are promoted in this way. Advertising on television clearly carries a relatively high cost, but when this is considered on a per person viewing basis, the cost of reaching each person becomes relatively small. If 15 million viewers tune in to watch *Coronation Street*, an advertisement during the half-time break will still have many potential customers glancing at the television screen. The advent of more television channels, which target specific viewing groups, may make television a more effective method to use.

Newspaper advertising

Newspaper advertising is a popular method of promoting goods, which works well for many products. Potential customers can look at the product and refer to its features at their leisure. Newspapers usually have quite specific target audiences, and this allows firms to use the newspaper that best suits them. Eye-catching adverts in glossy Sunday supplements can be particularly effective as these are more likely to be read at leisure.

Radio advertising

This has increased in popularity and the radio industry makes bold claims about the effectiveness of its use. The initial cost is less than for television advertising. As with television, the increase in the number of radio stations and the move to greater access via a digital framework mean that the significance of radio advertising is likely to increase.

Magazine advertising

Magazine advertising has the attraction of being highly targeted. Consumers tend to buy magazines to follow a specific interest. Firms that choose to advertise in magazines can therefore highlight products aimed at the people most likely to be interested in them. Many of the glossy magazines are crammed full of advertisements. Magazine advertising has the same advantage as newspaper advertising, in that the image remains as long as the magazine is available to read. Publications that end up in doctors' and dentists' waiting rooms can remain as adverts for several years!

Billboards and posters

These are highly effective and have the great advantage that they can be targeted at specific types of customer. Motorists may be targets for billboards sited at busy road junctions, while on a much smaller scale, the local village fete might be

Moveable posters can be extremely effective

promoted in the village store using a small poster in the shop window. The main requirement of this method is to make the poster as eye catching as possible. The image can be informative and/or persuasive. Posters can also be displayed effectively on the side of buses.

Electronic advertising

This involves the use of the internet and text messaging. Electronic advertising is a major growth area because the cost is relatively low and messages can be targeted depending on a previous indication of interests. The targeting aspect is an important advantage. The use of 'pop-up' adverts is widespread and, although they cause irritation to many who view them, they can have a great impact. Text message adverts also work well: additional ring tones, games and other products can be sold to mobile phone users. As new technology continues to evolve, it is likely that additional forms of electronic promotion will develop.

Cinema advertising

Cinema advertising has been around for many years. Watching adverts for the products on sale in the foyer, next week's film release or products available in the local area is one of the features of a cinema visit. Cinema advertising is a good way of reaching the specific audience type watching each film. Restaurants and takeaways are particularly good examples of firms that use cinema advertising to good effect.

Below-the-line methods

Personal selling

This involves using a fully trained team of staff who are prepared to work directly with a customer to ensure that the sale is made. The technique works well with some products. In some cases, customers expect it to happen. For example, if you were interested in buying a new car, you would probably expect to go for a test drive and have the sales person go over the features and functions of the car.

Sales promotions

Several techniques are used in a variety of situations:

- **Buy one, get one free (BOGOF).** This has become increasingly popular to encourage purchases of a product and develop greater brand loyalty. Boots the Chemist and Morrisons use this technique to great effect.
- **Free gifts.** These can be effective in creating increased awareness. Magazines often give away free merchandise to encourage customers to buy them, in the hope that they will continue to buy. The inclusion of free CDs and DVDs with weekend newspapers has become a popular method of encouraging greater sales.
- **Introductory offers.** An initial interest-free period on a credit card is one example of the use of an introductory offer. The launch of the PSP in September 2005 allowed customers to buy bundles of games cheaper than buying them separately.

■ **Money-off coupons or leaflets.** These are used to enhance sales and encourage brand loyalty. They are again targeted at specific groups through demonstrations, as inclusions in magazines or by direct mailing. They are excellent at creating specific additional demand, but often for only a short period of time.

■ **Competitions.** These help to stimulate demand and interest in a product, or themes related to a product. Some competitions give away special prizes, which raise the profile of the product. Other competitions ask for slogans, which can provide excellent future advertising material.

The Motor Show is a good example of an organised trade exhibition

■ **Trade fairs and exhibitions.** These methods, which are successful in some industries, involve a firm showing its products to potential buyers who have an interest in seeing many similar products displayed together. The Ideal Home Show and the Motor Show are good examples of international organised trade exhibitions.

Sponsorship

Many firms gain publicity by being associated with events either in their local area or at a national/international level. There is much to be gained by being one of the leading sponsors of major sporting events such as the Olympic Games. The Emirates shirt sponsorship of Chelsea FC raised the profile for both Emirates and Chelsea. For smaller firms, operating at a local level, giving money to a local football team or buying a bench in the local park also has advantages.

Publicity/public relations

All organisations like to present a good public image. There are many advantages in being able to demonstrate positive aspects of a firm's operations, and to encourage a 'feel good' view of the organisation as a whole and the individual products that it sells. Organisations such as the Body Shop have traded effectively on their ethically positive image. They continue to gain positive feedback, which enhances their sales.

Table 28.1 Summary of promotion methods

Above-the-line promotion	Below-the-line promotion
Television advertising	Personal selling
Newspaper advertising	Sales promotion (e.g. BOGOF)
Radio advertising	Sponsorship
Magazine advertising	Publicity/public relations
Billboards and posters	
Electronic advertising	
Cinema advertising	

Summary

Table 28.1 summarises the main methods of promotion.

Which promotion method?

All methods of promotion have their advantages and disadvantages and it is important to realise that firms combine and coordinate different methods into an overall promotion strategy. The **promotion mix** is the coordinated use of promotion methods.

The actual decision to use a particular promotion method is determined by a number of factors.

The nature of the product being sold

Heavy goods, such as farm machinery, are unlikely to be promoted on national television. A specialist farmers' magazine is a much more appropriate method because the market for farm machinery is relatively small.

The timescale

Some products need to be promoted quickly and to a wide audience. For example, the promotion of a new film will use a number of techniques in a relatively short time frame (7–10 days).

The finance available

Budgets can be a real constraint on the choice of promotion activities. Many firms would clearly like to be able to run a series of adverts during the Superbowl in the USA, but the cost of many millions of dollars is too much for most organisations.

The type of customer

All customers must be carefully analysed and the best way of communicating and selling to them must be found. If a typical customer group for a product tends to be professional, this will influence where, when and how the product is best promoted. The use of *market segmentation* (see Chapter 22) allows a firm to target customers and the choice of promotion method is critical in this targeting. Saga FM and Classic FM radio stations run advertising that targets their likely audiences.

The overall product strategy

The *product life cycle* (see Chapter 25) can have a significant influence on the different aspects of the marketing mix, particularly on the types and forms of promotion methods used.

External influences

Changes in new technology, legal factors and economic adjustments are just some of the external influences that may impact on the promotion method used. As stated earlier, advancements in technology have changed the way products are promoted. The law changes the rules that regulate advertising. For example, cigarette advertising is now not allowed in the UK. The Advertising Standards Authority (ASA) monitors all forms of advertising to ensure that the consumer is protected. Benetton has been the subject of many complaints regarding the nature of its advertising.

Size of the firm/location

If the firm is a small, locally based organisation, it will need to focus all promotion activities in its local area. Large, multinational organisations

e EXAMINER'S VOICE

In an examination situation, you might need to put together a promotion strategy or to comment on the existing methods employed by a firm in a case study. Be prepared to consider the list of factors above and try to apply them to the specific position in which the firm finds itself.

usually have a much wider range of promotion possibilities available to them.

Summary

The final choice of promotion method or methods should be a crucial component in the overall marketing strategy. It needs to fit in coherently with any changes that are made to the product, the price and the firm's distribution strategy. Direct Line Insurance, for example, is continually looking for new products to sell. It must ensure that the price is appropriate, but promotion of the new product is a crucial aspect of its success.

YOUR TURN

Questions

Time allowed: 35 minutes

1 Define above-the-line and below-the-line promotion. *(4 marks)*

2 List **three** methods of promotion available to a firm selling:
 a digital radios
 b a new magazine aimed at teenage girls *(6 marks)*

3 Justify the use of the promotion methods identified in question **2a**. *(6 marks)*

4 Explain why promotion has to be linked to the other aspects of the marketing mix. *(6 marks)*

5 Trade fairs and other exhibitions are a useful way of introducing new products to the market. Evaluate the reasons why new cars are often launched at major motor shows around the world. *(10 marks)*

(32 marks)

Case study

Time allowed: 35 minutes

The Kingswinford Balti

This Balti restaurant has an excellent local reputation. It provides good-quality but relatively inexpensive meals. The restaurant does not have a drinks licence. It has a regular clientele who delight in being able to take their own drinks. This feature helps to ensure that there is a good number of customers most nights of the week. The local area has several restaurants catering for all types of meals.

Unfortunately, the owner has noticed a worrying trend. The number of customers on Monday and Tuesday evenings has fallen in recent months and he

has been considering ways of increasing the number of diners on those two nights. He is aware that price reductions are unlikely to work given the cheap prices already on offer and he feels that a number of different promotional activities need to be considered.

Answer all questions.

1 State **three** examples of sales promotion techniques that the restaurant might use. *(3 marks)*

2 State **three** types of advertising that the restaurant might use. *(3 marks)*

3 Explain how the level of competition might affect the methods of promotion that the business might use. *(5 marks)*

4 Explain why below-the-line methods of promotion are more likely to be successful than above-the-line methods for this business. *(6 marks)*

5 Evaluate the extent to which other aspects of the marketing mix are more important than promotion in this situation. *(10 marks)*

(27 marks)

Group task

Consider a popular product such as Pepsi.
- List all the different ways of advertising the product that everyone in the group has seen.
- Assess the effectiveness of each method. Write down the good and bad aspects of the different methods listed.
- Assume that the group is now in charge of promotion at Pepsi. Develop an overall promotion strategy, this time considering aspects of sales promotion as well as advertising.

CHAPTER 29

Distribution

Distribution relates to the final 'P' in the marketing mix, which is usually referred to as *place*. Place is concerned with ensuring that products and services are available to consumers in a format and at a time that they want.

There are two aspects to distribution — distribution channels and physical distribution — and both are considered in this chapter. The chapter also considers the most appropriate ways of distributing goods in given situations.

Many students who learn about place make the assumption that it is concerned with the actual location of a particular shop or other site of the business. Place has much more to do with how a customer is able to interact with that business.

Physical distribution

Physical distribution is concerned with the physical movement of goods from the producers to the customers. There is a need to consider the methods of transport in terms of cost and overall efficiency. In recent years, there has been a tendency to buy goods in a wider variety of ways, including increased use of the internet. This has led to a need to develop more complex transport networks (e.g. to deliver goods around the world).

Firms must decide between various forms of national and local postal schemes, and different transport firms, using all modes of transport.

Distribution channels

A **distribution channel** comprises the different people or groups involved in the supply of goods to customers. It is a chain of all the different stages that exist in the distribution process. Each stage is referred to as an **intermediary**. The intermediaries each perform a different function and, while they can be given a variety of names, they tend to be wholesalers, retailers or agents.

Wholesalers
Wholesalers act as a link between the producers of a good and the retailer. They perform a number of key functions, but the two most important are breaking bulk and storing goods.

KEY TERMS

physical distribution: moving goods (e.g. using lorries)

distribution channel: the route taken from producer to final customer

intermediary: one link in the distribution chain

- **Breaking bulk** involves taking huge quantities of a range of products from producers and breaking them down into smaller quantities to allow retailers to buy them and store them effectively in their outlets. Wholesalers are particularly important to smaller retailers, which may only be able to stock a relatively small number of product ranges.
- Retailers are constrained by space and the need to use as much of this space in the selling function. A retailer that has good links with wholesalers tends to operate in an effective way by maximising sales floor space and encouraging wholesalers to store more of the goods.

Other functions of wholesalers include giving advice to retailers about the latest trends in the market and offering marketing support to retailers on certain product lines.

Retailers

Retailers perform the most obvious role of the distribution chain by giving consumers the opportunity to purchase goods in a familiar environment. They act as the link between the wholesaler and the customer and, because they deal with the customer directly, their role is particularly important.

There are many different kinds of retailer and they help to determine the tone and nature of the products sold in their outlets. Customers are often able to identify retailers by their position and status in the marketplace (e.g. high quality). Chapter 25 considered how certain products were perceived in terms of product positioning. This also applies to different types of retailer.

Retailers perform many of the same functions as wholesalers:
- The notion of breaking bulk is certainly a feature, but it happens at a smaller level. If you are interested in purchasing a chocolate bar, the shop is likely to have several choices available. You almost certainly only want to buy one and the shop will sell that one to you having 'broken the bulk' of the several that it has.
- Retailers effectively store the good until the consumer needs it.

OCR

AS Business Studies

KEY TERMS

wholesaler: a link in the distribution chain that usually takes goods from the producer, stores them and breaks bulk until a retailer needs them

breaking bulk: taking large quantities of a product and reducing them into a more manageable form for customers

retailer: a link in the distribution chain that usually deals directly with the final customer, making the product available to the customer as conveniently as possible

Retailers act as a link between the wholesaler and the customer

■ Retailers provide an outlet for producers. These producers must try to match the products that they are trying to sell to the types of retailer available. Producers of well-known goods have few problems in getting retailers to stock their products. Smaller producers often need to offer great incentives to entice retailers into stocking their products rather than the products of other firms.

Agents

Agents provide the link between sellers and buyers. An agent does not actually have ownership of the product, but ensures that the sale can take place. Agents are often used when firms are interested in selling goods abroad. They provide expertise in import and export legislation and are able to offer advice in a variety of areas. Agents are often specialists in language and culture, and can promote goods in an effective way. They take commission for providing this service.

Common channels of distribution

Channels of distribution show the possible links in the chain between producer and customer. The most common channels are shown in Figure 29.1.

Figure 29.1 Common channels of distribution

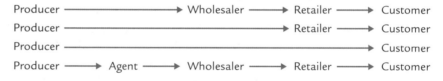

Each link in the chain adds value, but also adds costs to the finished product. Essentially, the more links in the chain, the higher the final price for customers. For example, a producer selling to a wholesaler, which sells to a retailer, which sells on to the final customer, has three lots of costs to take into account. Each link in the chain seeks a profit and this must add to the final price paid by the customer.

Perishable products, such as fresh flowers, must reach the customer quickly

Factors affecting the distribution of a product

A number of factors have an impact on the way that a product is distributed and the number of links in the distribution chain.

■ **Cost.** Shorter channels of distribution tend to be lower in cost.
■ **Type of product.** The nature of the product has considerable impact on the choice of channel. Perishable products must reach the customer quickly. Firms that export fresh flowers need to ensure that products reach customers as soon as possible. The size of the product can also make a difference. Firms selling tractors are likely to deal with customers directly. Coca-Cola will use a variety of different distribution methods to reach its customers because the product is available in so many different outlets.

- **Type of firm.** Larger companies are more likely to try to distribute goods themselves or to use established chains, such as the large-scale supermarkets. Smaller, independent firms must rely on developing links with top retailers, or use other methods of selling, such as the internet.
- **Spread of the market.** This relates to location and wider aspects of geography. A small, independent convenience store is only concerned with selling those products in demand in the local area. Similarly, a hairdressing salon is only likely to attract custom from a relatively local area. Coca-Cola, selling on an international basis, will need to have much more complex methods in place.
- **Technical aspects of the product.** A product in a very specific market is more likely to need to be 'sold' to the customer. The use of personal selling techniques will have an impact. With luxury cars, for example, the product needs to be demonstrated and delivered, and after-sales care needs to be provided.
- **Control required by the producer.** Firms that develop and produce goods and services are often unable to control how their products are eventually sold to customers. In a traditional chain of distribution, the product may pass through wholesalers and retailers before it reaches the final consumer. The product might be subjected to either positive or negative promotions, depending on the particular views of those wholesalers or retailers. Links in the distribution chain are much more likely to promote and try to sell a product where the possible return is high. If a producer is able to sell directly to a customer, or can control how the product is sold, it has much more chance of gaining a high return. Franchising can help, while the use of direct selling and distribution, as used by Dell Computers, ensures that the firm maintains control of the product and the way it is sold.

Ensuring good links with the intermediaries

It is vitally important to ensure that products are available to consumers when they need them; otherwise, they will be hard to sell. Producers that rely on intermediaries to help products reach consumers need to keep these intermediaries happy and promote the products in an effective way. This is particularly the case when producers are competing with others. They may need to offer retailers incentives to sell their own products rather than those from other producers. This can be achieved in a number of ways:

- **Providing specific product displays.** These can take up valuable space but also make the retail store more attractive. Soft drinks and ice-cream manufacturers often provide fridges and freezers to ensure that their products are stocked.
- **Offering retailer competitions.** It is quite common for a producer to offer retailers a chance to win free holidays — for example, to encourage them to sell more of its products.
- **Other promotions.** It can be difficult for a retailer not to be involved if there is a high-profile promotional campaign on offer in the market. Retailers can also be encouraged to push products on offer.

■ **Offering special deals or higher commission.** This can work in short bursts because it gives a specific focus on certain products for a short period of time. Establishing a positive view of a product in the thoughts of a retailer can be very effective in the longer term. Creating a degree of brand loyalty with the prospect of further discounts can also help.

■ **Offering training to retailers.** This can be extremely effective, particularly in aspects of merchandising. Merchandising is concerned with a variety of issues, but is relevant to retailers in terms of product display and positioning. Retailers need to be aware that products are more likely to sell when on display in some parts of the store than in others. There is a 'science' in finding the best position for each product to ensure that overall sales are optimised. One aspect of this relates to the racks of chocolates and sweets on the counter near the till in most small stores. Chocolate producers offer training to retailers to ensure that high-profit items are displayed in the best position to increase sales.

---

e EXAMINER'S VOICE

The marketing mix is made up of four variables (the four Ps), and each must play its part. However, 'place' is often the forgotten 'P'. It appears to be a variable that is tricky to change. 'The business is, where the business is' is a popular view developed by candidates in examinations. Place is much more than this. Be prepared to comment on how different retail outlets can change the way a product is sold; or how products are more likely to compete for space in a shop rather than on price.

Further sources

www.igd.com
— grocery trade

www.marketingteacher.com

www.thechannelinsider.com
— IT distribution

YOUR TURN

Questions
Time allowed: 35 minutes

1 Explain **two** functions of a wholesaler. *(4 marks)*

2 Discuss why a firm attempting to export furniture to Romania would be likely to use an agent. *(8 marks)*

3 Explain why a firm selling soft drinks is more likely to offer incentives to retailers than a firm selling sun cream. *(4 marks)*

4 Discuss why McDonald's ensures that its restaurants are carefully located. *(8 marks)*

5 Evaluate how greater use of the internet might impact on sales for hotel bookings. *(10 marks)*

(34 marks)

Case study

Time allowed: 30 minutes

Agent decline to stabilise by 2010

The decline in the number of travel agents will stabilise over the next 5 years, but the trade will still have to battle for survival, according to Euromonitor International. More than 600 agency locations are predicted to close by 2010 before a new breed of travel specialist takes hold, says the market analyst. Head of travel and tourism research, Caroline Bremner, said: 'We'll see a continued decline until all the less profitable businesses fall out, leaving behind the big groups, online companies and independent specialists, which will continue growing through providing a value-added service.'

The industry is expected to stabilise at 6,029 outlets — a drop of 12% from current levels of 6,658, according to Euromonitor's report, *Travel and Tourism in the Chaptered Kingdom*. However, the decline in retail sales is slowing, with 2009 registering a 1.6% drop on 2008, compared with a forecast decline of 2.8% for 2005 on 2004. Generally, independents are predicted to go more upmarket to differentiate themselves from online and larger retailers, and could specialise in areas such as adventure holidays, said Bremner. ABTA said the decline reflected the over-capacity for agents in the market. At the height of ABTA's membership numbers, it boasted 2,965 companies with 7,504 outlets. Today, this number is 1,426 with 6,164 shops.

Independent travel agents could specialise in areas such as adventure holidays

A spokesman said turnover had dramatically improved for remaining stores, with average turnover per company now £9 million, as opposed to £7.3 million in December 1999.

Source: **www.travelweekly.co.uk**, 4 August 2005

Answer all questions.

1 Discuss the different ways in which holidaymakers now book holidays. *(6 marks)*

2 How has this changed in the last 10 years? *(4 marks)*

3 Explain how the channel of distribution for holiday bookings is different from the channels used to sell tins of baked beans. *(5 marks)*

4 Explain how the changes highlighted in the case will affect a hotel owner in Majorca. *(5 marks)*

5 Evaluate whether the reduction in the number of retail outlets and the wider opportunities to buy holidays in other ways is good or bad for the consumer. *(10 marks)*

(30 marks)

Group task

In small groups, carry out some research on the different ways in which you can buy the following products:

- cut glass
- a new release DVD
- credit for your mobile phone
- a light bulb

Present to the other groups a chart showing the different methods of distribution used and suggest reasons why these are better than alternatives.

Would you recommend a different way of distributing the goods?

Module 2872
Business Decisions
Module 2873
Business Behaviour

Accounting and Finance

CHAPTER 30

Budgets

When you go to university or move away from home to start your first job, you will be faced with the task of organising your own money. You will need to ensure that you have sufficient money to cover the cost of your lifestyle. This chapter looks at the various types of budget and how they are used. It also explains how to analyse variance, which is the difference between budgeted figures and the actual figures achieved.

What is a budget?

A budget is an estimate or forecast of the income (revenue) and expenditure (costs) of a business for a given period of time (often 1 year). Budgets have the following functions:

- They are used to measure success in terms of to what extent objectives or targets are being met.
- They can be used to control expenditure or to ensure production is on target. If a business sees that its targets are unlikely to be met, then it can take remedial action.
- They provide a sense of direction for everyone in a business. Knowing what the targets for the business are enables the employees to be involved and to understand what is required. In several car assembly plants, the target for the production of cars is clearly displayed for all to see. Lights flash when the level of production is below the target rate.
- They can be used as the basis for 'management by exception' — dealing with areas of the business that fail to reach the budgets or targets set.
- They allow for delegation to departments within a business. Giving individuals or departments the responsibility for their own budgets or targets provides a high sense of involvement and responsibility. These are seen by theorists as important in motivating the workforce.
- They can be used to encourage efficiency within a business and thereby ensure targets are met. If targets are not being met, the business is likely to look for ways in which it can get on target. It is more likely that methods of increasing efficiency, improving output or reducing costs will be found if there is good reason to do so.

Setting budgets

It is important to understand that budgets are a *prediction* or *forecast*. Circumstances can change quickly, in a way that means the budget set is no longer realistic. For example, the budget set by British Airways for its sales

revenue during September 2001 was not achieved because sales fell massively overnight as a result of the 9/11 attack. No one within BA could have predicted such an event and therefore a calculation of how budgeted revenue differed from actual receipts would serve little purpose.

Limitations of budgets

Firms should be aware of several dangers and limitations when setting budgets:

- If the budget is unrealistic, it may demotivate employees.
- Changes in circumstances can make the budget set unrealistic, as described above.
- A sense of insecurity may develop if there is a threat of redundancy when targets are not met. According to Maslow, security is a significant motivational factor.
- If the budget is imposed by senior managers, it needs to be set in an informed manner. It is important for managers to know the needs of a particular department in order to set an accurate budget.
- Setting budgets can be a costly and time-consuming process.
- If the budget is for a new business, there will be no previous records to help gauge what is reasonable. This initial budget may therefore be of limited value.

What makes a good budget?

A good budget has the following characteristics:

- It fits the objectives of the business
- It balances the needs of the business and its employees in order to avoid stress and demotivation.
- It encourages the business to progress and yet remains realistic.
- It is continually monitored both to check that targets are being met and to allow for alterations to the budget as circumstances in the business environment change.

 TERM

variance: the difference between the predicted or budgeted figure and the actual figure achieved

Variance

The **variance** is the difference between the predicted or budgeted figure and the actual figure achieved. Measuring this difference enables a business to work out by how much it has exceeded or fallen short of its budget.

Table 30.1 shows the budget for the Penkridge Café for December 2005. Using the information in the table:

variance for sales revenue from teas and coffees

= actual level of sales − forecast level of sales

= £2,200 − £2,000 = +£200

The figure for the variance is positive because it is above the prediction. It shows that there is more revenue than expected coming into the business.

Table 30.1 Budget for the Penkridge Café, December 2005

Item	Forecast (£)	Actual (£)	Variance +/– (£)	Positive/ negative
Sales revenue				
Teas and coffees	2,000	2,200	+200	Positive
Soft drinks	400	300	–100	Negative
Food	4,000	4,500	+500	Positive
Total sales revenue	6,400	7,000	+600	Positive
Costs				
Wages	1,000	1,050	–50	Negative
Rent	800	800	0	–
Heating and lighting	100	110	–10	Negative
Advertising	50	50	0	–
Cost of food and drinks	1,900	2,010	–110	Negative
Total costs	3,850	4,020	–170	Negative
Profit	**2,550**	**2,980**	**+430**	**Positive**

 **EXAMINER'S VOICE**

It is important to be careful when commenting on the value of the variance. It is said to be positive when the *revenue* is *higher* than the forecast, as this is good news for a business. However, it is also positive when the *costs* are *lower* than the forecast. This is because with lower costs, less money is going out of the business. Do not just look for a minus or a plus sign.

Variance as a percentage

There are occasions when the variance is shown as a percentage. To calculate this, the variance is divided by the predicted figure. For example, using the information in Table 30.1:

$$\text{total sales variance} = \frac{600}{6,400} \times 100 = +9.38\% \text{ (positive)}$$

$$\text{total costs variance} = \frac{170}{3,850} \times 100 = +4.42\% \text{ (negative)}$$

$$\text{profit variance} = \frac{430}{2,550} \times 100 = +16.86\% \text{ (positive)}$$

Using a percentage figure makes it easier to compare the amount of variance between different elements of the budget.

Analysing the variance

It is important not to jump to the wrong conclusion. A negative variance is not always bad. If sales are higher than expected, which is positive, there will be an increase in the costs of buying the raw materials to produce the goods for sale. Although this extra cost will cause a negative variance, the reason for the increase in costs is positive.

A positive variance must also be treated with caution. If sales are lower than expected, which is negative, the costs associated with supplying these sales will be lower, which will appear as a positive variance. However, the cause of the decrease in costs is lower sales, which is not good for the business.

An increase in sales will appear as a positive variance. However, this increase needs to be analysed to ensure it is due to the effort of the business. An increase in sales revenue does not necessarily mean that the business has sold more goods. The increase may be due to inflation (see Chapter 10). Similarly,

the increase in sales revenue could be due to the fact that the government has increased the tax on products, which the business will not receive.

By looking again at Table 30.1, it is possible to build up a clear picture of what is happening to the Penkridge Café.

- It is December, so there are probably many people out shopping and therefore wanting refreshment.
- High sales of tea and coffee may be explained by the weather. It could be that the temperature was lower than expected and therefore more teas and coffees were sold.
- There is further evidence that this is the case, given that the sales of soft (cold) drinks have a negative variance.
- Another clue is the negative variance for heating and lighting costs. It could be that the café stayed open longer, or that more heating was needed because of the weather.
- The variance for rent and advertising is zero because this expenditure is fixed.
- The expenditure on advertising may be a reason why the sales are higher than budgeted.
- The increase in the cost of food and drinks may not be the same as the increase in the amount of food and drinks sold because of the advantages of economies of scale (buying in bulk).

EXAMINER'S VOICE

It is always worth considering whether the budget set was realistic. An apparently good performance by the business may be due, in part, to a pessimistic prediction for sales. Similarly, when the variance is negative it could be due to an over-optimistic budget. Knowing how the budget was arrived at will help when the analysis is undertaken.

YOUR TURN

Questions
Time allowed: 30 minutes

1 Why is it important for a business to set a budget? (5 marks)
2 Explain the term 'variance'. (4 marks)
3 Explain **three** problems facing a business when setting a budget. (6 marks)
4 Using Table 30.1, calculate the variance for wages as a percentage. (3 marks)
5 Comment on your answer to question 4. (6 marks)
6 Using the following information, calculate the variance and state whether it is positive or negative: budgeted costs £100,000; actual costs £105,000. (3 marks)

(27 marks)

Case study

Time allowed: 30 minutes

Wembley Stadium

The New Wembley Stadium, when completed, will be the largest stadium of its type in the world. Its seating capacity will be 90,000. It is hoped the stadium will be used for a wide range of sporting fixtures as well as other events such as concerts. Its special feature, the arch, which weighs a massive 1,650 tonnes, is designed to hold a sliding roof in place.

The project started in 1995 and by 2002 the old site had been demolished. By 2004, there were 1,500 construction workers on the site.

The total costs are expected to be £757 million. These comprise:

Purchasing the land and design fees	£120m
Building the stadium	£352m
Demolishing the old site and fitting the new	£99m
Infrastructure improvements	£21m
Finance and management costs	£165m
Total cost	**£757m**

However, several pundits suggest that the true cost will be much higher and may reach as much as £900 million. History supports the view that overspends are the norm. The Millennium Stadium in Cardiff suffered a serious underestimate of the final costs, which led to an overspend of between £26 and £70 million, depending on which report is read. The Scottish Parliament buildings and the Channel Tunnel were also both well over budget. Stadiums finished both on time and on budget are rarities.

Sources: **www.wembleystadium.com**; Simon Inglis, 'The New Wembley', *The Times*, 6 January 2006

Answer all questions.

1 Suggest some of the problems that the architects, Foster and Partners, and the builders, Multiplex Constructions (UK) Ltd, may have had in fixing the budget for building the New Wembley Stadium.

(6 marks)

2 Using the information in the case study, calculate the possible variance if the costs do reach £900 million.

(4 marks)

3 Discuss whether this possible variance is acceptable.

(14 marks)

(24 marks)

CHAPTER 31

Cash flow

Most firms that go out of business do so because of cash-flow problems rather than because they are not making a profit. Firms can carry on in business while making losses, but they cannot continue to trade if they are unable to pay their wages and suppliers due to a lack of cash. Cash-flow problems arise if there is insufficient money flowing into a business in relation to the amount that is flowing out in the form of payments for bills.

The example of MG Rover

In April 2005, it became clear that all was not well at MG Rover. A shortage of cash meant that the firm was forced to stop producing cars. There had not been enough money to pay the company's suppliers; nor was there enough money to pay its workers. Talks with a possible buyer or partner, Shanghai Automotive Industry Corporation (SAIC), broke down. The government agreed to provide a loan of £6.5 million to pay the staff for another week, but this was not the answer for a business that had creditors to the value of £1.4 billion. Some time later, MG Rover was sold to another Chinese carmaker, Nanjing, for £53 million.

All businesses have to ensure that they have enough money (working capital) to meet their daily bills — something MG Rover could not do.

Cash flow versus profit

An important distinction should be made between cash flow and profit. *Cash flow* is concerned with the day-to-day finances of an organisation. Ensuring that there are sufficient funds to pay the wages and the rent is all about having enough cash. Once the process of producing the goods has taken place, *profit* becomes a factor. However, it is difficult to make a profit if there is insufficient cash to buy the raw materials to enable production to occur, and a profit will only occur once the goods produced have been sold.

Cash-flow forecasts

A **cash-flow forecast** is a prediction of the values of money that are coming in (inflows) and going out (outflows) of a business. It is important to remember that it is just a forecast and therefore may not be accurate as circumstances change. The business environment (see Chapters 9–19) can affect both cash inflows and outflows. For example, a rise in interest rates may reduce sales and therefore reduce the flow of cash into a business. The rise

may also increase the payments on any loans that the business has, which will in turn increase the level of outflows.

Elements of a cash-flow forecast

The parts of a cash-flow forecast are as follows.

Cash inflow

Cash inflows represent the income that comes into a business, usually in the form of sales revenue (see Figure 31.1).

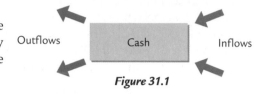

Figure 31.1

KEY TERMS

cash-flow forecast: prediction of cash movements in and out of a business

cash inflows: money coming into a business, usually in the form of revenue

cash outflows: money leaving a business to pay day-to-day bills

Cash outflow

Cash outflows represent the money that goes out of a business to pay for the costs of running the business, such as the materials needed to make the goods.

Net cash flow

This is found by deducting cash outflows from cash inflows. The result can be either positive or negative. *Positive cash flow* occurs when the value of cash inflows is higher than the value of cash outflows, as shown in Table 31.1. *Negative cash flow* occurs when the value of the outflows is higher than the value of the inflows. In Table 31.2, the net cash flow equals £110,000 − £130,000 = −£20,000.

> **EXAMINER'S VOICE**
>
> When the answer to a cash-flow calculation is negative (i.e. outflows are higher than inflows), you can show this either by using a minus sign or by putting the figure in brackets, as in Table 31.2. As long as it is clear to the examiner what you have done, either is acceptable.

January 2006	£	£	
Inflows			
Sales revenue	100,000		
Total cash inflows		100,000	(addition of all inflows)
Outflows			
Materials	40,000		
Wages	50,000		
Total cash outflows		90,000	(addition of all outflows)
Net cash flow		10,000	(inflows − outflows)

Table 31.1 Positive cash flow

January 2006	£	£	
Inflows			
Sales revenue	110,000		
Total cash inflows		110,000	(addition of all inflows)
Outflows			
Materials	80,000		
Wages	50,000		
Total cash outflows		130,000	(addition of all outflows)
Net cash flow		(20,000)	(inflows − outflows)

Table 31.2 Negative cash flow

Opening balance

This represents the amount of money a business starts with at a given point in time, usually the start of a financial year or the start of the month.

The opening balance of a cash-flow forecast for a new business represents any money that the business has before it begins trading. This usually takes the form of a loan.

Closing balance

This is the amount of money at the end of a given period of time — either the end of the financial year or the end of the month. The closing balance for the month of January will become the opening balance for February and so on. Using the example in Table 31.3, the closing balance for January is –£150 and therefore the opening balance for February is also –£150.

Item	January	February	March	April	May	June
Opening balance	1,500	(150)	(350)	(150)	250	900
Sales revenue	2,000	4,000	5,500	6,500	8,000	8,500
Bank loan	0	0	0	0	0	0
Total inflows	3,500	3,850	5,150	6,350	8,250	9,400
Raw materials	2,000	2,500	3,500	4,000	4,750	5,000
Labour costs	1,000	1,050	1,200	1,500	2,000	2,150
Rent	400	400	400	400	400	400
Gas and electricity	250	250	200	200	200	200
Total outflows	3,650	4,200	5,300	6,100	7,350	7,750
Net cash flow	(150)	(350)	(150)	250	900	1,650
Closing balance	(150)	(350)	(150)	250	900	1,650

Table 31.3
Cash-flow forecast (£)
for Bethany and Lauren's
Cards

e **EXAMINER'S VOICE**

The presentation of cash-flow forecasts and statements varies. Some, such as Table 31.3, include the opening balance as part of the cash inflows, in which case the net cash-flow figure will be the same as the closing balance. Others calculate the net cash flow by deducting the outflows from the inflows and *then* adding or subtracting the opening balance to work out the closing balance.

A **cash-flow statement** is a record of the actual amounts of inflows and outflows. This can be compared with the forecast.

The value of cash-flow forecasts

A cash-flow forecast helps a business to predict when, if at all, it may encounter a shortage of cash, shown by a negative cash flow. This means that the business can warn its bank that it might need to borrow some money in the form of an overdraft to cover the period when there is insufficient cash to meet its day-to-day costs.

The forecast can also be used as a means of control for the business. If outflows are growing faster than forecast, it may require remedial action to resolve the situation.

 KEY TERM

cash-flow statement: a record of the actual cash movements of a business over a specific period of time

What causes cash-flow problems?

Cash-flow problems have the following possible causes.

Too much stock

Overproducing means that the levels of stock start to pile up. This stock has been paid for, in the sense that the raw materials have been bought, wages have been paid to workers to transform the raw materials into finished goods, and other bills, such as utilities, have also been paid. However, until the stock is sold, the business is not gaining any revenue. As a consequence, there has been a large outflow of cash with no inflow.

Businesses are sometimes tempted to buy in more stock than they need, in order to benefit from buying in bulk savings (economies of scale). However, this may simply tie up cash in stock.

Poor (late) payers

In order to gain business, it may have been part of a firm's marketing strategy to offer buyers credit terms (e.g. giving them a month to pay). If debtors are slow to pay, the business may need to borrow cash in order to buy more materials and pay wages.

Poor economic conditions

If there is high unemployment or rates of interest are high, demand for goods and services will be lower, which in turn will reduce the likely revenues for businesses.

Seasonal demand

For businesses that rely on selling seasonal goods and services, cash-flow problems are more likely when their goods are out of season. During this time, the business will still be incurring costs such as rent, rates and some wages, and yet will have little revenue flowing into it.

HEMERA TECHNOLOGIES

Methods of improving the cash flow of a business

A firm's cash flow may be improved in several ways.

Working capital restructuring

The working capital of a business consists of cash, stock and debtors (see Chapter 4). Changing the amount of stock will alter the amount of cash available to the business.

Sainsbury's found that it had an excess amount of stock in its warehouses, some of which was out of date. Consequently, it had to change its storage and distribution methods in order to tie up less money in stock.

Increasing sales

By increasing sales, a business will increase the amount of cash inflows.

Although there will be some increase in outflows to pay for the necessary raw materials, the net cash flow should improve.

Selling off stock at sale prices

Many retail outlets, knowing that some of their stock is about to reach its sell-by date, will offer these items at drastically reduced prices in order to bring in some revenue rather than none at all.

Factoring

A business can sell its **debtors** to a factoring company. If business A is owed money by its debtors, but has yet to be paid, this may create a cash-flow problem, especially if business A has already paid for raw materials to make the goods that it has sold. The factoring company gives business A a percentage of the value of the debtors (as much as 90%) and keeps the other 10% as a charge for giving business A the money now. It is then up to the factoring company to get the debtors to pay as quickly as possible to enable the factoring company to make its money. By getting a prompter payment from the factoring company, business A will have money flowing into its business to help meet its bills and improve its cash flow.

Leaseback

A business can sell some of its assets, such as its land or a factory, and then lease them back by paying rent. This brings a substantial injection of money into the business (inflow) but creates a regular outflow in the form of the lease charge. This is a drastic step as it involves the business selling an asset that could have been used as security to borrow money. Nevertheless, in an emergency, many businesses have taken this step. Several football clubs, when cash flow has become a serious problem, have sold their ground and then leased it back.

Overdrafts

An overdraft is a short-term solution to a negative cash-flow problem. A bank lends a business money to cover its temporary negative cash flow and enable it to meet its day-to-day bills. The overdraft is helpful because it can be flexible in terms of the amount borrowed and the length of time for which the loan is required.

Reducing credit periods

By reducing the credit time offered to customers, a business should receive its revenue earlier. However, there is a risk that the customers may go to a rival business that offers a longer credit period.

Buying less stock and operating just-in-time

Although having less stock helps to reduce the amount of cash tied up in stock, it may create problems in terms of meeting customers' needs. Organising a just-in-time process can also be expensive initially (see Chapter 50).

Further sources

Company reports, which can be obtained direct from plc companies or from the *Financial Times*

YOUR TURN

Questions

Time allowed: 20 minutes

1 State **three** sources of cash outflows. *(3 marks)*

2 State **three** possible causes of a negative cash flow. *(3 marks)*

3 Explain how selling off stock will improve the cash flow of a business. *(5 marks)*

4 From Table 31.4, calculate the following. Show your working.
  a total expenditure for February
  b net cash inflow for March
  c opening balance for April

(6 marks)

(17 marks)

Table 31.4
Cash-flow statement
(£000)

Item	January	February	March	April
Opening balance	50			
Sales revenue	100	150	175	
Total cash inflows				
Wages	25	25	45	
Interest	10	10	10	
Fuel	5	5	10	
Total cash outflows				
Net cash inflow				
Closing balance				

Case study

Time allowed: 25 minutes

Red Letter Days

Rachel Elnaugh founded Red Letter Days in 1989. The business sold vouchers for exciting adventure days, including driving expensive sports cars, parachuting and hot-air ballooning, to name but a few.

The turnover of the business reached over £20 million, which having been achieved over such a short time, brought Rachel Elnaugh to the attention of the business press. She was seen as the modern entrepreneur. Such was her success that the BBC invited her to join a television programme, *Dragons' Den*, which allowed people with new business ideas to put their case and possibly receive financial backing.

By August 2005, Red Letter Days had gone into liquidation, owing £5 million to a range of suppliers of the adventure days. Cash-flow problems were cited as the main cause of the demise of a company that had been so successful that it floated on the stock exchange only a few years after it started.

As a result of the collapse, many suppliers of the adventure days were left with outstanding debts that Red Letter Days had not paid. Everyman Motor Racing suffered: by July

2005, it was owed £150,000. Headcorn Parachute Club was also owed money, as was Marine Connection, responsible for the Adopt a Dolphin charity. Although Marine Connection was only owed £15,000, this was sufficient debt to jeopardise the conservation project.

Answer all questions.

1 Explain the likely causes of the cash-flow problems experienced by Red Letter Days. *(6 marks)*

2 Evaluate the most appropriate methods of improving the company's cash flow. *(12 marks)*

(18 marks)

Costs

To make a profit, a business has to ensure that its revenue (the income from the sale of its products) exceeds its costs. Many people think that to increase profit, it is necessary for a firm to sell more goods and therefore gain more revenue. However, careful control of costs may be just as effective as higher revenue in adding to a business's level of profit.

Careful control of costs is essential if the business is operating in a competitive market where it is not easy to alter prices. Unfortunately, one of the most common ways for a business to cut costs is to reduce its number of employees. Headline news in August 2005 included the following:

- Metronet, which is helping to improve London's underground, announced that it was to cut nearly 300 jobs in an attempt to reduce costs.
- Ford Motors' Volvo cars division planned to lay off up to 1,500 workers to reduce costs by more than £72 million. Volvo had been hit by strong competition.

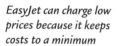

EasyJet has become a household brand because of its careful attention to costs, which has enabled it to charge low prices. Other products and services under the 'easy' name, such as the company's recent ventures into cruises and hotels, have relied on keeping costs to a minimum.

EasyJet can charge low prices because it keeps costs to a minimum

In order to keep a check on the level of costs, it is useful to classify them. This chapter looks at costs under a number of headings.

Fixed costs

KEY TERM

fixed costs: costs that are not directly related to the level of output (e.g. the factory, machines, business rates)

Fixed costs (also known as *overheads* or *indirect costs*) are costs that do not change as output or sales change. They have to be paid whether sales are 10 or 1,000. For example, factory buildings have to be paid for, usually in the form of interest on a loan. This interest is a fixed amount that the business pays on a regular basis (probably monthly), irrespective of the level of production. Similarly, the costs of the machines used to make the products are a fixed cost. Those who administer the business (e.g. the managers and secretaries) all have to be paid even before production has begun. Marketing activities are also a fixed cost because the advertising has to be paid for irrespective of the level of sales that is achieved.

Figure 32.1 shows that fixed costs remain constant as output changes.

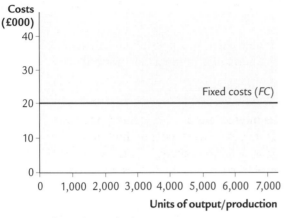

Figure 32.1 Fixed costs

Figure 32.2 An increase in fixed costs

Although these costs are referred to as fixed costs, it is more accurate to suggest that they are fixed *in the short term*. If production continues to increase, it might be necessary to purchase an additional machine to cope with the extra production required. In this instance, the fixed costs have increased, but only in order to meet the increase in production. The actual cost of purchasing the machine will remain the same regardless of whether the increase in production is 1 or 1,000. The fixed cost line will now change, as shown in Figure 32.2.

> **KEY TERM**
>
> **variable costs:** costs that are directly related to the level of output (the raw materials)

Variable costs

Variable costs are costs that are directly related to the level of output or sales. Variable costs increase when output increases and fall when output falls. A bakery will incur variable costs for the ingredients used in making bread. These raw materials, such as flour and yeast, change in proportion to the quantity of bread produced. Variable costs are often stated per unit — as the cost for each item produced. Unlike fixed costs, when production is zero, the variable costs are zero. Such costs can be shown as a straight line which slopes upwards as output increases (see Figure 32.3).

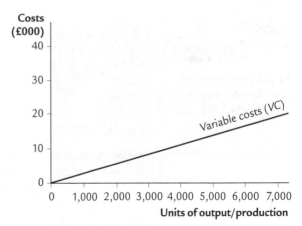

Figure 32.3 Variable costs

> **e EXAMINER'S VOICE**
>
> Ensure you are familiar with the alternative names for costs, as an examination question could use any of those mentioned here.

CHAPTER 32 Costs

KEY TERM

total costs: fixed costs
+ variable costs

Total costs

Having identified fixed and variable costs, it is possible to calculate the **total costs** for a business producing a particular product. The formula is:

$$\text{total costs} = \text{fixed costs} + \text{variable costs}$$

or

$$\text{total costs} = \text{direct costs} + \text{indirect costs}$$

The total cost line starts above zero because of fixed costs, as shown in Figure 32.4.

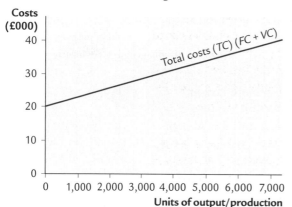

Figure 32.4 *Total costs*

Units of output	Fixed costs (£)	Variable costs (£)	Total costs (£)
0	100,000	0	100,000
100	100,000	1,000	101,000
200	100,000	2,000	102,000
300	100,000	3,000	103,000
400	100,000	4,000	104,000
500	100,000	5,000	105,000

Table 32.1 *Calculation of total costs*

Table 32.1 shows how total costs are derived from fixed and variable costs. Notice again that, even when no output is produced, costs are incurred. The fixed costs, probably for the factory, machines and administration, all have to be paid for. These costs do not change even as the output increases.

Unit cost

Table 32.1 helps to explain the significance of falling unit costs. The **unit cost** is the cost of producing one product and can be calculated using the formula:

$$\text{unit cost} = \frac{\text{total costs}}{\text{output}}$$

Reducing unit costs is a useful way for a business to survive in a competitive market. Using the figures in Table 32.1, when production is at 100 units:

$$\text{unit cost} = \frac{£101,000}{100} = £1,010$$

whereas when 500 units are produced:

$$\text{unit cost} = \frac{£105,000}{500} = £210$$

This fall in the unit cost is mainly due to the fixed costs being spread over a greater number of units.

An understanding of these costs will be useful when we come to consider the concepts of *contribution* and *breakeven* in Chapters 33 and 34.

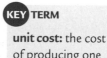

KEY TERM

unit cost: the cost of producing one unit = total costs ÷ output

Marginal cost

Marginal cost is the cost of producing one additional (extra) good. Using the information in Table 32.1, the total cost of producing 201 goods is:

£100,000 fixed costs + (£10 × 201 = £2,010) variable costs = £102,010

As fixed costs do not change, the marginal cost is the increase in variable costs, which is £10.

 KEY TERM

marginal cost: the cost of producing one extra unit

Social cost

The implications of a business decision are not always included in the business's own costs. There might be a significant cost to other stakeholders or to the country as a whole. For example, a tobacco company producing cigarettes has to pay for the manufacturing process and the marketing and distribution of its cigarettes. However, it does not pay the negative costs of treating people who are diagnosed with cancer as a result of smoking: this is a social cost.

Similarly, every time you or a member of your family drives a car, although some costs are paid by you, such as the cost of petrol, the damaging carbon dioxide emissions and the problems resulting from them are not charged to an individual driver, but are borne by society as a whole.

Opportunity cost

The opportunity cost is related to what a business could have spent money on. If a business such as McDonald's spends money on a new advertising campaign to highlight its range of healthy salad foods, it cannot spend that money on helping franchise owners improve the standard of their seats. The opportunity cost is the next best alternative (money towards new seats) that had to be given up in order to spend the money on its first choice (the advertising campaign).

YOUR TURN

Questions
Time allowed: 15 minutes

1 State **two** alternative names for indirect costs. *(2 marks)*

2 Suggest which type of cost best fits each of the following items. For example, raw materials are direct or variable costs.
   a cost of machinery
   b fuel for an airline such as British Airways
   c cost of an advertising campaign
   d salaries
   e wages of production workers *(5 marks)*

3 On Thursday, 4 August 2005, the Bank of England's Monetary Policy Committee announced a reduction in interest rates of 0.25%, bringing rates down to 4.5%. Suggest which type of costs of a business will have been reduced.

(3 marks)

Units of output (000s)	Fixed costs (£000s)	Variable costs (£000s)	Total costs (£000s)
0			200
10		20	
20			
30		60	

Table 32.2

4 Using Table 32.2, calculate:
  a total costs for an output of 10,000
  b variable costs for an output of 20,000
  c fixed costs
  d variable cost for 1 unit of output   *(4 marks)*

(14 marks)

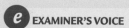 **EXAMINER'S VOICE**

Be careful to note the denominations given in the question. In question 4, output is given in thousands, as are the fixed, variable and total costs. Remember also to show your working. Laying your figures out clearly will help the examiner to see what you are doing.

Case study

Time allowed: 35 minutes

The national minimum wage

In October 2004, the government increased the national minimum wage level by nearly 8%. The new minimum wage for adult workers was set at £4.85 an hour. There were slightly smaller increases for workers up to the age of 21.

For many businesses, the increase was viewed as another problem to be faced. The retail sector, in particular, was greatly affected. With very small profit margins, any increase in retailers' costs was a problem, especially in a competitive market. The problem did not stop at having to find the extra money to pay those who were paid at the national minimum. In some areas, because of the high turnover of staff, especially in the retail sector, some employers were already paying above the minimum wage level in an attempt to increase their retention rates. Once their lowest-paid workers received an 8% pay rise, the rest of the workforce wanted a similar amount in order to maintain the difference between wage levels.

However, the dilemma facing the government is to balance the need to ensure that the national minimum wage is sufficient to maintain a decent standard of living, while being careful not to keep

increasing it to levels that add too much to the costs of businesses, which may then cut the number of staff they employ.

Amanda Aldridge, head of retail at KPMG, stated that 'the increases seen in the minimum wage over recent years cannot go on indefinitely. Further rises could cut profits, making business less disposed to take on labour'.

Source: adapted from *Marketing*, October 2004

Answer all questions.

1 State **two** costs that a retail business would have to pay.   *(2 marks)*

2 If the national minimum wage were £5 an hour and it was increased by 5%, calculate the new minimum wage.   *(3 marks)*

3 Explain why any increase in costs for a retailer is a problem.   *(5 marks)*

4 State which type of costs would be affected by an increase in the national minimum wage.   *(1 mark)*

5 Discuss the likely consequences of increasing the national minimum wage for the stake-holders of a retail business.   *(14 marks)*

                                          (25 marks)

CHAPTER 33

Contribution

A business needs to cover its costs in order to make a profit, but it is important to understand that a profit is not made as soon as goods start to be sold. The concept of *contribution* is useful in deciding whether a particular product is helping a business to make a profit.

Contribution is the revenue that is received from selling a product *less* the direct costs (or variable or unit costs) of producing that good. Assuming the revenue is greater than the direct costs of making the good or providing the service, the good is making a contribution to the overheads (fixed costs). In some cases, if the overheads have already been paid for, all revenue will be a contribution to profit.

Contribution or marginal costing

KEY TERM

contribution:
revenue – direct costs

To calculate the **contribution per unit** (i.e. how much each unit of production is contributing to overheads), the following formula is used:

contribution per unit (CPU) = price – direct or variable costs

For example, Jaskaren and Inderjit decided to run a disco for their GCSE business enterprise. They fixed the price of the tickets at £5. This price included entrance to the disco and some food. The cost of the food to be provided for each person was £2. The hire of the hall and the fee for the DJ came to £150. Therefore, to calculate the contribution for each ticket sold, the formula is:

CPU = price – direct costs
= £5 – £2 = £3

To calculate the **total contribution** (i.e. how much in total is being contributed to the overheads), the formula is:

total contribution = CPU × sales

Therefore if 70 tickets were sold, the total contribution would be:

CPU of £3 × sales of 70 = £210

To calculate the profit of the disco, the formula is:

KEY TERM

total contribution:
contribution per unit
× sales

profit = total contribution – overheads or fixed costs

In other words, the profit equals any revenue left after paying the overheads:

profit = £210 – £150 = £60

Remember to show your working clearly, so that the examiner can follow what you have done. If you do this, you may receive marks even if your answers are incorrect because examiners use the 'own figure rule'. This means that if you make a mistake in a calculation the examiner will take whatever figures you have used. It is also important to write out any formula you use, as this will show the examiner that you know how to calculate the answer, even if the figures you use are wrong.

The principle involved in the contribution method can be illustrated using the model shown in Figure 33.1.

The contribution method can be used both to calculate how much an individual product contributes to overheads or profits and to compare the contributions of more than one product to the overheads of the business. Table 33.1 shows the profit calculation for a barbecue set, while Table 33.2 compares the contributions of three models of the product.

From this, the business is able to see that model 1 is contributing the most: £40,000. However, all three models are contributing in a positive manner because the revenue from them is greater than the direct costs.

In Table 33.2, the overheads of the business have been shared equally between the three models, although it could allocate the overheads according to a percentage of sales or by any other means it chooses.

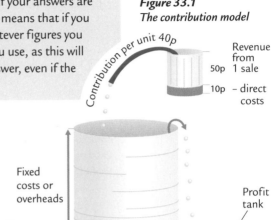

Figure 33.1
The contribution model

	Value (£)
Price	100
Direct costs	20
Contribution per unit (price – direct costs)	80
Sales (units)	500
Total contribution (sales × CPU)	40,000
Overheads	25,000
Profit (total contribution – overheads)	15,000

	Value (£)			
	Model 1	Model 2	Model 3	Total
Price	100	120	180	
Direct costs	20	25	35	
Contribution per unit (price – direct costs)	80	95	145	
Sales (units)	500	300	150	
Total contribution (sales × CPU)	40,000	28,500	21,750	
Overheads (£30,000)	10,000	10,000	10,000	
Profit for each model (total contribution – overheads)	30,000	18,500	11,750	
Total profit (models 1 + 2 + 3)				60,250

Table 33.1
Calculating the profit from a product: Bar-B-Q

Table 33.2
Comparing product contributions: three models of Bar-B-Q

However, the advantage of contribution costing is that the overheads do not have to be allocated at all. In most cases, a business will not worry about how much of the overheads an individual model should pay. Instead, the contribution from all three models can be added together:

total contribution = £40,000 + £28,500 + £21,750 = £90,250

and then the overheads can be deducted to produce the profit, as in Table 33.3:

profit = £90,250 – £30,000 = £60,250

Table 33.3
Deriving profit from total contribution

	Model 1	Model 2	Model 3	Total
		Value (£)		
Price	100	120	180	
Direct costs	20	25	35	
Contribution per unit (price – direct costs)	80	95	145	
Sales (units)	500	300	150	
Total contribution (sales × CPU)	40,000	28,500	21,750	
Total contribution (models 1 + 2 + 3)				90,250
Overheads				–30,000
Profit (total contribution – overheads)				**60,250**

Table 33.3 shows how contribution is usually used by business. As long as the overheads are covered, it is not important which of the products pays for them. The important thing is that the products are making a contribution to overheads. For many businesses, it is almost impossible to work out which product should pay what percentage of the overheads because sales vary, as do the direct costs, and therefore the best method of ensuring that the overheads are paid is for all the products that the business produces to contribute.

ⓔ EXAMINER'S VOICE

Most examination questions will concentrate on calculating the total contribution of products and then subtracting the value of the overheads (as in Table 33.3), to ascertain the level of profit or loss. Some questions may refer to labour costs and the cost of materials. Both are classed as direct costs unless otherwise stated.

Special orders

The concept of contribution can be used to decide whether it is worthwhile for a business to take on an additional or special order. We can see this with an example.

Go Nuts 4 Donuts, a business that produces cakes that are sold to a range of cake shops within the area, has overheads of £55,000. The business has not been trading for long but has already managed sales of 400,000.

The manufacturer already sells a range of doughnuts (12 different types in total, but with almost identical costs), but is keen to attract an order from a supermarket chain. Table 33.4 shows the sales and costs of the doughnuts.

INGRAM

The supermarket wants to place an order for an initial quantity of 25,000 doughnuts but is only prepared to pay 15p per doughnut. The owners are not sure what to do. For this type of business decision, contribution is particularly helpful. Calculating the contribution is done in exactly the same way as before. The result is shown in Table 33.5.

It is necessary to ascertain whether the total contribution from the firm's existing sales cover its overheads. Table 33.4 shows that the total contribution of £80,000 covers the overheads of £55,000 and therefore the business makes a profit of £25,000. By taking on the additional order, the business will receive an additional contribution of £1,250. This will add to the profit of the business because the overheads have already been covered.

This assumes that the business does not incur any additional overheads in fulfilling this special order, and that it has enough capacity spare to produce the 25,000 extra doughnuts. There are other factors to consider when taking on such an order, especially if this is only an initial order:

- How many doughnuts will the supermarket want in the future?
- Will Go Nuts 4 Donuts be able to produce the number of doughnuts that may be ordered in the future?
- How will its existing customers be affected?
- Will additional overheads be incurred?
- Will the business have enough staff to take on the potential increases in production?
- How keen is Go Nuts 4 Donuts to develop the supermarket as a long-term source of business?

Table 33.4 *Sales and costs of doughnuts: Go Nuts 4 Donuts, 2005*

Price of doughnuts	30p
Sales	400,000
Overheads	£55,000
Direct costs	10p per unit
Therefore:	
Contribution per unit (price 30p – direct cost 10p)	20p
Total contribution (sales × CPU)	£80,000
Profit (total contribution – overheads)	£25,000

Price of doughnuts for supermarket	15p
Sales for special order	25,000
Direct costs	10p per unit
Contribution per unit (price 15p – direct cost 10p)	5p
Total contribution (sales × CPU)	£1,250

Table 33.5 *Special order: Go Nuts 4 Donuts*

YOUR TURN

Questions

Time allowed: 25 minutes

1. State the formula for calculating contribution per unit. *(2 marks)*
2. total contribution – overheads = ? *(1 mark)*
3. Explain why contribution is an important decision-making tool for business. *(4 marks)*
4. If a business sells 10,000 roses at £1.50 each and the direct costs are 40p and fixed costs are £11,500, discuss whether the business should stop selling roses? *(14 marks)*

(21 marks)

Case study

Spiders

Oliver and Uzma have run their website business, 'Spiders', for just over 4 years with considerable success. It is operated from Oliver's home in order to reduce the overheads of the business. Most of its expenditure is on the equipment required to create the websites for its customers. There is some expenditure on marketing the business, but not a significant amount as it relies on word of mouth and the careful placement of pop-up adverts on the internet. Sales and costs data for three types of website that the company offers are presented in Table 33.6.

The overheads for the business are £45,000.

Oliver and Uzma have been approached to produce a new website for a client, who has asked for a special price because if the website is good, there will be the possibility of many more to follow.

However, the requirements are quite unusual and neither Oliver nor Uzma has tackled work of this kind before. Oliver is keen to try and thinks the business should accept the order. Uzma is much more cautious and does not think it is worth it.

'I've worked out the costs for this new order. The price wanted is £1,200 and our labour costs and raw materials will come to £1,150. We won't be making any money from the order.'

	Website A	Website B	Website C
Price (£)	1,500	2,000	2,400
Labour costs (£)	700	900	1,100
Sales (units)	50	10	5

Table 33.6 *Sales and cost data for Spiders websites*

Answer all questions.

1 Calculate the contribution per unit for each of the original three types of website, A, B and C. *(6 marks)*

2 Using the data in Table 33.6, calculate the level of profit from the original websites. *(4 marks)*

3 Calculate the contribution of the proposed new website. *(3 marks)*

4 Discuss the additional factors that might influence Spiders in deciding whether to take on this special order. *(14 marks)*

(27 marks)

Breakeven analysis

Breakeven analysis is another tool that businesses can use to aid the decision-making process. The **breakeven** point or level is the level of output at which total revenue covers (is equal to) total costs. In Table 34.1, it can be seen that breakeven output is 500 units, where total revenue and total costs are both £50,000.

Units of output	Sales revenue (£)	Fixed costs (£)	Variable costs (£)	Total costs (£)	Profit/loss (£)
0	0	25,000	0	25,000	–25,000
100	10,000	25,000	5,000	30,000	–20,000
200	20,000	25,000	10,000	35,000	–15,000
300	30,000	25,000	15,000	40,000	–10,000
400	40,000	25,000	20,000	45,000	–5,000
500	50,000	25,000	25,000	50,000	0
600	60,000	25,000	30,000	55,000	5,000
700	70,000	25,000	35,000	60,000	10,000

Table 34.1
Breakeven output

e EXAMINER'S VOICE

When looking at a table such as Table 34.1, be careful to read the correct amounts, whether they are in millions or thousands of pounds. Getting the right formula and making the right calculation, but writing out the wrong answer because you have not noted the denominations carefully, will cost you valuable marks.

Calculating breakeven

Producing a table in order to find the breakeven level is time consuming. A quicker method is to use a *formula for breakeven*, which includes the concept of contribution, introduced in Chapter 33. The formula is:

$$\text{breakeven output} = \frac{\text{fixed costs}}{\text{contribution per unit}}$$

Remember that:

contribution per unit = price – direct or variable costs

Here is a simple example. A business making teddy bears has fixed costs of £10,000 and the direct costs are £2.50 for each bear made. The intended selling price is £15.

e EXAMINER'S VOICE

When using the formula for breakeven, it is important to remember that it is *total* fixed costs divided by *unit* contribution. It is a common error to put the formula the wrong way round or to use total contribution.

Therefore the number of teddy bears that need to be sold to break even is:

$$\frac{£10,000}{(£15 - £2.50)} = \frac{£10,000}{£12.50} = 800 \text{ teddy bears}$$

This breakeven figure can now be used to assess whether it is possible to achieve this number of sales.

This formula can also be used to show the likely consequences for total revenue and breakeven output if there is a change in price. Increasing the price means that the contribution per unit will increase and, as a consequence, the number of goods that need to be sold to break even will fall.

Deriving breakeven graphically

Breakeven output can also be found graphically. First, we must remind ourselves how each of the curves on a breakeven graph is arrived at.

As we saw in Chapter 32, **fixed costs** (overheads or indirect costs) are costs that do not alter with the level of output and are therefore represented by a horizontal straight line. It is important to note that fixed costs exist even if no production is taking place. For example, if a business uses a machine (a fixed cost) that costs £25,000, fixed costs when output is 0 are £25,000, as shown in Figure 34.1.

Variable costs (direct costs) vary directly in proportion to the level of output. As output increases, the level of variable costs also increases, as shown in Figure 34.2.

Total costs are calculated by adding together fixed and variable costs. It is important to note that the total cost line does not start at zero. Even when a business is not producing any goods, it still has fixed costs. The business will have bought the factory premises and the machines necessary to produce the goods. In this case, the total cost curve starts at £25,000, as shown in Figure 34.3.

(e) EXAMINER'S VOICE

It is always worth commenting on an answer for breakeven. Is it very high or low? Is it possible to make this many units?

KEY TERMS

fixed costs: costs that do not vary with output

variable costs: costs that vary with output

total costs: fixed costs + variable costs

total revenue: price × sales or output

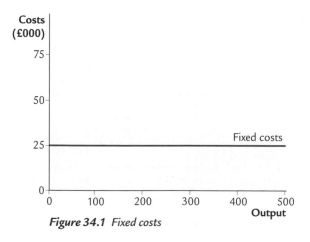

Figure 34.1 *Fixed costs*

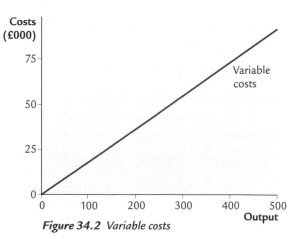

Figure 34.2 *Variable costs*

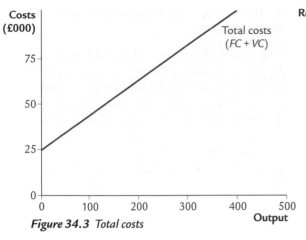

Figure 34.3 *Total costs*

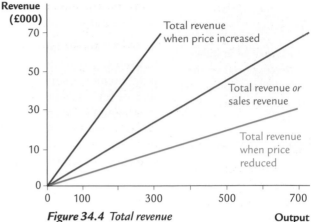

Figure 34.4 *Total revenue*

Total revenue for a business is calculated by the formula:

total revenue = price × level of output

The slope or gradient of the total revenue line is determined by the price: the higher the price, the steeper the total revenue line will be. This is shown in Figure 34.4.

The point at which the total revenue line cuts the total costs line (where $TR = TC$) is the breakeven point.

Knowing its breakeven level of output enables a business to assess its profit and loss at various levels of output. In Figure 34.5, any level of output to the right of the breakeven level will be profitable, whereas any level of output to the left of the breakeven level will mean that a loss is incurred.

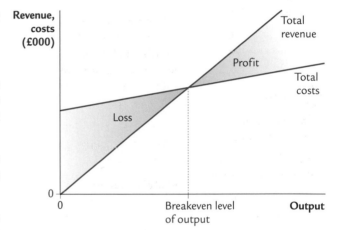

Figure 34.5 *Profit and loss*

Margin of safety

The concept of breakeven allows a business to assess the consequences of changing the conditions within which it operates. The **margin of safety** is the level of output in excess of the breakeven level (see Figure 34.6).

Knowing its margin of safety can help a business to assess the impact on its profits of any change in either the actual level of output

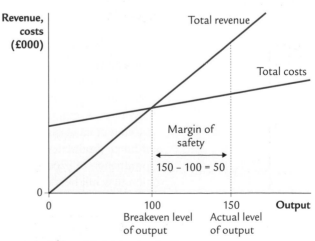

Figure 34.6 *Margin of safety*

KEY TERM

margin of safety: the difference between the actual level of output and the breakeven level

or the breakeven level. The smaller the margin of safety, the less flexibility the business has to deal with any change in circumstances.

Table 34.2 shows the margin of safety at various levels of actual output, for a business producing flags. At (b), there has been a fall in the level of output and therefore, assuming all other variables are constant, the margin of safety falls. At (c), a further fall in actual output now means that there is no margin of safety and therefore any other disruption to output will result in a loss being incurred.

𝑒 EXAMINER'S VOICE

Always state the formula in any question that requires a calculation. If you get the formula right, you will usually get some marks even if your subsequent calculations are wrong.

	Actual level of output	Breakeven level of output	Margin of safety
(a)	1,200	800	400
(b)	1,000	800	200
(c)	800	800	0

Table 34.2 Margin of safety at varying levels of output

Benefits and limitations of breakeven analysis

Benefits
Using breakeven analysis has several benefits for a business:
- Tables and diagrams are easy to view, comprehend and interpret.
- It is useful as a management tool to aid the decision-making process.
- It can be used to show the level of profit at a given level of output.
- The margin of safety can be established.

Limitations
However, breakeven analysis does have limitations:
- The direct or variable costs may change, depending on the quantities involved. A manufacturer is likely to be able to negotiate a discount for buying in large quantities.
- If batch production (see Chapter 46) is being used, which may involve the production of fixed quantities for each batch, the breakeven level of production may not be obtainable. Producing in quantities of 50 in each batch, with a breakeven level of 840, means that the business would have to decide whether to produce 800, which would mean a loss, or 850, which is beyond the breakeven output but may be more than the demand for the product.

- Calculating the total revenue relies on there being just one price. In business, this is unlikely as discounts may be offered for large purchases, or promotional offers may be used, especially in the early stages of the product life cycle.
- There is an assumption that if the price increases, total revenue will also increase. This is often not the case as an increase in price can lead to a fall in sales and therefore a fall in revenue.
- There is sometimes uncertainty as to whether costs are fixed or variable — labour is an obvious example.
- There is no certainty that all goods will be sold. Circumstances change and therefore may affect sales.

YOUR TURN

Questions

Time allowed: 25 minutes

1 State the formula for calculating the breakeven level of output. *(2 marks)*

2 Assuming Fiona sells only handbags, at £40 each, and her direct costs per item are £10, with fixed costs of £7,500, calculate the breakeven level of sales. *(4 marks)*

3 a If Fiona is able to sell 320 handbags, calculate the level of profit made. (Remember to show your working.) *(3 marks)*
  b What is her margin of safety? *(2 marks)*

4 If Fiona were to increase her prices, explain what would happen to her breakeven level of sales. Use a diagram. *(5 marks)*

5 Figure 34.7 shows total revenue and total cost curves for a firm. From the diagram:
  a calculate the selling price *(2 marks)*
  b calculate the total variable costs at the breakeven level of output *(2 marks)*

(20 marks)

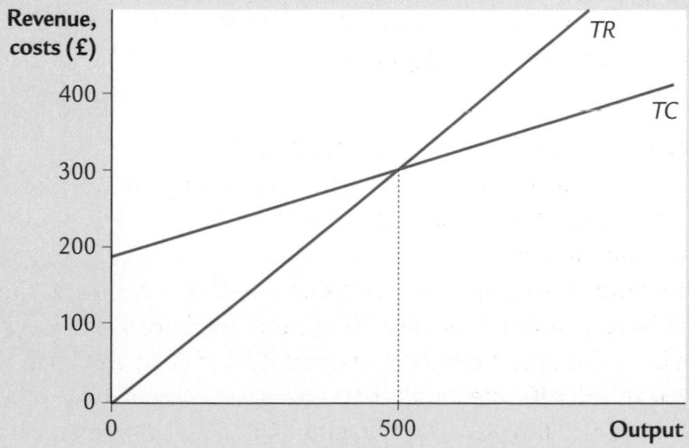

Figure 34.7
Revenue and cost curves

> **e EXAMINER'S VOICE**
>
> Whenever you include a diagram in your answer, ensure that you explain what has happened. Don't just draw it and assume it is obvious. Ensure that all parts of your diagram have clear labels.

Case study

Time allowed: 35 minutes

The business of revising

Deepa Patel was keen to set up her own business, providing revision courses for AS and A-level business studies students in her local area. She bought a laptop and PowerPoint projector for £1,500. After she had conducted some market research, she found the cost of hiring a suitable hotel conference room was £400, which included a sound system and a screen for the PowerPoint projection. The room would hold up to 300 students. Deepa had already spent £100 on a mailshot to schools in her region.

She had calculated that the cost of providing revision material in a folder worked out at £4 per student. This would cover the cost of a folder and all the photocopied revision sheets. In addition, the hotel would charge £4 per student for water and coffee.

Not having undertaken such courses before, Deepa wanted to make sure that she had some support and decided it would be a good idea to employ an assistant for the day of any revision course. In an attempt to keep her costs down, she chose to employ a student from her own school and agreed to pay her £50 for the day.

She was uncertain what price to charge, even after researching similar courses that had been advertised in a business studies magazine to which she subscribed. After considerable thought, Deepa decided to charge £18 for the full-day course.

Answer all questions.

1 Calculate the total fixed costs for Deepa's revision course.   *(2 marks)*

2 Calculate the breakeven number of students for her revision course.   *(4 marks)*

3 For her first revision course, a total of 245 students attended.
   a Calculate the level of profit she made.   *(4 marks)*
   b Calculate the margin of safety for the revision course.   *(3 marks)*

4 If Deepa decided to increase her prices to £20 for the day's course, calculate by how much the breakeven level of output would change.   *(3 marks)*

5 Using the breakeven information, analyse which price might be best for Deepa's revision course.   *(9 marks)*

                                                                                  (25 marks)

CHAPTER 35

Investment appraisal

Investment appraisal helps a firm to decide whether an investment is feasible. A business such as Cadbury requires capital equipment (machines) in order to produce the chocolate that it intends to sell. The decision about whether it should buy these machines is based on the costs of such machines and the likely revenue that they will generate.

It is important to note, however, that investment appraisal does not just apply to the purchase of a machine. The same technique can be applied to the purchase of new premises, or a marketing campaign.

A business needs to be able to judge whether an investment is going to be worthwhile. There are different ways of assessing the viability of such planned investments. The two main methods are *payback* and *accounting rate of return*. In order to apply these methods of investment appraisal, it is necessary to be able to calculate the likely cash flows from any investment.

Payback

The **payback** method of appraisal considers how quickly the cost of the investment will be covered or paid back. If two proposals are being considered, whichever pays back the faster is likely to be favoured (though there are exceptions to this, which will be considered later). Payback is sometimes seen as a measure of the amount of risk involved with an investment. The longer it takes to pay back the cost of the investment, the greater the risk involved. Payback is used as the first test of the viability of an investment.

We will look at three examples of investment appraisal, using the payback method. Note the following terms that will be used:

- *Net cash inflow* is the likely return on the investment per year, calculated by the formula:

    net cash inflow = revenue – direct costs

- *EOY* = end of year (by the end of the year, the cash flow will have occurred)
- *EOY 0* is when the investment takes place; in the tables that follow, the figure in this column represents the cost of the investment

Example 1
Table 35.1 shows the cash inflows resulting from an investment costing £50,000. The payback period is calculated by totalling the cash inflows until the cost of the investment is covered.

KEY TERMS

investment appraisal: methods of assessing whether an investment is a feasible option

payback: an investment appraisal technique used to assess the amount of risk involved, by calculating how long it takes to recover the cost of the investment

EXAMINER'S VOICE

Payback has nothing to do with whether a business can borrow the money or whether it can afford to pay back the loan.

Year	Net cash inflow	Cumulative cash inflow
EOY 0	0	(50,000) (the new investment)
EOY 1	10,000	(40,000)
EOY 2	20,000	(20,000)
EOY 3	20,000	0

Table 35.1
Payback calculation: example 1

EXAMINER'S VOICE

As usual, it is essential to show your working when calculating payback. The layout of your answer will not only help you to be organised and reach the right answer, but it will also help the examiner to see what you have done.

It is a good idea to write the figures for the cumulative inflows in brackets if they are negative. By doing this you will be able to see which figures are positive and which are negative, just as you did for a cash-flow statement.

For this particular investment, payback happens by the end of year 3. This is because, by the end of year 3, there is sufficient net cash inflow to pay back the £50,000 investment.

Example 2

There are occasions when the figures do not work out as simply as for the example above. In order to calculate exactly when the payback occurs *within* a given year, it is necessary to look at the year in which the payback occurs. Table 35.2 shows cash inflows resulting from another £50,000 investment.

Year	Net cash inflow	Cumulative cash inflow
EOY 0	0	(50,000) (the new investment)
EOY 1	20,000	(30,000)
EOY 2	20,000	(10,000)
EOY 3	20,000	10,000

Table 35.2
Payback calculation: example 2

In this example, the payback occurs within the third year. In order to calculate exactly when this happens, you need to look at the amount still to be paid back at the start of year 3 (10,000) and divide this amount by the cash inflow for the third year:

$$\frac{10,000}{20,000} = \frac{1}{2}$$

Half of a year is 6 months and therefore the payback period is 2 years and 6 months.

Example 3

The payback method can also be used to compare two possible investment plans in an attempt to ascertain which is the better option in terms of payback.

Emma runs a garden centre and is thinking about investing in a café to encourage her customers to stay longer. She has two

possible proposals, A and B. Idea A would cost £20,000 and idea B would cost £30,000. It is estimated that the revenues from these investments will be as shown in Table 35.3.

Year	Net cash inflow A	Cumulative cash inflow A	Net cash inflow B	Cumulative cash inflow B
EOY 0	0	(20,000)	0	(30,000)
EOY 1	5,000	(15,000)	10,000	(20,000)
EOY 2	5,000	(10,000)	10,000	(10,000)
EOY 3	5,000	(5,000)	10,000	0
EOY 4	5,000	0		

Table 35.3
Payback calculation: example 3

The payback period for idea A is 4 years, while for idea B it is only 3 years. Therefore, according to the payback method, idea B is the better option because the payback is quicker.

What this method does not tell Emma is whether she can afford the initial cost of idea B at £30,000. For a small business, idea A may be a more affordable option. There is also no information on the life of each investment. The equipment bought for Emma's garden centre café may last longer if idea B is pursued, in which case it will bring in revenue over a longer period of time.

Just as important is how quickly such equipment is changing. Technological progress may mean that the equipment for idea B becomes outmoded and therefore buying the cheaper option A may be advantageous.

Is payback a good investment appraisal technique?
Table 35.4 summarises the pros and cons of the payback method of investment appraisal.

Advantages	Disdvantages
• It is easy to use and understand. • It is a useful test of the amount of risk involved: the longer the payback, the greater the risk.	• It ignores the value of money over time – over time, the spending power of money falls as prices rise. • It does not take into account any cash inflows after the payback period. • It does not measure the profitability of the investment. • There is no indication of when the cash inflows occur.

Table 35.4
Advantages and disadvantages of the payback method

It is important to remember that there are other factors a business will need to consider in order to make an appropriate decision. The business's ability to borrow the capital needed to undertake the investment will depend on the nature of the business, its size and how long it has been trading. A small, newly established business will find it much harder to obtain a large loan or to afford the repayments than a multinational business like Shell.

The business will have to consider how long the investment will last, since the life expectancy of some machines may only be a few years. For example, a business thinking about buying a new van to distribute its goods will have

A payback period of 3 years may be quite acceptable for a café

to gauge how long the van will last and compare this with the payback period. The life expectancy of a vehicle will be a lot shorter than that of a new factory, which could last for 30 years.

The usefulness of the payback method may also depend on how quickly demand changes for the product or service in question. In other words, the volatility of the market is significant. A payback period of 3 years may be more than satisfactory for a café, but it will be far too long for a nightclub or garden centre, where fashions and tastes change very quickly.

Accounting rate of return (ARR)

Unlike the payback method, the **accounting rate of return** (ARR) measures the profitability of a particular investment. It looks at the profit generated from the investment as a percentage of the investment. Alternative names for this technique include: *annual average rate of return* and *average rate of return*.

KEY TERM

accounting rate of return: an investment appraisal technique used to assess the profitability of an investment

Example

An initial investment of £20,000 for an ice-cream van, which will be kept for 4 years, produces cash inflows of:

	£
EOY 0	(20,000)
EOY 1	11,000
EOY 2	12,000
EOY 3	13,000
EOY 4	14,000
Total cash inflows	50,000

Once the total inflows have been calculated, the initial investment cost is deducted to give the profit.

	£
Total cash inflows	50,000
Investment cost	(20,000)
Profit	30,000

To gain the annual average profit, the total profit is divided by the number of years: in this case, 4.

$$\text{annual average profit} = \frac{£30,000}{4} = £7,500$$

Finally, to gain the return on the investment, the annual average profit is divided by the original cost of the investment.

$$\text{accounting rate of return} = \frac{£7,500}{£20,000} = 0.375 = 37.5\%$$

To recap stage by stage:

1 Calculate the total cash inflows.
2 Subtract the cost of the investment to gain the total profit.
3 Divide the total profit by the life expectancy of the investment (in years)
4 Divide the answer by the initial cost of the investment to obtain the % ARR.

Is the ARR a good investment appraisal technique?

Table 35.5 summarises the pros and cons of accounting rate of return for investment appraisal.

e EXAMINER'S VOICE

As with all statistical techniques, it is important for you to state the formula or method of calculation and show all your working. There are usually more marks for showing how you have attempted the question than there are for the right answer.

Advantages	Disadvantages
• It takes into account all the cash flows throughout the life expectancy of the investment. • It measures the profitability of the investment.	• There is no indication of when the cash flows occur. • It ignores the value of money over time. • There is a need to know the life of the investment.

Table 35.5
Advantages and disadvantages of ARR

YOUR TURN

Questions

Time allowed: 35 minutes

1 State **two** methods used for investment appraisal. *(2 marks)*

2 Which method of investment appraisal considers the level of risk? *(1 mark)*

3 Calculate the payback period of an investment that costs £250,000 and generates the following net cash inflows:

EOY 1	£20,000
EOY 2	£40,000
EOY 3	£100,000
EOY 4	£120,000

(4 marks)

4 State **two** limitations of the payback method. *(2 marks)*

Year	Cash inflows (£000) Project 1	Project 2
EOY 0	(300)	(200)
EOY 1	50	30
EOY 2	60	30
EOY 3	70	50
EOY 4	90	60
EOY 5	80	80

Table 35.6 **Investment projects**

5 A business renting holiday homes has two options to consider. Using the accounting rate of return method and Table 35.6, suggest which investment the business should undertake. *(6 marks)*

6 Apart from the accounting rate of return, analyse other factors the business should consider before deciding which project to invest in. *(10 marks)*

(25 marks)

CHAPTER 36

Profit and loss

The profit and loss account (P&L) measures the level of profit or loss that a business has made in a given period of time. This period is often known as the trading or accounting period and is usually 1 year. The P&L is used to inform shareholders and other interested stakeholders of how well the business has performed.

The layout of the P&L is significant, as it allows the levels of revenue and costs in the business to be identified quickly. This may be helpful when it comes to assessing the level of company performance and how this can be improved.

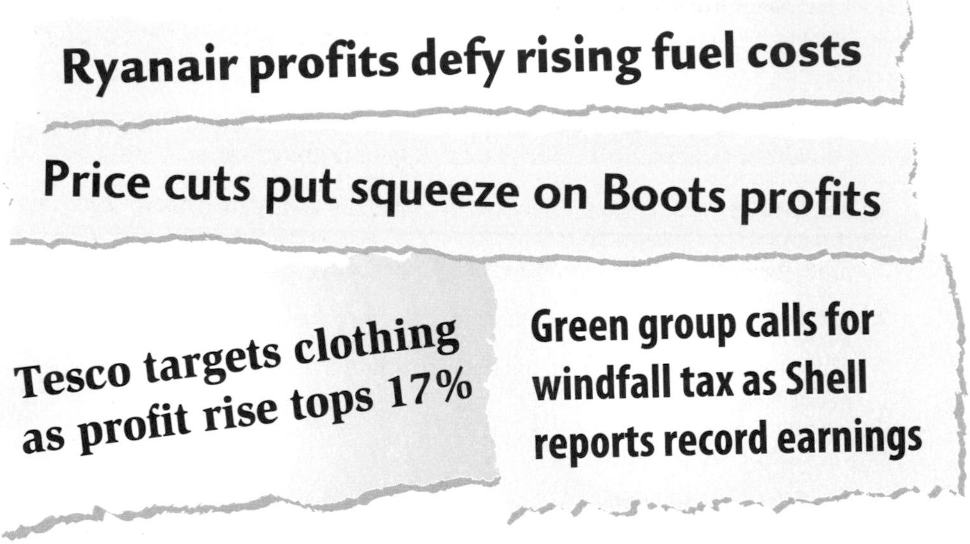

Figure 36.1 Profit levels are an indicator of company performance

Ryanair profits defy rising fuel costs

Price cuts put squeeze on Boots profits

Tesco targets clothing as profit rise tops 17%

Green group calls for windfall tax as Shell reports record earnings

The profit and loss account

First, it is important to establish exactly what is meant by the term 'profit'. Profit is the difference between the level of income generated and the costs incurred by the business. In its simplest form, profit is calculated by subtracting the total costs from the total revenue.

Table 36.1 sets out a typical P&L at the end of the accounting period. The heading, 'Profit and loss account, year ending December 2005', is important because it lets stakeholders know how the business has performed in a given time period. The financial year can start at any time, but the majority of businesses use either the tax year, which runs from April to April, or the calendar year, January to December.

Profits for public limited companies are normally declared every 6 months. Some of the larger companies declare their profits quarterly. The half-year profits are known as the 'interim results'.

(1) Sales revenue (or turnover)		200,000	
(2) *Minus* Cost of sales	80,000		
(3) Gross profit		120,000	(1 – 2)
(4) *Minus* Expenses	50,000		
(5) Operating profit		70,000	(3 – 4)
(6) *Minus* Interest payable	5,000		
(7) Net profit		65,000	(5 – 6)
(8) *Minus* Tax	10,000		
(9) *Minus* Dividends	20,000		
(10) Retained profit		35,000	(7 – 8 – 9)

Table 36.1 Profit and loss account, year ending December 2005 (£)

It can be seen from Table 36.1 that the figures start off high, but slowly get smaller, as deductions are made. The first deduction is for the *cost of the sales*, which is calculated in a special way:

cost of sales = opening stock (from previous year) +
        stock purchased in this year – closing stock (what stock is left)

It is only necessary to count the cost of the stock that was actually sold in the financial year. For example, if the business started with stock worth £50,000, bought £75,000 worth and at the end of the year had £45,000 left, then:

opening stock	£50,000
+ stock bought	£75,000
– closing stock	£45,000
cost of sales	£80,000

In the year, the actual amount of stock sold cost £80,000 and therefore that is the amount that has to be taken off the sales revenue of £200,000 to calculate the gross profit for 2006:

gross profit = sales revenue – cost of sales
        £200,000 – £80,000 = £120,000

Other items in the P&L are calculated as follows:

operating profit = gross profit – fixed costs (which include expenses)
        £120,000 – £50,000 = £70,000

net profit = operating profit – interest paid
        £70,000 – £5,000 = £65,000

retained profit = net profit – tax and dividends
        £65,000 – £30,000 = £35,000

Retained profit is money that the business can use in whatever way it wishes. It may be invested in the business in the form of new capital equipment or used to pay off debts.

> **EXAMINER'S VOICE**
>
> Amounts to be deducted can be put in brackets to signify that they are negative quantities, but in a P&L this is not essential. Again, the layout of your work is crucial to help both you and the examiner to see what you have done. You do not need to use two columns for the figures; however, by doing so it is easier for you to know what is a deduction and what is a running total.
>
> It is unlikely that you will be asked to undertake any calculations at AS. However, you should understand how the figures are arrived at because this will make it easier for you to analyse a P&L.

Interpretation of profit and loss accounts

A P&L often refers to at least 2 years' accounts. This enables a comparison to be made. For example, in Table 36.2, analysing how the figures for 2005 and 2006 differ is of interest. Although the amount of retained profit is the same at £5,000, the activities in the 2 years are different.

Table 36.2 shows that sales revenue increased by £10,000 between 2005 and 2006, while the cost of sales increased by only £2,000, and therefore the gross profit increased by £8,000.

The operating profit increased by £6,000 (expenses having increased by £2,000).

	2006	2005
Sales revenue	120	110
Cost of sales	65	63
Gross profit	55	47
Expenses	37	35
Operating profit	18	12
Interest payable	5	4
Net profit	13	8
Tax and dividends	8	3
Retained profit	5	5

Table 36.2 Profit and loss account for E & T Ltd, 2005 and 2006 (£000)

The retained profit was the same, possibly because the dividend paid increased (but the amount of tax paid could also have increased).

> **EXAMINER'S VOICE**
>
> Be careful when commenting upon any form of financial statement. Ensure you refer to the correct amount involved. In Table 36.2, the values are thousands of pounds.

The value of profit and loss accounts

The P&L serves the following purposes:
- It enables the business to make decisions. Being able to see the amount of profit made may affect any decisions on future expenditure.

e EXAMINER'S VOICE

It is important to ensure that you comment on profit and loss accounts in the context of the case information provided. Is the business in the case new or well established? The level of profit could vary according to the age of the business. Similarly, the level of profit could be affected by the nature of the product or service, and how competitive the market is in which the business is operating. A new business is likely to be concerned with survival, rather than making a huge profit.

If the case states that the business is hoping to expand, it is possible that the short-term level of profit will be low, due to the cost of expansion. In the long run, profits will be higher, once the benefits of the expansion (assuming it is successful) have had the chance to increase production and therefore profits.

- Management can use the P&L to monitor the progress of the business in terms of targets set. It also allows comparisons to be made between financial years.
- It provides other stakeholders with valuable information. A bank may be interested in the amount of profit a business has made in order to assess the amount of risk involved in lending money to the business.
- It helps investors to decide whether they should invest their money in the business. A profitable business is more likely to attract further investors.
- The Inland Revenue can see that the correct amount of tax is paid.
- The employees are able to see how much profit the business has made and therefore whether it is in a strong position to increase their wages and salaries.
- It is a legal requirement under the Companies Act to maintain financial records for certain types of business.
- Suppliers may want to see the P&L as evidence of the company's ability to pay for materials supplied.

Further sources

Company reports, which can be obtained direct from plc companies or from the *Financial Times*

YOUR TURN

Questions

Time allowed: 20 minutes

1 Given that sales revenue for 'Bags & All' in 2005 was £147,000, and that costs of sales were £49,000, calculate the firm's gross profit. *(2 marks)*

2 Outline the difference between gross profit and operating profit. *(4 marks)*

3 Outline **three** ways in which the P&L may be useful to external stakeholders. *(6 marks)*

4 Explain **two** ways in which internal stakeholders would be affected by a fall in the level of profit made by a company. *(4 marks)*

(16 marks)

Case study

Time allowed: 30 minutes

The Carphone Warehouse Group plc

Group revenues up 25% to £1,290.7 million!

Charles Dunstone, CEO, stated: 'These strong results show the continuing success of Carphone Warehouse's strategy...'

	October 2005	September 2004
Revenue	1,290,687	1,032,954
Cost of sales	877,875	715,746
Gross profit	412,812	317,208
Operating expenses	329,148	255,669
Other expenses*	48,018	34,029
Operating profit	35,646	27,510
Interest payable	5,724	4,334
Interest received	2,623	1,975
Profit before tax	32,545	25,151
Tax	7,921	6,689
Net profit	24,624	18,462

Table 36.3 *Profit and loss account, 26 weeks ended 1 October 2005 (£000)*

* The term 'Other expenses' is used for simplification.

Source: adapted from results issued in *The Times*, November 2005

Answer all questions.

1 Using the P&L shown in Table 36.3, calculate the percentage increase in net profit from 2004 to 2005.

(3 marks)

2 Explain which stakeholders will benefit from the results shown in the P&L.

(5 marks)

3 To what extent should Charles Dunstone, CEO, be pleased with the results shown in the P&L?

(12 marks)

(20 marks)

CHAPTER 37

Balance sheets

A **balance sheet** is a statement about the value of a business at a given point in time, showing what it owns (its assets) and what it owes (its liabilities). All private and public companies issue balance sheets for their shareholders.

The elements of a balance sheet

Table 37.1 shows a sample balance sheet. As with profit and loss accounts, it is normal for a balance sheet to be headed with the name of the company and the period covered.

Fixed assets	100,000	
Less Depreciation (10%)	10,000	(10% of 100,000)
		90,000
Current assets		
Cash	3,000	
Stock	40,000	
Debtors	12,000	
Total current assets		55,000	(adding cash, stock and debtors)
Current liabilities		
Overdraft	5,000	
Total current liabilities		5,000
Net current assets		50,000	(current assets – current liabilities)
Long-term liabilities	75,000	
Net assets		65,000	(fixed assets + net assets – long-term liabilities)
Shareholders' funds*		
Ordinary shares	50,000	
Retained profit	15,000	
		65,000

Table 37.1 Balance sheet for Snapshots Ltd, year ending 31 December 2005 (£)

*These amounts should balance (be equal to) the net assets.

The meanings of the various terms contained in the balance sheet are as follows:

- **Fixed assets** — the factory or buildings owned by the business. Fixed assets also include the fixtures and fittings of the business, such as the machines and equipment used. They can be classified into *tangible assets* — those that can be seen, such as the factory or machinery — and *intangible assets* — those that are not visible, such as a patent or the goodwill of the business (the value of its reputation or good name). It is difficult to put an accurate value on intangible assets.
- **Depreciation** — an allowance for wear and tear on the factory and/or the machines. This is subtracted to give a realistic value of the business.

As the factory and machines age, their value decreases. Depreciation reflects this, usually as a percentage of the assets.

- **Current assets** — assets that are not fixed. They can be converted into cash within the accounting period. The more easily these assets can be converted into cash, the better. This ability to convert assets into cash is known as *liquidity*.
- **Cash** — another term for money.
- **Stock** — materials, unfinished goods (work in progress) and finished goods.
- **Debtors** — money owed to the business.
- **Current liabilities** — what is owed by the business.
- **Overdraft** — a short-term loan for less than 1 year.
- **Net current assets** — current assets minus current liabilities.
- **Long-term liabilities** — loans for more than 1 year.
- **Net assets** — net current assets plus fixed assets minus long-term liabilities.
- **Capital employed or shareholders' funds** — the value of the funds tied up in the business as shares and retained profits.

One additional term used in connection with balance sheets is *prudence*. This is an accounting phrase that is used to indicate that there is a need to be cautious when valuing a business.

The balance sheet will balance in terms of the calculations. Net assets (what the business owns) will always be equal to (balanced by) the shareholders' funds. Hence balance sheets sometimes say that the net assets are 'financed by' the shareholders' funds, which are also referred to as the 'source of funds'.

For negative amounts — money that is owed — the figure is often shown in brackets. This makes it easier to remember that the figure is negative and needs to be subtracted to gain a realistic value of the business.

A considerable amount of information can be gained from the balance sheet for Snapshots Ltd about the value of the business. The owner may want to state that he or she owns a shop that is worth £100,000. However, because the shop is quite old and some of the fixtures are in need of replacing, the true value is less than this. Depreciation takes into account this ageing factor.

The current assets of the business total £55,000. This does not mean that the owners can go out and spend this amount of money. Some of the £55,000 is tied up in stock, which may or not be sold soon. A business selling food may have a lot of current assets tied up in stock that will not sell, perhaps due to the sell-by date being reached.

Debtors represent some of the current assets. This is money that is owed to the business. However, it is not certain that this money will be paid to Snapshots.

Even after noting these points, there are current liabilities to be taken into account. Liabilities represent money that is owed by the business — in this case, £5,000. As a consequence, the true value of Snapshots' current assets is £50,000 (assuming that stock can be sold and that debtors will pay up).

To gain a more realistic value of the business, any long-term liabilities (money that is owed for more than 1 year) also have to be taken into consideration. These amount to £75,000.

Thus, for Snapshots Ltd, the actual value of the business is £65,000. We can summarise the various calculations as follows:

		£
Fixed assets		90,000
+ Net current assets	(current assets − current liabilities) (£55,000 − £5,000)	50,000
− Long-term liabilities		75,000
Net assets		65,000

How useful is a balance sheet?

It is important to be able to look at a balance sheet and understand what is being stated. Do the figures make sense for this type of business selling this particular product? For Snapshots Ltd, a small retail outlet selling cameras and photographic equipment, the figures appear realistic. However, the make-up of the assets may vary depending on the type of business. A large supermarket chain such as Tesco would have a high proportion of its current assets in stock and cash, whereas a furniture chain such as DFS, which is often promoting its products with offers of 'buy now, pay later with 3 years' interest-free credit', will have a lot less in stock (products are made to order) and a high proportion of debtors.

The balance sheet is helpful if a business wants to obtain a loan from a bank. By looking at the balance sheet, the bank would be able to assess if the business had sufficient assets that could be used for security against the loan.

The balance sheet is also helpful to a business, as it can assess if it has enough cash to keep itself afloat. By looking at the current assets and liabilities, it can calculate its net current assets to see if it has enough cash (working capital) to keep the business going. All businesses need money on a day-to-day basis to be able to buy raw materials and pay bills and wages.

Further sources

Company reports from the *Financial Times*

Questions

Time allowed: 20 minutes

1 From the list below, state whether each item is an asset or a liability. You may want to say which category it belongs to. For example, cash = asset (current asset).
   a debtors   **c** loan for 4 years
   b overdraft   **d** machines   *(4 marks)*

2 State how to calculate net current assets.   *(2 marks)*

3 The figures in Table 37.2 are part of a balance sheet for two retail outlets. Comment on the figures.

(6 marks)

	Business A	Business B
Current assets (£000)		
Cash	112	10
Stock	600	112
Debtors	10	600

Table 37.2

Fixed assets	250
Current assets	
Cash	15
Stock	110
Debtors	60
Current liabilities	
Creditors	95
Net current assets	
Net assets	
Shareholders' funds	340

Table 37.3
Balance sheet for Techno Computers Ltd as at 31 March 2006 (£000)

4 Using the information in Table 37.3, calculate the following:

a net current assets

b net assets

Explain how you know your answer for **b** is correct.

(8 marks)

(20 marks)

Case study

Time allowed 35 minutes

Expansion at Hudsons

The Staffordshire garage, Hudsons Ltd, has decided to expand its sales rooms in order to display more cars, both new and second-hand. At present it has a small indoor showroom area, which can only house three cars. The planned extension would allow Hudsons to have three times as many cars on display and room for a comfortable sales office to provide prospective customers with a seating area and drinks facilities.

The cost of the extension is about £120,000. The shareholders of the company are unwilling to finance this extension plan, having recently financed a very successful new workshop for the repair and servicing of cars. In order to gain the necessary finance, Hudsons' finance director, Martin, has provided the

bank with its most recent balance sheet (Table 37.4).

'We need to remain competitive,' said Ian, the managing director. 'The bank manager will take one look at our balance sheet and lend us the money without hesitation.'

Fixed assets	600
Less Depreciation (10%)	60
Current assets	
Cash	10
Stock	250
Debtors	30
Current liabilities	80
Net current assets	
Long-term liabilities	110
Net assets	

Table 37.4
Balance sheet for Hudsons Ltd as at 31 March 2005 (£000)

Answer all questions.

1 Calculate Hudsons' net assets.

(4 marks)

2 Using the balance sheet, suggest whether the bank manager will be prepared to lend Hudsons the money it requires for the extension.

(9 marks)

3 Other than the balance sheet, evaluate the factors that are likely to affect Hudsons' decision about whether to borrow the £120,000 needed to build the proposed extension.

(12 marks)

(25 marks)

Module 2872
Business Decisions
Module 2873
Business Behaviour

People in Organisations

CHAPTER 38

Workforce planning

Workforce planning is concerned with how a business forecasts the quantity and quality of human resources that it needs to achieve its objectives. It is sometimes referred to as *human resource planning*. It is not just about the right number of people to employ and how suitable staff are hired. It has more to do with ensuring that the 'right' people are employed at the appropriate time. These people are those who will fit in with the ethos of the business and help the business achieve its goals.

KEY TERM

workforce planning: a process used to plan the number and quality of employees that will be required, in both the short and long term

The role of workforce planning has become much more important because the business world and the individual markets in which businesses operate are continually changing (see Chapters 8–19). Consequently, the human resource needs of a business will also change. The best businesses are those that can plan ahead and see what their needs will be as soon as possible in order to obtain the right staff at the right time.

What workforce does the business need?

In order to achieve the objectives of the business, a workforce needs to be effective and efficient. There are only so many workers who will fit the needs of a particular business, so ensuring that the right staff are employed is vital. Without having the right staff at the right time, a business may have problems meeting the needs of its consumers, or it may experience a high turnover of staff because they are overworked or not suitable for the business.

It is important to ensure there is a balance in the workforce in terms of both *age* and *skills*. If all the workers were aged over 50, there might be a problem in bringing new ideas and enthusiasm to the business. Similarly, if the entire workforce were under 25, there would probably be a lack of experience and a lack of authority.

Most businesses need to have a range of skills available. For example, Figure 38.1 shows the workforce at a motor sales, service and repair garage.

It is important to ensure there is a balance in the workforce in terms of age and skills

General Manager
Service Supervisor
Service Adviser
Workshop Controller
Sales Manager
Sales Adviser
Sales Administrator
Customer Care Manager
Accounts
Receptionist
Bodyshop Manager
Bodyshop Administrator
Mechanics
Parts Buyer
Cleaners

Figure 38.1 *The workforce at a motor sales, service and repair garage*

Each of these jobs requires different skills and therefore will need different training and working conditions. For instance, the mechanic will need the right tools in order to do the job properly and the receptionist will require telephone equipment and an environment that welcomes customers and makes them feel comfortable. Providing the right working conditions will help the business to retain its staff, and therefore help to reduce labour turnover. This will also make it easier for the business to forecast its demand for staff.

For a larger business, planning its staff requirements may be considerably more complicated. It is not easy to balance the human resource needs and financial constraints of a large business to ensure that its objectives can be achieved. Therefore, planning is essential.

What factors affect a business's human resource needs?

To gauge what the human resources needs of a business are, many factors need to be considered.

- **The changing needs of the business.** For example, a change in sales trends may mean that the business needs to increase the production of one product and decrease that of another. As a consequence, more workers with one particular skill may be needed. On the other hand, increased sales may just mean there is a need for more staff overall.
- **Staff turnover.** Staff may leave the firm due to retirement, promotion or being discontented with the job or environment in which they work. When staff leave, for whatever reason, they have to be replaced.
- **A change in technology.** Improved technology might mean that there is less need for labour, or that the existing workforce has to be retrained to work with the new equipment.
- **A change in the method of production.** For example, moving from batch to flow production (see Chapter 46) might mean that the workforce will need retraining or will be surplus to requirements.
- **Budgeting.** The level of the budget may alter the number of workers who can be employed. If there are financial problems within the business and costs have to be reduced, cutting the labour force is one possible method of achieving the necessary reductions.
- **The economy.** The state of the economy will affect the demand for labour. For example, if the economy is enjoying a boom situation, there will be a high level of economic activity and therefore there will be a high demand for labour. The converse is true during a recession.
- **Unforeseen circumstances.** Natural disasters and terrorist activities have greatly affected

Flooding in Cornwall in 2004 left many businesses without premises and led to the loss of many jobs

TOPFOTO

the human resource needs of business. Flooding in Cornwall and Carlisle in 2004 and 2005, for example, left many businesses without premises and led to the loss of many jobs.

Unfortunately for business, forecasting human resources needs is not straight-forward. Sometimes, without any real warning, circumstances arise that can alter a firm's workforce requirements.

What factors affect a business's ability to meet its human resource needs?

A firm's ability to meet its workforce needs depends on several factors:

- **The availability of potential workers.** Are there sufficient numbers of potential employees available?
- **The skills of the potential workers.** Are there sufficient numbers of workers available with the right skills?
- **The nature of the work required.** If the job involves unsociable hours or is unpleasant, the number of potential workers will be restricted. However, if the job is of a high status or has additional benefits, it is likely to attract a greater supply of interested people.
- **The demand for workers from other businesses.** This will affect the avail-ability of employees and the level of wages that they expect. If labour is scarce, the general wage level will be higher.
- **The location of the business.** Is the location attractive? If not, an insufficient number of workers will be willing to move to this area to gain employment.
- **The cost of living in the locality of the business.** The cost of housing is one reason why some businesses in the London area find it difficult to gain workers. To overcome this problem, some workers may choose to live some distance from the business. However, if this is to be possible, a convenient form of transport needs to be available.
- **Government legislation.** This may make it harder or more expensive to take on workers. An increase in the national minimum wage, for example, might discourage a business form taking on additional staff due to the increased costs.
- **EU regulations.** Regulations such as the Working Time Directive, which limits the permitted hours of work for many employees, may mean that additional workers are needed to complete the required tasks.

Strategies adopted by businesses to meet their human resource needs

The cost of trying to recruit labour, in terms of time and money, is significant. In addition, the cost of employing labour is expensive: not only do wages have to be paid, but also statutory working conditions have to be met. The rights of workers have been strengthened, making it harder to dismiss staff. It is for

these reasons that many businesses now consider alternatives to employing staff on a full-time basis.

Once the right staff have been recruited (see Chapter 39), it is important to ensure that they are looked after in an appropriate manner. If not, they will leave or not perform effectively. With this need to look after the workforce in mind, businesses have expanded the use of flexible working hours, job sharing and teleworking.

Outsourcing

A business normally has a number of employees who are important and employed on a permanent basis. However, usually in response to an upturn in business or for a one-off order, a business can subcontract work.

Outsourcing refers to the contracting of jobs to external labour. Instead of a business having to hire its own labour, it uses another business to undertake a specific job. This saves a business the difficulty of hiring staff, who may not be needed after a specific job or task has been completed. By outsourcing, the business also avoids incurring additional costs of having more permanent staff. This is particularly important for businesses whose trade is irregular.

In a competitive market, outsourcing is a way of reducing costs, and it has been undertaken by many UK businesses. Marks and Spencer's customer services department is run from India, as are several call centres, including National Rail Enquiries.

Flexible working hours

More businesses are now operating flexible working hours in order to gain and retain the right staff. Many potential employees, particularly women, have been tempted into the workforce by such an arrangement. A large number of businesses operate a 'core' time, which may be between 10 a.m. and 3 p.m., when employees have to be present. Apart from the core time, there is flexibility, allowing employees to work to suit their own particular lifestyles.

Although this system may be more expensive to administer and operate, as the place of work may need to be open for longer hours, there are benefits:

- The business may save some money by gaining or keeping good staff and not having to spend money on recruitment and training.
- There may be benefits for the economy as a whole if this system is adopted more widely, as the rush hour will become more staggered.

Job sharing

A variety of job-sharing schemes exist. Some employees share jobs on a morning/afternoon basis, while others share on a day-to-day basis. Which system is operated usually depends on the needs of

Job sharing schemes are common in nursing

KEY TERM

outsourcing: using external labour to undertake a specific job or contract

the business and how long a handover period is required. (A handover period may be needed to ensure continuity and that everyone has been informed about what has been done to date.)

Benefits of operating a job-sharing scheme include the following:
- Employees are able to work the hours or days that suit them, which means that a business is more likely to gain and keep the staff it needs.
- If one of the job sharers is absent, some of the tasks of the job will still be covered by the other job sharer, who may even be able to take on the extra work if it is for a short period of time.

There are, however, downsides of job sharing:
- There are additional administrative costs of employing two people instead of one.
- Careful planning may be required to ensure that job sharers take a similar approach to a given task.
- If the job sharers have managerial responsibilities, differing leadership styles may confuse staff under their supervision.

Teleworking

Teleworking involves allowing employees to work away from the business premises. It has been made a lot easier due to the level of communications technology now available. Teleconferencing (multiple-way conversations by phone) and video conferencing allow effective communication without it being necessary for all employees to be present at the place of work.

The advantages of teleworking are as follows:
- Many businesses have found that the productivity of employees increases, as there are fewer distractions and interruptions at home than at the place of work.
- Allowing employees to work at home saves valuable commuting time and allows the employee to choose when to work.
- A lower level of absenteeism has been recorded.

However, the following disadvantages have been identified:
- It is harder to check that employees are actually working.
- There is an initial set-up cost in providing the equipment necessary to facilitate the required level of communication.

Further sources

www.cipd.co.uk/default.cipd

YOUR TURN

Questions

Time allowed: 25 minutes

1 Define workforce planning. *(2 marks)*

2 State **four** factors that affect the human resource needs of a business. *(4 marks)*

3 Explain **two** benefits of operating a job-sharing scheme. *(4 marks)*

4 Why is it of benefit to a business to have employees of differing ages? *(4 marks)*

5 Explain how a business may benefit from outsourcing. *(4 marks)*

6 Outline how teleworking may help to motivate employees. *(4 marks)*

(22 marks)

Case study

Time allowed: 35 minutes

Labour turnover crisis hits personalised cards business

'Choose and Deliver' is a greeting cards service that specialises in hand-made cards. These are made to order and then delivered either to the customer or to a named address. The business was started from the home of Mr and Mrs Robinson, both artists who wanted to work for themselves. Customers now visit the shop in a large village in Staffordshire or their website to order cards for all occasions. The bulk of their sales are via their website. Such has been the growth in sales that the business now employs six staff, who spend most of their time designing and producing the specialist cards.

The business is run from the shop, which has a workroom at the back and a storeroom upstairs. The employees work in quite cramped conditions because the business expanded faster than the premises could really cope with. Mrs Robinson concentrates on the production of the cards, while Mr Robinson handles the ordering of supplies and is responsible for the finances of the business.

There have recently been problems with ensuring that all the orders are met on time. Mrs Robinson is adamant that the cramped conditions are hampering production, as is the lack of staff. Staff turnover has been a problem since the business expanded. Pay is reasonable for the area, but there are times when the demand for the personalised cards is so high that the employees struggle to meet it. Mrs Robinson will not compromise on the quality of the finished cards, as this is one of the unique selling features for the business.

Employees tend to stay for about 6–18 months before leaving for a range of reasons. All the employees are female and are working to help with the family finances. Most have young children and are keen to finish work on time to collect them from nursery or school. As a consequence, they are reluctant to undertake any overtime, even with a generous incentive to do so. Mrs Robinson has tried pressurising the staff to work longer hours, but this may be one of the reasons why employees leave.

Mr Robinson is reluctant to take on extra staff, as this would affect costs and therefore profits, which are very healthy. He recently tried to change the way in which employees operate, but the lack of space prevented any viable solution.

By accident, he discovered a possible solution. One of the staff, Danielle Taton, who had only just been recruited, broke a leg in a car crash. This came at a very busy time for the business and therefore Mr Robinson delivered materials to Danielle's house for her to produce the required cards.

'I think I have a solution to our problems,' Mr Robinson said eagerly.

Answer all questions.

1 Analyse the factors that will affect the ability of Choose and Deliver to meet it human resource needs. *(9 marks)*

2 Evaluate the possible solutions to Choose and Deliver's human resource problems. *(14 marks)*

(23 marks)

CHAPTER 39

Recruitment and training

Ensuring that the best possible candidate is obtained for any job advertised is crucial to all firms. The cost involved in advertising the post, sifting through job applications, interviewing applicants and selecting an employee is high, as is the cost of training the new employee. A business must give careful consideration to the process at each and every stage, as making a mistake could mean that the whole exercise has to be repeated, costing the business time and money.

KEY TERM

recruitment: the process of employing additional staff

Recruitment

The aim of **recruitment** is to employ and retain the best possible human resources. The stages of the recruitment process are shown in Figure 39.1. This section looks at each of these in turn.

Figure 39.1
Stages of recruitment

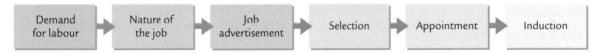

Demand for labour

Any business will need to establish that there is a demand for a particular job. This may arise from an increase in the demand for a product, which means that the firm needs to take on extra staff. Hotels often take on more staff during the summer months in order to meet demand.

The nature of the job

Once the need to take on additional staff is recognised, a **job description** should be drawn up. This consists of a job title, the name of the person to whom the employee will be responsible and some details of what the job entails. An example is given in Figure 39.2 on p. 278.

At this stage, the person or team involved with the selection process may also build a **person profile**, which will give a list of the personal qualities and qualifications for the ideal candidate. This is sometimes referred to as a **job specification**. For the senior physiotherapist post, the person profile may include:

■ qualified with a minimum of 2 years' experience
■ experience of working with a range of medical staff
■ able to motivate a team of physiotherapists who work in a busy department
■ able to communicate with consultants and patients in a supportive manner

KEY TERMS

job description: expectations for the job, usually including the tasks to be performed and the responsibilities involved

job specification or person profile: skills and characteristics of an ideal candidate for the job

Figure 39.2 *Example of a job description*

Job title: Senior physiotherapist (responsible to head of unit)

Location: Queen's Medical Centre, Nottingham

Tasks/duties: Working with acute respiratory patients on intensive care, high-dependency units and medical/surgical wards

Working conditions: Opportunities for in-service training and on-site courses
$37\frac{1}{2}$ hours a week
25 days' holiday plus bank holidays
Minimum of 2 years' experience

The business now has to decide whether the post can be filled from within the business (**internal recruitment**) or whether there is a need to appoint from outside the business (**external recruitment**).

Internal recruitment

Appointing from within the business may be considerably cheaper than appointing from outside, and it can act as a form of motivation to the existing workforce if they perceive that there is an opportunity for promotion. If it is considered that more than one candidate will apply, an advertisement for the job may be displayed within the business.

It is quite likely that there will be considerably fewer candidates if an internal appointment is made. In addition, the employers will already know which candidates are able to undertake the job, based on their previous experiences within the business. As a consequence, an internal appointment ought to be less risky than an external one, since, even after interview, knowledge of external candidates will not be as detailed. Finally, because the person appointed already knows the business and how it operates, the induction process ought to be shorter and therefore less expensive.

However, there are limitations in making an internal appointment. Appointing one internal candidate in preference to another may lead to jealousy and resentment on the part of the candidate who did not get the job. In addition, by not advertising externally, better candidates may be missed who could bring new ideas to the business. A further problem with making an internal appointment is that it is likely to create another vacancy, which then has to be filled.

External recruitment

If an external appointment is to be made, an advertisement will have to be drawn up and positioned in an appropriate medium (see the next section). There are also many employment and recruitment agencies that specialise in finding the right person for a specific job. Some of these agencies operate a system of 'headhunting', whereby the agency approaches someone whom it

KEY TERMS

internal recruitment: appointing from within the business

external recruitment: appointing from outside the business

thinks matches the job and person specification. In many instances, the headhunters find someone who is not actively seeking new employment. This process tends to be used for high status positions within industry.

Although external recruitment is more expensive than internal recruitment, it does offer the business a much higher chance of attracting a wide range of prospective candidates. An external candidate may not only bring new ideas to the business, but may also be able to tell it how other businesses are operating. However, there are sometimes restrictions on what information a person can take with them to a new job.

Job advertisement

Job advertisements normally appear in newspapers, professional magazines or the internet. It is important to balance the cost of the advertisement with the need to provide sufficient detail to screen out unsuitable candidates, while at the same time attracting those with the right qualities.

The advertisement should give prospective candidates some indication of what the post requires (a job specification) and what sort of person the business is looking for (a person profile). Figure 39.3 includes some sample job advertisements for designers.

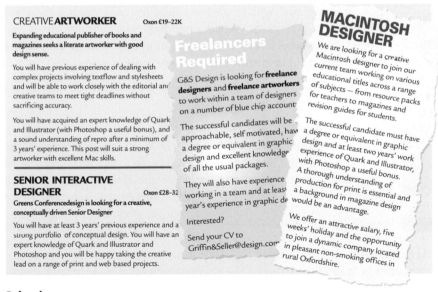

Figure 39.3
Job advertisements

Selection

For most jobs, candidates are asked to fill in an application form or compile a CV (curriculum vitae) and possibly send in a letter of application. These are used by the business to sift through the applicants before making a 'short list' of candidates to interview. In a large organisation, there may be a personnel department that is responsible for recruitment. This department will organise the selection process, which usually depends on the post to be filled.

Today, using just an interview to select the most appropriate person for a job is highly unusual. This is because interviews have been found to be unreliable in some instances, as people can be influenced by appearance and personal bias. Many firms now use a range of selection techniques. Which selection process is used will depend on:

- the nature of the job (e.g. management or shop-floor worker)
- the budget for recruitment (often influenced by the size of the business)
- the cost of the process
- the likely number of applicants

Aptitude tests (or role plays)

In an aptitude test or role play, a candidate is asked to deal with situations that he or she is likely to encounter in the job. This can be used to assess the level of skill that a candidate shows in a given situation.

Interview panels

Interviews are still an important assessment tool in the search for the right candidate for a job. However, great care has to be taken to ensure that the interview process is effective. It is important that there are not too many

Interviews are an important tool in the search for the right candidate for a job

people on the panel because the job applicant may be overwhelmed by facing several interviewers, and also there may be some duplication of questions, which wastes valuable time. Asking the right questions is essential. A good interview will combine open and closed questions. It will start with simple questions to put the applicant at ease before asking the more probing ones.

In order to save on costs, some interviews are now conducted via video links or by telephone.

Psychometric tests

These tests are designed to ascertain information about the personality of the applicant — whether the person is flexible or inflexible, assertive or passive, stable or unstable, a team player or a loner, and if he or she is able to solve problems. It is necessary for such tests to be interpreted by a trained person if they are to be effective.

Appointment

Care must be taken to ensure that the selection process is mindful of the legislation that exists to protect individuals from discrimination based on age, sex and race (see Chapter 16).

Whatever selection process has been used, and assuming that an appropriate applicant has been found, under the Employment Rights Act (1996) the employer must provide the new employee with a contract within 2 months of starting work. The contract must contain:

- job title
- location of employment

- hours of work
- rate and timing of pay
- holidays and other entitlements, such as pensions
- terms of notice

Induction

Assuming the right person has been selected, it is equally important to ensure that he or she is retained. Losing staff affects labour turnover and means that the whole recruitment process has to be repeated, at further expense to the business.

In order to help retention levels, induction programmes are implemented to ensure the successful applicant settles into the company environment and is aware of the ethos of the business. Induction concentrates on the business as a whole rather than the specific job and usually includes:

- how the particular business operates
- administrative procedures
- the location of different departments
- the corporate approach to differing situations
- the rules of the business

Training

Training benefits the business and the employee: the employer benefits from a more skilled worker and the employee benefits in terms of being more motivated.

There are two main types of training: **on-the-job** and **off-the-job**. Which of these is used depends on several factors:

- the size of the business
- the cost of the training
- the skills available to train employees
- the time available

On-the-job training

On-the-job training occurs at the place of work and is therefore more convenient and less time consuming than having to travel somewhere else. It can be organised to fit in with the other needs of the business. The effectiveness of this type of training depends on the skill and attitude of the trainer. Bad habits as well as good ones may be passed on if the training is not monitored carefully. Nevertheless, the training can benefit the trainer as well as the trainee, as the responsibility is viewed as a motivator (see Chapter 41).

Off-the-job training

Off-the-job training can take place either at the place of work or externally. It is training away from the actual job. It is more usual for the training to be done by someone who is not an employee of the business, although this

KEY TERMS

on-the-job training: learning the task at the place of employment by watching an experienced employee

off-the-job training: learning the task away from the job, either at the place of work or externally

Training benefits the business and the employees

depends on the size of the firm, as larger organisations may have their own training department.

If the training is external, the timing and details of the course will be outside the control of the employee and employer, and therefore may not be as convenient, with resulting loss of production and time. However, it will operate within a given time scale, unlike on-the-job training, which may be hampered by more pressing needs of the business and trainer. The trainee may also benefit from seeing other trainees, being able to share problems and learn about other people's work experiences.

Off-the-job training is relatively expensive and, although the course will be run by experts, the practices taught during external training may subsequently have to be adapted to suit the needs of the specific business.

The importance of training

If staff are to be retained, it makes sense to invest in them. Henry Dixon, managing director of a marketing communications agency, stated: 'It costs me £3,000 to £5,000 to recruit someone, so why not spend some or all of that on keeping your staff happy?'

Employees are more likely to be happy with companies that take the time and effort to develop them professionally and personally. Companies, large and small, can invest in their employees in order to improve retention. Procter and Gamble, for example, has an enviable reputation for staff retention and a policy of promoting from within the business.

The *Marketing* Employer of the Year online survey (17 November 2004) found that 82% of employees would prefer to stay with one company rather than take on a series of moves. The survey also stated that the majority of respondents thought that the key to professional development is training, with 65% preferring to train externally rather than be taught by senior managers from within their company. Claire Owen, managing director of Stopgap, believes that training makes employees feel valued.

Training is vital if the most is to be gained from each employee. Once trained, there is a danger that employees will demand higher wages or contemplate moving on to another business. Nevertheless, it is essential for all businesses to invest in all their available resources, including the labour force. The process of training is expensive and time consuming. It is therefore important to get the training programme right to help retain valuable employees. Offering them training will give them a feeling of involvement and an opportunity to better themselves. Motivation is covered in detail in Chapter 41.

Further sources

www.stopgap.co.uk

www.tt100.biz

Case study 1

Time allowed: 25 minutes

Online training, anytime, anywhere

Meeting the training requirements of a small business can be difficult. In particular, if demand for the company's products is unpredictable, knowing when it is a good time to run a training programme or allow staff out for training becomes almost impossible.

One solution is online training provided by the government-backed service Learn Direct. This training programme can be undertaken at home, at work or at one of several Learn Direct centres. To date, over a million employees have taken such a course since 2000.

Sarah Turpin, head of workforce development and policy at Ufi (University for Industry), the government-funded body that provides Learn Direct, stated that

Learn Direct was attempting to add to its resources in order to help small businesses with their training needs. With training offered at any time, anywhere and on almost anything, a small business employee can access knowledge in manageable amounts. Anything from spreadsheets to cash-flow forecasts can be taught. Everyone has access to a personal tutor to ensure that employees are motivated and feel supported.

Over 400 courses are available online at **www.learndirect-business.co.uk**

Source: adapted from Rachel Bridge, 'Online training, anytime, anywhere', *Sunday Times*, 31 October 2004

Answer all questions.

1 Outline **two** reasons why training is important. *(4 marks)*

2 Discuss the effectiveness of online training for employees of a small business. *(14 marks)*

(18 marks)

Case study 2

Time allowed: 25 minutes

Comet — training its staff to understand the products it sells

Comet, the electrical retail chain owned by Kesa, has decided that training its staff is the right way to compete with the growing threat from supermarkets.

Since demerging from the Kingfisher group in 2003, its strategies have changed drastically. The focus is now on the service that Comet offers to customers rather than just on the products that it sells. Coupled with a relaunch of its brand name and a change of colour scheme for its 250 stores throughout the country, Comet is investing in its staff.

Simon Fox, the managing director, wants the staff

to know about the products it is selling. He is hoping to change the views of his customers, who see the staff as inexperienced and underqualified in helping them select the right goods. Changing the image of Comet's staff will not be easy, according to Bryan Roberts, a consultant.

Comet has invested heavily in a new e-learning system, enabling the staff in each store to learn about the products being sold. Only when the staff have acquired enough knowledge of the products and passed a test to prove this will they be allowed to work with customers.

There will be two levels of understanding for the staff: 'proficient' and 'expert'. The latter can only be reached with further training and even meeting with the manufacturers of the products to be sold. It is thought that it will take about 18 months for half the staff to be at least 'proficient'.

Simon Fox, when asked about the time involved, suggested that this training strategy was essential if Comet was to get the maximum market share possible.

Source: adapted from Matthew Goodman, 'We understand our products', *Sunday Times*, 14 July 2005

Answer all questions.

1 State the difference between learning on and off the job. *(4 marks)*

2 Explain why governments spend money to finance training schemes. *(4 marks)*

3 Explain the difference between internal and external recruitment. *(4 marks)*

4 Discuss how training its employees will benefit Comet. *(9 marks)*

(21 marks)

CHAPTER 40

Employment law

Employment takes place when one person (the employee) supplies his or her labour to another (the employer) in return for payment. This chapter concentrates on the principles of employment law and the rights and duties of employers and employees.

All employers have a duty of care towards their employees. However, in addition to this duty of care, there exists a wide range of Acts to protect the employee. **Legislation** concerning employees can be conveniently divided into three categories:

- legislation relating to the recruitment of employees
- legislation relating to employees while at work
- legislation relating to the dismissal of employees (severance)

 KEY TERM

legislation: an alternative name for laws or Acts of Parliament

> ### ⓔ EXAMINER'S VOICE
>
> The Acts included in this chapter are only a selection of all the legislation that exists. They are meant to give you an idea of the range of Acts that have been passed. In an examination, knowledge of some legislation will be useful. However, you will not be expected to have an in-depth knowledge of all the legalities. Questions concentrate on how a business is affected by such legislation.

Recruitment legislation

Sex Discrimination Act (1975)

This Act makes it unlawful for employers to discriminate on the grounds of sex in advertising for and selecting employees. It is also illegal to discriminate on the grounds of gender in promotions, training opportunities and access to benefits.

Legislation had already been passed with regard to discrimination on pay, in the Equal Pay Act (1970).

Race Relations Act (1976)

This states that it is unlawful for an employer to discriminate against any employee on colour, race, ethnicity or nationality grounds.

It is unlawful for employers to discriminate on the grounds of sex or race

Legislation relating to employees while at work

Employment Rights Act (1996)

As stated in Chapter 39, within 2 months of starting employment, the employer must give the employee a written statement outlining the contract of employment. This document must include:

- the parties involved
- the starting date of employment
- a statement with regard to previous employment (if it affects the period of continuous employment)
- job title
- level of pay
- payment dates or intervals (e.g. monthly)
- hours of work
- holiday entitlement and holiday pay
- sick pay and pension entitlements
- length of notice by each party (employer and employee)

If the employer has at least 20 employees, the statement must include:
- disciplinary rules or procedures
- grievance procedures

Employees in such an organisation also have a right to an itemised pay slip showing:
- gross pay
- deductions
- net wages

Employees have an implied contractual duty to behave reasonably and responsibly towards their employers.

If no contract is given, once a pay slip has been received, there is an implied contract.

Trade Union and Labour Relations Act (1992)
This Act allows an official of a recognised trade union to take time off work without loss of pay to conduct certain types of union business. It also permits a recognised union official to undertake other union business by having a reasonable amount of time off work without pay.

It could hurt her employer too

Falls caused by slips and trips cost businesses £500 million each year. They are the most common type of workplace accident. If staff were encouraged to clean up spills and keep workplaces tidy, everyone could be saved a lot of unnecessary pain.

For free safety posters visit watchyourstep.hse.gov.uk or call 0845 345 0055.

Don't just see it, sort it.

HSE
Better health & safety
benefits everyone

COURTESY OF HEALTH & SAFETY EXECUTIVE

Disability Discrimination Act (1995)
This states that is it unlawful to discriminate on the grounds of a disability. The Act does not apply to businesses with fewer than 20 employees.

Health and Safety at Work Act (1974)
This Act is one of many pieces of legislation passed over the years to enhance the safety of employees. Its main aim is to improve the standard of protection for employees while at work, and to lay down the expectation that the employer has a 'duty of care'.

Protective clothing and safety equipment are highlighted, as is the need to have a written health and safety policy, where a business employs more than five people.

A health and safety officer (who is not a member of the management team) must be appointed to ensure that safety standards are enforced.

The legislation also lays out the need for the employees to take 'reasonable care' of their own safety.

The Health and Safety Executive is responsible for ensuring that safety standards are adhered to. This can be done via inspections of business premises, although there are problems in ensuring that all premises are inspected.

Additional duties of employers

Working Time Directive

This directive, issued by the European Commission, limits employees to working an average maximum of 48 hours a week. The UK currently has an opt-out clause which means that the directive does not apply in this country.

Maternity leave

Expectant mothers are entitled to 6 weeks' paid leave at 90% of their current earnings followed by up to about £100 a week for a further 20 weeks, and to return to work after the birth of their baby. In 2003, would-be parents were given the right to ask for flexible working. There are proposals to extend maternity leave from 6 months to 12 months.

Maternity rights start as soon as employment starts. This is unlike other rights regarding dismissal, where the employee needs to show continuous employment for a given period of time.

Paternity leave

Fathers are entitled to paid leave in order to be present at the birth of their baby and for up to 2 weeks afterwards. In 2005, proposals were made to increase paternity leave pay from the present rate of £105 a week to 90% of earnings, in line with the rate for maternity leave.

The national minimum wage

The national minimum wage is part of the government's strategy to ensure that employees are treated fairly in the workplace. This strategy includes ensuring that workers receive sufficient wages. In October 2005, the minimum wage was increased to £5.05 an hour (from £4.85) for persons over the age of 22. The government at this time announced that there would be a further increase in October 2006 to £5.35, subject to confirmation in February 2006. The other increases were:

- from £4.10 to £4.25 for workers aged 18–21 (this is known as the *development rate*)
- to a minimum of £3 for workers aged 16 and 17 (this is still to be finalised by the government)

It is small firms that find changes in employment legislation the hardest to deal with. Unlike larger businesses, such companies do not have legal departments to translate the legislation in order to ensure compliance.

Laws slow growth

Helen Rush and Jackie Wigley are co-founders of Chinasearch Ltd, a small business based in Warwickshire that sells discontinued china and tableware and employs 30 full- and part-time staff, mostly women. Rush said:

> Dealing with changes to employment legislation takes up quite a lot of our time and it's a worry to make sure we have understood and interpreted it properly.
>
> We have had to involve our solicitor to make sure we have got our terms of employment correct, and it's expensive.
>
> It's also very difficult as a small company because we have a small number of staff and so any changes affect us quite significantly.
>
> We're a growing company but we feel that our rate of growth will be constrained by having to work within these ever-changing employment laws because they slow us down and cost us money.

Source: *Sunday Times*, 26 September 2004

REPRODUCED WITH PERMISSION OF CHINASEARCH LTD, MAY 2006

Dismissal legislation

Employment Rights Act (1996)

Gross misconduct for which an employee may be sacked must be stated in the contract of employment. This might include stealing, destroying the property of the employer, and risking the lives of fellow employees.

Any claims for unfair dismissal must be made within 3 months. These cases are heard by an **industrial tribunal**.

There are four main stages that must be gone through when disciplining employees:

- The employer must write to the employee stating the reason for disciplinary action. The employee in question must be invited to meet the management.
- A meeting between the employee and management must discuss the issues surrounding the action. There must be an opportunity for the employee to put his or her viewpoint.
- A decision arising from the discussion must be given verbally and in writing.
- The action taken by the business must then be recorded, and any appeal process must be implemented.

Changes were introduced in 2004 to encourage employer and employee to meet in order to try to find a solution before expensive tribunals are called on to give a judgement.

> **KEY TERM**
>
> **industrial tribunal:**
> an independent body responsible for hearing claims for unfair dismissal

The legislative burden

Mike Huss of Peninsula, an employment consultancy based in Manchester, estimated that there have been about 100 new regulations introduced by the Labour government since 1997. Many small firms are finding these changes increasingly hard to deal with while at the same time trying to run the business.

In December 2005, a survey showed that nearly 85% of businesses asked intimated that they were reluctant to employ women workers of childbearing age. This was because of the potential costs of maternity leave.

Further sources
www.dti.gov.uk/employment/pay/national-minimum-wage/index.html
www.opsi-gov.uk
http://europa.eu
www.hse.gov.uk/watchyourstep

YOUR TURN

Questions
Time allowed: 20 minutes

1 According to the Employment Rights Act (1996), state **four** items that should be included in a contract of employment. *(4 marks)*

2 State **three** examples of legislation that is designed to protect people in the recruitment process. *(3 marks)*

3 Outline the difference between maternity and paternity leave. *(4 marks)*

4 Explain how a business may be affected by employment legislation. *(5 marks)*

(16 marks)

Case study
Time allowed: 30 minutes

Silent order of monks pays for ignorance of law on jobs

The Cistercian monks from the Welsh island of Caldey were ordered to pay compensation to an old couple who had been sacked in order to save money. The couple, Mr and Mrs McHardy, were given just 10 minutes' notice after working for the monks for 23 years!

The Cistercians were established on the island in 1929 and live to a strict no-speaking rule between the hours of 7 a.m. and 7 p.m.

Mr and Mrs McHardy, who cooked and cleaned for the monks, had been given a redundancy payment of only £675 following a short meeting with the abbot, Father Daniel Santvoort. Mrs McHardy was given £540. In addition, they were given a 'friendship' payment of £500 each.

Following the short meeting with the abbot, the McHardys were given just 4 weeks to leave their tied cottage and find another home.

The employment tribunal found that the couple had been unfairly dismissed because the monks had not followed the proper procedure. The chairman of the tribunal, Roger Jones, stated: 'The manner of their dismissal left a lot to be desired. It cannot be right to behave this way to people who had given 23 years of service. Procedurally, the position was flawed and flawed badly.'

At the hearing, a former abbot claimed that Mr McHardy had drunk excessively and suggested that the couple had embezzled money from the order. Mr and Mrs McHardy denied this. Mr McHardy admitted that he had been suffering from alcoholism but said that he was now recovering. He told the tribunal that, only 2 years previously, the monks had promised him and his wife a home for life on the island.

The former monk stated that the monks would face hardship because of the extra compensation, which was to be decided in the coming weeks.

Source: adapted from an article by Simon de Bruxelles in *The Times*, 8 January 2005

Answer all questions.

1 State **three** examples of legislation that aimed to protect Mr and Mrs McHardy while at their place of work. *(3 marks)*

2 Evaluate why the tribunal decided that Mr and Mrs McHardy had been unfairly dismissed. *(14 marks)*

(17 marks)

CHAPTER 41

Theories of motivation

Ensuring that its workforce is content is a vital concern for any business. A happy workforce is more likely to be a productive one and absenteeism is a lot higher among discontented workers. The level of labour turnover is thought to be greatly influenced by the level of motivation for the individual worker. The quality of the products or service may also be affected if workers are not motivated in what they do.

In answer to the 2005 *Marketing* Employer of the Year survey, when asked to make a choice between greater working flexibility and 10% more pay, 61% of employees were in favour of more pay. But pay can come in many forms. Employees in the field of marketing want not only pay but also a package including private healthcare, a bonus scheme and a company car. NatWest Primeline, an internet and telephone banking service, prides itself on financial and non-financial packages that include a pension package and a profit-sharing scheme that could add as much as 10% to an employee's salary.

Remuneration packages can include private healthcare

Paula Vennells, commercial director of Whitbread, suggests that it is the non-financial packages that help to retain staff: ‘We are not necessarily over-generous on financial benefits, but there are huge non-financial benefits. The culture of the company makes it a very exciting and happy place to work. The "Whitbread way" states that our people treat and respect each other.’

Paul Werb, head of marketing and public affairs at Action for Blind People, also suggests that his organisation has been successful because of its culture: ‘It is very inclusive and democratic, with everyone involved in decisions.’

Source: 'Show me the money', *Marketing*, 17 November 2004

What is motivation?

The quotations above indicate that there are many ways in which employees may be motivated. However, before discussing what motivates employers and employees, it is important to establish what *motivation* actually means.

Motivation is concerned with the behaviour of the individual person. It is often considered to be the forces that encourage and drive people to work hard. What those forces or influences are varies according to the range of theories that exist.

Motivation has been defined by Child (1973) as follows: 'It consists of internal processes which spur us on to satisfy some need.' Murray (1964) defines a motive as 'an internal factor that arouses, directs and integrates a person's behaviour'.

Theories of motivation

Motivational theories attempt to define what motivates people and, as a consequence, to explain how best to obtain our goals.

Taylor's scientific management

Frederick Taylor (1856–1915) was one of the first people to consider how to get the best out of employees. His perspective was based on using a scientific approach (hence the term 'scientific management') in order to increase output. He was an engineer and this background influenced his approach to making the most efficient use of the workforce.

His analysis involved a careful study of how long workers took to perform certain tasks and how they undertook such tasks. (*Work study* has evolved from Taylor's approach.) Taylor assumed that workers were lazy and needed directing in how to perform tasks. If workers were given the right equipment and work was divided into specialised, repetitive tasks, each worker would quickly become proficient in his/her job, and therefore more productive. In addition, the amount of training needed would be minimal, and this would help to keep costs down. This was known as the *division of labour*. Henry Ford later adopted this de-skilling of the workforce in his car plants in the USA.

Henry Ford adopted Taylor's division of labour methods in his car plants in the USA

Taylor suggested that, as long as management kept a tight control of the workforce, by ensuring that each worker performed his/her own small but clearly defined part of the productive process, then levels of production would increase. The last part of Taylor's theory was to encourage workers by paying them according to what they produced: the more they produced,

the more they were paid. (This is thought to be the origin of *piece rates*.) In theory, this may encourage a higher level of output by each worker, but it does not necessarily mean that the standard of the work will be satisfactory.

Taylor's theories were published in his book, *The Principles of Scientific Management*, in 1911. It is easy to dismiss some of his ideas, but it is worth noting that Taylor did establish an approach to the organisation of workers and, it could be argued, led others to consider how best to motivate them. However, this approach to the workforce, treating each worker as if he/she was a machine to be organised and 'programmed' to perform, was not considered by other theorists to be a good method of motivating workers.

Mayo and human relations management

Elton Mayo (1880–1949) was a supporter of Taylor, but his own experiments led him to believe that scientific management did not and could not explain why workers behaved as they did. Mayo considered that money was not as important as was first thought, and that one of the main motivators was the working environment.

He conducted a series of experiments in Chicago during the 1920s. He wanted to show that by altering the working environment he could increase the output of the workers. He selected two groups of female workers at a factory at Hawthorne, Chicago. One group was the control group, while the working conditions of the other group were altered. The latter group's first change involved altering the lighting conditions. Other changes involved the workers' break times, the number of hours worked, lunchtimes, free meals and even the elimination of rest breaks altogether.

After each change in working conditions, the two groups were interviewed and asked for their opinions. In all, over 20,000 interviews with the workforce were conducted.

During the period of the experiment, the level of absenteeism fell. Moreover, for every change that was introduced, the output of *both groups* increased. The only exception to this was when the number of breaks increased. In this case, the workers considered the increase in work breaks too disruptive to the flow of their work.

Mayo concluded that:
- as each member of the two groups had been interviewed on a regular basis, they felt a sense of recognition and belonging to the group and the company
- communication and expectations within the group and with management influenced productivity

As a consequence of the 'Hawthorne effect', businesses began to organise themselves differently. Human resources became an important department and the structure of businesses altered to reflect this. Improved facilities, such as canteens, were provided to increase the welfare of the workforce.

The relationship between management and the workforce changed as a result of more communication and consultation. All these changes recognised the fact that workers, according to Mayo, appreciated, and were motivated by, a sense of involvement and recognition.

Herzberg's two-factor theory

Research by Frederick Herzberg (1923–2000) in Pittsburgh, USA, established that the morale of the workforce was affected by two sets of factors, which Herzberg called *motivators* and *hygiene* or *maintenance factors*.

Motivators

These are factors that motivate workers and give an indication of job satisfaction. They include:

- a sense of achievement
- recognition of workers' contributions
- responsibility
- opportunities for promotion and self-improvement
- undertaking meaningful tasks

All of the above are related to the job that is performed and not the working environment in which the job is undertaken.

If the motivators are in place, Herzberg thought it was likely that workers would:

- use their initiative
- be more flexible in response to change
- be more positive in attempting to meet the objectives of the business
- take more care in their work

The business, as well as the individual worker, is likely to benefit from the presence of motivational factors. Contented and motivated workers will increase their productivity and consequently raise more revenue for the business. With a motivated workforce, the level of absenteeism will be lower. In addition, the level of labour turnover will be lower, so the business will incur lower costs by not having to cover for absent workers or spend more money on training new ones.

Hygiene or maintenance factors

These factors will *not* positively motivate the workforce, but have the potential to demotivate employees if they are inadequate or inappropriate. They are related to the working environment and not the actual job. In other words, they affect the conditions in which a particular job is undertaken. Hygiene factors are:

- working conditions
- pay
- company bureaucracy
- status
- job security

Tackling hygiene factors will improve the working environment and help reduce discontentment, as it is often these factors that lead to industrial action by workers.

Herzberg's work led to many changes in the workplace, including the introduction of *job enrichment* and a change away from the traditional assembly line (see Chapter 42). Herzberg's ideas have been criticised, particularly because his findings are based on research among a limited sample of 200 engineers and accountants. Nevertheless, the validity of his ideas is shown by the fact that industry has adopted many aspects of his suggestions.

McGregor's Theory X and Theory Y

These theories were developed by Douglas McGregor (1906–64). They concern the styles of leadership that could be adopted in order to achieve a motivated workforce, which are explained in Chapter 43.

It is sufficient to state that here that Theory X is a style of leadership that suggests that workers are motivated by money and need supervising because they are incapable of making decisions or using any initiative. This is the kind of leadership fostered by the work of Frederick Taylor. In contrast, Theory Y leadership assumes that workers are looking to gain job satisfaction and will seek and take responsibility, which is more in line with the work of Abraham Maslow (see below) and Frederick Herzberg.

Maslow's hierarchy of needs

Abraham Maslow (1908–70), an American psychologist, claimed that people's needs in the workplace could be organised into a hierarchy from lower-order needs up to higher-order needs. He classified these needs into five distinct levels, as shown in Figure 41.1:

- **Physiological needs.** These are the basic needs for food, clothing and shelter. At work, people need to earn sufficient money in order to meet these basic physiological needs.
- **Safety needs.** These include a safe, secure environment and job security. For many people, a secure job is preferable to a short-term contract on high wages. Of more concern in recent times is the need for a secure future, especially at retirement age. Having sufficient to live on once employment ends is now a concern for many workers.

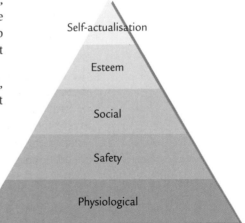

Figure 41.1 Maslow's hierarchy of needs

ⓔ EXAMINER'S VOICE

There is no need to draw this diagram in an exam unless you wish to make reference to the hierarchy being significant. It is more important to use Maslow's ideas in the context of the actual case and question.

- **Social needs.** People have a desire to be wanted, to have friends and to have a sense of belonging. Being part of a team and being able to integrate with fellow employees is considered to be important.
- **Esteem needs.** These are concerned with obtaining self-respect and enjoying a certain level of status. Status symbols such as company cars, an office and an impressive title are important to some employees.
- **Self-actualisation needs.** These relate to achieving one's full potential in life and are concerned less with achieving recognition from others than with achieving personal goals that an individual may set himself or herself. Maslow suggested that self-actualisation is concerned with the intellectual needs of an individual. He also suggested that self-actualisation needs are unlikely ever to be completely satisfied because once employees have achieved a certain target, they will set themselves a new one. (This is in direct contrast to the findings of Taylor, who suggested that employees lack initiative and need directing at all times.)

The hierarchy is usually shown in the form of a triangle because the number of people operating at the higher-level needs is less than at the lower level. However, it is important to realise that each need is not mutually exclusive.

The significance of Maslow's hierarchy is that, once people have achieved a lower-order need, they will no longer be motivated by that and will move on to a higher-level need in order to be motivated. Lower-order needs offer contentment rather than motivation, in a similar way to Herzberg's hygiene factors, while higher-order needs offer motivation.

Tom Peters

Although he is not listed in the exam specification, it is worth noting what one of the modern thinkers in the business world has to say about motivating the workforce. In his book *Thriving on Chaos* (1982), Tom Peters lists many methods of motivating employees. Many of his suggestions mirror the ideas of previous theorists. They include:

- recognising champions (sense of recognition)
- involving all workers in all aspects of the business (sense of involvement and belonging)
- offering financial incentives (hygiene factors and Taylor)
- encouraging participation (sense of involvement and responsibility)
- guaranteeing continuous employment (security)

Tom Peters

> **e EXAMINER'S VOICE**
>
> It is important to highlight similarities and differences between the different theories. Try to ensure that you refer to the theories that are best suited to the case involved. It may not be necessary to refer to all of them.

Summary

Table 41.1 summarises the key points for each of the named theorists.

Name	Theory	Key points	
Taylor	Scientific management	■ Organise employees like machines ■ Tight control and direction of workforce ■ Pay on the basis of piece rates	
Mayo	Human relations management	■ Hawthorne effect (Western Electric, Chicago) ■ Working conditions changed to improve productivity but motivated by: – recognition – sense of involvement	
Herzberg	Two-factor theory	Motivators: ■ sense of achievement ■ recognition ■ responsibility ■ promotion ■ meaningful work/tasks	Hygiene/maintenance factors: ■ working conditions ■ pay ■ company bureaucracy ■ status ■ job security
McGregor	Theory X and Theory Y	Theory X: ■ money motivates ■ supervision of workers required ■ workers have little initiative ■ workers do not make decisions	Theory Y: ■ job satisfaction motivates ■ workers are able to work on their own ■ workers have initiative and can make decisions ■ workers are motivated by rewards and recognition
Maslow	Hierarchy of needs	■ Physiological needs ■ Security needs ■ Social needs ■ Status needs ■ Self-actualisation needs	

Chapter 42 considers how firms use motivational theory to ensure that employees are content and therefore productive. The implications for the style of leadership are examined in Chapter 43.

Table 41.1
Theories of motivation: summary chart

e EXAMINER'S VOICE

You need to be able to write about how a business will be affected by the theories of motivation: in other words, the implications in terms of costs, manpower and management styles.

YOUR TURN

Questions

1 a Draw up a table showing a list of Herzberg's motivators and hygiene factors. *(4 marks)*
  OR
  b Explain the difference between Herzberg's motivators and hygiene factors. *(4 marks)*

2 Copy and complete the following table by suggesting an appropriate motivational theory for each situation described. (There may be more than one right answer.) *(6 marks)*

(10 marks)

Situation	Theory	Additional details
The human resources department has introduced a complicated four-page form to be filled in by all staff	Herzberg	Hygiene factor Company bureaucracy
Jim Harris, the owner of the local bakery, operates an employees' award evening		
Uzma Hassan, director of personnel, introduces a new pay deal with additional bonus payments		
Luci Widdows, the manager of a local business, always promotes staff from within the business		

Case study

B&Q staff to share £32 million

Shop-floor staff at the leading DIY chain are to share a bonus package of £32 million. This record payout to over 38,000 employees follows a successful year for the group, which recorded profits of over £370 million. This level of bonus represents an increase of nearly 13%. For the most junior of staff this could mean a bonus payment of around £900. For the more senior staff, the bonus payments may be equal to around 10% of their salary.

Volkswagen cuts bonus payments

Directors of the car group Volkswagen are cutting bonus payments by as much as 30% following the poor performance of the car group, whose sales fell last year. The chief executive of VW told a press conference that the directors would suffer a larger cut in bonus payments than other staff. This follows a fall in revenue from the sales of the Golf model and a consequential fall in profits.

Answer the following question.

EITHER
Discuss the likelihood of the B&Q staff being motivated by the introduction of the bonus package. *(14 marks)*
OR
Using appropriate motivational theory, discuss the likely effect on the Volkswagen workforce of cutting bonus payments. *(14 marks)*

Methods of motivation

Meeting the needs of employees is a vital part of human resource management. For example, providing a works canteen or restaurant can help to satisfy Herzberg's hygiene factors and achieve Maslow's social needs. However, it is not always easy to decide how best to meet the needs of the workforce and ensure that employees are motivated. This chapter looks at how theories of motivation may be applied in practice.

Personnel performance indicators

Ensuring that its workforce is not only contented but also highly motivated will aid a business in achieving success. There are several ways to establish if the workforce is 'happy', and these are referred to as **personnel performance indicators**.

- **Absenteeism.** This is defined as the number of staff absent as a percentage of the total number of staff employed. Absenteeism can be defined as absence without real reason ('throwing a sickie'). Some texts refer to this type of absenteeism as *casual absenteeism*. If the absenteeism level is high, this may indicate that workers are not content because of a lack of motivation or poor working conditions. It may also be caused by poor recruitment in the first place.
- **Labour turnover.** This is the number of staff who leave each year as a percentage of the total number of staff employed. The causes of high labour turnover could be many, but, as for absenteeism, they are probably a combination of Herzberg's hygiene factors and motivators.
- **Productivity of labour.** This is measured by the total level of output in a given period divided by the total number of staff employed (to give the output per employee). This is not only a useful measure of efficiency but, in this context, also a useful indicator of satisfaction. Contented employees tend to be more productive.

KEY TERM

personnel performance indicators: a method of assessing how content the workforce is, which involves measuring a range of indicators such as absenteeism

---

EXAMINER'S VOICE

Care should be taken with these indicators because all employees are different, as are the conditions in which they work. For example, high productivity could be due to the introduction of a new machine, making the level of output increase and therefore affecting the productivity of employees. However, the level of discontentment among employees might actually *increase*, if the machine has altered their jobs and fewer skills are required.

Job enrichment

The application of motivational theories — as suggested, for example, by Herzberg — is important to a business if its employees are to be productive. According to Herzberg, motivators are related to the actual job. Therefore, it is important to ensure that the job is interesting and enriches the employee. This approach to fulfilling Herzberg's motivating factors is called **job enrichment**.

Enrichment involves making the job more interesting, often by offering a wider range of tasks to be performed. This may then provide employees with more responsibility and involvement, and in turn may generate a higher level of achievement. Herzberg wanted workers to be given more responsibility by reducing the level of supervision and making the workers responsible for their own work. In addition, he suggested that workers should have a greater involvement in discussions with management. This would offer both involvement and recognition for the work they do.

Job enrichment involves allowing workers to be responsible for their own decision making and, if possible, enabling them to perform a complete task, rather than just one particular part of a task. Herzberg's ideas of how to achieve the 'motivators' in the working environment also included giving workers feedback on their performance, as this provides them with both recognition and a sense of achievement.

It is important to realise that job enrichment is not the same as *job enlargement*. Giving employees more of the task that they are already performing is not enrichment; it merely adds to their workload and may even cause frustration.

Job rotation and cell production

In many factories today, an attempt has been made to implement the ideas of Herzberg via **job rotation**, which gives employees a range of tasks. This is not the same as enrichment because it does not involve an increase in responsibility.

However, *cell production*, where workers are divided into teams, and each team is responsible for a set number of tasks in the production process, is a form of enrichment. This is because it gives workers autonomy and responsibility. Each team is responsible for the quality of its work and who does which particular job within the team. Jobs can also be rotated within the team.

Teamworking

Teamworking, a term coined by Charles Handy in 1990, involves groups of multi-skilled workers, who have a common objective and are encouraged

to apply a *kaizen* (continuous improvement) approach to their tasks (see Chapter 49). As they are multi-skilled, all the members of the group can undertake any of the tasks.

McDonald's, Rolls-Royce and Rover are examples of companies that have used teamworking and have reported improvements in personnel performance indicators. Teamworking increases employees' accountability for the final product and encourages them to take more pride in the work of their team.

Empowerment

Empowerment, described at length by Rosabeth Moss Kanter, the author of several books on business, means not only that employees are allowed to perform a task, but also that they can make the decisions about when and how the task is done. This takes advantage of the fact that employees are often in a much better position than managers to make such decisions, as they are the ones who have experience of performing the task.

Allowing the workforce to be involved in the decision-making process gives them responsibility, which according to Herzberg is a motivator. Empowerment also gives the workers a sense of involvement, which Mayo advocated as important in the motivation of workers.

Payment methods

Although there is disagreement about whether money, in any form, actually motivates a workforce, it is an important hygiene factor, according to Herzberg. In Maslow's view, payment helps to satisfy certain elements of the hierarchy of needs.

There are many possible payment methods, each of which can influence the performance of the workforce differently.

Piece rates

Piece rates tie pay to the level of output achieved. Taylor viewed such a system as a method of encouraging workers to produce more goods. However, such a system is fraught with dangers. The division of labour approach to production means that few, if any, workers are responsible for producing any product from start to finish. It is therefore difficult to gauge particular workers' input.

There are very few processes now where an individual worker's input is measurable. In the pottery industry, piece rates still exist, where individual workers produce individual items. But if a worker is reliant upon a machine to help produce goods, it may be difficult to decide what proportion of the good he or she was responsible for. Furthermore, if the machine breaks down, pay will be affected, regardless of the amount of effort made by the worker.

 KEY TERMS

empowerment: delegation of a task and the decision-making process about how the task is done

piece rates: a system of payment linked to output

Piece rates still exist in the pottery industry

Other factors that could affect the success of this system of payment include:

- regular and adequate supplies
- cooperation between workers
- the quality of the goods produced

Commission

Commission is a specific kind of piece rate system. It normally involves paying sales personnel a low basic wage or salary, which is topped up according to the number of sales they achieve.

Performance-related pay and bonus schemes

Tying pay to performance is a hazardous process. First, it is necessary to judge the performance of a worker. Who will do this and what criteria will be used to make this judgement? If one person gains additional payments, how will others react? Some companies have tied this type of payment system to appraisal (a system of monitoring performance on a regular basis). However, this is not thought to be sound practice.

Herzberg cites a further problem with such a pay scheme. He suggests that once additional payments are made, they become the norm in the eyes of the employee. Consequently, such payments will no longer have any incentive effects and will become a hygiene factor.

Profit sharing and profit-related pay

If the business makes a profit, employees may be given a proportion of this amount in an attempt to reward their efforts and to give them a sense of belonging to the business (one of Maslow's needs and a Mayo motivator).

Share ownership

As with profit-sharing schemes, share ownership offers employees an opportunity to become more involved with the business by actually owning a small part of it. Subsequently, the employee will be further rewarded if the business makes a profit by receiving a dividend from the shares owned.

Benefits (perks)

Many employers offer their employees a pension plan and make contributions to workers' pensions. Maslow would view this as satisfying their security needs. However, many firms are now finding it hard to continue such schemes, as they are turning out to be very costly. Since Gordon Brown, the chancellor of the exchequer, introduced an additional tax on share dividends, which has raised over £10 billion a year, companies have struggled to operate schemes with the same standard of benefits.

A traditional benefit for many employees was a company car. Here again, however, following a succession of tax increases on the ownership of company cars, the level of benefit perceived by the employee has diminished.

Private healthcare cover is a growing benefit, allowing employees to be

treated more quickly than on the National Health Service, and therefore meaning that they have less time off from work.

Many companies offer their employees attractive facilities at the place of work. Heavily subsidised restaurants, and sporting and recreational facilities abound. Gym facilities are seen not only as a benefit to the employees, but also as advantageous for the business, helping to keep the workforce fit and therefore reducing the probable number of days off for sickness. There are even examples in power-generation plants of golf courses being available for employees.

Prize incentives

Some businesses offer their employees holiday prizes for achieving or beating targets. Others offer a growing range of vouchers to be spent in well-known chain stores, in exchange for improved productivity, completing training programmes and good attendance at work. These are so popular with employees that vouchers totalling £1.38 billion were sold in 2004.

Incentives are no longer only available to sales staff. The director of motivation for the performance management agency P&MM has stated: 'Companies have had years of successfully using incentives for sales forces…they are now realising that they can get the same results within their own organisations.' MFI has used incentive schemes to good effect to motivate its cleaning staff.

Many companies provide gym facilities for their employees

The Royal Mail, one of the UK's largest employers, with approximately 170,000 employees, had a serious problem with casual absenteeism. On most days of the year, up to 10,000 employees could be absent, which affected the ability of the Royal Mail to meet its targets and literally 'deliver the goods'. As an incentive to cut absenteeism, in 2004 it introduced a nationwide programme for staff with a 100% attendance record to enter a draw to win Ford Focus cars and Thomas Cook holiday vouchers. Attendance increased by over 11%, which meant that at least an extra 1,000 employees a day were not absent. The scheme was so successful that, the following year, all those employees who managed 12 months without any absence were entered for another draw to win one of 39 cars.

Further sources

www.thetimes100.co.uk

YOUR TURN

Questions

Time allowed: 30 minutes

1 Explain the difference between job enlargement and job enrichment. *(4 marks)*

2 Analyse the advantages and disadvantages of implementing a piece rate system. *(9 marks)*

3 Suggest an appropriate method of payment for the following:
   a a car assembly worker
   b a shop assistant
   c a bus driver
   d a dentist *(4 marks)*

4 For one of your answers to question 3, analyse its likely effect on motivating the worker. *(9 marks)*

(26 marks)

Case study

Time allowed: 40 minutes

Motivation methods

Jack, Michael and Jason own a new business manufacturing and selling garden sheds and tree houses.

They are keen to establish themselves in the market and are hoping to gain a lot of sales quite quickly, especially as the month is April — when, according to research, customers start to think about their gardens. They advertise both locally and nationally, using local papers and the internet.

There is a team of assembly workers who make the sheds and tree houses, and another group of workers who go out to the customers' houses to erect them in their gardens.

Michael is keen to encourage the employees who make the sheds in the factory to produce more in order to meet the expected rush of orders. Jason, who is responsible for organising the team that delivers and assembles the sheds and houses, also wants these employees to complete their jobs more quickly. However, there is also concern about the quality of the assembly at customers' homes. Having to go back to a customer to sort out any problems is costly and time consuming.

Finding the right sort of staff for both the factory and delivery teams has become more of a problem. Even though the business has only been established for just over a year, labour turnover is very high. Staff often fail to turn up, making it difficult to meet orders on time. Michael wants to spend more time on the marketing of the business's products and developing a larger range of sheds to meet a wider range of consumer requirements.

Answer all questions.

1 State **two** methods of financial motivation that Jack could use. *(2 marks)*

2 Evaluate how Jack could effectively implement a job enrichment scheme for his workforce. *(14 marks)*

3 Explain a method of motivation that could be introduced to satisfy the ideas of Maslow. *(4 marks)*

4 Suggest the likely reasons for high labour turnover in this business. *(6 marks)*

(26 marks)

CHAPTER 43

Leadership

The following two extracts highlight the fact that there are different views on the most important attributes that a leader should have, and how leaders should operate.

‘You won't get someone more autocratic than me.’

Alan Sugar, ex-chairman of Tottenham Hotspur FC and chairman of Amstrad, who featured on *The Apprentice*, BBC 2, April 2005

‘Leaders make sure people not only see the vision, they live and breathe it. How do you do that? First of all, no jargon. Targets cannot be so blurry they can't be hit. And when people do live and breathe the vision, show them the money, be it salary, bonus or significant recognition…’

‘If you want people to experiment, set the example yourself…’

‘Work is too much part of life not to recognise moments of achievement.’

Jack Welch, quoted in Tony Allen-Mills, 'Neutron Jack (and his wife) tell it like it is', *The Sunday Times*, 3 April 2005

Responsibilities of leaders

Leaders are responsible for setting the objectives for the business, which are to be implemented by the firm's managers. Leaders are also responsible for coping with change.

It is important to be aware that the style of leadership will have an effect on the workforce and how the workforce responds to the leader will affect the ability of the business to achieve its objectives.

Leadership styles

Lewin, Lippett and White tested different leadership styles on groups of children, who were involved in making masks. Each group was subjected to a different style, which was changed every 6 weeks.

The conclusion reached by Lewin, Lippett and White was that the different styles of leadership dramatically affected the climate in which each group operated. They affected not only the personalities of the group members, but also the interpersonal relationships within the group.

Several styles of leadership have been identified.

Autocratic leadership

An **autocratic leadership** style has the following characteristics:

- It adopts a Tayloristic approach to management, in line with McGregor's Theory X (see Chapter 41).
- Tasks are set by the leader.
- Communication is likely to be one-way from the top down.
- The leader is often remote from the workers and does not appear on the factory floor.
- Work is supervised.
- There is little or no opportunity for workers to use their initiative.
- Little activity takes place once the leader leaves.
- The decision-making process is quick.

Democratic leadership

Democratic leadership is characterised by the following:

- It involves McGregor's Theory Y (see Chapter 41) and Herzberg's motivators.
- Work problems are discussed.
- Objectives and tasks are agreed between leader and workers.
- Communication is two-way.
- There are opportunities for workers to use their initiative.
- Workers are likely to have a greater sense of involvement and therefore to be more highly motivated.
- Responsibility is often delegated to the workers.
- The decision-making process takes longer because of the greater number of people involved.

Laissez-faire leadership

The features of **laissez-faire leadership** are as follows:

- The leader is a non-participant, who delegates nearly all responsibilities.
- The leader is available if required.
- Workers set their own objectives and tasks.
- There are many opportunities for workers to use their initiative.
- Workers may lack a sense of direction and cohesion.
- The decision-making process may take a very long time or not be made at all due to a lack of consensus or agreed sense of direction.

Paternalistic leadership

Paternalistic leadership has the following characteristics:

- The decision-making process is in the hands of the leader or management.

KEY TERMS

autocratic leadership: the leader takes all major decisions and there is little or no worker involvement

democratic leadership: delegation of the decision-making process allows the workforce to be involved and therefore increases motivation

laissez-faire leadership: the leader has little or no input in the decision-making process and the workforce is left without proper guidance

paternalistic leadership: although there are examples of consultation, the leader decides what is best for the workforce

- It recognises that hearing the needs of the workers is important and may encourage the workforce to feel wanted and important.
- However, regardless of the views of the workforce, the paternalistic leader will still decide what is best for the business.

There is a danger that the workforce may become frustrated with this style of leadership. They may quickly realise that the leader is not allowing them any real opportunity to be involved in the decision-making process and subsequently will not be motivated by such an approach. Many Japanese firms were once seen as being paternalistic. The workers were provided with excellent facilities at the place of work, but had little or no say in decision making.

Other approaches to leadership style

Contingency theory
Fiedler suggests that the best style of leadership depends on the type of task to be undertaken. In addition, the charisma and power of the leader are significant in deciding the most appropriate style of leadership to use.

McGregor's Theory X and Theory Y
Douglas McGregor, a social psychologist from Harvard, wrote *The Human Side of Enterprise*, in which he argued that there are two distinct styles of management. He called these Theory X and Theory Y (see Chapter 41):
- Theory X is an authoritarian approach to leadership, which is adopted by those leaders who believe that workers dislike work and therefore need to be controlled to improve their performance.
- Theory Y is an approach to leadership that assumes that workers have both initiative and self-control, which can be used to achieve the goals of the business. Consequently, the role of management is to maximise this commitment of the workers

Management grid
According to Tannenbaum and Schmidt, different leadership styles lead to different approaches to the decision-making process. They developed the **management grid** shown in Figure 43.1. The differing styles of leadership will also have an effect on the workforce in terms of their attitudes and degree of motivation.

> **KEY TERM**
>
> **management grid:** an analytical tool that highlights a range of management styles from leadership centred to group centred, according to which the process of management changes as the emphasis between leader and group changes

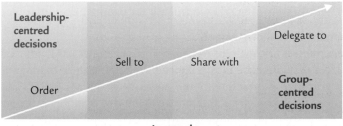

Approach

Figure 43.1 Tannenbaum and Schmidt's management grid

If the decision process is leadership centred, workers will not feel as involved (Mayo) or have as much responsibility (Herzberg), and therefore may not be as motivated. However, if the decision process is group centred, workers are more likely to be motivated because they are given responsibility and will feel involved.

Businesses today tend to concentrate on McGregor's Theory Y model and use a group-centred approach to the decision-making process. Teamworking is also commonplace in business, as firms attempt to line themselves up with Theory Y and a group-centred approach.

 EXAMINER'S VOICE

When explaining how different styles of leadership affect the workers, it is important to reinforce your argument with reference to the theorists you have learnt about. However, it is not a good examination strategy just to quote all the theories you know. Be selective and refer to the theories that best suit the context of the case and the particular question you are addressing.

Management by objectives

The **management by objectives** (MBO) approach is attributed to Peter Drucker. It relies on the workers agreeing with management what the objectives should be and then using these agreed objectives to track the progress of the business. The development and agreement of the objectives should involve the entire workforce.

KEY TERM

management by objectives: management on the basis of an agreed set of objectives

Such an approach means that all the workers are aware of where the business is going and why particular objectives have been set. A degree of delegation is necessary to ensure that the objectives are achieved. Involving all the workers and ensuring that everyone knows the direction of the business should enhance the morale and motivational strength of the workforce.

The more realistic the objectives by which the business is to be managed, the more likely it is that they will be achieved. Applying the 'SMART' approach to setting objectives (see p. 50) should ensure that the use of management by objectives is appropriate.

It is important for management to be seen not as an obstacle to completing tasks, but as a facilitator. According to Drucker, 'Most of what we call management consists of making it difficult for people to get their work done.'

Management by walking about

A management approach operated by Hewlett-Packard, the computer business, suggests that the most important requirement of management is to make face-to-face contact with the workforce on a regular basis. This approach means that workers and management can operate on the same level and that there are opportunities for two-way communication.

Factors affecting the style of leadership

Several factors affect the style of leadership adopted:

- personality of the leader
- skills of the leader
- size of the business
- skills of the workforce
- tasks to be performed
- organisational structure of the business

There may also be some conflict for management between the need to ensure the task is done and the need to consider the welfare of the employee. An autocratic style of leadership will place greater emphasis on completing the task (task orientated), whereas a democratic style of leadership may put greater emphasis on the employee (people orientated).

In an attempt to be conscious of both task and employee welfare, and to break the traditional 'management versus the workers' approach, more businesses are now sharing facilities such as dining rooms, whereas, historically, management and the workforce had separate facilities.

At the Dyson plant in Malmesbury, no employees wear ties and they all share the same facilities in an attempt to break down the barriers between management and the workforce. The company believes that task completion is assisted by the fact that all employees are considered to be important.

A natural-born leader?

There is a continuing debate about whether there is such a thing as a natural leader. Does any one person have all the right traits to be a leader? Or are different traits or characteristics required for different types of leadership? Most people today would argue that different characteristics are required to lead in different circumstances. The characteristics required to lead a sports team will be different from the those required to lead a multinational business.

What is not in dispute is that, whatever type of leader is in place, their style of leadership will affect how the people being led will behave.

The characteristics required to lead a sports team are different from those required to lead a multinational business

Further sources

C. Handy (1990) *Understanding Organisations*, Oxford University Press.

www.newscorp.com and **www.newsinternational.com** — companies owned by Rupert Murdoch, media tycoon

www.easygroup.co.uk — companies owned by Stelios Haji-Ioannou

YOUR TURN

Questions

Time allowed: 20 minutes

1 Explain the difference between an autocratic and a democratic style of leadership. *(4 marks)*

2 State **four** factors that may affect the style of leadership adopted. *(4 marks)*

3 Outline the likely style of leadership if the emphasis is 'group centred'. *(3 marks)*

4 Analyse why the use of 'management by objectives' will benefit a business. *(9 marks)*

(20 marks)

Case study

Time allowed: 25 minutes

Running Britain the Weinstock way

Lord Weinstock died in 2002, but the legacy of his approach lives on in some of the UK's biggest companies.

Some senior executives of Centrica, LogicaCMG and BAE Systems worked under Lord Weinstock while at GEC. Other companies have ex-GEC executives in post.

Sir Roy Gardner, who was the chief executive at Centrica and left to become chairman of the Compass group, was a GEC man. Mike Parton, Marconi's chief executive, was also a GEC man previously.

GEC was once regarded as one of the UK's finest companies, with operations ranging from electronics to telecommunications and aerospace. Lord Weinstock was managing director for 33 years, between 1963 and 1996. It was while he was in charge that many of the businessmen named above were gaining their experience at GEC.

Lord Weinstock presided over a decentralised company of smaller units, where employees, no matter how young, were encouraged to take responsibility:

'If you had the courage of your convictions, you would get lots of support from him and he'd try and help' (Martin Read, chief executive of LogicaCMG and an ex-GEC employee).

'At any one time he would have 10–15 bright young people on his radar whose careers he would follow... He was a fantastic teacher and he had a complete disregard for people's age' (Rupert Soames, chief executive of Aggreko).

Source: adapted from an article by Joe Bolger in *The Times*, 29 October 2005

Answer all questions.

1 To what extent could Lord Weinstock be viewed as a democratic leader? *(12 marks)*

2 From the case, suggest how GEC employees may be motivated. *(5 marks)*

(17 marks)

Organisational structures

The simplest way to show how a business is organised is by using an organisational chart. This is a diagram that shows the hierarchy within a business, usually from top to bottom, or from the board of directors to the shop-floor workers or operatives.

From this chart, it easy to see at a glance the other key concepts related to the organisation of a business. These include types of hierarchy, span of control, communication, line management, chain of command and accountability.

A typical **organisational structure** of a business may look like Figure 44.1. It is a hierarchy, with the managing director at the top and the workers at the bottom. Senior management followed by middle management are in between.

EXAMINER'S VOICE

It is important to remember that every time you have to analyse an organisational chart, you should consider the key concepts listed here.

KEY TERM

organisational structure: the way in which a business is organised

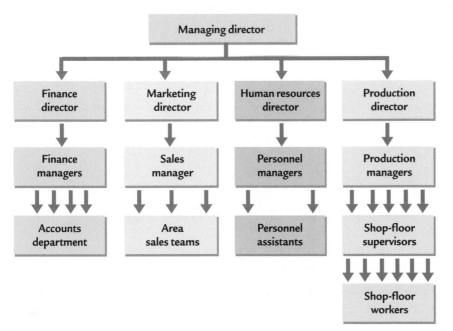

Figure 44.1
A traditional organisational structure: hierarchy with four and five levels

Organisational concepts

Span of control

The **span of control** is the number of employees for whom a manager or superior is responsible. A great or wide span of control means that the

KEY TERM

span of control: the number of employees (subordinates) for whom a manager is responsible

manager is responsible for many employees. A narrow or thin span of control means that the manager is responsible for relatively few employees.

Traditional approaches suggest that the best span of control is four or five. This is because, as the number in the span of control increases, the number of channels of communication increases rapidly, and therefore effective communication may break down. This is the dilemma for organisational structures. If a small span of control is required, the number of layers or levels in the hierarchy will increase. This means that there will be more layers for communication to pass through, thus making effective communication less likely.

Figure 44.2
Spans of control

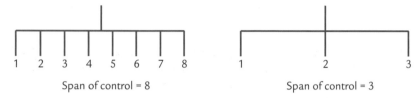

Span of control = 8   Span of control = 3

There is no correct number for an effective span of control. How many people are involved will depend on:

- the personality of the manager/superior
- the skill and experience of the employee or subordinate
- the size of the business
- whether or not the business is *centralised* (see below)
- the degree of competition in the market — if costs are an issue, this will encourage a wider span of control, which is often achieved through the process of *delayering* (see below)
- the extent to which the business has agreed and well-defined objectives — if all the employees are clear as to the direction of the business, less supervision will be required and therefore a wider span of control can be used

Chain of command

The chain of command is concerned with the way in which responsibility for employees is organised within a business. The organisational chart in Figure 44.3 shows that Judith is responsible for Tom, Harry, Francis and Sarah. It can also be seen that, in turn, Tom is responsible for Albert and Joe. Similarly, the chart shows that Tom, Harry, Francis and Sarah are accountable to Judith.

Figure 44.3
Chain of command

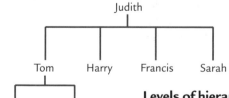

The chain of command can often serve as a useful guide to the lines of communication in an organisation.

Levels of hierarchy

This refers to the number of levels or layers within a business organisation. In Figure 44.1 there are five levels or layers. The number of levels or layers will depend on the type of organisational structure chosen by the business.

A horizontal or flat structure will have fewer levels than a vertical or tall structure.

Too many levels or layers in the hierarchy may not be good for a business. Addressing the annual conference of the Institute of Professional Qualified Secretaries (IPQS) in London, Chief Superintendent Helen Ball of the Metropolitan Police told delegates that hierarchical workplaces such as the police force and many 'old school' employers were in danger of stifling talent.

Delayering

Delayering often takes place as a result of rationalisation within a business. If the business is in a competitive market, it needs to ensure that its costs are kept under control, and one way to reduce costs is to remove a layer or tier of management.

A further advantage of delayering is that it provides an opportunity for employees to have more responsibility, which may be beneficial in terms of motivation. Delayering may also mean that the decision-making process is quicker, as there are fewer layers for decisions and messages to go through.

However, it is important to note that if delayering takes place, the span of control in the business will increase. There will also be implications for costs in the short term, as redundancies may be necessary to achieve the delayering. This may demotivate employees if they are fearful of losing their job, as it will reduce their sense of security (Maslow, see Chapter 41).

Delegation

The more delegation in an organisation, the bigger the span of control will be and the wider the organisational structure. How much delegation takes place will depend on:

- the leadership style — a democratic style will mean more delegation
- how busy the manager or leader is — if the leader is very busy, delegation is more likely to occur
- the ability and willingness of employees to take on additional responsibility
- the type of task that is to be delegated

Empowerment

As stated in Chapter 42, empowerment means giving employees responsibility for the tasks they perform. It is a form of delegation. By enriching employees' jobs, it is hoped that they will be more motivated (Herzberg and Mayo). Offering empowerment may also give a business the opportunity to reduce the number of levels in its organisational structure (delayering).

Types of organisational structure

Looking at an organisational structure chart can be misleading. However, each type of structure has implications for the likely style of leadership and the role of employees in such an organisation.

 TERM

delayering: reducing the number of levels in the hierarchy of an organisation

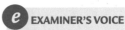 **EXAMINER'S VOICE**

When you look at a case study, note the implications of delayering for the business. Notice also how your points can be justified by naming a theorist.

1 — Only three levels of hierarchy
2
3

Wide span of control

Each manager is responsible for many employees

Figure 44.4 Organistic (horizontal or flat) structure

Management — 1
2 — seven levels of hierarchy
3
4
5
6
Shop-floor workers — 7

Narrow span of control

Figure 44.5 Mechanistic (vertical or tall) structure

Organistic (horizontal or flat) structure

The **organistic structure** is flat and has a large span of control (see Figure 44.4). Each manager is responsible for a large number of employees (subordinates). This type of structure is associated with a democratic style of leadership. Delegation is encouraged, allowing for a more motivated workforce.

Mechanistic (vertical or tall) structure

The **mechanistic structure** is more vertical than the organistic and consequently has a smaller span of control (see Figure 44.5). The style of leadership is less democratic than under the organistic structure. As there are a large number of layers in the structure, it is also more bureaucratic. An example is the civil service in the UK.

Centralised or entrepreneurial structure

Weinshall classified organisations as either *centralised* or *decentralised*. A **centralised structure** is associated with autocratic leaders who want to keep firm control of the business (see Figure 44.6). The leader is involved with everything and all communication goes through him/her. The decision-making process takes place at the top of the hierarchy.

Decentralised structure

A **decentralised structure** allows the decision-making process to take place away from head office.

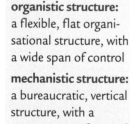

KEY TERMS

organistic structure: a flexible, flat organisational structure, with a wide span of control

mechanistic structure: a bureaucratic, vertical structure, with a narrow span of control

Marketing department

Finance department

Marketing director

Finance director

Chief executive

Production director

HRM director

Production staff

HRM staff

Figure 44.6 Centralised structure

The structure may be decentralised either by *product*, where each product has its own organisational structure (see Figure 44.7(a)), or by *area*, where each area or region has its own structure (see Figure 44.7(b)). Under a decentralised structure, the span of control will be wide. The style of leadership likely to be associated with this structure is democratic, as more employees will have responsibilities delegated to them.

KEY TERMS

centralised structure: the decision-making process is undertaken by the leader at the top of the hierarchy

decentralised structure: the decision-making process is delegated and undertaken on a regional or product basis

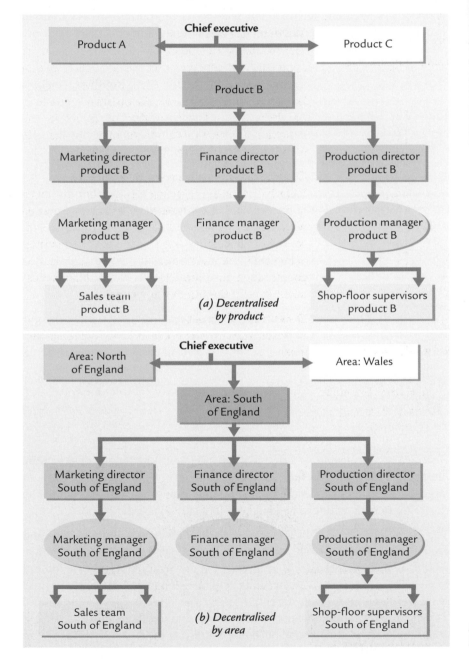

(a) Decentralised by product

(b) Decentralised by area

Figure 44.7 Decentralised structure

CHAPTER 44 Organisational structures

Marriott hotels are often quoted as an example of a successful decentralised structure. In addition, after the privatisation of the railways, the industry became a decentralised network as the ownership of the track went first to Railtrack and subsequently to Network Rail. Meanwhile, the ownership of running the routes was split up into franchises, which were bought by businesses such as Virgin.

There is considerable debate about whether a centralised or decentralised structure is the more appropriate. The main arguments on both sides are presented in Table 44.1.

Type of structure	Advantages	Disadvantages
Centralised	■ Decisions are quicker because there is no need to consult all areas or branches. ■ In the event of a crisis, there will be strong leadership. ■ There is a standardised approach in the way the business is operated. ■ Consumers will recognise the standardised approach and consistent organisation. ■ There is less duplication of resources, which may reduce costs.	■ Decisions are made without the benefit of local knowledge. ■ Lack of involvement in the decision-making process is demotivating. ■ Experts in a region may be ignored, resulting in mistakes. ■ Loss of goodwill in the regions may occur, as consumer needs are not met by centralised decisions.
Decentralised	■ Local regions or areas are better informed for some decisions. Regions will know local consumer needs and trends. ■ Being able to make decisions is a motivator (Mayo and Herzberg). ■ This delegation or empowerment will mean there are opportunities for local initiative to be used. ■ This is a more flexible approach, as decisions can be made for individual areas or products rather than having a standardised approach for all. ■ Less time is spent on communication and arguing a case for a specific region.	■ Consumers may not recognise the corporate identity as regions introduce variations. ■ Some decisions made at regional or product level may be appropriate for that region or product but not appropriate for the business as a whole (no overview). ■ Duplication of resources occurs, which could be reduced if centralised.

Table 44.1 Advantages and disadvantages of centralised and decentralised structures

Historically, organisational structures were rigid and had many layers in the hierarchy. As businesses became larger, more layers were added, leading to large, bureaucratic organisations. These large, rigid organisations lacked the flexibility to cope with change and consequently suffered.

The changing nature of business has led to a change in the structure and organisation of businesses. More businesses today have flatter structures, which suggests that the levels of hierarchy have been reduced in an attempt to give more employees a chance to take responsibilities. This delegation and empowerment, along with decentralisation, has altered the span of control and the lines of communication in businesses, making them more capable of adapting to the ever-changing business world.

Further sources

www.businesslink.gov.uk/bdotg/action

C. Handy (1990) *Understanding Organisations*, Oxford University Press.

YOUR TURN

Questions

Time allowed: 20 minutes

1 Define what is meant by the term organisation structure. *(3 marks)*

2 What information about a business can be found by looking at its organisational structure? *(4 marks)*

3 State what is meant by the term 'decentralisation'. *(2 marks)*

4 Explain why a flatter organisational structure is more likely to provide more opportunities to motivate employees. *(5 marks)*

5 Using Figure 44.8:
  a State the number of levels within the business. *(1 mark)*
  b Whom is the marketing director responsible for? *(2 marks)*
  c What is the span of control for the production managers? *(1 mark)*

(18 marks)

Figure 44.8 Organisation structure

Managing director — Marketing director — HRM director — Production director — Area sales manager A — Area sales manager B — Area sales manager C — Sales force — Production managers — Shop-floor supervisors — Shop-floor workers

Case study

Time allowed: 25 minutes

Poppies garden centres

Poppies is a growing chain of garden centres, selling a wide range of plants, gardening equipment, country clothes and fish, and in some of its 12 outlets, operating a restaurant. The owner, Tim, has built the business up from a small garden centre in Staffordshire to a nationwide chain with a growing reputation for meeting the needs of all lovers of gardens.

He has not been keen to reduce the amount of control he has over his growing retail empire, which has caused frustration at some of the outlets. The managers of these outlets have had to check with head office before buying stock to meet local needs. The majority of products are bought by Tim and his small team of buyers, who are based at the head office in Stafford.

Tim was concerned that his plans for further expansion might be jeopardised because of the difficulty of employing enough staff of the right quality. Steve, one of Tim's buyers at head office, hinted that there was a need to give the managers at the branches more control.

'Allowing them to run their own particular branch in their own way may be beneficial to us all,' stated Steve.

'I am not prepared to let the good name of the business be threatened by managers doing their own thing,' retorted Tim.

Emma, a business graduate working at Tim's head office, commented quietly, 'But I could save you

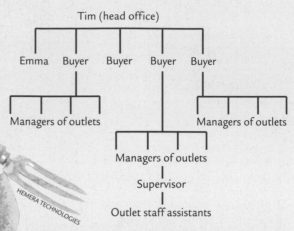

Figure 44.9 Poppies organisation chart

money, which could be used to finance your expansion plans. Look, I have drawn an organisation chart of the business. There are real opportunities for what is called delayering.'

Answer all questions.

1 State the number of layers within the organisation chart (Figure 44.9). *(1 mark)*

2 Outline which type of organisational structure best describes Poppies. Justify your answer. *(5 marks)*

3 Evaluate the consequences for Poppies if delayering is allowed to take place. *(14 marks)*

(20 marks)

Module 2872
Business Decisions
Module 2873
Business Behaviour

Operations
Management

CHAPTER 45

The scale of operation

The size of an organisation or part of an organisation can have a crucial impact on overall efficiency. Firms wanting to increase their productive efficiency try to reduce the cost of each item they produce. This chapter considers the factors that influence firms in trying to operate at their best level of production. It looks at the factors that encourage firms to increase their scale of production (economies of scale) and the reasons why firms might choose to operate at over and under full capacity.

Why do businesses grow?

Firms have an almost natural wish to grow. It is quite common for a firm to change from being a sole trader to a partnership to a limited company (private or public). This growth occurs as part of a natural progression. As the objectives of firms change, the desire to achieve greater profits encourages growth.

While there may be good reasons why a firm may choose to stay small, there are a number of benefits to growth. Firms will grow to achieve:
- **greater profits.** Larger firms are able to increase sales and this can often lead to higher profits.
- **increased market share.** This increases the relative and actual power of firms, which are then able to have a greater say in determining prices.
- **higher chances of survival.** Larger firms generally find it easier to survive. Firms often merge to increase their power and achieve longer lives for them both.
- **cost reductions.** Larger firms tend to be more efficient, as they are able to make better use of the resources they have available. They gain the benefits of economies of scale.

Types of growth

Organisations can grow in a number of ways, but they tend to fit into one of two categories.
- **Internal (organic) growth** is where a firm grows naturally over time. It does this simply by increasing in size to satisfy increases in demand. Many organisations have started small and have increased in size as the popularity of what they provide has increased. Even Microsoft started as a small organisation and achieved growth by essentially doing more of the same.

Bill Gates, creator of Microsoft

- **External growth** is where a firm is able to grow quickly by merging with or taking over another business, often a local or national competitor. External growth works well if firms can finance this expansion in an economical way. However, some firms find it difficult to manage this kind of sudden growth.

Capacity

What is capacity?

Capacity is the maximum amount of output that can be achieved over a period of time. The difficulty in trying to measure or establish this level of output is that the factors which can influence it vary so much. The measure relates mostly to the resources that are available to the firm. These resources include buildings, machinery and labour. Within a given time period, firms establish their maximum capacity by assessing what could be produced with those resources. Over time and with changed resources, the capacity can change.

Capacity utilisation

Capacity utilisation refers to the percentage of the agreed maximum capacity level that is actually being achieved in a given time period. A simple formula can be used to calculate capacity utilisation:

$$\text{capacity utilisation (\%)} = \frac{\text{actual level of output}}{\text{maximum possible output}} \times 100$$

For example, a firm producing 60,000 items in a given time period, when it is accepted that full capacity would allow 80,000 items to be produced, has a capacity utilisation of:

$$\frac{60,000}{80,000} \times 100 = 75\%$$

Capacity utilisation is often used as a measure of efficiency. Average costs tend to fall as the level of production increases. Ideally, therefore, firms will aim to produce as close to full capacity as possible in order to reduce costs. There may, however, be times when firms are unable to produce at this level of capacity.

Under-utilisation of capacity

There are a number of reasons why firms may have to produce at less than the desired maximum capacity level:

- **General reduction in demand.** The product may suffer from loss of customer demand due to changes in fashion, poor marketing or falling behind other products in the market.
- **Seasonal variation in demand.** Service industries, in particular, suffer from seasonal variation. A seaside hotel may have to turn customers away in the summer months, but may consider shutting altogether in the winter.

KEY TERMS

internal growth: natural growth of a firm achieved by increased production and sales

external growth: growth achieved by takeover and merger

capacity: the maximum that a firm can produce in a given period of time with the available resources

capacity utilisation: the percentage of total capacity that is actually being achieved in a given time period

- **Overall increase in capacity.** This can be caused by over-investment in new technology, which can make production more efficient but will reduce capacity utilisation if a similar increase in demand is not required.
- **Inefficiency in the production process.** This could be due to insufficient maintenance, poor labour relations, stock control problems or inadequate quality control.

Football clubs must have full stadiums to maximise revenue

Under-utilisation of capacity can be both good and bad for the organisation.

- On the positive side, it allows for routine maintenance and other machinery checking to take place. A lower level of output can reduce the stress on staff and allows a firm to cope with sudden increases in demand.
- On the negative side, low capacity levels can cause unit costs to rise. Fixed costs still have to be paid and these are spread out over fewer units of output. Staff can also become insecure and demotivated if they are not fully utilised. Ultimately, prices may have to rise to cover the increase in unit costs.

Over-utilisation of capacity

Some firms push the boundaries of possible production to cope with increasing demand. This may be a short-term issue, but it can develop into a medium- to long-term problem.

Firms can produce at higher than the nominal capacity level by:

- **increasing the hours of the workforce.** This might involve working overtime or taking on temporary or part-time staff.
- **reallocating workers.** This can be achieved by making staff more flexible in the way that they work.
- **subcontracting work to others.** This can be an effective way of dealing with short-term surges in demand. Other firms or individuals can often be very skilled and specialist in particular areas.

The main drawbacks of operating at high capacity levels are:

- **poorer quality of output and customer service.** Firms that operate at full capacity and beyond may produce goods too quickly or with less care than when there is less rush. This can have a negative impact on quality. Delays and the need for customers to 'queue' for their goods also have a negative effect on customer relations.
- **stress and strain on staff and other resources.** Working at high capacity levels can be stressful for staff, who experience constant pressures to produce. Overused capital equipment is more likely to break down and there may be little or no time for routine maintenance.
- **possible loss of sales.** Firms that operate at high levels of output are unable to cope with sudden increases in demand. All flexibility is lost and some customers may go elsewhere.

Economies and diseconomies of scale

The theory of economies of scale relates to the benefits that firms can gain by increasing the scale of production. In simple terms, the theory suggests that, as the scale of production increases, the *average* or *unit costs* of production fall. It is crucial that the definition is stated carefully. Missing out the word 'unit' in the definition completely changes the meaning and makes it incorrect.

The benefits of **economies of scale** can be explained in a number of ways. It is normal to distinguish between internal and external economies of scale.

Internal economies of scale

Internal economies of scale are achieved as a result of a firm growing internally. There are many examples:

- **Purchasing economies.** These are gained as a benefit of being able to purchase raw materials and other supplies in larger quantities. The larger the firm, the greater the likely discount that can be achieved.
- **Financial economies.** Larger firms are able to negotiate cheaper loans and are more likely to get a loan in the first place because lending institutions are likely to experience a lower level of risk with them.
- **Managerial economies.** Larger firms are able to employ specialist managers. This allows the firms to operate more effectively. Each of these managers can carry out his/her role in an efficient way.
- **Technical economies.** As a firm gets bigger, it can gain the benefit of buying more effective capital equipment. Smaller firms are unable to invest in the same way.
- **Marketing economies.** Larger firms can benefit from being able to use more effective methods of marketing. Above-the-line methods such as television advertising are only available to larger firms.
- **Risk-bearing economies.** Small firms tend to concentrate on a limited range of products, while larger firms can spread the risk by expanding into different products. They may even expand by taking over their suppliers. This allows the firms to reduce their costs.

External economies of scale

External economies of scale are achieved by a firm as a result of growth in the industry in which it operates. Many of these advantages occur if the firm is located close to other competing firms. Examples include the following:

- **Concentration economies.** Firms benefit as an industry grows in a specific region because skilled labour tends to move to that area. Local training colleges run specialist courses and suppliers to that industry tend to locate nearby. All these factors reduce costs.
- **Information economies.** Firms can benefit as information services are set up for the benefit of the industry. The internet has provided firms with many advantages of this kind.

 KEY TERM

economies of scale: a reduction in unit costs achieved as the scale of production increases

EXAMINER'S VOICE

Remember to define economies of scale carefully. Unit costs, not just costs, are falling as a result of increased size.

KEY TERM

diseconomies of scale: an increase in unit costs as a result of an increased scale of production

Diseconomies of scale

Economies of scale suggest that unit costs fall as the scale of production increases. However, beyond a certain level of output it becomes less likely that further cost savings can be achieved. A point is eventually reached where unit costs start to rise. **Diseconomies of scale** occur for a number of reasons:

- **Communication problems.** As a firm increases in size, it becomes more difficult to communicate in an effective way. The increased number of staff makes decision making more complex. The organisational structure of the firm develops increased levels of hierarchy and communication slows down.
- **Problems in managing the production process.** Large-scale production can be difficult to manage. Storage costs may increase and, as the firm reaches full capacity, there is a need for physical growth, which can involve additional fixed costs.
- **Reduction in morale.** Workers tend to lose their sense of belonging to the organisation as the firm gets bigger. As workers feel less important, they will be less inclined to push themselves and work hard. Labour turnover and absentee rates will increase, and therefore costs will rise.

Diseconomies of scale must be monitored carefully. Larger firms need to review the impact on costs when they take the decision to increase the overall size of the firm.

Further sources
www.growthbusiness.co.uk
www.growingbusiness.co.uk
www.moneyterms.co.uk/economies-of-scale

YOUR TURN

Questions

Time allowed: 30 minutes

1 Explain the difference between internal and external growth. *(4 marks)*

2 Explain **two** advantages for a firm of operating at full capacity. *(4 marks)*

3 Calculate the capacity utilisation of a firm producing 60,000 units when full capacity suggests that 90,000 units could be made. *(4 marks)*

4 Define the term 'economies of scale'. *(2 marks)*

5 Analyse **two** problems faced by an airline operating below full capacity. *(6 marks)*

6 Analyse **three** economies of scale that a hotel may gain by taking over another hotel. *(9 marks)*

(29 marks)

Case study

Time allowed: 30 minutes

Valueflora increases sales with Nochex

Russell Hirst founded Valueflora.com in 2003, having already worked in the online flower industry. As the name suggests, Valueflora.com is a dedicated online florist, but the unusual part is that the business gets many of the flowers that it sells sent direct from the growers to customers using arrangements designed by Valueflora.com. This means that customers get fresher, longer-lasting blooms at great prices because Valueflora.com is cutting out the middlemen's costs.

Russell says, 'We studied the online flower market closely before we started. We found some offered very good quality at a price, while many of the cut-price brigades had service issues. That's a real problem in our trade, as flowers are often ordered to celebrate a special day: a birthday or an anniversary.

'I decided there was no point in starting unless I could find ways to be the very best on quality, value for money and, in particular, back all that up with excellent customer service. And with the Valueflora.com concept, that's exactly what we've done. By selling straight from the growers to the customer we cut out a huge swathe of costs and we are left free to concentrate on delivering customer service and efficiency.

'Of course, things occasionally can go wrong, but if they do, it's how you put things right that counts. We have every incentive to sort things out quickly, as we are totally dependent on customer recommendations to build the business.'

And that's a strategy that seems to be paying dividends for this Manchester-based company that started by offering just four types of flowers. Spurred on by customer recommendations, Valueflora.com now serves over 30,000 repeat customers with an exciting range of exotic flora imported from South America as well as UK-grown farm-fresh flowers. It also offers fine wines, fruits and a range of gifts, including cakes and chocolates.

Russell says that this remarkable business performance in just two and a half years is all down to organic growth driven by the company's focus on high-quality customer service and great value. He points out, 'We don't advertise or use mass-marketing gimmicks. We do reward repeat customers and those who recommend us with our Petal Points loyalty scheme. Plus we e-mail half-price offers out to those who subscribe to our free newsletter.'

Switching to Nochex 18 months ago has also had a positive effect on the business. Valueflora.com can now, thanks to Nochex, accept payment for flowers in 120 different countries. Russell says, 'Our previous payment services provider was very restrictive, limiting us to accepting payments from just 13 countries. Their systems were also quite complex and required customers to register with them before they could send the payment.

'I'd say that sales increased by more than 25% as a direct result of fully integrating Nochex into our website. This was due to the streamlined checkout process, removal of the need for customers to register before paying and, later on, the acceptance of cards from any country. That international card acceptance will continue to assist growth, as we are now able to expand further internationally with Nochex handling all payments.'

To that end, Valueflora.com now has partners in India, Australia and Germany.

'Our previous payment service provider was US-based and if we e-mailed an enquiry to them, we were lucky to get a reply within 4 days. With Nochex, a response is more likely to come back within half an hour. And they are pleasant people to deal with.

'I get the impression they really value our business, which is a rare thing for a small company to experience with a financial services provider.

They really have the human touch and are obviously dedicated to the same business values as us: quality at competitive prices backed by great service.'

To date Valueflora.com has delivered flowers to celebrities such as Shirley Bassey and successfully located Michael Jackson after his recent trial to have a bouquet delivered. It also offers a corporate flower service, but the bulk of its orders come from private individuals who tend to favour roses, closely followed by exotic pale green carnations flown in from South America. The stunningly scented huge bunch of 150 freesias for £22 is also a winner and Nochex is determined to help Valueflora.com keep delivering its winning flowers.

Source: adapted from **www.nochex.com**

Answer all questions.

1 Explain why Valueflora's growth has been organic. *(3 marks)*

2 Analyse the possible economies of scale that Valueflora might have achieved by growing in this way. *(8 marks)*

3 Discuss the circumstances that might cause Valueflora to experience diseconomies of scale. *(9 marks)*

4 How could Valueflora determine its full capacity level? *(4 marks)*

5 Evaluate the problems that seasonal demand might cause Valueflora. *(10 marks)*

(34 marks)

CHAPTER 46

Types of production

Firms produce goods in a variety of ways. In order to decide on the most appropriate way of producing their goods and services, all firms must look at the resources they have at their disposal. These include labour, land, machinery and other physical resources. This chapter considers different methods of production and how they make use of these inputs. There is also a consideration of how to decide on the most appropriate method of production in given situations.

Should production be labour or capital intensive?

Production involves combining several resources (inputs) in order to produce goods. The four factors of production, land, labour, capital and enterprise highlight different resources that can be utilised (see Chapter 3).

A firm that makes greater use of labour than machinery in the production process is said to be **labour intensive**. Examples include wedding cake making and dressmaking.

The alternative is to make greater use of capital machinery in the production process. In this situation, a firm is said to be **capital intensive**. Examples include car production and microchip manufacturing.

Manufacturing microchips is capital intensive

Some firms have seen a slow but dramatic move from labour-intensive to capital-intensive production. The modern car, for example, used to be produced in a fairly labour-intensive way. Greater use of automation in firms that produce on a mass scale has meant that staff are now needed far less.

Methods of production

The mix of capital and labour used in the production process is linked to the choice of production method. Several different methods exist and the OCR specification requires a consideration of four of these: job, batch, flow and cell production (see Figure 46.1).

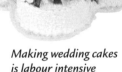

Making wedding cakes is labour intensive

KEY TERMS

labour intensive: involving a high proportion of workers in the production process compared with machinery or other capital equipment

capital intensive: involving a high proportion of capital equipment in the production process compared with the use of labour

> ### *e* EXAMINER'S VOICE
>
> Do not include lean production as a method of production. Lean production is an overall philosophy, which includes cell production (see Chapter 47).

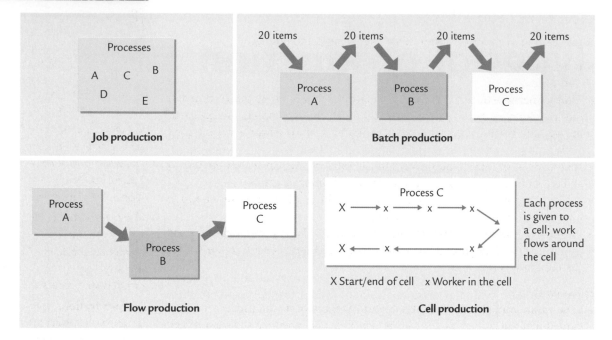

Figure 46.1
Methods of production

Job production

Job production involves producing a single item, such as a designer dress, to fit in with the specific needs of a customer. A single product is manufactured in its entirety before the firm goes on to produce another.

Batch production

In **batch production** a whole group (or batch) of items is produced together. These items move around the production process as a group, and the entire group must complete one stage of the process before any of the items move on to the next stage. Examples of batch production are bread making and the production of other food items.

Flow production

In **flow production** goods move through the production process in a continuous way. The process is mostly used by firms that produce a high proportion of standardised products, such as personal computers.

Cell production

Cell production involves the organisation of multi-skilled workers into work cells. A work cell is defined as a collection of equipment and workstations arranged in a single area, which allows a product or group of similar products to be processed completely from start to finish. The cell, in which workstations are usually arranged in a U-shaped layout, is essentially a self-contained mini-production line that caters for a group of products undergoing the same production process. Several manufacturers have begun using this approach, including Canon (cameras) and Lucas Industries (car components).

A designer dress is made using job production

Which method is best?

Each method of production has advantages and disadvantages.

Job production

Advantages

- **A large increase in added value.** The specialist nature of job production and the individuality of the product usually mean that customers are prepared to pay high prices. A designer dress worn by a top celebrity carries a high price.
- **Increased staff motivation.** Workers in job production are often highly skilled and take great pride in producing the finished goods.
- **A high level of quality.** The specification of the work is often set at a high level, which results in a high-quality product.
- **Increased customer satisfaction.** Customers always welcome a good product. Job production is likely to encourage brand loyalty and enhance the company's reputation.

Disadvantages

- **Time-consuming production.** The nature of the production process tends to slow down the level of output. When workers take great care to ensure high quality, it is much more difficult to produce quickly.
- **Higher production costs.** Production costs are higher because job production is highly labour intensive. Producing at lower levels of output reduces the possibility of benefiting from economies of scale. The use of highly skilled workers also increases costs.
- **Poor use of capital resources.** Job production is likely to use machinery and capital equipment, but it is unlikely to use it in the same way as other methods of production, and for much of the time it may lie idle.
- **Customers may have to wait.** The one-off (bespoke) nature of job production means that waiting lists may develop for certain products. This may be a positive selling feature in some markets, but it could encourage some customers to look elsewhere.

Batch production

Advantages

- **Faster than job production.** Producing goods in larger quantities allows firms to produce them more quickly than if they used job production.
- **Lower costs than job production.** Firms using batch production can benefit from economies of scale, which reduces unit costs. Batch production is also a little more capital intensive than job production and this is likely to reduce overall costs.
- **Greater ability to meet customer demand.** Using batch production means that customers are less likely to have to wait. Batch production is often linked with just-in-time methods of production (see Chapter 51), where specific customer orders are satisfied as required. The production line must be flexible to ensure that each batch meets the needs of the specific customer

KEY TERMS

job production: goods are produced one at a time to match the specific needs of customers

batch production: each group of goods passes through every stage of the production process together

flow production: goods 'flow' in a continuous fashion through the production process

cell production: small teams or 'cells' of workers are located close together; each group produces whole units or carries out one of the processes in a larger facility

order. For example, if a local police force orders a specific model of car, it is likely to have very individual needs, such as no sunroof, a specialist radio system and white paintwork. After producing the cars for this order, the machine settings will need to be changed before production switches to more general customers or to the next order from another customer.

Disadvantages

- **Lower motivation.** The workforce can be less skilled and this makes the work less interesting. Greater specialisation in the production process may lead to lower morale and possibly lower-quality working.
- **Increased 'downtime'.** Batch production tends to involve a much greater degree of stop–starting. This is due to constant changes being made to the production process to allow for the necessary flexibility. Work for the day must be scheduled carefully.

Police cars are likely to be made using batch production

- **Higher stock levels.** More stock needs to be held on site. The quantity of work-in-progress is greater, as the batch production process requires each item in the batch to be stored, waiting for the other items in the batch to complete that process.
- **Loss of individuality and quality.** Batch production requires a number of products to be produced to the same specification. The individual nature of the product is lost. This can also mean that the quality of output falls.

Flow production
Advantages

- **Low unit costs.** If the firm is producing at a high level of capacity, economies of scale will be high and unit costs will be low. The use of unskilled or semi-skilled workers means that labour costs will be relatively low. The process is likely to be highly capital intensive, making the most efficient use of machinery and other resources.
- **High level of standardisation.** Flow production works well when multiple versions of the same product are produced. A continuous production line operates efficiently when it remains in use.
- **Increased levels of output.** Flow production is generally fast and allows for a greater number of units of production to be made. High-volume production coupled with a high volume of sales is the key to mass-market success.

Disadvantages

- **Inflexible production.** Flow production thrives on being continuous; it is not efficient when stopped and started again. Therefore, it is more difficult to satisfy the specific requirements of individual customers when using flow production.
- **Lack of worker motivation.** Workers who operate on a flow production line are often given few different tasks during their working day and this can

cause them to become demotivated. Flow production workers are often unskilled, but it is still necessary to try to motivate them.

■ **Problems of breakdowns.** Machinery breakdowns and stock hold-ups can cause real problems in trying to keep production continuous. A problem at any point on the production line can cause difficulties for the whole process.

■ **High initial costs.** Firms have to be sure that high levels of production can be sustained. If not, it can be difficult to justify making such a large investment in the capital equipment required.

■ **Less worker responsibility.** This means that the quality of the finished goods may be lower.

Cell production

Advantages

■ **Greater teamwork.** The workforce in cell production works very closely together, both in terms of physical location and in terms of working as a team. This improves communication between the team (cell) members.

■ **Improved quality.** Workers are responsible for producing high-quality goods and are encouraged to reduce wastage to a minimum. They are likely to take a greater pride in their work.

■ **Workers become multi-skilled.** The workforce is likely to be able to carry out a number of different tasks. All requirements of the cell can be carried out by all workers in that cell.

■ **Reduction in stock requirements.** Cell production fits in with the overall philosophy of lean production and waste reduction. Stock is kept to a minimum in the production process.

Disadvantages

■ **Requires teamwork.** Not all workers work well together. Teams that do not gel will not be able to operate effectively in a cell.

■ **Output can be less than flow production.** The need to produce in small teams means that production output tends to be much lower.

■ **More complex factory layout.** It may be necessary for the factory to be given a new layout. The U-shaped cells can require a considerable amount of space. Not all organisations will be able to make this change.

How do firms choose the best method?

The decision about which method of production to use can be affected by a number of different factors. These factors must be evaluated carefully to help determine the best method of production in a given situation.

■ **Type of product.** This can be looked at in many ways, including size, shape and complexity of styling. A firm producing a one-off design for a new building such as the stadium for the 2012 Olympic Games in London is likely to use job production. For Cadbury's chocolate bars, on the other hand, flow or batch production is more likely to be used because of the standardised nature of the product.

- **Demand for the product.** High demand makes flow production more likely. Lower demand means that firms will be unwilling to invest in capital equipment, making flow production less likely. The individual needs of customers can also encourage firms to use job or batch production rather than flow production.
- **Quality level demanded by customers.** If the consumer wants high levels of quality, there will be a greater requirement to use job, cell or batch production. Where production is more standardised, it may be difficult to employ flow production.
- **Size of the firm.** This can have an impact because larger firms gain the benefit of technical and financial economies of scale. These economies make flow or batch production more likely.
- **Availability of technology.** The market may be relatively new, with few or no opportunities to exploit advances in technology. As microchip technology became more popular and advanced, it was more possible to use it in the production process.

The best method of production can be tricky to determine. Most firms have evolved over time and have developed by using the available technology and the latest concepts at each stage in their growth. In any production facility, it is therefore quite possible to see examples of job, batch, cell and flow production under the same roof.

Car production is a good example to cite when considering flow production. A modern car plant will tend to adopt the best aspects of flow production to generate the basic framework for production, but in different departments or sections there may be aspects of batch production in evidence. For example, in the paint shop, it makes sense to paint the cars in colour batches: 20 red cars followed by 20 silver ones, and so on.

In contrast, Volvo has teams of workers who produce the engines together from start to finish. The teams take great pride in their workmanship and put their own stamp on the engine, so they become directly responsible for the quality.

Volvo has teams of workers who produce the engines together from start to finish

The design of cars invariably takes place through job production, and in some parts of a car plant it may be possible to witness cells. A modern facility must strive to produce in the most effective way possible, balancing the needs of customers with the need to produce effectively.

> ### ⓔ EXAMINER'S VOICE
>
> Be careful not to suggest a clear-cut example for each method of production. The examination will tackle this topic in relation to an actual firm. Assess what that firm is doing and be prepared to offer suggestions for improvement.

Further sources
www.manufacturingtalk.com/news/abd/abd159.html — leading product information
www.themanufacturer.com/uk/magazines/themanufacturer.html — manufacturing desisions
www.businessweek.com/magazine

YOUR TURN

Questions

Time allowed: 30 minutes

1 Explain the difference between labour-intensive and capital-intensive production. *(4 marks)*

2 Give **three** advantages of batch production. *(3 marks)*

3 Explaining why, suggest the best method of production to use for:
  a frozen chicken curries
  b cruise ships
  c boxes of matches
  d plasma screen televisions *(12 marks)*

4 What are the drawbacks of trying to use flow production when making handbags? Can you suggest a better method? *(8 marks)*

(27 marks)

Case study

Time allowed: 30 minutes

Pod production

Pod (cell) production is the latest method adopted by R. Griggs, the company behind Dr Martens. The Dr Martens factory in Whetstone, Leicestershire, employs more than 300 people, producing 55,000 pairs of shoes a week. It has recently introduced pod production, where workers are divided into individual cells made up of 17 people. Each pod is responsible for its own production. Staff work 39 hours a week, but each pod can divide that time how it wishes.

For example, if a pod wants to work 4 long days and have a day off, it can do so. And for every extra 100 pairs of shoes each pod makes over its target,

it gets extra money. Workers can earn up to £411 a week or £20,000 a year — a good rate for shoe workers.

But Griggs has had its share of troubles. It recently announced that it was closing its Somerset plant because of the downturn in the US market. That leaves it with four factories in the East Midlands. R. Griggs isn't alone. The shoe industry, like many others, has declined substantially. There are now only about 20 shoe manufacturers left in the UK. The decline began in the 1950s, when cheaper imports began coming into the country.

The mass market for shoes is very price sensitive, and in the UK, labour is 30% of the cost of production. Those shoemakers who have survived tend to be at the high-margin, craft end of the market (e.g. Church & Co., now a subsidiary of Prada) or in a niche market (e.g. Griggs)

Bristol used to be an international shoe making centre, with more than 10,000 people working in the industry before the Second World War. Now there are none, although 100 workers are still employed at a shoe manufacturer's distribution depot. Northampton is probably the town most associated with the industry in the UK. But times have changed. In the late 1990s, manufacturing employed 27% of the working population in this town of about 200,000. Now it's 20% and falling.

Source: adapted from **http://news.bbc.co.uk/1/hi/programmes/working_lunch/education/1763720.stm**

Answer all questions.

1 Explain whether you think Griggs is a labour-intensive business. *(4 marks)*

2 Analyse the advantages to Griggs of using pod (cell) production. *(6 marks)*

3 Evaluate the pros and cons of being an employee at Griggs. *(10 marks)*

4 Discuss whether batch production would be more appropriate to use at Griggs. *(10 marks)*

(30 marks)

CHAPTER 47

Lean production

Lean production is a collection of techniques that has been developed to minimise the amount of 'waste' on the shop floor. Waste is defined as anything that slows down production or which stops production operating at low cost. Lean production also attempts to improve the quality of output and overall efficiency.

Lean production includes the following elements:
- continuous improvement/kaizen (see Chapter 49)
- cell production (see Chapter 46)
- just-in-time (see Chapter 51)
- time-based management

History of lean production: from Ford to Toyota

The starting point for **lean production** goes back to Henry Ford. Ford developed the first flow production system in the 1940s. The aim was to ensure that all material was always moving down the production line. This worked well until the Ford Motor Company decided to move away from the vision of Henry Ford by increasing production. All aspects of the production process were kept very busy even if the next stage in the process was not ready to accept the work. Stocks increased at all stages of the process through to the end retailer and inefficiencies crept into the system. Genuine flow production had developed into **mass production**.

While all this was happening, Taiichi Ohno at Toyota was given the task of trying to increase productivity to catch up with the rates achieved by US companies. The managers at Toyota were encouraged to study Ford. They learned that the supermarket principle of putting out small quantities of items for customers to buy and constantly replenishing them helped to improve the efficiency of space usage. Between 1945 and 1970, Toyota developed its lean production techniques into the **Toyota Production System (TPS)**, which is a model of efficiency still considered highly today. Toyota was able to develop systems that ensured it was doing more with less of everything. The company used less space, fewer staff, less capital and less stock.

Advantages of lean production

Lean production offers the following advantages:
- **Increased motivation of the staff.** Workers like to be part of a successful organisation. The focus on efficiency encourages the workforce to maintain its interest in the job.

KEY TERMS

lean production: a collection of methods that attempt to reduce waste in the production process

mass production: use of flow production techniques in large-scale markets

Toyota Production System (TPS): a system operated by Toyota in its production facility, which developed the concept of lean production

- **Increased quality of output.** The increased focus on waste reduction tends to focus the workforce on the production of high-quality goods.
- **Improvement in cash flow.** Better stock control and waste reduction releases money to be spent elsewhere in the organisation.
- **Higher level of worker participation.** Workers are more likely to be involved in the decision-making process through techniques such as quality circles (see Chapter 48), which in turn can improve motivation (Mayo).
- **Increased level of output.** Lean production reduces production bottlenecks by setting output according to actual demand.

Disadvantages of lean production

Lean production nevertheless suffers from the following disadvantages:

- **Can reduce the opportunity to gain economies of scale.** The need to order stock in smaller quantities but more frequently reduces the prospect of gaining purchasing economies of scale.
- **Requires all staff to be in favour.** Some staff find it difficult to sustain the constant demand to improve and develop. Management, in particular, must be in favour to maintain the focus on lean production.
- **May not be able to meet customer demand.** The need to reduce wastage and minimise stock levels tends to reduce the ability of firms to cope with sudden changes in customer demand.
- **Relies on a good supply chain.** The business may be reliant on the efficiency of the suppliers in replenishing stocks.

Time-based management

Time-based management is a feature of lean production that tends to focus on the need to reduce the time it takes to produce goods. This reduction in time relates to all aspects of production, from initial product development right through to delivery of the finished product to the final customer. Time-based management ties in with other aspects of lean production because of the need to reduce waste. Reductions in time, by definition, reduce waste.

By matching customer needs with the output of the business, a more effective organisation is developed. The business becomes more competitive in markets in which it can more readily meet customer demand.

Effective time-based management also makes use of *simultaneous engineering*. This concept involves product planning and includes all departments within an organisation and customer representatives. The goal is to share information to make the design, development and production of the product more streamlined and to make the end product meet final customer expectations and needs.

KEY TERM

time-based management: methods that reduce the time it takes to develop and produce a product in order to reach the market more quickly

A key factor in the success of Xbox was getting to the market before PS3

Lean production versus mass production

Lean production and mass production are often chosen for comparison in examination questions. The key features of each method are listed in Table 47.1.

Mass production	Lean production
High levels of stock	Reduced stock levels (just-in-time?)
Flow production (continuous)	Adaptable production (often cell and/or batch)
Quality inspection	Inbuilt defect prevention
Low skill level of workforce	Highly skilled workers
Large-scale deliveries	Small-scale deliveries
Higher economies of scale	Lower economies of scale

Table 47.1
Mass production and lean production compared

Chapters 48–51 consider wider aspects of lean production. The important point to note here is the efficiency improvements that stem from a philosophy of waste reduction.

Further sources

www.leanuk.org/pages/lean_books_lean_solutions.htm

www.themanufacturer.com/

www.ims-productivity.com/productivity/tools/tools8.htm

EXAMINER'S VOICE

Lean production is not necessarily the best method for all firms. You should look at the firm being used in the case study or data-response question and assess what is right for that firm.

YOUR TURN

Questions
Time allowed: 30 minutes

1 Define the term 'lean production'. *(3 marks)*

2 Explain **three** benefits of lean production. *(6 marks)*

3 Explain **three** differences between mass production and lean production. *(6 marks)*

4 Evaluate the advantages of developing time-based management techniques for a firm producing a new games console. *(10 marks)*

5 'Economies of scale are more important than lean production.' Evaluate this statement. *(10 marks)*

(35 marks)

Case study
Time allowed: 30 minutes

The Kodak experience of lean production

Kodak has been the leading name in the production of camera film for many years. Faced with increased competition and falling sales, the company looked at several ways of improving its trading position.

The company overhauled its manufacturing process as well. That task fell to an old-timer, Charles Brown, who is today the chief administrative officer. A chemical engineer, Brown spent much of his career in manufacturing, ultimately developing a lean production system in 1997 that was based on Toyota's acclaimed continuous improvement approach. He dubbed it the Kodak Operating System. KOS forces managers to look at everything that happens in a plant in terms of waste — waste of time, waste of space and so on. They then analyse every step in a process — down to the hand movements of assembly-line workers — to look for a better way. Everything goes that does not 'create value for the customer', says Brown.

The progress has been measurable. In 1997, for instance, 100 days passed from the first step of making film to when the little yellow box reached the customer; today such cycle times are half as long. So far, says Brown, KOS has saved 'tens of millions of dollars worth of capital and hundreds of millions

in inventory' and has contributed 'hundreds of millions in productivity'. The directors, impressed by such stats, asked Brown in late 2003 to inject KOS into Kodak's entire corporate plumbing, from human resources management to product development to the products themselves. 'It's an entire management philosophy,' says Brown.

Kodak's workers understand the pressure the company is under. But that does not necessarily mitigate their misery. The tyranny of micromanaged productivity, says a veteran employee, hangs like a cloud over Kodak's rank and file: 'You're accountable for everything you do, or don't do, all the time. You're worried that you may not have a job from one week to the next, and you don't know whether, if you come up with a good idea to save the company money, you could cost people their jobs.'

It's a leaner and meaner company, no doubt. Yet Wall Street still isn't convinced that Kodak can compete in the digital marketplace. Its latest camera, EasyShare-One, available this summer for $600, features the largest display screen around, a memory capable of holding 1,500 high-resolution images and, for an extra $100, wireless communication. But competition is intense, especially in photo printing, which is still where the money is. In film, Kodak had only two major competitors, Fuji Photo Film in Asia and Agfa-Gevaert in Europe. Now, both its old foes are in the printing market, as is the giant HP. And Sony and Canon aside, there are at least a dozen firms making digital cameras.

Source: adapted from **www.time.com/time/insidebiz/printout/0,8816,1025191,00.html**

Answer all questions.

1 Explain the advantages of lean production to Kodak. *(6 marks)*

2 Evaluate the impact on the workforce of Kodak following the implementation of KOS. *(10 marks)*

3 Discuss why lean production is likely to be more important to Kodak than to a firm in a less competitive market. *(10 marks)*

4 Analyse the use of time-based management at Kodak. *(6 marks)*

(32 marks)

CHAPTER 48

Quality

This chapter considers what consumers and producers understand by quality, and how increased motivation of staff and a better-trained workforce can impact on the quality of output. This chapter and the next also look at why quality is so important in the world of business.

What is quality?

Quality can be defined as *ability to satisfy the expectations of consumers*. However, the level of customer satisfaction can be very difficult to measure. Quality control is a mechanism for ensuring that an output (product or service) conforms to a predetermined specification. It tends to involve some means of judging the products purchased or the service that has been provided. Different consumers are likely to judge products in different ways.

quality: features of a product that allow customers to be satisfied with their purchase

Chapter 25 considered the factors that might be used to judge whether a product is a good product. The value analysis process described there took into account function, economic production and aesthetics. When individuals judge products and services on the basis of quality, the value analysis framework is a useful starting point.

Product quality tends to be judged on the basis of:

- good function
- durability
- reliability
- image
- after-sales service
- value for money

It could be argued that value for money is the most important criterion. Good quality does not necessarily mean the very best that can be achieved. The notion of 'satisfying the expectations of consumers' is concerned with producing a product or providing a service with which customers will be happy. If a customer is unhappy, it suggests that the provision of a good-quality product or service has broken down.

Advantages of producing quality goods

The production of high-quality goods has several benefits to a firm:

- **Higher prices.** Many customers associate a higher level of quality with a higher price. If there is a general perception that quality has improved, the potential to raise prices often goes with it, as in the case of BMW cars.

BMW can sell its cars for high prices because customers associate them with high quality

■ **Reduction in waste.** In line with the ethos of lean production (see Chapter 47), a higher-quality product produced in a lean environment is often produced more efficiently. There is less need to rework materials or replace scrapped products.

■ **Less need to advertise.** This has much to do with a stronger brand image. Customers are inclined to buy the product based on their perception of its brand name, as with Dyson.

■ **Reduction in customer complaints.** This has the advantage of reducing the need to replace or repair defective products. There is also less chance of firms facing legal problems as a result of poor production. The business is therefore operating with lower costs.

■ **Increased guarantee periods.** Firms are able to offer increased warranty or guarantee periods, since better-quality products are less likely to need to be repaired during this warranty period. This can have a positive impact on sales.

The importance of the workforce in improving quality

Different organisations use a variety of techniques to improve overall quality. A clear focus is needed to enhance the effectiveness of staff in achieving quality improvements and workers must be encouraged to push for such improvements. Many of the aspects of *lean production* require the full cooperation of staff to ensure success. *Total quality management* (see Chapter 49) is an approach that encourages the workforce to play a full role in achieving quality improvements. *Kaizen* (also Chapter 49) suggests that the workforce should be striving for improvements in the workplace. Workers may also be able to improve their approach to the *management of waste* in the workplace (see Chapter 51).

Quality circles

Quality circles are regular short meetings set up to resolve work-related problems. The key feature of a quality circle is that it gives a range of workers the opportunity to contribute to the quality improvement debate.

A typical quality circle meeting may have the following characteristics:
■ 6–10 members of staff from different parts/levels of the organisation
■ a supervisor nominated to take charge of that meeting
■ the discussion of particular problem areas
■ prioritising other issues or problems
■ collation of information following open discussions
■ putting forward final solutions to management

 KEY TERM

quality circles: meetings of groups of workers from different levels and sections of an organisation to seek improvements in quality

Advantages of quality circles

The use of quality circles offers a business the following advantages:

- **Increase the motivation of staff.** Workers are more involved in the decision-making process and have a greater sense of pride in their work. They are therefore more likely to produce effectively.
- **Improve communication.** As more staff are talking to each other across different departments, there is bound to be a stronger sense of working as a team.
- **Unlock worker potential.** The use of quality circles can improve the overall performance of individual workers. Those directly involved are able to develop their skills and hidden talent can sometimes be discovered.
- **Put quality on the agenda.** The formalised nature of quality circles gives a renewed focus to quality in the workplace.

Disadvantages of quality circles

A number of disadvantages can arise from the use of quality circles:

- **Cost and time.** Meetings take time and can be viewed as costly if little is achieved.
- **Resentment among staff not involved.** Those staff not invited to take part might be unhappy and this could decrease the overall level of motivation.
- **Potential mismatch of staff involved.** The make-up of some quality circles can put together staff from very different levels in the organisation. These workers have very different objectives and the meetings that follow could reflect this. Staff have to be chosen carefully to ensure this does not happen.

The importance of training

Training can be defined in several ways and takes many forms (see Chapter 39). The aim of all training is to change or reinforce behaviour and/or to increase skills. In the area of quality, workers need to be made aware of the improvements they can make in their performance and the positive impact these can have on sales, profit and, ultimately, return for the worker.

Quality training should be continuous and must adapt to any changes in the business environment. Firms should ideally have a quality policy in place, of which training should be an integral part. The needs of the workforce should be considered and individual plans should be set out. These plans can be developed as a result of worker appraisal schemes. All training should be monitored and new quality training objectives should be set on a regular basis.

Investors in People

Investors in People is the national standard set to achieve a good level of training and development of staff. It provides a framework for improving the performance of an organisation through the setting of clearly planned objectives. The improvement of quality is an integral component of the

Investors in People: a national scheme designed to develop good practice in training and development of staff

framework, with specific attention to how staff can achieve higher perform-ance levels for themselves and the organisation as a whole. The culture of continuous improvement is a key feature of the standard.

Staff motivation

A happy and contented worker is generally a productive worker. Chapter 41 considered the full range of motivation theories and techniques. Any approach designed to improve the ability or the desire of the worker to work more effec-tively is likely to increase quality. The motivation of staff remains a crucial factor in achieving results. Techniques such as job enrichment (see Chapter 42) and job enlargement help to improve motivation and at the same time increase motivation.

> **ℯ EXAMINER'S VOICE**
>
> The theories of lean production and quality circles give good reasons why they should be adopted, but part of the skill required by the examination is to relate the theory to an actual firm. Be as prepared to say why a particular technique will not work as to say that it will.

Further sources

www.brecker.com/quality.htm

www.see.ed.ac.uk/~gerard/Management/art3.html

www.organisationalchange.co.uk/tqm/index.htm

www.investorsinpeople.co.uk/

YOUR TURN

Questions   Time allowed: 35 minutes

1 Give a definition of quality as it relates to:
   a baked beans
   b a hairdressing salon   (4 marks)

2 Discuss the advantages and disadvantages of trying to use quality circles at a local restaurant.   (10 marks)

3 Explain why it is important to have the support of the workers when trying to improve quality.   (5 marks)

4 Using the example of a fast-food restaurant, explain why it is important to train staff carefully when trying to increase quality.   (4 marks)

5 Assess whether quality circles would work in your school or college.   (10 marks)

                                                            (33 marks)

Case study

Time allowed: 30 minutes

Quality circles at Ricoh

Ricoh (UK) Products Ltd was established in 1984 and has since become one of the world's leading suppliers and manufacturers of office automation systems. The company is a leading innovator in office equipment technology with a research and development programme that introduced the first digital copier and a complete range of original engines.

Ricoh has been using continuous improvement in many guises for its 20-year life at Telford. The journey to a climate of continuous improvement had its very beginning with quality circles, then kaizen, and on to today's more advanced activities such as 'lean' concepts and 'business process engineering'.

The management objectives are deployed through to continuous improvement activities. Employee participation is key, and good use is made of the employee suggestion scheme and other employee incentive-based approaches.

The Ricoh mission statement reads as follows:

To develop and deploy robust strategic plans and sound management information systems, to help us continue to win and retain an increasingly satisfied customer base, enabling us to be recognised as 'the market leading supplier of Document Solutions, committed to outstanding service and support, delivered by motivated employees, providing our customers with tangible business benefits' through the provision of the most effective levels of order fulfilment and services.

Source: **www.ricoh.co.uk**

Answer all questions.

1 Ricoh strives to increase customer satisfaction. Explain how the use of quality circles could enhance this. *(8 marks)*

2 Assess why lean production techniques to improve quality are more likely to work at Ricoh than at other firms. *(6 marks)*

3 Evaluate why Ricoh considers employee participation as key to continuous improvement. *(8 marks)*

4 Discuss to what extent motivation of staff and improvement in quality are linked at Ricoh. *(10 marks)*

(32 marks)

CHAPTER 49

Quality assurance, kaizen and benchmarking

This chapter focuses on the concept of quality assurance, contrasting its emphasis on prevention with traditional methods of quality control that emphasise inspection. It also explains the benefits and problems of kaizen and benchmarking as methods of increasing the overall effectiveness of the production process.

Approaches to improving quality

There are several ways in which quality can be improved. This section considers two principal methods: quality control and quality assurance.

The traditional **quality control** method concentrates on trying to reduce the number of defective products by testing or observing a sample of them at the end of the production process. This process of *inspection* is designed to find out if any workers have produced products that fail to meet the specification required.

Production process
........................▶ Inspection

Figure 49.1
Quality control

In contrast, **quality assurance** seeks to emphasise quality improvement at all stages of the production process. The focus is on using a policy of *prevention* to reduce the number of defective products. The aim is to ensure that quality is important to all workers. This model reduces the need to inspect, as quality has been built into the process.

KEY TERMS

quality control: inspection of products as part of a sampling process to ensure that agreed standards have been reached

quality assurance: instilling quality throughout the organisation as part of the process of production

Production process
Prevention Prevention Prevention
........................▶
Prevention Prevention Prevention

Figure 49.2
Quality assurance

The quality control approach is similar to the principle of the traffic police patrol. The police patrol the roads, spotting motorists who drive badly or who commit traffic offences. Not every motorist who breaks the law is stopped. The traffic police are encouraged to catch as many as they can. This

process of sampling from the total number of drivers helps to reduce the number of people who drive badly.

The quality assurance approach is widely accepted as being more professional. Placing the emphasis on each worker reduces the need to inspect and each worker is rewarded with an enhanced role. This method is similar to encouraging people to drive safely and not to break the speed limit.

Quality control

This method checks the effectiveness of production by sampling finished products. It assumes that workers are not able to monitor quality themselves in an effective way. It has a number of advantages and disadvantages.

Patrol of the roads by traffic police is a form of quality control

Advantages of quality control

- **Quality is the job of experts.** Quality control puts the process of judging quality in the hands of specialist staff. Trained specialists are best placed to judge consistency in quality.
- **Patterns of inconsistent production can be spotted.** Quality control experts are able to discover problems that occur on a regular basis. Common problems that crop up can be dealt with in a consistent way.
- **Defective products are spotted.** The process of sampling allows those products not up to the required standard to be removed.

Disadvantages of quality control

- **'Big Brother'.** Checking for defective products is considered to be a negative way of monitoring performance. Inspectors are seemingly rewarded for catching out the poor performance of others.
- **The workforce becomes sloppy.** Placing the function of quality with one department removes the need for others to look after quality. If workers are aware that work is being checked by others, they have little need to monitor quality themselves.
- **Not every product is checked.** The sampling process involved in checking does not allow for every product to be considered fully. Defective products can easily slip through and into the hands of customers. This has a negative impact on the business's reputation.

Quality assurance

The move towards a philosophy of quality assurance shifts the emphasis away from checking at the end of the process, and towards monitoring quality throughout the process of production.

Quality assurance places an increased emphasis on customer requirements, building the notion of an *internal customer* into the process. The internal

customer idea encourages workers at each stage in the production process to view the next stage as a customer. This focus tends to improve the care that workers take with their output. This culture of respect for the next stage in the process means that each process is gradually improved. This concept of 'total quality' removes the need to inspect at the end.

Advantages of quality assurance

- **Workers take more care.** Every worker is given greater responsibility to produce at a consistent level.
- **Increased motivation of workforce.** The greater role of staff increases their status and recognition within the firm. This process of job enrichment helps to improve overall morale.
- **Reduced costs.** Costs tend to fall because there is no need to employ the inspection team. Reductions in the number of defective products can also have a dramatic impact on the need to rework or replace them.
- **Workers are best placed to improve quality.** The workforce is in the best position to improve quality. They do the job and they are most aware of what can go wrong. They can monitor the process most carefully.

Disadvantages of quality assurance

- **The workforce may reject it.** In many jobs, there is a greater focus on increased output than on improved quality. If staff are paid for the numbers produced (piece rate), they are more likely to concentrate on output rather than quality.
- **Increased demands on the workers.** The workforce may find the quality focus too stressful. The continual pressure on staff to produce at a high level can result in demotivation.
- **Increased initial cost.** The switch to a system of quality assurance can be quite costly in terms of training and implementation.
- **Some products may not need it.** In some markets there may be less requirement to produce products that are at a high standard. Cheaper product lines may work well with a limited sampling process of quality control rather than needing quality assurance.

The choice of a particular method of quality monitoring will depend on a variety of factors. The nature of the product is clearly central to this discussion. If you produce a range of cheap-selling potato snacks, you are unlikely to check each packet produced to ensure that whatever shapes are portrayed are actually in the packet. In contrast, Boeing and Airbus, which manufacture aircraft, are likely to test every single component several times to ensure that the aircraft fly safely.

Total quality management

The philosophy of **total quality management (TQM)** is an extension of the principle of quality assurance . This was developed by the management guru

Dr W. Edwards Deming, who produced a 14-point plan for management that focused on the improvement of quality in the production process:

1 'Right first time' — aim for defect prevention rather than detection.
2 Provide a consistent, clear message on quality.
3 All staff must share a commitment to continuous improvement and change.
4 Build partnerships with suppliers (many companies have extended this to apply to the supply chain within an organisation).
5 Constantly improve.
6 Educate and train staff to take responsibility for their own quality.
7 Supervisors should encourage and help.
8 Encourage change by eliminating the 'fear of failure' factor when introducing improvements.
9 Integrate departments and share problem solving.
10 Set clear, achievable goals.
11 Avoid setting global standards of work.
12 Help employees to take pride in their work.
13 Train and educate.
14 Establish a structure and culture to support these aims.

The plan gives a clear measure of quality in the production process. Workers are driven by improved quality. The culture of total quality provides an excellent working environment for all staff.

 KEY TERM

total quality management (TQM): an extension of quality assurance in which everyone in the production process is encouraged to produce the required product first time

Kaizen

What does kaizen mean?

Kaizen means 'continuous improvement'. It comes from the Japanese words *kai* meaning 'school' and *zen* meaning 'wisdom'. Under kaizen, all workers are involved in making regular, ongoing improvements to the production process. The changes made tend to be quite small, but they occur on a regular basis. Kaizen is one of the most commonly used words in Japan: it is constantly in the newspapers, on the radio and on television. In business, the concept of kaizen is so deeply ingrained in the minds of managers and workers that they often do not even realise they are 'thinking kaizen'.

KEY TERM

kaizen: the process of achieving continuous improvements in the workplace through workers regularly finding small ways of improving what they do

Advantages of kaizen

Kaizen offers the following benefits:

- Where kaizen is introduced for the first time, improvements in productivity of 30% or more are not uncommon, without any capital investment.
- It helps lower the breakeven point.
- It helps eliminate waste and improve processes.
- It helps management become more attentive to customer needs and to build systems and processes that take customer requirements into consideration, resulting in improved quality and greater customer satisfaction.

- The system can be applied to any workplace due to its simple nature and low day-to-day cost.
- Kaizen has been implemented around the world as a way of improving production and quality, while also improving safety and employee morale.

Disadvantages of kaizen

Kaizen is subject to the following disadvantages:

- Some staff may be unhappy or unwilling to get involved.
- Kaizen can be tricky to implement.
- The cost of setting up a kaizen system can be a problem.

Benchmarking

Firms that get involved with **benchmarking** monitor best practice in their industry. In simple terms, benchmarking involves finding the best way to carry out a task by looking at other firms in the same industry. The tasks observed can be quite small, but benchmarking could include monitoring the whole production line. Performance standards are established and the firm is then 'scored'. Areas where the firm scores lower than the industry average are looked at first. Other tasks are also monitored to identify areas for possible improvement.

Advantages of benchmarking

- By observing good practice elsewhere, a firm can learn how to improve its own systems and procedures.
- Clear and attainable targets can be set, based on the experience of others.
- Benchmarking reduces the cost and wastage of performing unnecessary activities.

Disadvantages of benchmarking

- It may be tricky to gain accurate data.
- Some firms just copy others. This will not lead to development in the market. The firm will be a follower and never a leader.
- The information gathered must be acted upon to justify the expense.

Summary

The techniques of lean production are geared to achieve the combined objectives of waste reduction and quality improvements. Total quality management, benchmarking and kaizen have a clear focus to achieve these objectives. However, different situations might require different interpretations of the techniques in practice.

For example, it may be difficult for Boeing to use benchmarking in a specific production activity because its main competitor, Airbus, is unlikely to allow direct access to the production facility. Boeing may, however, look at wider aspects of the Airbus operation (e.g. marketing) and learn much from these.

The nature of the firm's product and the level of competition in its market may also have an impact on the use of quality-specific techniques such as TQM and kaizen.

AIRBUS S.A.S. 2005©

Airbus is unlikely to allow rival firms access to its production facility

Further sources

www.benchmarking.gov.uk

www.themanufacturer.com/uk/detail.html?contents_id=6156

www.businessballs.com/dtiresources/total_quality_management_TQM.pdf

e EXAMINER'S VOICE

Avoid the temptation to assume that lean production techniques are the answer to all production and quality problems faced by firms. In the examination, you may score more marks for being able to discuss the disadvantages of these techniques and for stating the reasons why a particular approach may not work.

YOUR TURN

Questions

Time allowed: 30 minutes

1 Explain the main differences between quality control and quality assurance. *(4 marks)*

2 Why do some firms use quality control rather than quality assurance? *(5 marks)*

3 Analyse **three** benefits to BMW of using total quality management. *(6 marks)*

4 Explain **one** benefit and **one** difficulty for Sony of using benchmarking. *(4 marks)*

5 Evaluate how a McDonald's restaurant might make use of kaizen. *(8 marks)*

(27 marks)

Case study

Time allowed: 30 minutes

Nissan flies the flag for UK efficiency

The UK's biggest car plant, Nissan in Sunderland, is more than 5% more productive than the most efficient car plant in North America, according to a major international study.

The 2005 Harbour Report measures the productivity of car plants on a labour hours/vehicle basis. It shows that in 2004 the average combined time it took Sunderland to build its three models (Micra, Almera and Primera) was a fraction over 15 hours per car. This was 5.1% better than the top-ranked plant in North America, which averaged 15.85 hours per car.

Taken in isolation, the Micra supermini took just 13 hours to build – over 21% more efficient than the combined volume of the most productive plant in North America.

Sunderland was ranked as the most productive car plant in Europe from 1997 through to 2003 by the World Markets Research Centre. Last year, Nissan submitted data to the Harbour Report, which studied more than 30 plants across Europe (although comparisons among European plants are private) and every domestic and major foreign manufacturer in North America.

The Sunderland plant's managing director, Colin Dodge, said: 'I'm delighted that we've improved on our productivity record from 2003. It's a good indication that you're building cars well, achieving an excellent standard of quality and working efficiently. If you get any of those things wrong, you won't be productive, so obviously I'm pleased.

'The key to our continued success is the thorough application of the world-renowned Nissan Production Way, a long history of improvement based on benchmarking, the skill and dedication of the management team and the high integrity and motivation of the workforce.

'As ever, it's the workforce who should take the lion's share of the credit. Their hard work is ensuring we remain competitive and are in a good position to attract new models to the UK.'

Recently, Nissan unveiled the coupé/convertible Micra C+C, which Sunderland will build from September onwards. This will be followed in January 2006 by the Tone 'mini-MPV' and the 4×4 crossover car, provisionally called Qashqai, in December 2006.

The Micra too has recently benefited from extensive 'refreshment' with improvements both inside and out. Last week a Micra became the four millionth vehicle to be built at Sunderland since production began in 1986.

Source: **www.prnewswire.co.uk/cgi/news/release?id=149585**

Answer all questions.

1　Explain how Nissan is calculating production efficiency. *(4 marks)*

2　Analyse how Nissan might be making use of benchmarking. *(6 marks)*

3　Assess how Nissan might be able to create 'high integrity and motivation of the workforce'. *(6 marks)*

4　Evaluate the extent to which Nissan could make use of a kaizen approach in its production. *(9 marks)*

(25 marks)

CHAPTER 50

Stock types and levels

Stock and its management are major issues for many firms. This chapter considers the different types of stock that firms hold and the decisions that they take in trying to determine how much of each to keep. The issue of drawing up stock control charts is also considered.

Efficient stock control means that a business has the right amount of stock in the right place at the right time. It ensures that capital is not tied up unnecessarily, and protects production when there are problems with the supply chain.

The role and purpose of stock

All businesses have to keep some stock. Large retail organisations such as Tesco must have huge quantities of items in stock to ensure that demand can be satisfied.

Stock is used in an organisation to keep the flow of production going. Many organisations are required to carry many different types of stock items. A small car has as many as 3,000 different components, each of which is designed separately to work in perfect coherence with the others. Each item of stock must be carefully monitored and controlled.

Essentially, stock can be put into one of three categories:
- stocks of raw materials
- stocks of finished goods
- stocks of **work-in-progress**

Each type of stock can be managed in different ways. The business needs to consider these different ways in terms of cost and overall efficiency.

The cost of stock

Firms must try to consider how much it costs to keep different levels of stock. The relationship between the amount of stock held and the cost of stock is shown in Figure 50.1. The graph suggests that the higher the stock level, the higher the cost. This reflects the high cost of storing goods and raw materials.

KEY TERM

work-in-progress: the amount of stock tied up as it moves through the factory

Large retail organisations such as Tesco must have huge quantities of items in stock to meet demand

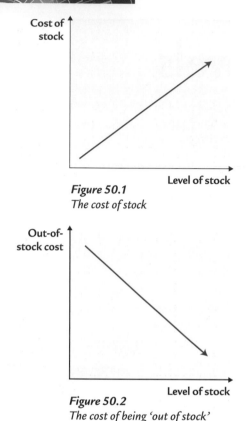

Figure 50.1
The cost of stock

Figure 50.2
The cost of being 'out of stock'

Based on Figure 50.1, it could be suggested that firms should minimise the amount of stock held. This forms the basis of the just-in-time principle of stockholding (see Chapter 51).

However, it is also useful to consider the cost of stock in another way: in terms of the cost of being 'out of stock'. This is shown in Figure 50.2.

Here the relationship between stock level and cost is considered in terms of the possible cost of being unable to satisfy the business's customers. This **out-of-stock cost** can be looked at in the same way as a profit that has not been gained. The higher the level of stock, the less likely it is that a firm will be unable to satisfy demand.

The two diagrams therefore conflict with each other about the ideal level of stock to keep in an organisation. In some markets, demand can be unpredictable or the product may be seasonally demanded. In every case, it is necessary to determine the ideal level of stock to keep.

In practice, firms establish a maximum and a minimum level of stock. They must also decide how many items of stock to order. The following must be taken into account:

■ **Storage facilities.** These help to set the maximum stock level. The physical storage space and the cost of having it are important factors.
■ **Economies of scale.** Bulk buying generates cost savings. This cost reduction could be important in deciding on stock levels.
■ **Opportunity cost.** The decision to purchase additional stock items means that this money cannot be spent on other things.
■ **Fluctuations in demand.** Firms must be responsive to changes in demand where possible.

Stock control charts

A **stock control chart** attempts to monitor the level of stock over time (see Figure 50.3). The chart plots the likely pattern of stock usage in an attempt to show the maximum and minimum stock levels and a reorder point.

■ The *maximum stock level* is the highest level of stock kept by the firm.
■ The *minimum stock level* (also known as the **buffer stock level**) is the lowest level of stock that the firm considers is safe to ensure that orders can be satisfied or production kept going.
■ The *reorder level* is the level of stock at which the firm feels it necessary to reorder.
■ The *lead time* is the time it takes for an order to be received by the firm.

The stock control chart assumes that stock is used evenly over time. The usage of stock causes the stock level to drop. To ensure that stock does not run out completely, it is necessary to reorder. This reordering must be set so that the level of stock does not go down below the minimum stock level. There is often a delay after ordering before the new stock arrives. This is known as the **lead time** and explains why the stock does not rise immediately on the graph. Care must be taken to set the reorder level at the ideal point.

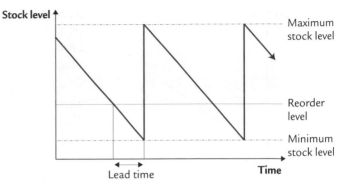

Figure 50.3 *Stock control chart*

Example

A firm sets the minimum or buffer stock level at 500 units. The maximum stock level is 3,000 units. The firm uses 500 items per day. Stock takes 1 day to arrive. The stock control chart is shown in Figure 50.4. This chart sets the reorder level at 1,000 units. If the lead time were set at 2 days, the reorder level would go up to 1,500 units.

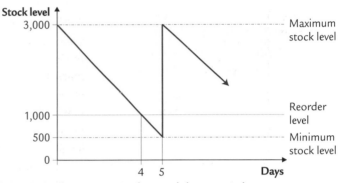

Figure 50.4 *Stock control chart: example*

Stock control charts give a useful indication of likely stock movements assuming that stock usage remains constant. This assumption may be unrealistic. In real-life business, there are likely to be problems with breakdowns, holiday shutdowns, difficulties in supply and so on.

Managing stock usage

The nature of the products that are made and the different types and numbers of stock that a firm has will influence how stock is managed. The issue of setting an 'ideal' stock level can be a function of several factors. Stock wastage, for example, can occur due to theft in the workplace, poor-quality output or stock becoming out of date.

Food retailers need to make sure they put new stock at the back of the shelves to encourage sale of the oldest stock first

A number of methods can be used to improve overall stock efficiency.

- **Stock rotation.** This can be used to tackle the problem of out-of-date stock. The method ensures that the oldest stock is sold first and often involves moving stock items around. In the case of food retailers, for example, it is important to fill the shelves carefully. Care should be taken to pull the oldest stock to the front of the shelves to encourage its sale ahead of the newer stock.

- **Computer-based stock control.** Retailers also use computer-based systems such as **electronic point of sale (EPOS)** to assist in the tracking of stock. The bar code system monitors sales and therefore stock movements in the store.

- **Reducing the overall level of stock.** Methods such as just-in-time (see Chapter 51), which try to minimise the amount of stock kept, help to reduce some of the costs of high stockholding.

Stock control is an area of the business that has an impact on many functions. From cash management through to levels of production and aspects of marketing, the correct management of stock can be crucial.

KEY TERMS

stock rotation: a method designed to ensure that the earliest stock bought in by the firm is the stock that is used up first

electronic point of sale (EPOS): a computer-based stock system that monitors movements of stock in and out of the firm

EXAMINER'S VOICE

Remember that there are different forms of stock. The policy that a firm has for its raw materials could be very different from the one that it uses for its finished goods. In the examination, be careful not to assume that one solution will fit all problems.

Further sources

www.businesslink.gov.uk/bdotg/action/layer?topicId=1074039371

www.thetimes100.co.uk/theory/theory.php?tID=257

www.is4profit.com/busadvice/epos/epos3.htm

www.thebarcodewarehouse.co.uk/solutions/warehouse-management-software/

YOUR TURN

Questions

Time allowed: 40 minutes

1 List **three** different types of stock. *(3 marks)*

2 Explain the difference between the cost of holding stock and the out-of-stock cost. *(4 marks)*

3 a Draw a stock control chart using the following information:
- buffer stock level = 1,000 units
- maximum stock level = 10,000 units
- lead time = 1 week (5 days)
- stock usage = 500 per day

Assume a 5-day working week. *(8 marks)*

b What will happen to the reorder point if the lead time is **(i)** increased, **(ii)** reduced? Explain your answer. *(4 marks)*

4 Discuss the factors that will influence the reorder level of stock for a firm producing **(i)** wing mirrors for Ford, **(ii)** business studies textbooks. *(10 marks)*

5 Explain the reasons why Morrisons uses stock rotation. *(4 marks)*

(33 marks)

Case study

Time allowed: 35 minutes

Daryl Industries

Daryl Industries manufactures up-market shower enclosures. Three years ago, it was manufacturing its product 'families' in batches determined by the materials it had in stock. Customers often change their requirements and the company's response times were slow when operating this type of manufacturing system.

Daryl knew it had to move towards 'mass customisation', to respond quickly to individual customers' needs while still benefiting from the efficiencies of mass production. The company lacked the expertise to tackle this itself, and sought assistance from Liverpool University's Agility Centre. The problems identified by the centre's audits were more fundamental and the changes recommended more demanding than Daryl had anticipated. The company implemented a cellular layout and had its staff trained to operate the new cells and use spreadsheets to plan and control stock levels for each cell. These changes helped Daryl to increase its turnover by almost 15% per employee, and achieve gearing 20% ahead of budget.

The next recommendation related to the products themselves. The agility audits highlighted the need to redesign the shower enclosures to minimise the number of components and make them as generic as possible. The solution involved creating a common chassis which could be customised through add-ons such as handles and hinges. Components were redesigned to fit as many models as possible. Daryl also updated the company's IT system.

'The help from Liverpool University was fantastic,' says Daryl's technical director, John Porter. 'They guided us with great skill through massive changes to the business. We now hold about half our previous stock levels. We achieve 100% accurate stock counts. We deliver on time. We rarely have overdue orders. As a result, we've reduced debt and improved profitability.'

Source: adapted from **www.liv.ac.uk/2004/businessgateway/casestudies/daryl.htm**

Answer all questions.

1 Explain why it is important for a firm such as Daryl Industries to meet the individual needs of customers. *(4 marks)*

2 Explain why the move to a cellular layout might have improved stock control at Daryl Industries. *(5 marks)*

3 Discuss the link between improved use of IT and higher profitability. *(8 marks)*

4 Evaluate whether the reduction in the number of components is a good idea in a competitive market. *(9 marks)*

(26 marks)

CHAPTER 51

Just-in-time and waste management

This chapter focuses on the remaining aspects of lean production. The philosophy of just-in-time (JIT) has had a dramatic impact on firms in many different markets. Just-in-time is customer driven and slots into the notion of waste reduction by removing the need for firms to carry stock. The overall reduction of waste can also improve efficiency. Both JIT and waste management can help to make an organisation leaner.

Just-in-time

What is just-in-time?
Just-in-time aims to reduce all types of stock so that, at all stages of the production process, stock is only ordered to ensure its arrival exactly when it is needed. This approach follows the 'internal customer' principle identified in Chapter 49. Each stage in the process requires the components and raw materials from the previous stage at the right time for them to satisfy that stage.

The customer focus is crucial to the JIT approach. Production should only commence when there is a specific customer order. This order generates a requirement for a finished product. This, in turn, generates the need for the partly finished components to be ready for that final stage. In turn, this creates the need for the earlier components and raw materials to be ready, and so on. The principle is that, in each case, the different stages are ready 'just in time' to be used. The left-hand side of Figure 51.1 shows the focus of just-in-time. The right-hand path shows the actual process of production.

Japanese manufacturing firms, such as Toyota, developed a system of cards known as **kanban**, which accompany each item through the production process. The kanban card is the trigger for the required components and raw materials to be delivered to the stage in the process that needs them.

KEY TERM

just-in-time: a production system in which raw materials, work-in-progress and finished products are delivered at the precise time they are required

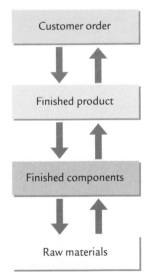

Figure 51.1 Just-in-time

KEY TERM

kanban: a card system used in just-in-time, whereby a card follows each item through the production process and is the trigger for stocks to be ready

Advantages of just-in-time
Firms using just-in-time derive the following benefits:

- **Reduced stock levels.** JIT can reduce the costs of holding stock and allows any storage facility to be used for profit-generating production.

- **Avoids overproduction.** The customer focus eliminates the need to produce goods just in case they might need to be sold.
- **Promotional benefits.** The closer links made with customers can improve brand loyalty and be used positively in the future promotion of goods.
- **Reduction in waste.** All items of stock can be accounted for and this will reduce staff pilferage and loss due to damage.
- **Quality improvements.** Production of goods with a specific customer in mind often encourages workers to take more care in the actual production process.
- **Overall cost reduction.** The reduction in waste and the need to store less or no stock must have an impact on costs.

Disadvantages of just-in-time

Just-in-time production nevertheless suffers from several disadvantages:

- **Requires good communication.** There is a crucial need to have good supply links. The firm must communicate effectively with its suppliers; failure to do this will result in production stops.
- **Supply problems.** If the suppliers have difficulty in meeting the needs of the firm, this can bring a halt to the overall production.
- **Machine breakdown.** A similar situation can arise if there is any form of machine stoppage. The highly planned nature of production means that any minor break affects the whole production process.
- **Lack of workforce commitment.** The workers must be flexible in their approach. The just-in-time philosophy is often tied in with other aspects of lean production and these techniques may not appeal to all types of worker. Workers need to be multi-skilled.
- **Loss of economies of scale.** The need to buy in smaller quantities but more frequently may reduce the benefits of bulk buying.

A fitted kitchen can be made and delivered using just-in-time production

Evaluation

Just-in-time is not the ideal solution for all firms. It works well for organisations that can identify specific customers who demand particular products. For example, a customer interested in buying a fitted kitchen will place an order having discussed the specific requirements with the retailer. That order will then be specifically made and delivered and fitted some weeks later. The order reaching the factory triggers the need to produce.

By contrast, it would be more difficult to identify specific customers in a high-volume market. Pepsi, for example, cannot hope to know who will consume each of its cans. This makes the use of just-in-time less certain.

Waste management

Why reduce waste?

Waste reduction is the central element of lean production. The term 'waste' is used to describe anything that is inefficient in the production process. It can take several forms:

- **Overproduction.** This means producing more than the customer requires.
- **Waiting.** This can include waiting for the production process to begin or excessive machine time/downtime.
- **Transportation.** This includes work in progress, bad organisation and double handling. Handling products more than once increases the costs and the likelihood of damage occurring. Having to move things over long distances must also increase costs.
- **Over-processing.** There can be marketing advantages in giving the customer 'extra' satisfaction, but generally doing more than is necessary is inherently wasteful.
- **Stock.** Keeping stocks of parts or materials that are not being worked upon and which are stored between operations ties up space and capital.
- **Poor factory layout.** This can involve excessive movement of staff and components around the factory. Tools and spare parts may need to be searched for.
- **Scrapping/reworking defective products.** Poor quality of production leads to reworking or even disposing of partly or fully produced products.

The lean production approach encourages the reduction of all aspects of waste. No firm is able to achieve zero waste, but this can act as a strong aim.

Efficiency is about making the best use of resources. Waste reduces the effectiveness of the inputs that are used to create the firm's outputs. Moving stocks unnecessarily around the factory is a good example of the ineffective use of one of the inputs in production.

Moving stocks around the factory unnecessarily is a good example of the ineffective use of one of the inputs in production

How can waste management be improved?

Firms might adopt any of the following in order to improve their **waste management**:

- **Introducing just-in-time.** This stops the need to overproduce.
- **Improving links with suppliers.** Better communication with the supply chain reduces the problems of having idle machinery.
- **Better factory layout.** This minimises the need to have inefficient movement of goods around the factory.

■ **Closer links with marketing.** Production should work in a coordinated way with marketing. The firm should produce exactly what the customer wants — no more and no less.

■ **Improved quality control.** This reduces the need to scrap or rework materials.

Adopting these improvement methods will ensure that waste is reduced and productive efficiency is improved. Waste reduction is clearly important in achieving the overall aim of operations management — to improve inputs in order to achieve better satisfaction of customers.

> **ⓔ EXAMINER'S VOICE**
>
> Just-in-time and waste management must be considered in relation to the specific case study used in the examination. As with other aspects of lean production, it is important to note that these methods will not be used by every firm. Some organisations simply will not be able to make full use of either technique. You may be able to score marks by being able to criticise the techniques in relation to a particular firm.

Further sources

www.rusi.org/downloads/pub_rds/8foulkes.pdf

www.leanuk.org

www.themanufacturer.com/us/detail.html?contents_id=3724

YOUR TURN

Questions
Time allowed: 35 minutes

1 Explain the main differences between just-in-time production and a 'just-in-case' method of stock control. *(4 marks)*

2 Give **two** examples of firms that are more likely to use:
a just-in-time
b just-in-case *(4 marks)*

3 Explain why efficient factory layout is so important to the achievement of waste reduction. *(5 marks)*

4 Analyse the problems of just-in-time as a method of production for a house-building firm such as Barratt Homes. *(8 marks)*

5 Evaluate the extent to which Microsoft could use just-in-time and waste management techniques. *(10 marks)*

(31 marks)

Case study

Time allowed: 40 minutes

Corus to establish dedicated distribution facility

Corus, the international metals company, has announced that it is to establish a just-in-time (JIT) supply facility in Coventry. The facility will improve efficiency and increase flexibility to enhance service levels in delivering steel skin panel blanks from its dedicated Automotive Service Centre in Wolverhampton to Mayflower Vehicle Systems.

The 1,200m^2 satellite facility, located at Swallow Gate Business Park adjacent to the Mayflower operation, will be fully networked with the Automotive Service Centre, which is based at the Corus Steelpark, a 50-acre steel supply and processing hub, in Wednesfield in the West Midlands. The networked JIT facility will allow Corus to provide Mayflower with full functionality, including complete visibility and traceability of stock, the processing of orders and even invoicing.

The JIT facility will stock Mayflower's complete requirement of 206 different sizes and specifications of automotive steel blanks for more than 100 different body parts, which the company supplies to several leading vehicle manufacturers.

With a 2,000-tonne stock capacity, the distribution satellite will provide a flexible and efficient supply of blanks timed to meet Mayflower's specific manufacturing schedule. A back-to-back loading and off-

loading system will operate between the Corus Automotive Service Centre, the JIT facility and Mayflower. This further streamlines the supply chain, allowing materials to flow in a more efficient and reliable way, thereby reducing storage, handling and transport costs.

Locating the facility on Mayflower's doorstep has enabled the company to eliminate its own steel stocks and release both capital and space tied up in this area. In particular, the new facility will help to alleviate the specific logistics problems posed by the almost constant traffic congestion on the M6 motorway between Coventry and Wolverhampton. The JIT facility is expected to be operational from the end of May 2003.

Commenting on the supply facility and the added value of working with a material supplier such as Corus, Dave Watson, general manager supply, Mayflower Vehicle Systems, said: 'Reducing costs through the supply chain is a major challenge facing the automotive industry, and the investment and commitment Corus has made in establishing this facility will help us to achieve this. Corus has worked closely with us to understand our specific needs as a tier one supplier, which helps us deliver the quality of products and service demanded by vehicle manufacturers.'

Source: adapted from an article dated 28 May 2003 online at **www.corusautomotive.com**

Answer all questions.

1 Explain why JIT is a good idea for Corus. *(4 marks)*

2 Explain why the location of the sites is so important in making JIT work for Corus. *(4 marks)*

3 Analyse the problems of coordinating supply to the customers of Corus. *(6 marks)*

4 Discuss aspects of waste management/waste reduction identified in the case study. *(10 marks)*

5 Evaluate the cost implications of introducing the JIT facility to Corus. *(10 marks)*

(34 marks)

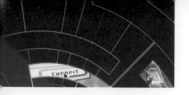

Index

Note: page numbers in **bold** type refer to key terms (where these occur more than once only the first occurrence is given); page numbers in *italic* type refer to illustrations and diagrams.

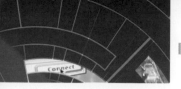

Index

Index